These Notes refer to the Companies Act 2006 (c.46)
which received Royal Assent on 8 November 2006

COMPANIES ACT 2006

EXPLANATORY NOTES

INTRODUCTION

1.   These explanatory notes relate to the Companies Act 2006 (c.46) which received Royal Assent on 8 November 2006. They have been prepared by the Department of Trade and Industry (DTI) in order to assist the reader in understanding the Act. They do not form part of the Act and have not been endorsed by Parliament.

2.   The notes need to be read in conjunction with the Act. They are not, and are not meant to be, a comprehensive description of the Act. So where a section or part of a section does not seem to require any explanation or comment, none is given. Further, where provisions in the Act restate what was in the Companies Act 1985 (the 1985 Act) an explanation is not always given, except to the extent required to explain changes to associated provisions.

BACKGROUND

3.   The UK was one of the first nations to establish rules for the operation of companies. Today our system of company law and corporate governance, setting out the legal basis on which companies are formed and run, is a vital part of the legal framework within which business is conducted. As the business environment evolves, there is a risk that the legal framework can become gradually divorced from the needs of companies, in particular the needs of smaller private businesses, creating obstacles to ways that companies want and need to operate.

4.   In March 1998, the DTI commissioned a fundamental review of company law. An independent Steering Group led the "Company Law Review" (CLR) whose terms of reference required them to consider how core company law could be modernised in order to provide a simple, efficient and cost effective framework for British business in the twenty-first century. After extensive consultation with interested parties, the CLR presented its Final Report to the Secretary of State for Trade and Industry on 26 July 2001. The report contained a range of recommendations for substantive changes to many areas of company law, and a set of principles to guide the development of the law more generally, most notably that it should be as simple and as accessible as possible for smaller firms and their advisers and should avoid imposing unnecessary burdens on the ways companies operate.

5.   Many of the provisions of the Act implement CLR recommendations. The Government set out and consulted on its intentions in this regard in the White Papers "Modernising Company Law" (July 2002) and "Company Law Reform" (March 2005). The 2005 White Paper included approximately 300 draft clauses and described in detail the policy intention for other areas. Further clauses were made publicly available for comment in July, September and October 2005. The Companies Bill, then titled the Company Law Reform Bill, was introduced to the House of Lords on 4 November 2005.

OVERVIEW OF THE STRUCTURE OF THE ACT

6.   The general arrangement of the Act is as follows:

PART	SUMMARY
Parts 1 to 7	The fundamentals of what a company is, how it can be formed and what it can be called.
Parts 8 to 12	The members (shareholders) and officers (management) of a company
Parts 13 and 14	How companies may take decisions
Parts 15 and 16	The safeguards for ensuring that the officers of a company are accountable to its members
Parts 17 to 25	Raising share capital, capital maintenance, annual returns, and company charges
Parts 26 to 28	Company reconstructions, mergers and takeovers
Parts 29 to 39	The regulatory framework, application to companies not formed under the Companies Acts and other company law provisions
Parts 40 to 42	Overseas disqualification of directors, business names and statutory auditors
Part 43	Transparency obligations
Parts 44 to 47	Miscellaneous and general

SUMMARY OF LEGISLATIVE CHANGES

7.   The company law provisions of the 2006 Act (Parts 1 to 39) restate almost all of the provisions of the 1985 Act, together with the company law provisions of the Companies Act 1989 (the 1989 Act) and the Companies (Audit, Investigations and Community Enterprise) Act 2004 (C(AICE) Act 2004). Paragraphs 9 and 10 below contain details of the provisions that remain in those Acts. The company law provisions also codify certain aspects of the case law.

8.   Tables of origins and destinations are available that show the origins of the company law provisions of the Act by reference to enactments in force on 8 November 2006. The tables identify where provisions of the existing law have been re-enacted with or without changes and where provisions of the new law have no predecessor or are fundamentally different from their predecessors.

9.   Of company law provisions in the Acts referred to in paragraph 7, the only ones that remain are those on investigations that go wider than companies (Part 14 of the 1985 Act) and the provisions on community interest companies in Part 2 of the C(AICE) Act 2004.

10.   The non-company law provisions in those Acts that remain are:

   a) Part 18 of the 1985 Act (floating charges and receivers (Scotland)),

b) Part 3 of the 1989 Act (powers to require information and documents to assist overseas regulatory authorities),

c) Section 112 to 116 of the 1989 Act (provisions about Scottish incorporated charities)

d) Part 7 of the 1989 Act (provisions about financial markets and insolvency)

e) Schedule 18 of the 1989 Act (amendments and savings consequential upon changes in the law made by the 1989 Act)

f) Sections 14 and 15 of the C(AICE) Act 2004 (supervision of accounts and reports), and

g) Sections 16 and 17 of the C(AICE) Act 2004 (bodies concerned with accounting standards etc).

11.   In non-company law areas the Act makes amendments to other legislation, in particular the Financial Services and Markets Act 2000, and also makes new provision of various kinds. The main areas in which provision of this kind is made are:

- overseas disqualification of company directors (Part 40),

- business names (Part 41) – replacing the Business Names Act 1985,

- statutory auditors (Part 42) – replacing Part 2 of the Companies Act 1989, and

- transparency obligations (Part 43) – amending Part 6 of the Financial Services and Markets Act 2000.

TERRITORIAL EXTENT AND DEVOLUTION

Northern Ireland

12.   Company law is a transferred matter. Currently, the provisions of GB company law are generally replicated, some time later, in separate Northern Ireland legislation. The Act provides for a single company law regime applying to the whole of the UK, so that companies will be UK companies rather than GB companies or Northern Ireland companies as at present. This does not affect the legislative competence of Northern Ireland: company law remains a transferred matter, and the Act could be separately amended or repealed in Northern Ireland if that were so desired.

13.   Where a note describes a particular section as restating or replacing a provision in the 1985 Act, the 1989 Act or the C(AICE)Act 2004, this should be read as applying equally to the corresponding provision of the Companies (Northern Ireland) Order 1986, the Companies (Northern Ireland) Order 1990 or the Companies (Audit, Investigations and Community Enterprise) Order 2005.

Scotland

14.   Company law is a reserved matter and Companies Acts extend to the whole of Great Britain. However, there are several areas where, in legislating about companies, the Act deals with matters that are devolved:

- changes (in Part 41) to the regulation of business names (a devolved matter) – these correspond to changes (in Part 5) to the regulation of company names (a reserved matter);

- statutory guidance to prosecutors and other enforcement authorities in relation to a new offence of knowingly or recklessly causing an audit report to be misleading, false or deceptive – although the offence itself is a reserved matter, guidance is to be issued by the Lord Advocate in Scotland (see section 509);

- changes relating to exemptions from audit requirements for companies that are charities (see section 1175);

- conferral of a power on the Auditor General for Scotland to specify public bodies for his audit (see section 483).

These were the subject of a legislative consent motion agreed to by the Scottish Parliament on 16 March 2006.

Wales

15.   Company law is not transferred to the Welsh Assembly. There are no provisions that impact on devolved competences.

Crown Dependencies

16.   Part 28 of the Act (takeovers) contains provision enabling it to be extended by Order in Council to the Isle of Man or any of the Channel Islands. This reflects the existing jurisdiction of the Takeover Panel (as the takeover regulator) and has been agreed by the relevant Island authorities. If the power were to be exercised, there would be further consultation with the Island authorities beforehand.

PART 1: GENERAL INTRODUCTORY PROVISIONS

Section 1: Companies

17.   This section restates section 735(1)(a) and (b) of the 1985 Act. It defines "company" and provides signposts to provisions in the Act which relate to companies that are registered but not formed under the Act or former Companies Acts, to unregistered companies and to overseas companies.

Section 2: The Companies Acts

18.   This section replaces section 744 of the 1985 Act. The Act does not restate or replace all existing companies legislation and section 2 makes it clear that any reference to "Companies Acts" in the Act includes those provisions of the Acts listed in *subsection (1)(c)* that remain in force as well as the company law provisions of the Act and Part 2 of the C(AICE) Act 2004.

19.   The CLR recommended that the law should provide for the formation of new companies of each of the types that are currently available (Final Report, paragraph 9.2). This

recommendation is taken forward in the following group of sections, which retains all of the current forms of companies.

Section 3: Limited and unlimited companies

20.   This section restates section 1(2) of the 1985 Act. It updates the Companies Acts definitions of "limited company" and "unlimited company" to reflect changes to what is to be included in a company's memorandum of association (see section 8). As now, a company may be limited by shares or by guarantee. Where there is no limit on the liability of the company's members, a company is an "unlimited company."

Section 4: Private and public companies

21.   This section restates section 1(3) of the 1985 Act. It provides definitions of "private company" and "public company."

22.   A "private company" is any company that is not a public company.

23.   A "public company" is a company whose certificate of incorporation states that it is a public company. To obtain this certificate the company will need to comply with the provisions of the Act (or former Companies Acts) as regards registration or re-registration as a public company. There is a minimum share capital requirement (the "authorised minimum"), which is currently set at £50,000, and remains unchanged under the Act. In future the authorised minimum will however be capable of being satisfied in sterling or the euro equivalent to the prescribed sterling amount (see Chapter 2 of Part 20).

24.   Section 4 also provides a signpost to Part 20 of the Act, which sets out key differences between public and private companies, for example, a private company may not offer shares to the public.

Section 5: Companies limited by guarantee and having share capital

25.   This section restates section 1(4) and section 15(2) of the 1985 Act. It makes it clear that a company can no longer be formed (or re-register) as a company limited by guarantee and with a share capital. This provision has been in force in Great Britain since 22nd December 1980 and in Northern Ireland since 1st July 1983.

Section 6: Community interest companies

26.   The C(AICE) Act 2004 came fully into force on 1 July 2005. Part 2 of that Act created a new company vehicle, the "community interest company" or "c.i.c.", which is designed for use by social enterprises.

27.   This section provides a signpost to the provisions in the C(AICE) Act, which enable a company to be formed as or become a community interest company. Such companies are registered under the same legislation as other registered companies, but have to complete certain additional formalities and are subject to certain additional elements of regulation. *Subsection (2)* of this section highlights the fact that in some respects the requirements imposed on community interest companies are different from the requirements imposed on other registered companies.

PART 2: COMPANY FORMATION

28.   This Part of the Act is about how companies are formed. It replaces or, as the case may be, restates equivalent provisions in the 1985 Act.

Section 7: Method of forming company

29.   This section replaces sections 1(1) of the 1985 Act. It retains the current requirement that individuals who wish to form a company must subscribe their names to the memorandum of association ("memorandum"). *Subsection (1)* introduces the new provisions about forming a company. In line with the recommendations of the CLR, it is provided that a single person is able to form any sort of company (not just a private company) (Final Report, paragraph 9.2).

30.   *Subsection (2)* reproduces the existing requirement that a company may not be formed for an unlawful purpose.

Section 8: Memorandum of association

31.   This section replaces section 3(1) of the 1985 Act.

32.   Under the Act, the memorandum serves a more limited, but nonetheless important, purpose: it evidences the intention of the subscribers to the memorandum to form a company and become members of that company on formation. In the case of a company that is to be limited by shares, the memorandum will also provide evidence of the members' agreement to take at least one share each in the company.

33.   The memorandum of a company formed under the Act will, therefore, look very different from that of a company registered under the 1985 Act. In addition it will not be possible to amend or update the memorandum of a company formed under the Act.

34.   These changes to the memorandum are based on the CLR's recommendation that there should be a single constitution (Final Report, paragraph 9.4). In line with the principles behind this recommendation, in future key information regarding the internal allocation of powers between the directors and members of a company will be set out in one place: the articles of association ("articles").

35.   By virtue of section 28, provisions in the memoranda of existing companies will be treated as provisions in the articles if they are of a type that will not in be in the memoranda of companies formed under the Act. Existing companies will, therefore, not be required to amend their articles to reflect these changes, but they can do so if they wish. They will however be able to alter or update provisions in their constitution which are now set out in their memoranda by amending their articles, for example to reflect changes to the law made by the Act.

Section 9: Registration documents

36.   This section replaces various provisions in sections 2 and 10 of the 1985 Act. It prescribes the types of information or "documents" that must be delivered to the registrar when an application for registration is made and the registrar to whom the information must be delivered.

37.   The changes to the way in which certain information is delivered to the registrar are required as a result of the changes that have been made to the memorandum. In future, information which is currently set out in the memorandum will be provided to the registrar in accordance with the provisions of this section, which prescribes, amongst other things, the contents of the application for registration. In all cases this application must state:

- the company's proposed name;

- whether the company's registered office is to be situated in England and Wales (or Wales), in Scotland or in Northern Ireland;

- whether the liability of the company's members is to be limited and if so whether it is to be limited by shares or by guarantee;

- whether the company is to be a private or a public company.

38.   In the case of a company that is to have a share capital, the application must also contain a statement of capital and initial shareholdings (see section 10). In the case of a company that is to be limited by guarantee the application must also contain a statement of guarantee (see section 11).

39.   In all cases the application must also contain a statement of the company's proposed officers (see section 12) and a statement of the intended address of the company's registered office (that is, the postal address of the company's registered office as opposed to a statement confirming the jurisdiction in which the company's registered office is to be situated – which is also required).

40.   The application for registration must also contain a copy of any proposed articles (to the extent that the company does not intend to use the model articles (see sections 19 and 20) and must be accompanied by the memorandum (see *subsection (1)*) of this section and a statement of compliance (see section 13).

41.   In future it will be possible to form a company on-line and the various types of information referred to in the section are, therefore, capable of being delivered as a series of data entries as well as in paper or such other form as the registrar may permit or prescribe. The registrar has power under section 1068 to prescribe the form and manner in which documents are to be delivered to her.

Section 10: Statement of capital and initial shareholdings

42.   This section is a new provision. It sets out the contents of the statement of capital and initial shareholdings.

43.   Currently, in the case of a limited company with a share capital the memorandum is required to state the amount of the share capital with which the company proposes to be registered and the nominal amount of each of its shares. This is known as the "authorised share capital" and acts as a ceiling on the amount of capital which can be issued (although this limit can be increased by ordinary resolution). The CLR recommended that the requirement for a company to have an authorised share capital should be abolished (Final Report, paragraph 10.6).

44.   The Act gives effect to this recommendation and in future, information about the shares subscribed for by the subscribers to the memorandum, which is currently set out in the memorandum itself, will be provided to the registrar in the statement of capital and initial shareholdings.

45.   Like the statement of guarantee (see section 11), the statement of capital and initial shareholdings must contain such information as may be prescribed by the Secretary of State, in regulations made under the Act, for the purpose of identifying the subscribers to the memorandum (i.e. the founder members of the company).

46.   The statement of capital and initial shareholdings is essentially a "snapshot" of a company's share capital at the point of registration. For public companies, this requirement is linked to the abolition of authorised share capital (see above). It implements (as far as public companies are concerned) Article 2 of the Second Company Law Directive (77/91/EC) (the "Second Directive") which states:

> "the statutes or instruments of incorporation of the company shall always give at least the following information...(c) when the company has no authorized capital, the amount of the subscribed capital....".

47.   The statement of capital and initial shareholdings must contain the following information:

- the total number of shares of the company to be taken on formation by the subscribers to the memorandum;

- the aggregate nominal value of those shares;

- for each class of shares: prescribed particulars of the rights attached to those shares, the total number of shares of that class and the aggregate nominal value of shares of that class; and

- the amount to be paid up and the amount (if any) to be unpaid on each share (whether on account of the nominal value of the shares or by way of premium).

48.   The reference to *"prescribed particulars of the rights attached to the shares"* in this section (and elsewhere in the Act where a statement of capital is called for), refers to such particulars as may be prescribed by the Secretary of State by statutory instrument (see section 1167).

49.   Whilst the Second Directive only applies to public companies it is important that the information on the public register is up-to-date for both public and private companies. A statement of capital will, therefore, be required where it is proposed that a company formed under the Act will have a share capital on formation and, with limited exceptions (in particular, where there has been a variation of class rights which does not affect the company's aggregate subscribed capital) whenever a limited company having a share capital makes an alteration to its share capital (and in certain cases where an unlimited company makes a return to the registrar).

Section 11: Statement of guarantee

50.   This section replaces section 2(4) of the 1985 Act. It sets out the contents of the statement of guarantee that must accompany the application for registration where it is proposed that a company will be limited by guarantee on formation.

51.   The statement of guarantee is essentially an undertaking, given by the founder members of the company, to contribute to the assets of the company up to a specified amount in the event of it being wound up. New members must also agree to make the same contribution.

52.   A member of a company limited by guarantee is only liable to contribute to the assets of a company if it is wound up during the time that he is a member or within one year of him ceasing to be a member.

53.   Like the statement of capital and initial shareholdings the statement of guarantee must contain such information as may be prescribed by the Secretary of State, in regulations made

under the Act, for the purposes of identifying the subscribers to the memorandum (i.e. the founder members of the company).

Section 12: Statement of proposed officers

54.   This section replaces section 10(2) and (3) of the 1985 Act and contains a new provision. Under section 10, details of the first director(s) and the secretary or joint secretaries must be given to the registrar at the time of application for registration. That requirement is carried forward but there are two changes:

- firstly, to the required particulars. These are specified in relation to directors in sections 163 to 166. The main change is that a service address must be provided for each director who is a natural person. This is in addition to the requirement for the usual residential address;

- secondly, as recommended by the CLR (Final Report, paragraph 4.7), there is no requirement for a private company to have a company secretary but it may do so if it wishes (see section 270(1)). As now, a company which proposes to be registered as a public company must have a company secretary (see section 271).

Section 13: Statement of compliance

55.   This section replaces section 12(3) and (3A) of the 1985 Act. At present, where an application for registration of a company is made in paper form, the application must be accompanied by a statutory declaration (made before a solicitor or commissioner of oaths) confirming that the requirements of the 1985 Act in respect of registration, and of matters precedent and incidental to it, have been complied with (see section 12(1) of that Act). This statutory declaration must be made by one of the persons whom it is proposed will be a founder director or secretary of the company (that is, on registration) or a solicitor engaged in the formation of the company.

56.   Where the application for registration is made in electronic form, in place of the statutory declaration required under section 12(3) of the 1985 Act, the same persons may, alternatively, deliver an "electronic statement" to the registrar. This statement must confirm that the requirements referred to in section 12(1) have been met.

57.   Based on the recommendations of the CLR (Final Report, paragraph 9.5), the current requirement for a statutory declaration or electronic statement, here and elsewhere in the Act, is replaced by a requirement to make a statement of compliance. This statement does not need to be witnessed and may be made in paper or electronic form. It will be for the registrar's rules under section 1068 to specify who may make this statement (and the form of it). As with all documents delivered to, or statements made to, the registrar, it is an offence to make a false statement of compliance – see section 1112.

Section 14: Registration

58.   This section restates section 12(1) and (2) of the 1985 Act. As now, where the registrar is satisfied that all of the requirements of the Act as to registration have been met she will register the documents delivered to her and issue a certificate of incorporation under section 15.

Section 15: Issue of certificate of incorporation

59.   This section restates section 13(1)(2) and (7)(a) of the 1985 Act and contains a new provision in *subsection (2)*, which prescribes the contents of the certificate of incorporation issued by the registrar on registration of a company. The certificate of incorporation is conclusive evidence that the requirements of the Act as to registration have been met, that the company has been registered, and (where relevant) that the company has been registered as a limited company or a public company.

60.   There is one change to what the certificate of incorporation is required to state: in future this will include details of whether the company's registered office is situated in England and Wales (or in Wales), in Scotland or in Northern Ireland. The certificate will also state, where the company is limited, whether it is limited by shares or by guarantee.

Section 16: Effect of registration

61.   This section replaces section 13(3) to (5) of the 1985 Act. It provides, amongst other things, that the subscribers to the memorandum, together with such other persons as may from time to time become members of a company, are a body corporate by the name stated in the certificate of incorporation and, in the case of a company having a share capital, that the subscribers to the memorandum become holders of the shares specified in the statement of capital and initial shareholdings. This means that on registration a company becomes a legal person in its own right, which is distinct from the people who own it (the members) and the people who manage it (the directors).

PART 3: A COMPANY'S CONSTITUTION

62.   This Part deals with various matters relating to a company's constitution. It replaces similar provisions in the 1985 Act. It starts by defining (non-exhaustively) *"a company's constitution"* and then makes provision about the main constituent parts of a company's constitution (the articles of association and certain classes of members' resolutions and agreements), including their legal effects, how they are to be notified to the registrar and made available to members, and how changes to them are to be dealt with.

CHAPTER 1: INTRODUCTORY

Section 17: A company's constitution

63.   This section is a new provision. It sets out a definition of *"a company's constitution"* which will apply throughout the Act, and the other "Companies Acts" (defined in section 2), unless the context requires a wider or more restricted meaning (see for example section 257, which expands the definition of a company's constitution for the purposes of Part 10). The concepts of a company's constitution and the rights and obligations arising under it are used both in this Part and elsewhere in the Act.

64.   The definition is expressed to be non-exhaustive. In addition to the provisions of companies' articles and the resolutions and agreements to which Chapter 3 of this Part applies (described in section 29), the contents of certain other documents are clearly of constitutional relevance for certain purposes. For example the certificate of incorporation summarises key information pertaining to the company such as whether it is public or private limited – see section 15.

CHAPTER 2: ARTICLES OF ASSOCIATION

65.   A company's articles are rules, chosen by the company's members, which govern a company's internal affairs. They form a statutory contract between the company and its members, and between each of the members in their capacity as members, and are an integral part of a company's constitution. At present, companies may divide their constitutional rules between their memoranda and their articles, with the terms of their memoranda being capable of being altered after formation in some respects but not in others. In future, the memorandum will be a very simple document of purely historic significance, evidencing an intention to form a company, and all the company's key internal rules on matters such as the allocation of powers between the members of a company and its directors will be set out in the articles – see notes on sections 8 and 28.

Section 18: Articles of association

66.   This section replaces section 7(1) and (3) and section 744 of the 1985 Act. It carries forward the requirement that all registered companies must have articles. The provisions of this section have been updated to reflect the changes made by section 19, which gives the Secretary of State the power to prescribe "default" model articles for different descriptions of companies. As a result of this change, some types of company that are currently required to register articles with the relevant registrar of companies (for example, private companies limited by guarantee) will have the option of not registering articles but relying on the "relevant model articles" for that description of company.

67.   As now, the articles must be contained in a single document and must be divided into consecutively numbered paragraphs.

68.   Generally speaking, companies formed under the 1985 Act have freedom to make such rules about their internal affairs as they see fit, subject to the qualification that if a company's articles contain anything that is contrary to the provisions of that Act, or against the general law, then it will have no effect. This principle will also apply to the articles of companies which are formed and registered under the Act.

Section 19: Power of Secretary of State to prescribe model articles

Section 20: Default application of model articles

69.   Section 8 of the 1985 Act enables the Secretary of State to prescribe model forms of articles for companies registered under that Act (see the Companies (Tables A to F) Regulations 1985 (SI 1985/805)). Articles for certain special types of companies used in particular sectors, for example, commonhold associations, right to manage ("RTM") companies, and right to enfranchise ("RTE") companies are prescribed by regulations made under the Acts of Parliament that created these types of company.

70.   Although sections 8 and 8A of the 1985 Act allow the Secretary of State to prescribe forms of articles (and memoranda) for a number of different types of company under section 8, he is only able to prescribe "default" model articles for companies limited by shares. "Default" model articles are model articles which apply to companies of a particular description where they have not registered any articles of their own, or have not made provision for a particular matter for which there is a corresponding model article. "Default" model articles apply to a company of the description for which they are prescribed only to the

extent that it has not modified the default provision in question in its own registered articles or excluded it, or the model articles in their entirety, from the registered articles.

71.   The rationale behind this is that the model articles should operate as a "safety net" which enables the members and directors of such companies to take decisions in circumstances where a company has failed to provide the appropriate authority in its registered articles (or failed to register articles at all).

72.   These two sections replace section 8 of the 1985 Act. In line with the CLR's recommendations (Company Formation and Capital Maintenance, paragraph 2.22), the Secretary of State will have the power to prescribe model articles, including "default" model articles, for different descriptions of companies formed under the Act.

73.   For existing companies, there will be no change. The principle is maintained that the version of the model articles that was in force at the time that a particular company was originally registered will continue to apply to that company. For the majority of companies limited by shares on the register at the date that the Act comes into force, the "default" model articles will continue to be the Companies Act 1985 Table A ("Table A").

74.   Existing companies will be free to adopt, wholly or in part, the model articles prescribed for companies of a particular description formed under the Act (see *subsection (3)* of section 19). For example, an existing private company limited by shares may prefer to adopt the new model articles for private companies limited by shares, or indeed the new model articles for public companies formed under the Act (with or without modification) in place of the current Table A articles, or previous articles of its own devising.

75.   As with Table A, the adoption of model articles by companies formed under the Act will be entirely a matter for individual companies. They will be able to incorporate (with or without amendment) provisions from the model articles, and/or add to those provisions, and/or exclude such provisions as they think fit.

76.   They will also be able to adopt the provisions of model articles by reference. This is a common practice, which enables a company that wishes to incorporate specific provisions of the model articles into its own registered articles to do this without having to copy out the provision in question. To take an example, a company's registered articles may say something to the following effect: *"the model articles apply except for articles x, y and z"*, or *"the company's articles are A, B and C, plus model articles g, p and q. Model article n applies but is amended as follows: …"*. Companies have found such techniques useful in the past and they will continue to be permitted.

Section 21: Amendment of articles

77.   *Subsection (1)* provides that, as now, a company's articles can in general be amended by special resolution. This restates section 9(1) of the 1985 Act.

78.   *Subsections (2) and (3)* make it clear that this general principle is subject to certain rules in charities legislation about the ability of companies which are charities to change their constitutions and the effects which such changes have. There are separate but broadly similar rules for English and Welsh, Scottish and Northern Irish charities.

Section 22: Entrenched provisions of the articles

79.   Section 22 is a new provision. It replaces the current practice (provided for in section 17(2)(b) of the 1985 Act), whereby companies are able to entrench certain elements of their constitution by putting them in their memoranda and providing that they cannot be altered.

80.   This section permits companies to provide in their articles that specified provisions may be amended or repealed only if conditions are met that are more restrictive than would apply in the case of a special resolution. Such a provision is referred to as a "provision for entrenchment". As a result of this section companies formed under the Act will not be permitted to provide in their articles that an entrenched provision can never be repealed or amended.

Section 23: Notice to registrar of existence of restriction on amendment of articles

81.   This is a new provision that requires a company to give notice to the registrar when an entrenching provision is included in its articles (whether on formation or subsequently) or where the company's articles are altered by order of a court or other authority so as to restrict or exclude the power of the company to amend its articles. There is a corresponding requirement as to notice where the company amends its articles so as to remove a provision for entrenchment or where the articles are altered by order of a court or other authority so as to remove a provision for entrenchment or any other restriction on, or any exclusion of, the power of the company to amend its articles.

Section 24: Statement of compliance where amendment of articles restricted

82.   This is a new provision. Where a company's articles contain provision for entrenchment or where the articles are subject to an order of a court or other authority restricting or excluding the company's power to amend its articles and the company subsequently amends its articles, it is required to send to the registrar the document making or evidencing the amendment. This document must be accompanied by a "statement of compliance" (see note on section 13).

83.   The statement of compliance must certify that the amendment to the articles has been made in accordance with the company's articles (including any provision for entrenchment) or, where relevant, in accordance with any order of the court or other authority that is in force at the time of the amendment.

84.   The purpose of the provisions in sections 23 and 24 is to ensure that the registrar, and any person searching the public register, is on notice that the articles contain entrenching provisions and that special rules therefore apply to the company's articles.

Section 25: Effect of alteration of articles on company's members

85.   This section restates section 16 of the 1985 Act. The only difference is that section 16 also applied to alterations of a company's memorandum. A company formed under the Act will not be able to (or need to) alter its memorandum.

86.   This section retains the principle that a member of a company is not bound by any alteration made to the articles subsequent to his becoming a member if the alteration has the effect of increasing his liability to the company or requires him to take more shares in the company. A member may however give his written consent to such an alteration and, where he does, he will be bound by it.

Section 26: Registrar to be sent copy of amended articles

87. The First Company Law Directive (68/151/EEC) requires Member States to take such measures as are required to ensure that companies disclose certain constitutional information which will then be made available to the public in a central register. In particular, companies are to be required to disclose (i) their *"instrument of constitution, and the statutes if they are contained in a separate instrument"*; (ii) *any amendments to these instruments*; and (iii) *"after every [such] amendment...the complete text of the instrument or statutes as amended to date"*. For UK companies, the "instrument of constitution" equates to the memorandum and the "statutes" equate to the articles. The central registers are those kept by the registrars of companies for England and Wales, Scotland and Northern Ireland.

88. This section replaces equivalent provisions in section 18(2) and (3) of the 1985 Act and Schedule 24 to that Act.

89. Where a company fails to comply with the provisions of this section, the company and every officer of the company who is in default commits an offence. The penalty for this offence is set out in *subsection (4)*.

Section 27: Registrar's notice to comply in case of failure with respect to amended articles

90. This section is a new provision. It gives the registrar a means of ensuring that companies comply with the obligation set out in section 26 without having to resort to criminal proceedings. (However, the offence of failing to file amended articles is retained: see of section 26(3)).

91. Where the registrar becomes aware of any default in complying with section 26 (or any similar provision of another enactment that was in force at the time of the default, for example, section 18(2) of the 1985 Act), she may give notice to the company requiring it to rectify the breach within 28 days. Where the company complies with the notice, the company will avoid prosecution for its initial failure to comply. If the company does not comply, it will be liable to a civil penalty of £200, recoverable by the registrar as a debt, in addition to any criminal penalty that may be imposed (see, for example, section 26(4)).

Section 28: Existing companies: provisions of memorandum treated as provisions of articles

92. For companies formed under the Act, the memorandum will contain limited information evidencing the intention of the founder members to form a company. The memoranda of existing companies, on the other hand, will contain key constitutional information of a type which will in future be set out in the articles or provided to the registrar in another format (see Part 2). *Subsection (1)* of this section provides that such material is to be treated for the future as part of the company's articles.

93. *Subsection (2)* of this section makes it clear that where the memorandum of an existing company contains a provision for entrenchment (see note on section 22) at the date that this part of the Act comes into force, this will be deemed, with effect from that date, to be a provision for entrenchment in the company's articles.

CHAPTER 3: RESOLUTIONS AND AGREEMENTS AFFECTING A COMPANY'S CONSTITUTION

94.   This Chapter replaces equivalent provisions in the 1985 Act on the registration of resolutions and agreements and on making these available to members.

Section 29: Resolutions and agreements affecting a company's constitution

95.   This section replaces section 380(4) and (4A) of the 1985 Act. It lists the resolutions and agreements that must be forwarded to the registrar for registration (see section 30) and made available to members on request (see section 32).

Section 30: Copies of resolutions or agreements to be forwarded to registrar

96.   This section restates section 380 (1), (5) and (7) of the 1985 Act and Schedule 24 to that Act. Where a company passes a resolution or enters into an agreement of the type listed in section 29, it must forward a copy of the resolution or agreement to the registrar for registration within 15 days of the date on which the resolution was passed. If a company fails to do this, the company, and every officer of it who is in default, commits an offence. For the penalty, see *subsection (3)*.

97.   Where a resolution or agreement which affects a company's constitution is not in writing, the company is required to provide the registrar with a written memorandum setting out the terms of the resolution or agreement in question.

CHAPTER 4: MISCELLANEOUS AND SUPPLEMENTARY PROVISIONS

Section 31: Statement of company's objects

98.   This section provides for a new approach to the question of a company's objects. Under the 1985 Act all companies are required to have objects and these objects are required to be specified in the memorandum. The 1985 Act also makes specific provision for where a company states its objects to be to carry on business as a general commercial company (see section 3A of the 1985 Act).

99.   Based on a recommendation of the CLR (Final Report, paragraph 9.10), under the Act a different approach is taken. Instead of companies being required to specify their objects, companies will have unrestricted objects unless the objects are specifically restricted by the articles (see *subsection (1)*). This will mean that unless a company makes a deliberate choice to restrict its objects, the objects will have no bearing on what it can do. Some companies will continue to restrict their objects. Companies that are charities will need to restrict their objects (under charities legislation) and some community interest companies may also choose to do so.

100.   *Subsection (2)* provides that where a company changes its articles to add, remove or alter a statement of the company's objects, it must give notice to the registrar. The registrar is to register that notice, and the alteration does not take effect until it has been so registered.

101.   *Subsection (3)* ensures that such an amendment to the company's articles will not affect any rights or obligations of the company or render defective any legal proceedings by or against it.

102.   For companies which are charities, the effect of this section is subject to section 64 of the Charities Act 1993 in England and Wales and in Northern Ireland subject to the Charities (Northern Ireland) Order 1987 (SI 1987/2048 (NI 19)) *(subsection (4))*.

103.   *Subsection (5)* makes equivalent provision for Scotland. These provisions impose additional requirements in the case of companies which are charities when changing certain aspects of their constitutions, including their objects.

104.   The directors of a company are under a duty to observe the company's constitution (see section 171) although restrictions in objects will, as now, have little effect outside of the internal workings of the company because of the effect of sections 39 and 40 (except in the case of charities where modified rules again apply – see section 42).

Section 32: Constitutional documents to be provided to members

105.   This section replaces section 19 of the 1985 Act and Schedule 24 to that Act. It gives members the right to obtain from the company copies of the company's articles and certain other documents of constitutional importance (see *subsection (1)*).

106.   The provision in the 1985 Act which enables a company to charge its members 5p for a copy of its articles and/or memorandum has been removed. This information must in future be provided to the members (on request) free of charge.

107.   Where a company fails to comply with the provisions of this section, every officer of the company who is in default commits an offence. For the penalty for this offence, see *subsection (4)*.

Section 33: Effect of company's constitution

108.   *Subsection (1)* of this section replaces section 14(1) of the 1985 Act. Its effect is that the provisions of a company's constitution constitute a special kind of contract, whose terms bind the company and its members from time to time. Like section 14(1), the provisions of this section are excepted from the general principle set out in section 1 of the Contracts (Rights of Third Parties) Act 1999, so that provisions of a company's constitution will not confer any rights on persons other than the company and its members. Unlike section 14(1), section 34 refers to "*a company's constitution*", rather than its "*memorandum and articles*". This reflects the new division of formation and constitutional information between the memorandum, articles and other constitutional documents noted above.

109.   The language in *subsection (1)* has been updated but there is no change to the law (the provision continues to reflect what the law has always been: in particular a company's constitution binds both the company and its members).

110.   *Subsection (2)* replaces section 14(2) of the 1985 Act. It provides that amounts which a member of a company is obliged to pay to it under its constitution are debts due to the company. In England and Wales and Northern Ireland, such debts are ordinary contract debts.

Section 34: Notice to registrar where company's constitution altered by enactment

111.   This section replaces section 18 of the 1985 Act and Schedule 24 to that Act.

112.   The provisions of a company's constitution may be altered by legislation, rather than by a resolution or agreement of the company's members. Such legislation will either be of general relevance to all companies (for example, a new Companies Act provision that

provisions of a certain type in any company's articles are void), or to all companies of a particular type (for example, new commonhold legislation changing the provisions prescribed for inclusion in the articles of all commonhold associations) or it will be relevant only to a particular company (for example, a private Act of Parliament amending the articles of a specific company established by an earlier Act).

113.   In keeping with the principles underlying section 26, it is important that those searching the register of companies should be able to be made aware of the changes to companies' articles which legislation may effect. However, there is a balance to be struck between maintaining transparency on the one hand and inundating the registrar and searchers with mountains of paper which will be of little practical use to persons searching the public register (and whose contents are generally available in any event). The section therefore does not require companies to send copies of most public general Acts which alter their articles (such as Companies Acts or new commonhold legislation) to the registrar. It does however require "special enactments" (as defined in *subsection (4)*) to be sent to the registrar by companies whose articles are altered by the enactment in question.

114.   Where an enactment to which this section applies alters a company's articles, or where such an enactment alters a resolution or agreement affecting the company's constitution, the company is obliged to send a copy of the articles, or the resolution or agreement in question, as altered, to the registrar.

115.   The procedural rules for sending such legislation to the registrar, and the penalties for non-compliance with them, are as for section 26.

Section 35: Notice to registrar where company's constitution altered by order

116.   This is a new provision which provides a mechanism for registering alterations which are made to a company's constitution by an order of the court or other authority (for example, the Charity Commission). It obliges companies to give notice of such alterations to the registrar, and to supply a copy of the articles, or the resolution or agreement in question, as altered to the registrar.

Section 36: Documents to be incorporated in or accompany copies of articles issued by company

117.   This section replaces section 380(2), (6) and (7) of the 1985 Act and Schedule 24 to that Act. It provides that every copy of a company's articles which it issues must be accompanied by various documents: in particular resolutions, agreements, enactments or orders which affect or evidence alterations to the company's constitution (see *subsection (1)*) unless the effect of the resolution, agreement, enactment or order has been incorporated into the company's articles or is no longer in force.

118.   The intention behind this provision is that information provided on a request for a copy of the company's articles should be up-to-date but the company should not be obliged to provide the same information twice (i.e. in different forms).

Section 37: Right to participate in profits otherwise than as member void

119.   This section restates section 15(1) of the 1985 Act. It provides that a company limited by guarantee without a share capital cannot, by means of a provision in its articles or a resolution of its members, confer on any person a right to participate in its divisible profits otherwise than as a member. As under the 1985 Act, there is no statutory restriction on the

members of such companies participating in their profits, unless they have sought exemption from the use of the word "limited" in their names.

Section 38: Application to single member companies of enactments and rules of law

120.   Under section 7 it will be possible for a single person to form any type of company. This section provides that in future any enactment or rule of law that is applicable to companies formed by two or more persons (or having two or more members) applies (with any necessary modifications) to companies formed with one member (or having only one person as a member). This is already the case in respect of private limited companies: see the Companies (Single Member Private Limited Companies) Regulations 1992 (SI 1992/1699).

PART 4: A COMPANY'S CAPACITY AND RELATED MATTERS

121.   This Part replaces various provisions in the 1985 Act about a company's capacity and related matters, including in particular those in Chapter 3 of Part 1 of that Act.

Section 39: A company's capacity

122.   This section provides that the validity of a company's acts is not to be questioned on the ground of lack of capacity because of anything in a company's constitution. It replaces the present section 35(1) and (4) of the 1985 Act, which made similar provision for restrictions of capacity contained in the memorandum.

123.   The section does not contain provision corresponding to section 35(2) and (3) of the 1985 Act. It is considered that the combination of the fact that under the Act a company may have unrestricted objects (and where it has restricted objects the directors' powers are correspondingly restricted), and the fact that a specific duty on directors to abide by the company's constitution is provided for in section 171, makes these provisions unnecessary.

124.   *Subsection (2)* indicates that the section, like section 35 of the 1985 Act, is modified in its application to charities.

Section 40: Power of directors to bind the company

125.   This section provides safeguards for a person dealing with a company in good faith and restates section 35A and 35B of the 1985 Act. The power of the directors to bind the company, or authorise others to do so, is deemed not to be constrained by the company's constitution. This means that a third party dealing with a company in good faith need not concern itself about whether a company is acting within its constitution.

126.   *Subsection (2)(b)(i)* of the section replaces part of section 35B of the 1985 Act: an external party is not bound to enquire whether there are any limitations on the power of the directors. The first limb of section 35B (which refers to the memorandum) has not been carried forward. This is concerned with restrictions in a company's constitution that limit a company's ability to act and consequently the powers of the directors to bind the company (the so called "ultra vires rule"). Under the Act, the objects no longer affect the company's capacity to act and so this limb is not necessary.

Section 41: Constitutional limitations: transactions involving directors or their associates

127.   This section restates section 322A of the 1985 Act. It applies to a transaction if, or to the extent that, its validity depends on section 40 and provides that where the party to a

transaction with a company is an "insider" (for example, a director of the company or person connected to such a director – see *subsection (2)(b)(i) and (ii)*), then the protection afforded by that section will not apply. Instead, the transaction will be voidable at the instance of the company.

128.   Irrespective of whether the transaction is avoided, the "insider" and any director who authorised the transaction is liable to account to the company for any gain he has made as a result of the transaction and to indemnify the company for any loss or damage that the company has incurred (see *subsection (3)*). However, where the "insider" is not a director of the company, it may be possible for him to avoid liability if he can show that at the time he entered into the transaction with the company he was unaware that the directors were exceeding their powers (see *subsection (5)*).

129.   As now, under *subsection (4)*, a transaction will cease to be voidable in certain circumstances, for example, if restitution is no longer possible.

Section 42: Constitutional limitations: companies that are charities

130.   This section restates section 65 of the Charities Act 1993. It is a qualification of the rules in sections 39 and 40.

131.   It provides that the protection afforded to an external party by sections 39 and 40 will not apply where the company in question is a charity, unless:

- the external party was unaware (at the time that the act was done) that the company was a charity; or

- the company has received full consideration in respect of the act done, and the external party was unaware that the act in question was beyond the company's capacity or beyond the powers of the directors.

132.   Corresponding provisions for charities that are registered in Scotland can be found in section 112 of the Companies Act 1989 (see *subsection (5)*).

Section 43: Company contracts

133.   This section restates the provisions of section 36 of the 1985 Act.

Section 44: Execution of documents

134.   This section largely restates section 36A of the 1985 Act. It provides that a company may execute a document under the law of England and Wales or Northern Ireland by affixing the company seal or by signature by two directors or by one director and a secretary (or joint-secretary) or (for the first time) by a single director if that signature is witnessed and attested.

Section 45: Common seal

135.   This section replaces the provisions of sections 36A(3) and 350 of the 1985 Act. It permits but does not require a company to have a common seal. If a company has a common seal, it requires the seal to include the company's name: failure to do so is an offence.

Section 46: Execution of deeds

136.   This section restates section 36AA, inserted into the 1985 Act by the Regulatory Reform (Execution of Deeds and Documents) Order 2005 (SI 2005/1906). The only change is to extend the application for the purposes of the law of Northern Ireland.

Section 47: Execution of deeds and other documents by attorney

137.   This section replaces section 38 of the 1985 Act. The 1985 Act does not require the appointment of the attorney to be by deed nor does it say anything about deeds executed on behalf of the company in the United Kingdom. This section provides that a company may appoint, under the law of England and Wales or Northern Ireland, attorneys to execute deeds or other documents on its behalf, and that documents executed in this manner, whether in the UK or abroad, have effect as if executed by the company. It also makes clear that the method for a company appointing an attorney is by instrument executed as a deed, which is the same method by which an individual appoints an attorney.

Section 48: Execution of documents by companies

138.   This section restates section 36B of the 1985 Act. It makes clear that no seal is required regardless of any other statutory provision. The only change is the addition of *subsection (1)* which makes clear that this section forms part of the law of Scotland only.

Section 49: Official seal for use abroad

139.   This section replaces section 39 of the 1985 Act. It sets out the circumstances and manner in which a company may use its common seal outside the UK.

Section 50: Official seal for share certificates etc

140.   This section restates section 40(1) of the 1985 Act. It enables a company that has a common seal to have an official seal for sealing securities issued by the company and for sealing documents creating or evidencing securities so issued.

Section 51: Pre-incorporation contracts, deeds and obligations

141.   This section restates section 36C of the 1985 Act. A company is not bound by a contract purportedly made on its behalf before it came into existence unless the obligations are novated, i.e. a new contract must come into existence after incorporation on the same terms as the old one. Novation may be express or implied.

Section 52: Bills of exchange and promissory notes

142.   This section restates section 37 of the 1985 Act. A bill of exchange is an unconditional order in writing, addressed by one person to another, signed by the person giving it, requiring the person to whom it is addressed to pay on demand or at a fixed or determinable future time a sum certain in money to or to the order of a specified person, or to its bearer. A promissory note is an unconditional promise in writing made by one person to another, signed by the maker, engaging to pay, on demand or at a fixed or determinable future time, a sum certain in money to, or to the order of, a specified person or to its bearer. Where someone acting under a company's authority makes, accepts, or endorses such an instrument in the name of the company, or on its behalf, this section treats this as if these actions had been done by the company.

PART 5: A COMPANY'S NAME

143.   This Part applies to the name under which a company is registered, sometimes called the "corporate name". This Part regulates the choice of name. The rules are primarily intended to ensure that third parties are not misled. There are no property rights in companies' registered names as such. While there is no requirement for a company to use its

registered name in the course of business, this Part also requires a company to disclose its name in specified circumstances.

144.   Sections 70 to 74 provide for the appointment of adjudicators in cases where there is dispute over the registering of a company name. Section 71 safeguards the independence of the adjudicators and section 74 provides a right of appeal to the court.

CHAPTER 1: GENERAL REQUIREMENTS

Section 53: Prohibited names

145.   This section replaces section 26(1)(d) and (e) of the 1985 Act. It retains the existing prohibition of companies registering names that cannot be used without commission of an offence and of those that are offensive.

Section 54: Names suggesting connection with government or public authority

146.   This section replaces section 26(2)(a) of the 1985 Act. It prevents a name being registered without the Secretary of State's approval if it suggests a connection with Her Majesty's Government, a local authority or – which represents a change from the 1985 Act – any part of the Scottish administration, or Her Majesty's Government in Northern Ireland. A new power allows similar protection to be extended to other public authorities.

Section 55: Other sensitive words or expressions

147.   This section replaces sections 26(2)(b), 29(1)(a) and 29(6) of the 1985 Act.

148.   *Subsection (1)* requires prior approval for the adoption of a name that includes words or expressions specified in regulations. *Subsection (2)* provides for the procedure to be used for making the regulations. The words and expressions protected by the current Regulations (the Company and Business Names Regulations 1981, SI 1981/1685) include British, English, Scottish and Welsh; chamber of commerce, charity, Her Majesty, midwife, police, and university.

Section 56: Duty to seek comment of government department or other specified body

149.   This section replaces section 29(1)(b) and (2) and (3) of the 1985 Act. It provides power for the Secretary of State to specify whose view must be sought when seeking approval for a name. For example, under the present Regulations, the approval of the General Dental Council is required for the use of either "dental" or "dentistry". Regulations under the new power would be able to replicate this. They could also require the approval of, say, the House Authorities for names suggesting a connection with Parliament.

150.   When a request is made under section 56 in connection with the registration or the change of name of a company, the registrar must be sent a statement that a request has been made, and a copy of the response (see *subsections (3) and (4)*). But the registrar must no make the response available for public inspections (see section 1087(1)(a)).

Section 57: Permitted characters etc

151.   This section is a new provision. It provides power for regulations to specify what letters, symbols, etc may be used in a company's registered name; the regulations may also specify a permitted format for a name (for example, to prevent the use of superscript or subscript).

CHAPTER 2: INDICATIONS OF COMPANY TYPE OR LEGAL FORM

Section 58: Public limited companies

152.   This section replaces section 25(1) of the 1985 Act (and also section 27(4)(b) and (d) in its application to public limited companies). It brings together in a single provision all the alternative statutory indicators of legal status that must be used by a public company as part of its registered name, i.e. "public limited company" or the Welsh equivalent or the specified abbreviations. This section does not apply to community interest companies.

Section 59: Private limited companies

153.   This section replaces section 25(2) of the 1985 Act (and also section 27(4)(a) and (c) in its application to private limited companies). It brings together in a single provision all the alternative statutory indicators of legal status that must be used by a private company as part of its registered name, i.e. "limited" or the Welsh equivalent or the specified abbreviations. Certain companies are exempt (see section 61). This section does not apply to community interest companies.

Sections 60 to 62: Exemption from requirement as to use of "limited"

154.   These sections replace section 30 of the 1985 Act. Section 30 exempts certain companies from the requirement for their names to conclude with "limited". Exempt companies are also exempt under the 1985 Act from some of the requirements regarding publication of their name but they still have to disclose their limited status in correspondence. Those currently exempt are those with a licence granted under section 19 of the Companies Act 1948 which have delivered a statutory declaration to the Registrar that the company complies with the requirements for the exemption. These requirements are, in effect, that the company is non-profit-making and its objects are the promotion of commerce, art, science, education, religion, charity or any profession.

155.   Section 60 continues the exemption for companies already exempt so long as they continue to meet the conditions and until they change their registered name. It also provides an exemption for charities and allows the Secretary of State to make regulations exempting other companies. Only private companies may be exempt

156.   Sections 61 and 62, which replace section 30(2) and (3), specify the conditions that must be met for a company currently exempt to continue to qualify for the exemption: its objects must continue to satisfy the criteria for their exemption and its articles must both preclude distributions of dividends to its members and also, in the event of it being wound up, require its assets to be passed to a body with similar objects. For companies limited by shares benefiting from an exemption under the 1948 Act (or its Northern Irish equivalent), there is a new requirement that the articles prevent a distribution of capital. This is linked to the change in section 63(4) (see below).

Section 63: Exempt company: restriction on alteration of articles

157.   This section replaces section 31(1) and (5). It prohibits a company benefiting from an exemption under the 1985 Act or the 1948 Act (or their Northern Irish equivalents) from changing its articles in such a way that it no longer meets the requirements for the exemption. It is an offence to change the company's articles in such a way. Many companies with an exemption under the 1948 Act (or its Northern Irish equivalent) were made to include a provision in their memoranda preventing an amendment to their memoranda or articles

without the consent of the Board of Trade (there were a number of variations on this theme). *Subsections (4) and (5)* make provision to remove this administrative burden.

Section 64: Power to direct change of name in case of company ceasing to be entitled to exemption

158.　This section replaces section 31(2) to (6). It gives the Secretary of State power to withdraw a private company's exemption from the requirement for its name to conclude with "limited" and to direct it to change its name if it no longer meets the criteria that applied when it was granted the exemption.

Section 65: Inappropriate use of indications of company type or legal form

159.　This section replaces section 26(1)(a), (b), (bb) and (bbb) of the 1985 Act. These paragraphs restrict the use of various words, expressions and abbreviations that are indicators of legal status for various types of commercial entity, e.g. p.l.c., community interest company, open-ended investment company, etc. Some of the restrictions apply to the use of the particular indicator at the end of a company's name; some anywhere other than the end of the name; and some anywhere in a company's name.

160.　This section provides power to make regulations prohibiting the inclusion in a company's name of specified words, expressions and abbreviations. The only words etc that can be specified in the regulations are those associated with a particular type of company or form or organisation or those confusingly similar to such words and expressions. This section also provides power to require or prohibit the statutory indicators of legal status being used in conjunction with specified other words.

CHAPTER 3: SIMILARITY TO OTHER NAMES

Section 66: Name not to be the same as another in the index

161.　This section replaces section 26(1)(c) and (3) of the 1985 Act.

162.　*Subsection (1)* retains the present prohibition, in section 26(1)(c), on a company adopting a name that is already on the registrar's index of company names – which includes not only the names of Companies Act companies but various other business entities (see section 1099). *Subsections (2) and (3)* provide power for the Secretary of State to make regulations to replace the detailed rules presently contained in section 26(3) of the 1985 Act as to:

- what is to be disregarded; and

- what words, letters and symbols are to be taken as the same, or as not the same,

when comparing a proposed and an existing name. At present only "and" and "&" are taken as the same.

163.　The section provides power also to treat as the same:

- currency symbols (e.g. £, $) and their respective English word equivalents;

- "%" and "per cent";

- "1", "2", "3" etc and "one", "two" "three".

164.   The prohibition of names that, under these rules, are the same as an existing name will not be discretionary. But in future, it will be possible for there to be exceptions: *subsection (4)* provides that the regulations may provide that names which would otherwise be prohibited as being the same may be permitted in specified circumstances, or with specified consent, and that a subsequent change of circumstances or withdrawal of consent will not affect the company's registration.

Section 67: Power to direct change of name in case of similarity to existing name

165.   This section replaces section 28(2) of the 1985 Act which provides power for the Secretary of State to direct a company to change its name if the name is the same as or too like a name already on the registrar's index of company names (or one which should have been there). The objective is to prevent the public being confused by the simultaneous appearance on the register of two very similar names when the similarity is such that the later name was not caught by the non-discretionary prohibition of adopting a name effectively the "same as" an existing name (see section 66).

166.   The section is intended to cover two circumstances. First, any delay in the entry on the index of company names of new names of entities that are not UK companies. Companies House enter all names immediately but there may be delays outside their control. If the name had already been taken by the other entity before the company adopted it, then the Secretary of State will direct the company to change its name. Second, the visual difference between the new name and an existing name being so small that third parties are likely to be confused by the simultaneous appearance of both names on the index of company names.

167.   *Subsections (2) and (3)* provide power to make regulations, corresponding to that provided by section 66, to replace the detailed rules presently contained in section 26(3) of the 1985 Act as to:

- what is to be disregarded; and

- what words, letters and symbols are to be taken as the same

when comparing a proposed and an existing name. As in section 67, *subsection (4)* provides for a power to make regulations permitting names that would otherwise be regarded as "too like" in certain circumstances or where consent is given.

Section 68: Direction to change name: supplementary provisions

168.   This section replaces section 28(4) and (5) of the 1985 Act as they apply to section 28(2). It provides a deadline of 12 months for the Secretary of State to direct a change of name under section 67, and for the Secretary of State to specify a period for the company's compliance. It makes failure by the company to comply an offence.

Similarity to other name in which person has goodwill

169.   Sections 69 to 74 are new provisions. They respond to the CLR recommendation (Final Report, paragraph 11.50) that there be provision so that a person can apply for a company to be directed to change its name if the applicant can show that the name was chosen with the principal intention of seeking money from him or preventing him registering the name where it is one in which he has previously acquired reputation or goodwill.

Section 69: Objection to company's registered name

170.   This section provides for any person, not just a company, to object to a company names adjudicator if a company's name is similar to a name in which the objector has goodwill. There is list of circumstances raising a presumption that a name was adopted legitimately. The respondent must show that one of these applies, or otherwise that he acted in good faith or that the interests of the applicant are not significantly affected (for example, where the applicant has hardly used the name at all). The objection will be upheld if the respondent cannot do so, or if the objector can show that the name was registered either to obtain money from him or to prevent him using the name.

Section 70: Company names adjudicators

171.   This section provides power for the Secretary of State to appoint company names adjudicators and their staff and to finance their activities. One of the adjudicators is to be appointed Chief Adjudicator.

Section 71: Procedural rules

172.   This section provides the Secretary of State with power to make rules for the proceedings before a company names adjudicator. The list of matters which the rules may cover is not exhaustive. It also enables the rule to confer on the Chief Adjudicator power to determine any matter that could be the subject of the rules made under this power.

Section 72: Decision of adjudicator to be made available to public

173.   This section requires the adjudicator to publish his decision and his reasons for it, possibly through a website. The publication must be within 90 days of the decision.

Section 73: Order requiring name to be changed

174.   This section is a new provision. If an objection made under section 69 is upheld, then the adjudicator is to direct the company with the offending name to change its name to one that does not similarly offend. A deadline must be set for the change. If the offending name is not changed, then the adjudicator will determine a new name for the company.

Section 74: Appeal from adjudicator's decision

175.   This section enables appeal to a court against the decision of the company names adjudicator. The court will either uphold or reverse the adjudicator's decision, and may make any order that the adjudicator might have made.

CHAPTER 4: OTHER POWERS OF THE SECRETARY OF STATE

Section 75: Provision of misleading information etc

176.   This section replaces section 28(3) of the 1985 Act and, insofar as they support that subsection, section 28(4) and (5). It provides power for the Secretary of State to direct a company to change its name within a specified period in two circumstances. First, if misleading information was given to enable the adoption of the name. Second, if an undertaking or assurance given to enable the adoption of the name has not been fulfilled. The direction can only be made up to five years after the adoption of the name. It is an offence not to comply with the direction.

Section 76: Misleading indication of activities

177.   This section replaces section 32 of the 1985 Act. It provides power for the Secretary of State to direct a company to change its name, regardless of how long the company has had the name, in the specified circumstances. The circumstances are that, in his opinion, not only does the name give a misleading indication of the nature of the company's activities but also that the public are likely to suffer harm as a result. The company may appeal to the court, who may either confirm the direction or set it aside. It is an offence not to comply with the direction.

178.   The section also sets time limits for compliance with the direction (6 weeks) and the application to the court (3 weeks). If the court confirms the direction, it specifies the deadline for compliance.

CHAPTER 5: CHANGE OF NAME

Section 77: Change of name

179.   This section replaces section 28(1) of the 1985 Act. Under the existing provision, companies can only change their names:

- by special resolution; or

- following a direction by the Secretary of State in the restricted circumstances provided by section 31 of the 1985 Act, which apply only to companies exempt from their name concluding in "limited."

180.   This section also provides for the following means:

- whatever means are provided in the company's articles (this means that the company will be able to determine the procedures for changing its own name);

- by an order of the company names adjudicator if an objection under section 73 is upheld, or by a court following an appeal against the adjudicator's decision under section 74; and

- under section 1033 on the company's restoration to the register.

Section 78: Change of name by special resolution

181.   This section is a new provision. It requires the company to notify the registrar of a change of name when it has been agreed by special resolution. This requirement is in addition to the obligation under Chapter 3 of Part 3 to forward a copy of the special resolution to the registrar. *Subsections (2)* and *(3)* address the particular situation where a company has passed a special resolution to change its name but the change is not to take place until some other event has occurred (e.g. a merger). The notice of change of name must say that the change is conditional and whether the event has occurred. If the event has not yet occurred, the registrar will not act on the notice to change the name until she has received a second notice stating that the specified event has occurred. The registrar may rely on that statement without further evidence.

Section 79: Change of name by means provided for in company's articles

182.   This section is a new provision, supplementing the new provision (section 77(1)(b)) whereby a company may change its name by any means provided for in its articles.

Subsection (1) requires the company to provide the registrar with both a notice of the name change and a statement that the change has been made in accordance with the company's articles. *Subsection (2)* ensures the registrar may rely on that statement without further evidence.

Section 80: Change of name: registration and issue of new certificate of incorporation

183.　This section, which partly replaces sections 28(6) and 32(5) of the 1985 Act, provides for the procedures that the registrar must perform before a company's proposed new name is effective. *Subsection (2)* provides for the checks both that the name meets all the requirements for a company's name in this Part of the Act and that the necessary documents have been provided. *Subsection (3)* provides for the company to be issued with a certificate of incorporation with the new name.

Section 81: Change of name: effect

184.　This section, which replaces sections 28(6) and 32(5) in part and, in total, section 28(7) of the 1985 Act, provides that the new name is effective as soon as the altered certificate of incorporation is issued. It also provides that the change of name does not affect the company's rights or obligations or legal proceedings by or against it in its previous name.

CHAPTER 6: TRADING DISCLOSURES

Section 82: Requirement to disclose company name etc

185.　This section replaces sections 348(1), 349(1), and 351(1) and (2) of the 1985 Act and, insofar as it applies to companies, section 4(1) of the Business Names Act 1985. It provides power for the Secretary of State to make regulations requiring every company:

- to display a sign with its name and specified other information at specified locations;

- to include its name and specified other information in specified documents and communications;

- to provide its name and specified other information to those who request it in the course of business (this is a new provision insofar as it applies to companies doing business under their registered names).

Section 83: Civil consequences of failure to make required disclosure

186.　This section replaces section 5 of the Business Names Act 1985, so far as it applies to companies. As recommended by the CLR (Final Report, paragraph 11.57), it follows the precedent of the Business Names Act as regards the civil consequences of failure to comply with the information requirements made in regulations under section 82: the provision for personal civil liability of officers in default in section 349(4) of the Companies Act 1985 is not included.

Section 84: Criminal consequences of failure to make required disclosures

187.　This section replaces sections 348(2), 349(2) and (3) and 351(5) of the 1985 Act and, insofar as it applies to companies, part of section 7 of the Business Names Act 1985. It makes it an offence not to comply with the requirements, to be specified in regulations under section 82, for every company to disclose its name and specified other information.

Section 85: Minor variations in form of name to be left out of account

188.   This section is a new provision. It means that the company's name as used to comply with the disclosure requirements need not be exactly the same as the registered name. The permitted differences are the case of the letters, the use of punctuation, accents, etc and formatting. However the differences must not result in there being a risk of confusion.

PART 6: A COMPANY'S REGISTERED OFFICE

Section 86: A company's registered office

189.   This section restates section 287(1) of the 1985 Act. It requires every company to have a registered office and provides for that office to be an address to which communications and notices may be sent. Section 1139 provides that the service of a document on a company is effective if it is sent to its registered office.

Section 87: Change of address of registered office

190.   This section restates section 287(3) to (6) of the provisions of the 1985 Act. It provides the means by which a company may change the address of its registered office.

Section 88: Welsh companies

191.   This section provides a definition of a Welsh company. A company can be set up as a Welsh company by delivering to the registrar a statement on formation that its registered office is to be situated in Wales (see section 9(2)(b)). *Subsection (2)* restates section 2(2) of the 1985 Act whereby a company may become a Welsh company by passing a special resolution (so that the register states that its registered office is to be situated "in Wales"). As recommended by the CLR, *subsection (3)* provides a mechanism whereby a company can cease to be a Welsh company (i.e. so that the register states that its registered office is to be situated in "England and Wales"). This is new. At present, while a company may choose to restrict the address of its registered office to Wales on formation or subsequently by special resolution, it is not possible under the 1985 Act for a Welsh company to drop the restriction so that its registered office address can be changed to anywhere in England and Wales.

192.   Welsh companies may deliver documents to the registrar in Welsh (see section 1104). Welsh companies may also end their company name with Welsh versions of the statutory indicators of legal status. For example, "cyfyngedig" in place of "limited" or "c.c.c." in place of "p.l.c." (see sections 58 and 59). When a company ceases to be a Welsh company using the procedure under this section, it may no longer take advantage of these provisions.

193.   Where a company passes a special resolution under subsection (2) or (3) (and so becomes or ceases to be Welsh company) *subsection (4)* provides that the registrar will amend the register and issue the company with a new certificate of incorporation.

PART 7: RE-REGISTRATION AS A MEANS OF ALTERING A COMPANY'S STATUS

194.   This Part of the Act is about the re-registration of companies. It replaces equivalent provisions in Part 2 of the 1985 Act. There are some substantive changes as well as amendments reflecting the new provisions of the Act about registration which are carried through to the re-registration provisions.

Introductory

Section 89: Alteration of status by re-registration

195.   This section provides for various ways under the Act by which a company may alter its status. As recommended by the CLR (Final Report, paragraph 11.6) it retains the current possibilities for re-registration, but there is one significant change to the 1985 Act regime: in line with the recommendations of the CLR (Final Report, paragraph 11.11), in future a public company will be able to re-register as an unlimited private company without first having to re-register as private limited – see section 109.

Private company becoming public

Section 90: Re-registration of private company as public

196.   This section restates section 43(1) and (2), and section 48 of the 1985 Act. It enables a private company (whether limited or unlimited) to re-register as a public company providing that certain conditions are met. These conditions are set out in *subsections (2) to (4)*. They include a requirement for the company to make such alterations to its name and articles of association ("articles") as are necessary to reflect the fact that the company will be a public company. This will be particularly important for private companies formed under the Act who are using the model articles: in particular, the new model articles for private companies limited by shares formed under the Act will be written with such companies in mind and are unlikely to be suitable for use by a newly re-registered public company – see notes on sections 19 and 20.

197.   As now (see section 48 of the 1985 Act), an unlimited private company with a share capital will be able to re-register as a public company and this is reflected in *subsection (4)* of this section.

198.   *Subsection (2)(e)* retains the requirement that a private company may not re-register as a public company if it has previously re-registered as an unlimited company. The intention behind this provision is that a company should not be able to enjoy the benefits of limited liability or avoid the obligations that are attached to this, for example, the increased reporting requirements, by continually swapping from limited to unlimited status.

Section 91: Requirements as to share capital

199.   This section restates sections 45, 47(3) and 48(5) to (7) of the 1985 Act. It sets out the requirements as to share capital of a company that it is proposing to re-register as a public company. These requirements carry forward the provisions of current companies legislation, for example, the company's share capital must not be less than the authorised minimum (defined in section 763) and each of the company's allotted shares must be paid up at least as to a quarter of the nominal value of that share and the whole of any premium on in.

200.   *Subsection (5)* of this section replaces section 47(3) of the 1985 Act. It provides that the registrar must not issue a new certificate of incorporation on re-registration if the court has made an order confirming a reduction of capital which has the effect of bringing the company's allotted share capital below the authorised minimum (which remains at £50,000 but may be satisfied in sterling or euros – see section 763) or if the company has reduced its capital via the new solvency statement procedure for capital reductions (see section 642) or in connection with a redenomination of share capital (see section 626).

Section 92: Requirements as to net assets

201.   This section restates section 43(3)(b), (c) and (e), and (4), and section 46 of the 1985 Act. The requirements as to net assets for a public company remain unchanged (as now, these are determined by reference to the company's most recent balance sheet).

Section 93: Recent allotment of shares for non-cash consideration

202.   This section restates section 44 of the 1985 Act. As now, where there has been an allotment of shares for non-cash consideration between the date of the balance sheet required under section 92 and the date that the company passed the resolution to re-register as a public company, the registrar will not entertain an application for re-registration unless the consideration for the allotment has been valued in accordance with section 596.

Section 94: Application and accompanying documents

203.   This section restates sections 43(3)(a) to (e) and 47(2) of the 1985 Act. It prescribes the contents of the application for re-registration where a private company is proposing to re-register as public. There is one important change, which is required as a result of the abolition of the current requirement for private companies to have a company secretary – see section 270. In future, where a private company is proposing to re-register as a public company the application for re-registration must include a statement of the company's proposed secretary where the company does not already have a secretary. The contents of this statement are prescribed in section 95.

204.   The application for re-registration must be accompanied by a statement of compliance – see section 90(1)(c)(ii) – which replaces the present requirement for a statutory declaration (or its electronic equivalent), contained in subsections 43(3)(e) and (3A) of the 1985 Act, with a requirement to make this statement (see note on section 13).

Section 95: Statement of proposed secretary

205.   This section is a new provision, which is required as a result of the abolition of the requirement for private companies to have a company secretary – see section 270. Where a private company is proposing to re-register as a public company and the company does not already have a company secretary, the application for re-registration must include details of the person or persons who will act as company secretary or joint secretaries on re-registration. The statement of proposed secretary must also contain a consent, given by the person or each of the persons named in the statement, to act as company secretary or joint secretaries. If all the partners in a firm are to be joint secretaries, one partner in the firm may give consent to act on behalf of all of the partners.

Section 96: Issue of certificate of incorporation on re-registration

206.   This section replaces section 47 of the 1985 Act. As now, where the registrar is satisfied that a company is entitled to be re-registered as a public company, she will issue a new certificate of incorporation (which must state that it is being issued on the re-registration of the company). On the issue of a new certificate of incorporation under this section: the company becomes a public company; the change to its name and any amendments that were made to the company's articles take effect; and the person (or persons) named as secretary (or joint secretaries) in the statement of proposed secretary (see section 95) is deemed to have been appointed as such.

207.   As now, the certificate of incorporation on re-registration is conclusive evidence that the company is now a public company and that the requirements of the Act as regards re-registration have been met.

Public company becoming private

Section 97: Re-registration of public company as private limited company

208.   This section replaces section 53 of the 1985 Act. It enables a public company to re-register as a private limited company if the conditions specified in *subsection (2)* are met. The conditions are the same as those which are presently set out in section 53 but there are two important changes:

- Consistent with the approach taken elsewhere in the Act, for example the sections on the re-registration of a private company as public, *subsection (1)(c)(ii)* of this section introduces a new requirement for a statement of compliance (see note on section 13).

- *Subsection (2)* introduces new provisions which enable the registrar to process an application for the re-registration of a company from public to private limited within the 28-day period during which dissenting members may apply to the court, under section 98, for an order cancelling the resolution for re-registration, providing that she is satisfied that such an application cannot be made. This change reflects the registrar's current practice.

209.   As now, the company must make such changes to its name and articles as are necessary in connection with it becoming a private company limited by shares or, as the case may be, a private company limited by guarantee.

Section 98: Application to court to cancel resolution

210.   This section restates section 54(1) to (3) and (5) to (6) of the 1985 Act. As now, where a public company has passed a special resolution to re-register as a private limited company, the requisite majority of the company's members (see *subsection (1)*) may apply to the court for the cancellation of this resolution. Such an application to the court must be made within 28 days of the resolution to re-register being passed and on hearing the application the court may confirm or cancel the resolution or make such other order as it thinks fit.

Section 99: Notice to registrar of court application or order

211.   This section replaces section 54(4) (7) and (10) of the 1985 Act. It makes it clear that, as now, where an application is made to the court under section 98 (that is, to cancel a resolution for re-registration as a private limited company), the company must immediately give notice to the registrar. Similarly, where the court has made an order in connection with such an application, the company must deliver a copy of that order to the registrar within 15 days of the order being made (or such longer time as the court may direct).

212.   *Subsection (1)* of this section is a new provision which requires the dissenting members, on making an application to court seeking to cancel the resolution for re-registration from public to private, to give notice direct to the registrar. This ensures that the registrar is aware of any applications which have been made under section 98 and therefore will enable the registrar to process the application for re-registration without further delay where she is satisfied that no application to court may be made – see note on section 97.

213.   *Subsection (4)* carries forward the offence in section 54(10) of the 1985 Act. Where the company fails to give notice to the registrar or fails to deliver a copy of the order made by the court under section 98 within the prescribed time limits (see *subsections (2) and (3)*), the company and every officer of the company who is in default commits an offence. The penalty for this offence is set out in *subsection (5)*.

Section 100: Application and accompanying documents

214.   This section replaces section 53(1)(b) of the 1985 Act and contains new provisions. It prescribes the documents/information that must accompany the application for re-registration where a company is proposing to re-register from public to private limited. Consistent with the approach taken in the Act with other forms of re-registration, in future the application for re-registration as a private limited company must be accompanied by a statement of compliance – see note on section 13. (There is currently no requirement for a statutory declaration (or electronic equivalent) where a public company re-registers as a private limited company).

Section 101: Issue of certificate of incorporation on re-registration

215.   This section restates section 55 of the 1985 Act. As now, where the registrar is satisfied that a company is entitled to be re-registered as a private limited company, she will issue a new certificate of incorporation (which must state that it is being issued on the re-registration of the company). On the issue of a new certificate of incorporation under this section, the company becomes a private limited company and the change to its name and any amendments that were required to be made to the articles take effect.

216.   As now, the certificate of incorporation on re-registration issued under this section is conclusive evidence that the company is now a private limited company and that the requirements of the Act as regards re-registration have been met.

Private limited company becoming unlimited

Section 102: Re-registration of private limited company as unlimited

217.   This section replaces section 49, of the 1985 Act. As now, this section permits a private company that is limited by shares or, as the case may be, by guarantee, to re-register as an unlimited private company, providing that certain conditions are met (see *subsection (2)*) and all of the members have given their assent to the company being so re-registered. In the case of a deceased member, assent may be given by the personal representative of the deceased member's estate. Where a member is bankrupt, assent may be given by his trustee in bankruptcy (to the exclusion of the member in question).

218.   An "unlimited company" is a company not having any limit on the liability of its members.

219.   As now, a company may not re-register as an unlimited company, if it has previously been re-registered as limited (having previously been unlimited) or as unlimited (having previously been limited).

220.   The application for re-registration as an unlimited company must be accompanied by a statement of compliance (see note on section 13).

Section 103: Application and accompanying documents

221.   This section replaces section 49(8) and (8A) of the 1985 Act. It prescribes the contents of the application for re-registration where a company is proposing to re-register from private limited to unlimited and the documents/information that must accompany this application. The current requirement for a statutory declaration made by the directors on application for re-registration as an unlimited company is replaced by a requirement for a statement of compliance. Unlike other statements of compliance made under the Act (see, for example, section 13) the statement of compliance made on application for re-registration as an unlimited company must contain a statement made by the directors confirming that:

- the persons by whom or on whose behalf the form of assent is authenticated constitute the whole membership of the company; and

- if any of the members have not authenticated that form themselves, that the directors have taken all reasonable steps to satisfy themselves that each person who authenticated it on behalf of a member was lawfully empowered to do so.

222.   The contents of the directors' statement carry forward the provisions of section 49(8) of the 1985 Act.

Section 104: Issue of certificate of incorporation on re-registration

223.   This section restates section 50 of the 1985 Act. As now, where the registrar is satisfied that a company is entitled to be re-registered as an unlimited company, she will issue a new certificate of incorporation (which must state that it is being issued on the re-registration of the company). On the issue of a new certificate of incorporation under this section, the company becomes an unlimited company and the change to its name and any amendments that were required to be made to the articles take effect.

224.   As now, the certificate of incorporation on re-registration is conclusive evidence that the company is now an unlimited company and that the requirements of the Act as regards re-registration have been met.

Unlimited private company becoming limited

Section 105: Re-registration of unlimited company as limited

225.   This section replaces section 51(1) to (3) of the 1985 Act. As now, this section permits an unlimited company to re-register as a private limited company if certain conditions are met (see *subsection (2)*). As now, a re-registration from unlimited to limited requires a special resolution of the company's members, (which must specify whether the company is to be limited by shares or limited by guarantee). The company must also make such changes to its name and articles as are required to reflect the change in the company's status. As is the case under section 51(6) of the 1985 Act, this section does not permit the re-registration of an unlimited company as a public company (this section provides for the re-registration of an unlimited company as a *private* limited company). There is a new requirement for a statement of compliance (see note on section 13).

Section 106: Application and accompanying documents

226.   This section replaces section 51(5) of the 1985 Act and contains new provisions. It prescribes the contents of the application for re-registration where an unlimited private company is proposing to re-register as private limited and the documents/information that

must accompany this application. Where the company is to be limited by guarantee, *subsection (2)(b)* requires the application for re-registration to be accompanied by a "statement of guarantee" (see note on section 11). It should be noted that there is <u>no</u> requirement for a statement of capital and initial shareholdings where the company is to be limited by shares. This is unnecessary because the company will be required to make a return of allotments to the registrar, under section 555 as soon as it allots shares subsequent to its registration and the return must be accompanied by a statement of capital.

Section 107: Issue of certificate of incorporation on re-registration

227. This section restates section 52 of the 1985 Act. As now, it provides that, where the registrar is satisfied that a company is entitled to be re-registered as a private company, she will issue a new certificate of incorporation (which must state that it is being issued on the re-registration of the company). On the issue of a new certificate of incorporation under this section, the company becomes a private limited company and the change to its name and any amendments that were required to be made to the articles take effect.

228. As now, the certificate of incorporation on re-registration issued under this section is conclusive evidence that the company is now a private limited company and that the requirements of the Act as regards re-registration have been met.

Section 108: Statement of capital required where company already has share capital

229. This section is a new provision which requires a company that has re-registered from unlimited having a share capital to private limited by shares to file a statement of capital with the registrar in certain circumstances. The statement must be delivered to the registrar within 15 days of the company's re-registration and, where the company fails to observe this requirement, the company and every officer of the company who is in default, commits an offence (see *subsection (4)*).

230. The provision is necessary because unlimited companies are required to provide a statement of capital to the registrar in a limited number of circumstances only: in particular, where the company has a share capital on formation (see section 10) or where an unlimited company having a share capital makes an annual return to the registrar under section 854. Consequently, where an unlimited company having a share capital re-registers as private limited by shares under section 107, in contrast to other companies that are limited by shares, the information on the public register pertaining to the company's subscribed capital may be out of date (in particular if the company has allotted further shares subsequent to its formation or, as the case may be, its last annual return).

231. The requirement for a statement of capital in this section puts companies which have re-registered as private limited by shares under section 107 on the same footing as other companies limited by shares on the register and ensures that the information on the public register is up-to-date. The company will, however, be exempted from the requirement to provide a statement of capital on re-registration where there has been no change to the company's total subscribed capital since it was first formed and registered or, as the case may be, since the company filed its most recent annual return (see *subsection (2)*).

Public company becoming private and unlimited

Section 109: Re-registration of public company as private and unlimited

232. This section is a new provision, which, as recommended by the CLR (Final Report, paragraph 11.11), enables a public company to re-register as a private unlimited company with a share capital without first having to re-register as a private limited company. The conditions specified in *subsection (2)* must be met and all of the members must give their assent to the company being so re-registered. In the case of a deceased member, assent may be given by the personal representative of the deceased member's estate. Where a member is bankrupt, assent may be given by his trustee in bankruptcy (to the exclusion of the member in question).

233. A public company may not re-register as an unlimited private company under this section if it has previously been re-registered as limited or as unlimited (see *subsection (2)*). The intention behind this subsection (which is based on the provision in *subsection (2)(e)* of section 90) is that a company should not be able to enjoy the benefits of limited liability or avoid the obligations that are attached to this, for example, the increased reporting requirements, by continually swapping from limited to unlimited status.

Section 110: Application and accompanying documents

234. This section is a new provision. It prescribes the contents of the application for re-registration where a company is proposing to re-register from public to unlimited private and the documents/information that must accompany this application. There is a requirement for a statement of compliance (see note on section 13) and, in contrast to the statements of compliance that are required elsewhere in the Act, the statement of compliance that is required here must contain a statement made by the directors confirming that:

- the persons by whom or on whose behalf the form of assent is authenticated constitute the whole membership of the company; and

- if any of the members have not authenticated that form themselves, that the directors have taken all reasonable steps to satisfy themselves that each person who authenticated it on behalf of a member was lawfully empowered to do so.

235. This mirrors the requirements of the directors' statement in section 103(4).

Section 111: Issue of certificate of incorporation on re-registration

236. This section is a new provision which requires the registrar to issue a new certificate of incorporation is she is satisfied that a public company is entitled to register as private and unlimited. On the issue of a new certificate of incorporation (which must state that it is being issued on the re-registration of the company), the company becomes a private unlimited company and the change to its name and any amendments that were made to the articles take effect.

237. The certificate of incorporation on re-registration is conclusive evidence that the company is now a private unlimited company and that the requirements of the Act as regards re-registration have been met.

PART 8: A COMPANY'S MEMBERS

238.   This Part of the Act defines who are a company's members, provides rules relating to a company's register of members and overseas branch registers and, subject to certain exceptions, prohibits a company from being a member of its holding company.

CHAPTER 1: THE MEMBERS OF A COMPANY

Section 112: The members of a company

239.   This section restates section 22 of the 1985 Act. There are additional words to make it clear that the subscribers to the memorandum become members on registration of the company, even if the company fails to enter their names in the register of members.

CHAPTER 2: REGISTER OF MEMBERS

Section 113: Register of members

240.   This section restates section 352(1) to (5) of the 1985 Act. The only new provision is *subsection (5)* which makes it clear that, for the purposes of this Chapter, joint holders of a share fall to be treated as a single member, so the register need only show a single address although all their names must be stated in the register.

Section 114: Register to be kept available for inspection

241.   This section replaces section 353 of the 1985 Act. Currently, the register of members is required to be kept at the registered office of the company, except that if the company has appointed a third party to maintain or update the register, it may be kept at the office where that work is done, subject to that office being in the jurisdiction where the company is registered. Under the Act, it is immaterial where the work of compiling or updating the register is carried out. *Subsection (1)* provides that the register must be kept available for inspection either at the company's registered office or at a place permitted under regulations made under section 1136.

Section 115: Index of members

242.   This section replaces section 354 of the 1985 Act. There is no change in the obligation of a company with more than 50 members to maintain an index of the names of the members (which the company is obliged to do unless the register itself is kept in such a form as to constitute an index).

Section 116: Rights to inspect and require copies

243.   This section replaces section 356 of the 1985 Act. Under section 356, the obligation to make the register available for inspection is subject to an exception when the register is closed under section 358 of the 1985 Act. The power to close the register has not been carried forward in the Act and so the obligation in *subsection (1)* is absolute. The CLR recommended that information in a company's register of members should be made available only for certain specified purposes (Final Report, paragraph 11.44). This section follows this recommendation. It modifies the rights of inspection and to be provided with copies of the register of members and its index. (Section 1137 provides power for the Secretary of State to make regulations about the inspection of records and provision of copies and to set fees.) *Subsections (3) and (4),* which are new, require those seeking to inspect or to be provided with a copy of the register of members to provide their names and addresses, the purpose for

which the information will be used, and, if the access is sought on behalf of others, similar information for them.

Section 117: Register of members: response to request for inspection or copy

244.   This is a new provision. This section provides a procedure by which the company can refer the matter to the court if it thinks that the request may not be for a proper purpose. It replaces the 10-day deadline for compliance with a request with a 5-day period within which the company must either comply with the request or apply to the court for relief from the obligation. If the company opts for the latter, then *subsections (3), (4) and (5)* apply. Under subsection (3), if the court is satisfied that the access to the register of members is not sought for a proper purpose, it will require the company of the obligation not to comply with the request and may require that the person who made the request pay the company's costs. Under subsection (4), the court may also require the company not to comply with other requests made requests for similar purposes. If the court does not make an order under subsection (3), or the proceedings are discontinued, then, under subsection (5), the company must immediately comply with the request.

Section 118: Register of members: refusal of inspection or default in providing copy

245.   This section replaces section 356(5) and (6) of and Schedule 24 to the 1985 Act. It retains the existing sanctions for the company's failure to comply with a request. They do not apply if the court has directed that the company need not comply with the request.

Section 119: Register of members: offences in connection with request for or disclosure of information.

246.   This is a new provision. It creates two offences. First, in relation to the new requirement in section 116 to provide information in a request for access, it is an offence knowingly or recklessly to make a statement that is misleading, false or deceptive in a material particular. Second, it is an offence for a person to disclose to another person information from a company's register of members obtained under section 116 knowing or having reason to suspect that the other person may use the information for a purpose that is not a proper purpose.

Section 120: Information as to state of register and index

247.   This is a new provision. It implements the CLR recommendation that companies be required to advise anyone exercising their right of inspection or right to demand a copy of the register or index whether the information is up-to-date and, if not, the date to which it has been made up (Final Report, paragraph 11.43). Failure to provide this information renders the company and any officer in default liable to a fine.

Section 121: Removal of entries relating to former members

248.   This section replaces section 352(6) of the 1985 Act. Based on a recommendation by the CLR (Final Report, paragraph 11.40), it reduces the period for which the entry of a past member must be kept on the register from 20 years to 10 years.

Section 122: Share warrants

249.   This section replaces section 355 of the 1985 Act and implements the CLR recommendation (Completing the Structure, paragraph 5.41) in making clear that shares need not first be issued in registered form, but can be issued directly in warrant to bearer form.

Section 123: Single member companies

250.   This section replaces section 352A of the 1985 Act, which implements the Twelfth Company Law Directive (89/667/EEC) on single member private limited liability companies. This section requires a statement to be entered in a company's register of members that it has only one member if that is the case on incorporation or at a later date – if the latter, the date on which it so became must also be entered. It also requires a statement that the company has ceased to have only one member together with the date of the increase. Section 352A of the 1985 Act applies to private companies alone, but this section applies to both private and public companies.

Section 124: Company holding its own shares as treasury shares

251.   This section replaces section 352(3A) as regards the entries required to be made in the register of members where a company holds treasury shares. The effect of that provision is unchanged.

Section 125: Power of court to rectify register

Section 126: Trusts not to be entered on register

Section 127: Register to be evidence

252.   These sections restate sections 359, 360 and 361 of the 1985 Act.

Section 128: Time limit for claims arising from entry in register

253.   This section replaces section 352(7) of the 1985 Act. Based on a recommendation by the CLR (Final Report, paragraph 11.40), it reduces the time limit for claims relating to entries in the register from 20 years to 10 years.

CHAPTER 3: OVERSEAS BRANCH REGISTERS

254.   This Chapter restates the 1985 Act's provisions (section 362 and Parts I and II of Schedule 14) regarding overseas branch registers. It enables companies in specified circumstances to keep in a specified country or territory a register of those members resident in that country or territory. An overseas branch register is deemed to be part of the company's register of members. It differs from the provisions of the 1985 Act in two respects.

- First, rather than providing for an Order in Council, section 129(3) provides the Secretary of State with power to make regulations as to the circumstances in which a company is to be regarded as keeping an overseas branch register.

- Second, section 131 provides power to modify the provisions of Chapter 2 of this Part (relating to the company's register of members) in their application to overseas branch registers.

CHAPTER 4: PROHIBITION ON SUBSIDIARY BEING MEMBER OF ITS HOLDING COMPANY

255.   This Chapter is a restatement of the provisions of section 23 of the 1985 Act and Schedule 2 to that Act as it applies for the purposes of that section. Unless in circumstances covered by an exception, a company cannot be a member of its own holding company. There is no change of substance to the provision in the 1985 Act.

PART 9: EXERCISE OF MEMBERS' RIGHTS

256. The CLR considered the rights of persons other than the registered shareholders, presenting their recommendations in Chapter 7 of the 'Final Report'. The new provisions in Part 9 have been developed with these recommendations in mind and are designed to make it easier for investors to exercise their governance rights fully and responsibly. Nowadays when investors, whether major institutional investors or retail investors, buy shares in a listed company they are increasingly likely to hold their shares through an intermediary or a chain of intermediaries. This means that it is an intermediary's name that appears on the company's register of members. As a result investors typically have to rely on contractual arrangements with the intermediaries both to obtain information from the company and also to give any instructions they wish about how shares should be voted.

257. This Part of the Act introduces new provisions dealing with the ability of indirect investors to exercise governance rights. The first section in the Part removes any doubts as to the ability of companies to make provision in their articles for others to enjoy and exercise membership rights and enables indirect investors to enjoy information rights via the registered member. The next group of sections provides that indirect investors in traded companies can be nominated by the registered member to receive company documents and information. It is up to the registered member, typically a broker, to decide whether to nominate or not. The last two sections in the Part make it easier for registered members to exercise rights in different ways to reflect the underlying holdings and allow indirect investors to participate in, for example, requests for resolutions at the AGM. The provisions of this Part should be looked at together with sections 324 to 331 on proxies in Part 13, which enable the registered member to appoint indirect investors as proxies to exercise voting rights.

258. An important principle to note is that the information rights and exercise of other rights where shares are held on behalf of others can be initiated and enforced with the company only by the registered member. This Part does not compel the registered member to confer such rights on third parties. It will be for indirect investors, such as shareholders holding through a nominee, to choose a nominee operator who offers such rights as part of their service.

Effect of provisions in company's articles

259. Section 145 protects arrangements through company articles to enfranchise indirect investors and provides that where a company makes provision, through its articles, to extend rights to those holding shares through intermediaries, the provision is legally effective in relation to various statutory requirements.

Section 145: Effect of provisions of articles as to enjoyment of exercise of members' rights

260. This section (*subsection (1)*) allows a company's articles to enable a member to identify another person or persons as entitled to enjoy or exercise all or any specified rights of a member. The articles may specify that this entitlement can apply only to certain rights or to all rights, except the right to transfer the shares. As *subsection (4)(b)* makes clear, the right to transfer shares must remain, as under the 1985 Act, with the member whose name is on the register.

261.   *Subsection (2)* provides that where a company makes relevant provision in its articles, all the relevant references in the Companies Acts to 'member' should be read as if the reference to member was a reference to the person or persons nominated by the member. *Subsection (3)* provides a non-exhaustive list of the provisions in question.

262.   *Subsection (4)(a)* makes clear that non-members do not have direct enforceable rights against the company. They should enforce their rights through the member whose name is on the register and who has the right to enforce the articles.

Information rights

263.   Sections 146 to 150 introduce new provisions enabling indirect investors to be appointed by the registered member to receive information that is sent to members by the company. These provisions apply only to companies traded on a regulated market. The Secretary of State may extend or limit the classes of companies to which these provisions apply through the power provided under section 151.

Section 146: Traded companies: nomination of persons to enjoy information rights

264.   *Subsections (1) and (2)* provide new rights for members of companies whose shares are traded on regulated markets to nominate those on whose behalf they hold shares to receive information that is sent to members direct from the company and to exercise certain rights.

265.   *Subsection (3)* sets out what is meant by 'information rights', namely the right to receive all communications that the company sends to members, the right to require copies of accounts and reports (as in section 431 or 432), and the right to require hard copy versions of documents (section 1145).

266.   *Subsection (4)* refers to section 426, which allows under certain circumstances for summary financial statements rather than full accounts to be sent out as part of the general information. These must also be sent to nominated persons.

267.   *Subsection (5)* provides that the company does not need to respond to a nomination that specifies only certain information rights.

Section 147: Information rights: form in which copies to be provided

268.   This section deals with the way in which information is to be provided to a nominated person. *Subsection (2)* explains that if a nominated person wants communications to be in hard copy, they must ask the member, providing a postal address, before the nomination is made. If the member then passes this on to the company, under *subsection (3)* the nominated person will have the right to receive hard copy communications.

Section 148: Termination or suspension of nomination

269.   This section provides that a nomination will stop having effect on the request of the nominated person or the member (*subsection (2)*), or on the death, bankruptcy or winding up of the nominated person or the member (*subsection (3)*).

270.   *Subsection (5)* explains that all nominations made by member will be suspended if there are more nominations that the total number of shares, and *subsection (6)* makes similar provision where there are different classes of shares.

Section 149: Information as to possible rights in relation to voting

271.   This section requires the company, when sending a meeting notice to nominated persons, to include a statement that the nominated person may have voting rights that he can exercise through the person who nominated him.

Section 150: Information rights: status of rights

272.   This section deals with the rights arising from a nomination under section 146, and in particular provides that it is the member, rather than the nominated person, who can enforce the rights against the company.

Section 151: Information rights: power to amend

273.   This section gives a power for the Secretary of State to amend the provisions of sections 146 to 150. The power allows for changes in the companies covered, the circumstances in which nominations can be made and the rights conferred by nomination.

Effect of rights where shares held on behalf of others

274.   Sections 152 and 153 enable indirect investors, via the registered member, to exercise voting and requisition rights by making it easier for registered members to exercise rights in different ways to reflect underlying holdings and by allowing those on whose behalf they hold shares to participate in requisitions. These two sections apply to all companies.

Section 152: Exercise of rights where shares held on behalf of others: exercise in different ways

275.   This section provides that a member can choose to split his holding and exercise rights attached to shares in different ways. This is to accommodate members who hold shares on behalf of more than one person, each of whom may want to exercise rights attaching to their shares in different ways. So, for example, it enables votes to be cast in different ways. *Subsection (4)* provides that if the member does not make it clear to the company in what way he is exercising his rights the company can assume that all rights are being dealt with in the same way.

Section 153: Exercise of rights where shares held on behalf of others: members' requests

276.   This section deals with four situations where the shareholder threshold required to trigger a right is 100 shareholders holding £100 each on average of paid-up capital. Indirect investors are able to count towards the total subject to certain conditions, intended to ensure that only genuine indirect investors are allowed to count towards the total, that the same shares cannot be used twice and that the indirect investor's contractual arrangements with the member allow the former to give voting instructions.

PART 10: COMPANY DIRECTORS

277.   This Part replaces Part 10 of the 1985 Act (enforcement of fair dealing by directors), the provisions relating to directors in Part 9 of that Act and the provisions relating to confidentiality orders in Part 25 of that Act. It also introduces a statutory statement of directors' general duties to the company.

Who is a director?

278. Section 250 defines a director as including any person occupying the position of director, by whatever name called. This is the same as the definition contained in section 741(1) of the 1985 Act. The Act does not attempt a more detailed definition of a director because it is important to ensure that the term is applied to anybody who exercises real power within the company, particularly in relation to decision taking. The term "director" therefore includes:

- an executive director who has been properly appointed by the company;

- a non-executive director who has been properly appointed by the company;

- a de facto director (that is, a person who has assumed the status and functions of a company director even though he has not been properly appointed).

279. A "shadow director" is defined by section 251 as "a person in accordance with whose directions or instructions the directors of the company are accustomed to act". The section provides that a person is not to be regarded as a shadow director by reason only that the directors act on advice given by him in a professional capacity. This definition is the same as the definition contained in section 741(2) of the 1985 Act.

Powers of directors

280. This Part of the Act does not generally directly give powers to the directors, but, under the draft model articles of association for private companies limited by shares, the directors' functions are:

- to manage the company's business; and

- to exercise all the powers of the company.

CHAPTER 1: APPOINTMENT AND REMOVAL OF DIRECTORS

Section 154: Companies required to have directors

281. This section replaces section 282 of the 1985 Act. It distinguishes between private and public companies. It retains the requirement for a private company to have at least one director and requires all public companies to have at least two. There will no longer be an exception for public companies registered before 1st November 1929 (or before 1st January 1933 in Northern Ireland).

Section 155: Companies required to have at least one director who is a natural person

282. This section is a new provision. It introduces a requirement that every company have at least one director who is a natural person, ie an individual. Subject to this requirement being satisfied, any legal person, including one that is a company or a firm, can be a director but one company cannot be the sole director of another company. *Subsection (2)* provides that the requirement that the director be a natural person is met if the director is a corporation sole (for example, the Archbishop of Canterbury) or someone appointed on the basis of some other appointment that they hold.

Section 156: Direction requiring company to make appointment

283. This section is a new provision, enabling enforcement of the existing requirement for a private company to have at least one director and a public company to have at least two

directors and of the new requirement for every company to have at least one director who is an individual. Where it appears to the Secretary of State that any of these requirements is not met, the Secretary of State will be able to direct the company to comply by issuing a notice. It will be an offence not to comply.

Section 157: Minimum age for appointment as director

284.   This section is a new provision. It introduces a minimum age of 16 for a natural person to be a director. *Subsection (2)* provides that prohibition will not prevent the appointment of a younger person provided it is not to take effect until that person is 16. *Subsection (3)* provides that the age limit applies even if the director's appointment is a consequence of some other appointment. *Subsection (5)* provides that this prohibition on under-age directors does not provide protection from criminal prosecution or civil liability if he or she were to act as director, i.e. as a de facto director, or if the company's directors usually act on that young person's instructions.

Section 158: Power to provide for exceptions from minimum age requirement

285.   This section is a new provision. It provides for an exception from the prohibition in section 157 on anyone under 16 being appointed a director of a company. It provides a power for the Secretary of State to make regulations specifying circumstances in which a younger person may be a director. The regulations may differ for different parts of the UK.

Section 159: Existing under-age directors

286.   This section is a new transitional provision. *Subsections (1) and (2)* provide that where a person under 16 has been appointed as director (or holds the office of director by virtue of another office or is a corporation sole) prior to the prohibition on under age directors coming into force, that person will cease to be a director when the prohibition in section 157 comes into force. *Subsection (3)* makes it the company's responsibility to amend its register of directors accordingly but the company is not required to notify the registrar of the change. *Subsection (4)* gives the registrar power to amend the register without a notification by the company of the director's removal but rather on the basis of information already held (i.e. the date of birth as provided when the appointment was notified).

Section 160: Appointment of directors of public company to be voted on individually.

287.   This restates section 292 of the 1985 Act: the appointment of each proposed director of a public company must be voted on individually unless there is unanimous agreement to a block resolution. Without such consent, any appointment of a director that is not voted on individually is void. This ensures that members can express their disapproval of any particular director without having to reject the entire board.

Section 161: Validity of acts of directors

288.   This section, which replaces section 285 of the 1985 Act, provides that a director's actions are valid even if his or her appointment is subsequently found to have been defective or void.

Section 162: Register of directors

289.   This section replaces part of section 288 of the 1985 Act. It imposes on every company a requirement to keep a register of its directors (secretaries are dealt with in Part 12). This register need not contain particulars of shadow directors.

290.   This section requires the register to be kept available for inspection either at the company's registered office or at a place specified in regulations made under section 1136. It must be available for inspection by members (without charge) or the public (for a prescribed fee, set under powers provided under section 1137). Refusal to permit inspection is an offence for which every officer in default (including a shadow director) can be liable. In addition, the court may compel immediate inspection of the register if the company has refused.

Section 163: Particulars of directors to be registered: individuals

291.   This section replaces section 289 of the 1985 Act so far as it applies to individuals. It specifies the particulars that must be entered in the register of directors for each director who is an individual (as opposed to a company or similar entity). The most significant change is the requirement for companies to provide a service address for a director rather than, as now, the director's usual residential address. A director may give the company's registered office as his or her service address; the service address may also be the same as the director's residential address – but this will not be apparent from the public record. In addition, in fulfilment of a Government commitment given in March 1998, the particulars no longer include details of other directorships held. There are also changes to the requirement to provide the director's name. The requirement is now to include any name by which the individual was formerly known for business purposes. As recommended by the CLR (Final Report, paragraph 11.38), there is no longer an exception for a married woman's former name. However the section retains a protective provision relating to the former names of peers.

Section 164: Particulars of directors to be registered: corporate directors and firms

292.   This section replaces section 289(1)(b) of the 1985 Act. It retains the requirement for the corporate or firm name and the registered or principal office to be recorded where the director is either a body corporate or a firm that is a legal person under the law by which it is governed. In addition, as recommended by the CLR (Final Report, paragraph 11.38), it requires for EEA companies the register where the company is registered and its registration number; for all others, particulars of the legal form of the company or firm, the law by which it is governed, and, if applicable, where it is registered and its registration number.

Section 165: Register of directors' residential addresses

293.   This section is a new provision. It requires companies to keep a register of the usual residential addresses of directors who are individuals. Provided that a director's service address is not the company's registered office, if his/her residential address is the same as his/her service address, then the register need only contain an entry making that clear. This register is not to be open to public inspection, but can be used in accordance with Chapter 8 of this Part.

Section 166: Particulars of directors to be registered: power to make regulations

294.   This section is a new provision. It provides power for the Secretary of State to make regulations that add or remove items from the particulars that have to be entered in a company's register of directors and register of directors' residential addresses.

Section 167: Duty to notify registrar of changes

295.   This section replaces section 288(2) of the 1985 Act insofar as it applies to directors. It retains the requirement that the appointment of a director, or a director's ceasing to hold office, and any change in an existing director's particulars, be notified to the registrar within 14 days. This requirement does not extend to shadow directors. Default is an offence. This section also requires a notice of appointment to be accompanied by the appointee's consent. This provision ensures that the public record is kept up to date. There is also a requirement to notify the registrar of changes to information in the register of directors' residential addresses (but this information is not to be open to public inspection at Companies House).

Section 168: Resolution to remove director

296.   This section replaces section 303 of the 1985 Act. *Subsection (1)* provides that an ordinary resolution is sufficient to remove a director, but requires that it be at a meeting so as to ensure the director's right to be heard.

Section 169: Director's right to protest removal

297.   This section replaces section 304 of the 1985 Act. The only change is to be found in *subsection (5)*; the court need no longer be satisfied that the rights conferred by the section are being abused to secure needless publicity for defamatory matter, so long as it is satisfied that they are being abused

CHAPTER 2: GENERAL DUTIES OF DIRECTORS

Sections 170 to 181: General comments

298.   The general duties form a code of conduct, which sets out how directors are expected to behave; it does not tell them in terms what to do. More particularly, the duties address:

- the possibility that a director may put his own or other interests ahead of those of the company;

- the possibility that he may be negligent.

299.   The duties are derived from equitable and common law rules, and are not at the moment written down in statute.

300.   The Law Commission and the Scottish Law Commission recommended that there should be a statutory statement of a director's main fiduciary duties and his duty of care and skill in their joint report *Company Directors: Regulating Conflicts of Interests and Formulating a Statement of Duties*. The CLR's main recommendations in respect of directors' general duties are summarised in chapter 3 of the Final Report.

301.   The CLR recommended that there should be a statutory statement of directors' general duties, and that this should, with two exceptions, described in the next paragraph, be a codification of the current law. In particular they wanted:

- to provide greater clarity on what is expected of directors and make the law more accessible. In particular, they sought to address the key question "in whose interests should companies be run?" in a way which reflects modern business needs and wider expectations of responsible business behaviour;

- to make development of the law in this area more predictable (but without hindering development of the law by the courts);

- to correct what the CLR saw as defects in the present duties relating to conflicts of interest.

The Government has accepted these recommendations.

302.   There are two areas, both relating to the regulation of conflicts of interest, where the statutory statement departs from the current law:

- under section 175, transactions or arrangements with the company do not have to be authorised by either the members or by the board; instead interests in transactions or arrangements with the company must be declared under section 177 (in the case of proposed transactions) or under section 182 (in the case of existing transactions) unless an exception applies under those sections;

- section 175 also permits board authorisation of most conflicts of interest arising from third party dealings by the director (e.g. personal exploitation of corporate resources and opportunities). Such authorisation is effective only if the conflicted directors have not participated in the taking of the decision or if the decision would have been valid even without the participation of the conflicted directors. Board authorisation of conflicts of interest will be the default position for private companies, but public companies will need to make provision in their constitutions to permit this. Board authorisation is not permitted in respect of the acceptance of benefits from third parties (section 176).

303.   Both reforms implement recommendations of the CLR, which noted that the basic principles in the current law relating to directors' conflicts of interest are very strict:

- they noted that in practice most companies permit a director to have an interest in a proposed transaction or arrangement with the company, provided that the interest is disclosed to his fellow directors. The statutory statement therefore reflects the current position in most companies;

- they also took the view that the current strict rule relating to conflicts of interest in respect of personal exploitation of corporate opportunities fettered entrepreneurial and business start-up activity by existing company directors. The statutory statement therefore provides for board authorisation of such conflicts.

304.   These reforms are modified for charitable companies in England and Wales and Northern Ireland by section 181.

Codification of common law rules and equitable principles

305.   Codification is not a matter of transposing wording taken from judgments into legislative propositions. Judgments are, of necessity, directed at particular cases. Even when they appear to state general principles, they will rarely be exhaustive. They will be the application of (perhaps unstated) general principles to particular facts. In the company law field, the principles being applied will frequently be taken from other areas, in particular trusts and agency. It is important that these connections are not lost and that company law may continue to reflect developments elsewhere. Frequently the courts may formulate the same idea in different ways. In contrast legislation is formal. It is not easy to reconcile these

two approaches but the draft sections seek to balance precision against the need for continued flexibility and development. In particular:

- *subsection (3)* of section 170 provides that the statutory duties are based on, and have effect in place of, certain common law rules and equitable principles;

- *subsection (4)* of section 170 provides that the general duties should be interpreted and applied in the same way as common law rules and equitable principles. The courts should interpret and develop the general duties in a way that reflects the nature of the rules and principles they replace;

- *subsection (4)* of section 170 also provides when interpreting and applying the statutory duties, regard should be had to the common law rules and equitable principles which the general duties replace; thus developments in the law of trusts and agency should be reflected in the interpretation and application of the duties;

- section 178 provides that the civil consequences of breach (or threatened breach) of the statutory duties are the same as would apply if the corresponding common law rule or equitable principle applied. It also makes clear that the statutory duties are to be regarded as fiduciary, with the exception of the duty to exercise reasonable care skill and diligence which is not under the present law regarded as a fiduciary duty.

306.   The statutory duties do not cover all the duties that a director may owe to the company. Many duties are imposed elsewhere in legislation, such as the duty to file accounts and reports with the registrar of companies (section 441). Other duties remain uncodified, such as any duty to consider the interests of creditors in times of threatened insolvency.

Duties owed to the company

307.   Section 170(1) makes it clear that, as in the existing law, the general duties are owed by a director to the company. It follows that, as now, only the company can enforce them. Part 11 (derivative claims and actions by members) describes the mechanism whereby members may be able to enforce the duties on behalf of the company.

Who are the duties owed by?

308.   The duties are owed by every person who is a director of a company (as defined in section 250). They are therefore owed by a de facto director in the same way and to the same extent that they are owed by a properly appointed director.

309.   Certain aspects of the duty to avoid conflicts of interest and the duty not to accept benefits from third parties continue to apply even when a person ceases to be a director; this is necessary to ensure that a director cannot, for example, exploit an opportunity of which he became aware while managing the company's business without the necessary consent simply by resigning his position as director. The closing words of section 170(2) provide that these duties apply to a former director subject to any necessary adaptations. This is to reflect the fact that a former director is not in the same legal position as an actual director.

310.   The statutory duties apply to shadow directors where, and to the extent that, the common law rules or equitable principles which they replace so apply (section 170(5)). This means that where a common law rule or equitable principle applies to a shadow director, the statutory duty replacing that common law rule or equitable principle will apply to the shadow

director (in place of that rule or principle). Where the rule or principle does not apply to a shadow director, the statutory duty replacing that rule or principle will not apply either.

The relationship between the duties

311.   Many of the general duties will frequently overlap. Taking a bribe from a third party would, for example, clearly fall within the duty not to accept benefits from third parties (section 176) but could also, depending on the facts, be characterised as a failure to promote the success of the company for the benefit of its members (section 172) or as an aspect of failing to exercise independent judgment (section 173).

312.   The effect of the duties is cumulative, so that it is necessary to comply with every duty that applies in any given case. This principle is stated in section 179. One exception relates to the duty to avoid conflicts of interest (section 175). This particular duty does not apply to a conflict of interest arising in relation to a transaction or arrangement with the company. In such cases the duty to declare interests in proposed transactions or arrangements (section 177) or the requirement to declare interests in existing transactions or arrangements (section 182) will apply instead. Section 181 modifies these provisions for charitable companies in England and Wales and Northern Ireland.

313.   The cumulative effect of the duties means that where more than one duty applies, the director must comply with each applicable duty, and the duties must be read in this context. So, for example, the duty to promote the success of the company will not authorise the director to breach his duty to act within his powers, even if he considers that it would be most likely to promote the success of the company.

314.   As well as complying with all the duties, the directors must continue to comply with all other applicable laws. The duties do not require or authorise a director to breach any other prohibition or requirement imposed on him by law.

Relationship between the duties and the company's constitution

315.   Under section 171 a director must act in accordance with the company's constitution.

316.   Companies may, through their articles, go further than the statutory duties by placing more onerous requirements on their directors (e.g. by requiring shareholder authorisation of the remuneration of the directors). The articles may not dilute the duties except to the extent that this is permitted by the following sections:

- section 173 provides that a director will not be in breach of the duty to exercise independent judgment if he has acted in a way that is authorised by the constitution;

- section 175 permits authorisation of some conflicts of interest by independent directors, subject to the constitution;

- *subsection (4)(a)* of section 180 preserves any rule of law enabling the company to give authority for anything that would otherwise be a breach of duty;

- *subsection (4)(b)* of section 180 provides that a director will not be in breach of duty if he acts in accordance with any provisions in the company's articles for dealing with conflicts of interest;

- section 232 places restrictions on the provisions that may be included in the company's articles. But nothing in that section prevents companies from including in their articles any such provisions as are currently lawful for dealing with conflicts of interest.

317. The company's constitution may also set out the purposes of the company, especially in the case of an altruistic company which has purposes other than the benefit of the company's members. It is very important that directors understand the purposes of the company, so that they are able to comply with their duty to promote the success of the company in section 172.

Relationship between the duties and the detailed rules requiring member approval of conflicts of interest

318. Under the provisions in Chapter 4 of this Part, the directors must sometimes obtain prior shareholder approval for the following types of transaction involving a director (or, in some cases, a person connected to a director): long-term service contracts; substantial property transactions; loans, quasi-loans and credit transactions; and payments for loss of office.

319. Section 180 provides that:

- compliance with the general duties does not remove the need for member approval of such transactions (*subsection (3)*);

- (subject to the exception set out in the bullet point below) the general duties apply even if the transaction also falls within Chapter 4 (because it is a long-term service contract, substantial property transaction, loan, quasi-loan, credit transaction or payment for loss of office). So, for example, the directors should only approve a loan to a director if they consider that it would promote the success of the company. This is so, even if the loan does not require the approval of members under Chapter 4 because it falls within a relevant exception, such as the exception for expenditure on company business in section 204;

- if the transaction falls within Chapter 4 (because it is a long-term service contract, substantial property transaction, loan, quasi-loan, credit transaction or payment for loss of office) and approval of the members is obtained to the transaction in accordance with that Chapter, or an exception applies, so that approval is not necessary under that Chapter, then the director does not need to comply with the duty to avoid conflicts of interest (section 175) or the duty not to accept benefits from third parties (section 176) in respect of that transaction. All other applicable duties will still apply. For example, a director would not be acting in breach of the duty to avoid conflicts of interests if he failed to obtain authorisation from the directors or the members for a loan from the company in respect of legal defence costs. Section 181 modifies this provision for charitable companies in England and Wales and Northern Ireland.

Relationship between the duties and the general law

320. Section 180(5) provides that the general duties have effect notwithstanding any enactment or rule of law except where there is an express or implied exception to this rule. For example, section 247 provides that directors may make provision for employees on the cessation or transfer of a company's business even if this would otherwise constitute a breach of the general duty to promote the success of the company.

Consequences of breach

321.   Section 178 preserves the existing civil consequences of breach (or threatened breach) of any of the general duties. The remedies for breach of the general duties will be exactly the same as those that are currently available following a breach of the equitable principles and common law rules that the general duties replace.

322.   *Subsection (2)* of that section makes it clear that the duties are enforceable in the same way as any other fiduciary duty owed to a company by its directors (except for the duty to exercise reasonable care, skill and diligence, which is not considered to be a fiduciary duty). In the case of fiduciary duties the consequences of breach may include:

- damages or compensation where the company has suffered loss;

- restoration of the company's property;

- an account of profits made by the director; and

- rescission of a contract where the director failed to disclose an interest.

COMMENTARY ON INDIVIDUAL DUTIES

Section 171: Duty to act within powers

323.   This duty codifies the current principle of law under which a director should exercise his powers in accordance with the terms on which they were granted, and do so for a proper purpose. What constitutes a proper purpose must be ascertained in the context of the specific situation under consideration.

324.   This duty codifies the director's duty to comply with the company's constitution. The constitution is defined for the purpose of the general duties in section 257. As well as the company's articles of association it includes:

- decisions taken in accordance with the company's articles; and

- other decisions taken by the members (or a class of them) if they are to be treated by virtue of any enactment or rule of law as decisions of the company, for example a decision taken by informal unanimous consent of all the members.

Section 172: Duty to promote the success of the company

325.   This duty codifies the current law and enshrines in statute what is commonly referred to as the principle of "enlightened shareholder value". The duty requires a director to act in the way he or she considers, in good faith, would be most likely to promote the success of the company for the benefit of its members as a whole and, in doing so, have regard to the factors listed.

326.   This list is not exhaustive, but highlights areas of particular importance which reflect wider expectations of responsible business behaviour, such as the interests of the company's employees and the impact of the company's operations on the community and the environment.

327.   The decision as to what will promote the success of the company, and what constitutes such success, is one for the director's good faith judgment. This ensures that business decisions on, for example, strategy and tactics are for the directors, and not subject to decision by the courts, subject to good faith.

328. In having regard to the factors listed, the duty to exercise reasonable care, skill and diligence (section 174) will apply. It will not be sufficient to pay lip service to the factors, and, in many cases the directors will need to take action to comply with this aspect of the duty. At the same time, the duty does not require a director to do more than good faith and the duty to exercise reasonable care, skill and diligence would require, nor would it be possible for a director acting in good faith to be held liable for a process failure which would not have affected his decision as to which course of action would best promote the success of the company.

329. In requiring directors to have regard to the interests of employees, this provision replaces section 309(1) of the 1985 Act.

330. *Subsection (2)* addresses the question of altruistic, or partly altruistic, companies. Examples of such companies include charitable companies and community interest companies, but it is possible for any company to have "unselfish" objectives which prevail over the "selfish" interests of members. Where the purpose of the company is something other than the benefit of its members, the directors must act in the way they consider, in good faith, would be most likely to achieve that purpose. It is a matter for the good faith judgment of the director as to what those purposes are, and, where the company is partially for the benefit of its members and partly for other purposes, the extent to which those other purposes apply in place of the benefit of the members.

331. *Subsection (3)* recognises that the duty to promote the success of the company is displaced when the company is insolvent. Section 214 of the Insolvency Act 1986 provides a mechanism under which the liquidator can require the directors to contribute towards the funds available to creditors in an insolvent winding up, where they ought to have recognised that the company had no reasonable prospect of avoiding insolvent liquidation and then failed to take all reasonable steps to minimise the loss to creditors.

332. It has been suggested that the duty to promote the success of the company may also be modified by an obligation to have regard to the interests of creditors as the company nears insolvency. *Subsection (3)* will leave the law to develop in this area.

Section 173: Duty to exercise independent judgment

333. This duty codifies the current principle of law under which directors must exercise their powers independently, without subordinating their powers to the will of others, whether by delegation or otherwise (unless authorised by or under the constitution to do so).

334. The section provides that directors must not fetter the future exercise of their discretion unless they are acting:

a) in accordance with an agreement which has been duly entered into by the company; or

b) in a way authorised by the company's constitution.

335. The duty does not confer a power on the directors to delegate, nor does it prevent a director from exercising a power to delegate conferred by the company's constitution provided that its exercise is in accordance with the company's constitution. Under the draft model articles of association for private companies limited by shares, the directors may delegate their functions in accordance with the articles.

Section 174: Duty to exercise reasonable care, skill and diligence

336.   This duty codifies the director's duty to exercise reasonable, care, skill and diligence. Traditionally, the courts did not require directors to exhibit a greater degree of skill than may reasonably be expected from a person with their knowledge and experience (a subjective test). More recently, the courts have said that the common law standard now mirrors the tests laid down in section 214 of the Insolvency Act 1986, which includes an objective assessment of a director's conduct. This section is modelled on that section.

337.   The section provides that a director owes a duty to his company to exercise the same standard of care, skill and diligence that would be exercised by a reasonably diligent person with:

   a) the general knowledge, skill and experience that may reasonably be expected of a person carrying out the same functions as the director in relation to that company (an objective test); and

   b) the general knowledge, skill and experience that the director actually has (a subjective test).

Section 175: Duty to avoid conflicts of interest

338.   This duty replaces the no-conflict rule applying to directors. Under the current no-conflict rule, certain consequences flow if directors place themselves in a position where their personal interests or duties to other persons are liable to conflict with their duties to the company, unless the company gives its consent. A conflict of interest may, in particular, arise when a director makes personal use of information, property or opportunities belonging to the company or when a director enters into a contract with his company. Conflicts of interest may also arise whenever a director makes a profit in the course of being a director, in the matter of his directorship, without the knowledge and consent of his company.

339.   This duty covers all conflicts, actual and potential, between the interests of the director and the interests of the company. This includes conflicts relating to the exploitation of the company's property, information or opportunity for personal purposes. The only conflicts not covered by this duty, are those relating to transactions or arrangements with the company (interests in transactions or arrangements with the company must be declared under section 177 in the case of proposed transactions or under section 182 in the case of existing transactions unless an exception applies under those sections).

340.   Section 180(4) preserves any current ability of the members of a company to authorise conflicts that would otherwise be a breach of this duty.

341.   Under *subsections (4) to (6)* the duty is also not infringed if:

- the situation cannot reasonably be regarded as likely to give rise to a conflict of interest;

- in the case of a private company, unless its constitution prevents this, authorisation has been given by directors who are genuinely independent (in the sense that they have no direct or indirect interest in the transaction);

- similarly, in the case of a public company, but only if its constitution expressly permits this, authorisation has been given by the independent directors.

342.   The present law is that in all cases, conflicts of interest must be authorised by the members of the company, unless some alternative procedure is properly provided. The CLR were concerned that this strict requirement might stifle entrepreneurial activity; and therefore recommended that, in the case of a private company, it should be possible for conflicts to be authorised by independent directors unless the company's constitution prevents this.

343.   Under *subsection (6)*, board authorisation is effective only if the conflicted directors have not participated in the taking of the decision or if the decision would have been valid even without the participation of the conflicted directors: the votes of the conflicted directors in favour of the decision are ignored and the conflicted directors are not counted in the quorum.

Section 176: Duty not to accept benefits from third parties

344.   This section codifies the rule prohibiting the exploitation of the position of director for personal benefit. This duty prohibits the acceptance of benefits (including bribes). The acceptance of a benefit giving rise to an actual or potential conflict of interest will fall within the duty to avoid conflicts of interest (section 175) as well as this duty. This specific duty dealing with benefits from third parties is not subject to any provision for board authorisation.

345.   Any current ability of the members of a company to authorise the acceptance of benefits which would otherwise be a breach of this duty is preserved by section 180(4).

346.   The duty is not infringed if the acceptance of the benefit cannot reasonably be regarded as likely to give rise to a conflict of interest. Benefits conferred by the company (and its holding company or subsidiaries) do not fall within this duty.

Section 177: Duty to declare interest in proposed transaction or arrangement

347.   The equitable rule that directors may not have interests in transactions with the company unless the interest has been authorised by the members is replaced by this duty. This section requires a director to disclose any interest, direct or indirect, that he has in relation to a proposed transaction or arrangement with the company. The director does not need to be a party to the transaction for the duty to apply. An interest of another person in a contract with the company may require the director to make a disclosure under this duty, if that other person's interest amounts to a direct or indirect interest on the part of the director.

348.   Under the current equitable rule, shareholder approval is required for transactions between a company and a director. Company articles often modify the equitable rule, requiring disclosure of the conflict instead. As proposed by the CLR, shareholder approval for the transaction is not a requirement of the statutory duty. The members of the company may however still impose requirements for shareholder approval in the articles.

349.   The duty requires directors to disclose their interest in any transaction before the company enters into the transaction (*subsection (4)*). The duty does not impose any rules on how the disclosure of interest must be made, but *subsection (2)* allows the disclosure to be made by written notice, general notice or disclosure at a meeting of the directors.

350.   Disclosure to the members is not sufficient. The director must declare the nature and extent of his interest to the other directors. It is not enough for the director to merely state that he has an interest.

351.   If after he has disclosed his interest, he becomes aware that the facts have changed, or for some other reason the earlier disclosure is no longer accurate or complete, the director must make a further declaration, correcting the earlier one (*subsection (3)*). However, this is only necessary if the company has not yet entered into the transaction or arrangement at the time the director becomes aware of the inaccuracy or incompleteness of the earlier declaration (or ought reasonably to have become so aware).

352.   As the duty requires disclosure to be made to the other directors, no disclosure is required where the company has only one director. There is no need to disclose anything the other directors already know about or ought reasonably to have known (*subsection (6)(b)*). A director will breach the duty if he fails to declare something he ought reasonably to have known, but the duty does not otherwise require a director to declare anything he does not know. *Subsection (6)(c)* makes special provision for service contracts that are considered by a meeting of the directors or a committee appointed for the purpose (such as a remuneration committee).

353.   No declaration of interest is required if the director's interest in the transaction cannot reasonably be regarded as likely to give rise to a conflict of interest (*subsection (6)(a)*). Currently regulation 85 of Table A imposes a materiality test.

354.   Conflicted directors may, subject to the company's articles of association, participate in decision-taking relating to such transactions with the company.

Section 181: Modification of provisions in relation to charitable companies

355.   This section reverses certain relaxations made to the no-conflict rule as it applies to the directors of charitable companies in England and Wales and Northern Ireland.

356.   *Subsection (2)(a)* replaces section 175(3) which excludes conflicts of interest arising out of transactions or arrangements with the company. The replacement excludes such conflicts of interest from the duty only if or to the extent that the charitable company's articles so allow. The articles must describe the transactions or arrangements which are to be so excluded from the duty.

357.   *Subsection (2)(b)* replaces section 175(5) which allows authorisation for conflicts of interest to be given by the directors. The replacement only allows authorisation to be given by the directors where the charitable company's constitution expressly allows them to do so.

358.   *Subsection (3)* restricts the application of section 180(2)(b) which disapplies sections 175 and 176 in relation to those matters excepted from the requirements for member approval under Chapter 4. Section 180(2)(b) is restricted so that it only applies if or to the extent that the charitable company's articles allow the duties in sections 175 and 176 to be disapplied. The articles must describe the transactions or arrangements which are to be so excluded from those duties.

359.   *Subsection (4)* amends the Charities Act 1993 to give the Charity Commission the power to authorise acts that would otherwise be in breach of the general duties. This is necessary to preserve the current power of the Charity Commissioners to do so, in the light of the statutory statement of the general duties.

CHAPTER 3: DECLARATION OF INTEREST IN EXISTING TRANSACTION OR ARRANGEMENT

Section 182: Declaration of interest in existing transaction or arrangement

360.   This section requires a director to declare the nature and extent of any direct or indirect interest that he has in any transaction or arrangement entered into by the company. It replaces the provision made by section 317 of the 1985 Act.

361.   This chapter differs from the provisions of that section in a number of important respects. The main points are summarised below.

What should be declared?

362.   Directors are required to declare any interest, direct or indirect, that they have in an existing transaction or arrangement entered into by the company. This section only applies to transactions or arrangements already entered into by the company. Section 177 (duty to declare interests) applies in the case of proposed transactions or arrangements with the company.

363.   The director does not need to be a party to the transaction with the company in order for a declaration to be required under this section. For example, where the director's spouse enters into a transaction with the company that may (but need not necessarily) give rise to an indirect interest on the part of the director in that transaction.

364.   The declaration must be of the nature and extent of the director's direct or indirect interest.

365.   If the director has declared his interest in accordance with section 177 at the time the transaction was proposed, and before it was entered into by the company, the director does not need to repeat that declaration once the transaction becomes an existing transaction to which this section applies (*subsection (1)*).

366.   Furthermore, a director need not declare any interest:

- that cannot reasonably be regarded as likely to give rise to a conflict of interest;
- that the other directors already know about, or ought reasonably to know about; or
- that concerns the terms of his service contract, considered (or to be considered) by a meeting of directors or by the relevant committee of directors.

367.   A director is regarded as failing to make the declarations required by this section if he fails to declare something that he ought reasonably to have known. But the director is not otherwise expected by this section to declare things he does not know (*subsection (5)*).

When should the declaration be made?

368.   The declaration should be made as soon as is reasonably practicable. But even if the declaration is not made as soon as it should have been, it must still be made (*subsection (4)*). If after a declaration has been made the director's interest in the transaction or arrangement changes, or the director realises that his interests were not as originally declared, the director must make another declaration of interest, correcting or updating the earlier one (*subsection (3)*).

How should the declaration be made?

369.   The declaration of interest must be made to the other directors using one of the following three methods:-

- at a meeting of the directors; or

- by notice in writing (in accordance with the requirements of section 184); or

- by general notice (in accordance with the requirements of section 185).

Section 183: Offence of failure to declare interest

370.   This section restates section 317(7) of the 1985 Act. A director who fails to comply with the requirements of section 182 commits an offence. On conviction on indictment the maximum liability is an unlimited fine. On summary conviction the fine must not exceed the statutory maximum (currently £5,000). This section does not affect the validity of the transaction or impose any other civil consequences for a failure to make the declarations of interest required by section 182.

Section 184: Declaration made by notice in writing

371.   This section provides a new written procedure for the declarations of interest required by section 182. A written notice declaring the nature and extent of the director's interest must be sent to all the other directors. It may be sent in hard copy form or, if the recipient agrees, in electronic form. It may be posted, delivered by hand or, if the recipient agrees, by electronic means. When this is done, the notice is treated as forming part of the proceedings of the next meeting of the directors, and so should form part of the minutes of that meeting (*subsection (5)*).

Section 185: General notice treated as sufficient declaration

372.   This section replaces section 317(3) and (4) of the 1985 Act. It enables a director to give a general notice of his interests. A general notice is a declaration that the director is interested in another body corporate or firm, or that the director is connected with another person. If the company enters into a contract with the body corporate, firm or other person named in the general notice, the director does not need to declare any direct or indirect interest that he has in that contract arising as a result of his interest in the body corporate or firm named in the general notice or arising as a result of his connection to the person named in the general notice.

373.   In order to be effective, the general notice must state the nature and extent of the director's interest in the body corporate or firm (for example, sole shareholder of the company) or the nature of his connection with the person (for example, spouse or other connected person as defined in section 253). The requirement to disclose the extent of the interest implements a recommendation of the Law Commissions.

Section 186: Declaration of interest in case of company with sole director

374.   This is a new provision. Where a company has only one director, it is not possible for the director to declare his interests to the other directors, because there are no other directors. Therefore, a sole director does not need to comply with section 182 (declaration of interest in existing transaction or arrangement).

375.   The section makes special provision where the company has only one director, when it should in fact have more than one director (for example, because it is a public company). In such a case, the sole director must record in writing the nature and extent of his interest in any transaction or arrangement that has been entered into by the company.

Section 187: Declaration of interest in existing transaction by shadow director

376.   This section replaces section 317(8) of the 1985 Act. It extends this Chapter to shadow directors, so that a shadow director must also declare the nature and extent of his interest in any transaction or arrangement that has been entered into by the company, in accordance with section 182. The declaration must be made by notice in writing (section 184) or by general notice (section 185).

377.   The declaration is not made at a meeting of the directors, as this is not appropriate in the case of a shadow director. If the shadow director makes the declaration by general notice, that notice must be given in accordance with the notice in writing procedure set out in section 184. This means that a general notice given by a shadow director must comply with both section 184 and the first three subsections of section 185.

378.   Otherwise, apart from section 186 (declaration of interest in case of company with sole director), which is not relevant to a shadow director, all the other provisions of this chapter apply to a shadow director, including the exemptions in section 182.

GENERAL INTRODUCTION TO CHAPTERS 4 AND 5

379.   These Chapters contains several provisions designed to deal with particular situations in which a director has a conflict of interest. They replace provisions of Part 10 of the 1985 Act, but with a number of changes. The aim of the changes is:

- to improve accessibility and consistency. The Law Commissions commented that Part 10 of the 1985 Act "is widely perceived as being extremely detailed, fragmented, excessive, and in some respects, defective, regulation of directors"; and

- to implement various recommendations of the Law Commissions and the CLR (see in particular section B of the Law Commissions' joint report *Company Directors: Regulating Conflicts of Interests and Formulating a Statement of Duties*, annex C of *Developing the Framework*, chapter 4 of *Completing the Structure* and chapter 6 of the Final Report).

380.   Provisions regulating directors' conflicts of interest fall into two main categories:

- requirements for disclosure to members;

- requirements for member approval.

381.   The four types of transaction requiring the approval of members (long-term service contracts; substantial property transactions; loans, quasi-loans and credit transactions; and payments for loss of office) have been brought together within Chapter 4.

382.   Provision for disclosure to members in respect of directors' service contracts is contained in Chapter 5.

383.   On the other hand, the requirements in Part 10 of the 1985 Act to disclose, and maintain a register of, share dealings by directors and their families are repealed (see section 1177).

CHAPTER 4: TRANSACTIONS WITH DIRECTORS REQUIRING APPROVAL OF MEMBERS

Structure

384.   This Chapter sets out requirements for member approval in relation to four different types of transaction by a company:

- long-term service contracts;

- substantial property transactions;

- loans, quasi-loans and credit transactions;

- payments for loss of office.

385.   The rules relating to each type of transaction tend to adopt the following structure: they begin with the rule requiring member approval, followed by exceptions to that rule and finally the consequences of breaching that rule.

Alignment of provisions

386.   The provisions of this Chapter have been aligned wherever appropriate so as to achieve greater consistency of approach. Particular examples of alignment are mentioned below.

Criminal penalties

387.   This Chapter no longer imposes any criminal penalties for a failure to comply with its requirements.

Civil remedies

388.   The civil consequences of a failure to comply with the requirements for member approval of substantial property transactions and loans, quasi-loans and credit transactions have been aligned.

Approval by holding company

389.   This Chapter applies to long-term service contracts, substantial property transactions, loans etc and payments for loss of office entered into by a company and involving either a director of the company or a director of the company's holding company. In the latter case, the transaction must be approved by both the company and the holding company (unless an exception applies).

Transactions between a company and the director of a fellow subsidiary

390.   This Chapter does not normally apply to transactions entered into by a company that is neither the company of which the person is a director nor a subsidiary of the company of which the person is a director. The two exceptions are section 218 (payment for loss of office in connection with transfer of undertaking) and section 219 (payment for loss of office in connection with share transfer), where member approval is required for such a payment by any person to a director.

Exception for wholly-owned subsidiary

391.   Approval is never required under this Chapter on the part of the member of a wholly-owned subsidiary or on the part of the members of an overseas company.

Shadow directors

392.   Section 223 applies all the requirements of this Chapter to shadow directors (with a small modification in the case of payments for loss of office).

Approval required

393.   Section 281(3) applies so that the member approval required is an ordinary resolution, but the company's articles may require a higher majority or even unanimity

394.   Where approval for a transaction or arrangement is required under more than one set of rules in Chapter 4, all relevant sets of rules should apply, unless otherwise provided (section 225). For example, if the matter involves both a substantial property transaction and a loan, approval should be required under section 190 and under section 197 unless in each case a relevant exemption applies. Approval may be given for both purposes by a single resolution.

Memorandum with details of the transaction

395.   In the case of long-term service contracts, loans etc and payments for loss of office, a memorandum setting out certain particulars about the transaction requiring approval of the members must be made available to the members.

396.   If the approval is to be given by way of written resolution, the memorandum must be sent to the members able to vote on the written resolution no later than when the written resolution is sent to them. Section 224 provides that any accidental failure to send the memorandum to one or more members will not invalidate the approval given by the members, unless the company's articles state otherwise.

Requirement for Charity Commission consent for charitable companies

397.   Section 66 of the Charities Act 1993 renders prior authorisation by the members for certain transactions invalid unless the Charity Commissioners have given their prior written consent. This reflects concern that, in some cases, the members of a charitable company are not independent of the directors, and that requiring their approval would not provide sufficient protection for the charity. Section 226 inserts two new sections into the Charities Act 1993 in place of section 66 of that Act to reflect the changes made by this Chapter.

COMMENTARY

Sections 188 and 189: Service contracts

398.   These sections replace section 319 of the 1985 Act and require member approval of long-term service contracts. In broad terms, these are contracts under which a director is guaranteed at least two years of employment with the company of which he is a director, or with any subsidiary of that company.

399.   A director's "service contract" is defined in section 227 to include a contract of service, a contract for services and a letter of appointment as director.

400.   Failure to obtain approval allows the company to terminate the service contract at any time by giving reasonable notice. The purpose of this section is to limit the duration of directors' service contracts, as a long-term contract can make it too expensive for the members to remove a director using the procedure in section 168 (ordinary resolution to remove director) while allowing the members to approve longer arrangements if they wish.

401. The length of service contract for which member approval is required has been reduced from those longer than five years to those longer than two years.

Sections 190 to 196: Substantial property transactions

402. These sections require member approval to substantial property transactions. These are transactions where the company buys or sells a non-cash asset (as defined in section 1163) to or from:

- a director of the company;

- a director of its holding company;

- a person connected with a director of the company; or

- a person connected with a director of its holding company.

Approval is only required where the value of the asset exceeds £100,000 or 10% of the company's net assets (based on its last set of annual accounts or called-up share capital if it has not yet produced any accounts). No approval is required if the value of the asset is less than £5,000.

403. These sections replace sections 320 to 322 of the 1985 Act. The changes include:

- permitting a company to enter into a contract which is conditional on member approval (section 190(1)). This implements a recommendation of the Law Commissions. In cases where the approval of the members of the holding company is also required, the company may enter into arrangements conditional on approval being obtained from the members of the holding company (section 190(2)). The company is not to be liable under the contract if member approval is not forthcoming (section 190(3));

- providing for the aggregation of non-cash assets forming part of an arrangement or series of arrangements for the purpose of determining whether the financial thresholds have been exceeded so that member approval is required (section 190(5));

- excluding payments under directors' service contracts and payments for loss of office from the requirements of these sections (section 190(6)). This implements a recommendation of the Law Commissions;

- raising the minimum value of what may be regarded as a substantial non-cash asset from £2,000 to £5,000 (section 191);

- expanding the exception for transactions with members to include the acquisition of assets from a person in his character as a member of the company (section 192(a));

- providing an exception for transactions made by companies in administration (section 193). This implements a recommendation of the Law Commissions;

- not requiring approval on the part of the members of a company that is in administration or is being wound up (unless it is a members' voluntary winding up) (section 193).

Sections 197 to 214: Loans, quasi-loans and credit transactions

404.   In the case of a private company which is not associated with a public company, section 197 requires member approval for loans and related guarantees or security made by a company for:

- a director of the company; or

- a director of its holding company.

405.   In the case of a public company, or a private company associated with a public company, sections 197, 198, 200 and 201 require member approval for loans, quasi-loans (as defined in section 199), credit transactions (as defined in section 202) and related guarantees or security made by the company for:

- a director of the company; or

- a director of its holding company;

- a person connected with a director of the company; or

- a person connected with a director of its holding company.

406.   Section 256 explains what is meant by references to associated companies. A holding company is associated with all its subsidiaries, and a subsidiary is associated with its holding company and all the other subsidiaries of its holding company.

407.   Member approval is not required by these sections for:

- loans, quasi-loans, credit transactions and related guarantees or security to meet expenditure on company business. The total value of transactions under this exception made in respect of a director and any person connected to him must not exceed £50,000 (section 204);

- money lent to fund a director's defence costs for legal proceedings in connection with any alleged negligence, default, breach of duty or breach of trust by him in relation to the company or an associated company (section 205) or in connection with regulatory action or investigation under the same circumstances(section 206);

- small loans and quasi-loans, as long as the total value of such loans and quasi-loans made in respect of a director and any person connected to him does not exceed £10,000 (section 207(1));

- small credit transactions, as long as the total value of such credit transactions made in respect of a director and any person connected to him does not exceed £15,000 (section 207(2));

- credit transactions made in the ordinary course of the company's business (section 207(3));

- intra-group transactions (section 208); and

- loans and quasi-loans made by a money-lending company in the ordinary course of the company's business (as long as the requirements of section 209 are met).

408.   These sections replace sections 330 to 341 of the 1985 Act. The changes include:

- abolishing the prohibition on loans, quasi-loans etc to directors and replacing it with a requirement for member approval. This implements a recommendation of the CLR;

- abolishing the criminal penalty for breach;

- replacing the concept of relevant company in section 331 of the 1985 Act with associated company, as defined in section 256;

- removing some of the requirements currently imposed by section 337 of the 1985 Act on the exception for expenditure on company business (section 204);

- widening the exception for expenditure on company business to include directors of the company's holding company and connected persons (section 204);

- creating a new exception specifically for expenditure in connection with regulatory action or investigations (section 206);

- restricting the exceptions for expenditure on defending legal or regulatory proceedings to proceedings in connection with any alleged negligence, default, breach of duty or breach of trust by the director in relation to the company or an associated company (sections 205 and 206);

- widening the exception for small loans to include small quasi-loans (section 207(1)) in place of the current exception for short-term small quasi-loans in section 332 of the 1985 Act;

- widening the exception for small loans and quasi-loans to include transactions with connected persons (section 207(1));

- widening the exception for "home loans" to include those connected persons who are employees (section 209(3));

- raising the maximum amounts permitted under the exception for expenditure on company business (section 204), the exception for small loans and small quasi-loans (section 207(1)) and the exception for small credit transactions (section 207(2));

- widening the exceptions for intra-group transactions (section 208);

- abolishing the maximum amounts permitted under the exception for money-lending companies (section 209); and

- allowing affirmation of loans, quasi-loans and credit transactions entered into by the company in line with the provision in respect of substantial property transactions (section 214).

Sections 215 to 222: Payments for loss of office

409.   These sections require member approval for payments for loss of office. These are payments made to a director (or former director) to compensate them for ceasing to be a director, or for losing any other office or employment with the company or with a subsidiary of the company. They also include payments made in connection with retirement. In the case of loss of employment or retirement from employment, the employment must relate to the management of the affairs of the company.

410.   Member approval is required under section 217 if a company wishes to make a payment for loss of office to:

- one of its directors;

- a director of its holding company.

411.   Member approval is also required if any person (including the company or anyone else) wishes to make a payment for loss of office to a director of the company in connection with the transfer of the whole or any part of the undertaking or the property of the company or of a subsidiary of the company (section 218).

412.   In the case of a payment for loss of office to a director in connection with the transfer of shares in the company or in a subsidiary of the company resulting from a takeover bid, approval is required of the holders of the shares to which the bid relates and of any other holders of shares of the same class (section 219).

413.   These sections replace sections 312 to 316 of the 1985 Act. The changes include:

- extending the requirements to include payments to connected persons (section 215(3));

- extending the requirements to include payments to directors in respect of the loss of any office, or employment in connection with the management of the affairs of the company, and not merely loss of office as a director as such (section 215). This implements a recommendation of the Law Commissions;

- extending the requirements to include payments by a company to a director of its holding company (section 217(2));

- extending the requirements in connection with the transfer of the undertaking or property of the company to include transfers of the undertaking or property of a subsidiary (section 218(2));

- extending the requirements in connection with share transfers so as to include all transfers of shares in the company or in a subsidiary resulting from a takeover bid (section 219(1));

- excluding the persons making the offer for shares in the company and any associate of them from voting on any resolution to approve a payment for loss of office in connection with a share transfer (section 219(4)). This implements a recommendation of the Law Commissions;

- setting out the exception for payments in discharge of certain legal obligations (section 220);

- creating a new exception for small payments (section 221);

- clarifying the civil consequences of breach of these sections (section 222(1) to (3)); and

- resolving conflicts between the remedies where more than one requirement of these sections is breached (section 222(4) and (5)). For example, if the payment contravenes both section 217 and section 219 because it was a payment by a company to one of its directors and it was a payment in connection with a takeover bid, and none of the required member approvals have been obtained, then the payment is held on trust for the persons who have sold their shares as a result of the offer and not on trust for the company making the payment.

CHAPTER 5: DIRECTORS' SERVICE CONTRACTS

Section 227: Directors' service contracts

414.   This section is a new provision. It defines what is meant in this Part by references to a director's service contract. The term is used in sections 177, 182, 188 and 190 and in this Chapter. It includes contracts of employment with the company, or with a subsidiary of the company. It also includes contracts for services and letters of appointment to the office of director. The contract may relate to services as a director or to any other services that a director undertakes personally to perform for the company or a subsidiary.

Section 228: Copy of contract or memorandum of terms to be available for inspection

415.   This section requires a company to keep available for inspection copies of every director's service contract entered into by the company or by a subsidiary of the company. If the contract is not in writing, the company must keep available for inspection a written memorandum of its terms. This section, together with sections 229 and 230, replace section 318 of the 1985 Act.

416.   *Subsection (3)* is new. It requires the service contracts to be retained and kept available for inspection by the company for at least one year after they have expired, but the subsection does not require the copies to be retained thereafter. As a result of the expanded definition of service contract in section 227, this section now applies to contracts for services and letters of appointment, as recommended by the Law Commissions.

417.   As recommended by the Law Commissions, the exemption for contracts requiring a director to work outside the UK (section 318(5) of the 1985 Act) and the exemption for contracts with less than 12 months to run (section 318(11) of the 1985 Act) have not been retained.

418.   Failure to comply with the requirements of this section is a criminal offence for which every officer of the company who is in default may be held liable on summary conviction to a fine not exceeding level 3 on the standard scale (currently £1,000) or in cases of continued contravention a daily default fine not exceeding one-tenth of that. In a change from the current position under section 318 of the 1985 Act, the company will no longer be liable under the criminal offence.

Section 229: Right of member to inspect and request copy

419.   This section gives members a right to inspect without charge the copies of service contracts held by the company in accordance with section 228. *Subsection (2)* creates a new right for members to request a copy of the service contracts on payment of a fee set by regulations under section 1137.

Section 230: Directors' service contracts: application of provisions to shadow directors

420.   This section applies the requirements of this Chapter to service contracts with shadow directors.

CHAPTER 6: CONTRACTS WITH SOLE MEMBERS WHO ARE DIRECTORS

Section 231: Contract with sole member who is also a director

421.   Under this section, contracts entered into by a limited company with its only member must be recorded in writing if the sole member is also a director or shadow director of the

company. This does not apply to contracts entered into in the ordinary course of the company's business. The purpose of this section is to ensure that records are kept in those cases where there is a high risk of the lines becoming blurred between where a person acts in his personal capacity and when he acts on behalf of the company. This may be of particular interest to a liquidator should the company become insolvent.

422.   This section replaces section 322B of the 1985 Act, which implements article 5 of the 12th Company Law Directive (89/667/EEC). As the Act will permit public companies to have a single shareholder, this section applies to both private and public limited companies.

423.   A failure to record the contract in writing will not affect the validity of the contract (*subsection (6)*) but other legislation or rules of law might (*subsection (7)*).

424.   If there is a breach of this section, every officer of the company in default is liable on summary conviction to a fine not exceeding level 5 on the standard scale (currently £5,000). In a change from the current position under section 322B of the 1985 Act, the company will no longer be liable under the criminal offence.

CHAPTER 7: DIRECTORS' LIABILITIES

425.   The sections in this Chapter (sections 232 to 239) deal with two matters:

- they restate sections 309A to 309C of the 1985 Act (provisions relating to directors' liability). The only substantive changes to those sections are a new provision permitting companies to indemnify the directors of companies acting as trustees of occupational pension schemes (section 235), the creation of a right for members to request a copy of a qualifying third party indemnity provision (section 238(2)), the removal of criminal liability on the part of the company for failures to comply with the requirements of section 237 (copy of qualifying indemnity provision to be available for inspection), provision for regulations to specify places in addition to the registered office where inspection may take place (section 237(3)) and a requirement for all qualifying indemnity provisions to be retained by a company for at least one year after they have expired (section 237(4));

- they introduce a substantive reform of the law on ratification of acts giving rise to liability on the part of a director (section 239).

Section 232: Provisions protecting directors from liability

426.   This section prohibits a company from exempting a director from, or indemnifying him against, any liability in connection with any negligence, default, breach of duty or breach of trust by him in relation to the company. *Subsection (2)* prohibits indemnification by an associated company as well as by his own company. "Associated company" is defined in section 256 as, in effect, a company in the same group.

427.   Any provision, whether in the company's articles, in a contract or otherwise, attempting to exempt or indemnify a director in breach of this section is void. But this does not apply to lawful provisions in the articles for dealing with conflicts of interest.

Section 233: Provision of insurance

428.   This section permits a company to purchase and maintain insurance for its directors, or the directors of an associated company, against any liability attaching to them in

connection with any negligence, default, breach of duty or breach of trust by them in relation to the company of which they are a director.

Section 234: Qualifying third party indemnity provision

429. This section permits (but does not require) companies to indemnify directors in respect of proceedings brought by third parties (such as class actions in the US). It also permits (but does not require) companies to indemnify directors in respect of applications for relief from liability made under section 1157 (general power of the court to grant relief in case of honest and reasonable conduct) or under section 661(3) or (4)(power of court to grant relief in case of acquisition of shares by innocent nominee).

430. The indemnity may cover liability incurred by the director to any person other than the company or an associated company. This may include both legal costs and the financial costs of an adverse judgement. But the indemnity must not cover liabilities to the company or to any associated company (*subsection (2)*).

431. Another condition is that the indemnity must not cover criminal fines, penalties imposed by regulatory bodies (such as the Financial Services Authority), the defence costs of criminal proceedings where the director is found guilty, the defence costs of civil proceedings successfully brought against the director by the company or an associated company and the costs of unsuccessful applications by the director for relief (*subsection (3)*).

432. *Subsections (4) and (5)* explain when legal proceedings will be considered to have concluded for the purpose of the conditions imposed by subsection (3).

433. An indemnity that complies with these conditions is described as a qualifying third party indemnity provision.

Section 235: Qualifying pension scheme indemnity provision

434. This section permits (but does not require) companies to indemnify a director of a company acting as a trustee of an occupational pension scheme against liability incurred in connection with the company's activities as trustee of the scheme. An indemnity that complies with the conditions set out in this section is described as a qualifying pension scheme indemnity provision.

Section 236: Qualifying indemnity provision to be disclosed in directors' report

435. If a qualifying indemnity provision is in force for the benefit of one or more directors or was in force during the previous year, this must be disclosed by the company in the directors' report (as to the directors' report, see Chapter 5 of Part 15). Where the director is of one company but the qualifying indemnity provision is provided by an associated company, then it must be disclosed in the directors' reports of both companies. Companies which choose not to indemnify directors will not have to make any disclosure.

Section 237: Copy of qualifying indemnity provision to be available for inspection

436. This section requires a company to keep available for inspection copies of all the qualifying indemnity provisions it has made for its own directors, and also copies of all those it has made for directors of associated companies.

437. *Subsection (4)* is a new provision. It requires all qualifying indemnity provisions to be retained and made available for inspection for a further year after they have expired or

terminated. But the company is not required by this section to retain copies of the indemnity provision thereafter.

438. *Subsection (6)* makes a failure to comply with the requirements of this section a criminal offence. The maximum penalty that can be imposed on summary conviction is a fine not exceeding level 3 on the standard scale (currently £1,000) or in cases of continued contravention a daily default fine not exceeding one-tenth of that. In a change from the current position under section 309C of the 1985 Act, the company will no longer be liable under the criminal offence.

Section 238: Right of member to inspect and request copy

439. This section gives members a right to inspect without charge the copies of the qualifying indemnity provisions (or where they are not in writing, the written memorandum of their terms) held by the company in accordance with section 237.

440. This section also creates a new right for members on payment of a fee to request a copy of the copy or memorandum held by the company. The fee will be set by regulations made under section 1137.

Section 239: Ratification of acts of directors

441. This section preserves the current law on ratification of acts of directors, but with one significant change. Any decision by a company to ratify conduct by a director amounting to negligence, default, breach of duty or breach of trust in relation to the company must be taken by the members, and without reliance on the votes in favour by the director or any connected person. Section 252 defines what is meant by a person being connected with a director. For the purposes of this section it may also include fellow directors (*subsection (5)(d)*).

442. If the ratification decision is taken by way of a written resolution (see Chapter 2 of Part 13) the director and his connected persons may not take part in the written resolution procedure (*subsection (3)*). This means that the company does not need to send them a copy of the written resolution, and they are not counted when determining the number of votes required for the written resolution to be passed.

443. If the ratification decision is taken at a meeting, those members whose votes are to be disregarded may still attend the meeting, take part in the meeting and count towards the quorum for the meeting (if their membership gives them the right to do so).

444. *Subsection (6)* makes clear that nothing in this section changes the law on unanimous consent, so the restrictions imposed by this section as to who may vote on a ratification resolution will not apply when every member votes (informally or otherwise) in favour of the resolution. The subsection also makes clear that nothing in this section removes any powers of the directors that they may have to manage the affairs of the company.

445. *Subsection (7)* explains that the requirements imposed by this section are in addition to any other limitations or restrictions imposed by the law as to what may or may not be ratified and when.

CHAPTER 8: DIRECTORS' RESIDENTIAL ADDRESSES: PROTECTION FROM DISCLOSURE

446.   Under the 1985 Act (and previous Companies Acts), the usual residential address of every director must be entered on the public record held by:

- the registrar; and

- each company of which he is a director in its register of directors.

Access to the public record held by the registrar is made in a variety of ways, including daily bulk downloading by some subscribers. There is also a public right to inspect companies' registers of directors.

447.   There is an exception for directors at serious risk of violence or intimidation, e.g. from political activists and terrorists. Under sections 723B – 723E of the 1985 Act, introduced by the Criminal Justice and Police Act 2001, they may apply for a "confidentiality order". A director with a confidentiality order provides a single service address in addition to his usual residential address. The service address is entered on the public record; the usual residential address is kept on a secure register to which access is restricted to specified enforcement authorities. The historic record is not affected by the confidentiality order. By October 2006, nearly 11,000 Confidentiality Orders had been issued of which, it is estimated that nearly 7,000 were to directors (certain other individuals, eg partners in Limited Liability Partnerships, are also eligible).

448.   The CLR considered it essential that directors' residential addresses be filed with the central register, so that enforcement and regulatory bodies as well as liquidators and, in some circumstances, creditors and shareholders can discover the individual's residential address. However they were concerned that unrestricted public access to directors' residential addresses had been abused. They considered that there should not be any discretion as to whether particular addresses should or should not be placed on the public record. Therefore, while welcoming the introduction of the confidentiality order regime, they recommended **all** directors be given the option of:

- either, as now, providing their residential address for the public record;

- or, providing both a service address and their residential address, with the service address being on the public record and the residential address being on a separate secure register to which access would be restricted. Access to the restricted register would be available to certain public authorities. Other parties, such as members and creditors, should have a right to apply to the court for access to a director's residential address. (Final Report, paragraph 11.46)

449.   This Chapter of the Act, together with the provisions on the register of directors' residential addresses in Chapter 1 of this Part, is based on this recommendation. These provisions, which are all new, replace the confidentiality order regime.

Section 240: Protected information

450.   This section sets out the information about directors' usual residential addresses, recorded under Chapter 1 of this Part, that will be protected under the new provisions.

Section 241: Protected information: restriction on use or disclosure by company

451.   This section provides for the protection that a company must give to the information covered by section 240. It prohibits the company from using or disclosing an individual director's home address without his consent except for communicating with him, or to comply with an obligation to send information to the registrar or when required by a court.

Section 242: Protected information: restriction on use or disclosure by the registrar

452.   This section provides for protection by the registrar of information that is covered by section 240. The registrar need only protect information where it is submitted on a form where directors' usual residential addresses are required and entered in the appropriate place. The registrar is not obliged to check all documents submitted to her to ensure that an address has not been inadvertently disclosed. The protection is not retrospective: it does not apply to information on the public record when these provisions come into force. The Act makes separate provision, in section 1088, for removal of addresses from the register in circumstances specified by regulations.

Section 243: Permitted use or disclosure by the registrar

453.   This section provides for certain kinds of permitted use or disclosure of protected information, ie directors' home addresses and whether a service address is a home address. *Subsection (1)* provides that the registrar may use the protected information for communicating with the director in question. *Subsection (2)* provides that the registrar may disclose protected information to a public authority or credit reference agency (the definition of the latter is drawn from the Consumer Credit Act 1974) but this should be read with *subsections (3)* and *(4)*. Subsection (3) confers power on the Secretary of State to make regulations specifying conditions that must be met before the registrar may disclose protected information. The regulations may also provide for fees to be paid by the authority or agency seeking the address. Subsection (4) provides power to make regulations specifying the circumstances in which an application can be made for a director's address not to be revealed to a credit reference agency.

Section 244: Disclosure under court order

454.   This section provides for two circumstances in which the court may require the company to disclose protected information. The first circumstance is that the service address is not effective; the second is that the home address is needed for the enforcement of an order or decree of the court. If the company cannot provide the address, the court may require the registrar to reveal it. *Subsection (3)* provides that the application for the order may be made not only by a liquidator, creditor or member of the company but also by anyone with sufficient interest.

Section 245: Circumstances in which registrar may put address on the public record.

455.   This section provides that if a service address is not effective, then the home address can be put on the public record. It provides for the registrar to send a warning notice, with a specified period for representations before the intended action, both to the director and to every company of which he is a director. The registrar must take account of any representations made within the specified period in deciding whether to proceed as provided by the next section.

Section 246: Putting the address on the public record

456.   This section provides that, if the registrar is putting a director's home address on the public record under the previous section, then the registrar updates the public record as if she had been notified that the service address is the director's home address. She must also notify both the director and every company of which he/she is a director. The companies must each put the director's home address on its register of directors as his/her service address. And for the next five years, the director may not register a service address other than his usual residential address.

CHAPTER 9: SUPPLEMENTARY PROVISIONS

Section 247: Power to make provision for employees on cessation or transfer of business

457.   This section confers a power on the directors to make provision for the benefit of employees (including former employees) of the company or its subsidiaries on the cessation or transfer of the whole or part of the undertaking of the company or the subsidiary (*subsection (1)*).

458.   The directors may exercise this power, even if it will not promote the success of the company. The directors' general duty under section 172 to act in the way they consider would be most likely to promote the success of the company for the benefit of its members as a whole, does not apply when the directors exercise this power to make provision for employees (*subsection (2)*).

459.   There are a number of conditions to the exercise of this power. It must be authorised by a resolution of the members or, if the articles of the company allow it, by the board of directors. The company's articles may also impose further conditions on its use (*subsection (6)*).

460.   Any payments made by the directors using the power conferred by this section must be made before the commencement of the winding up of the company and can only be made out of profits available for dividend. Section 187 of the Insolvency Act 1986 confers power to make provision for employees once the company has commenced winding up.

461.   This section replaces section 719 of the 1985 Act. In a change from that section, the directors can no longer use the power conferred by this section to make payments to themselves or to former directors or to shadow directors, unless the payments are authorised by the members. The CLR recommended that directors should be prevented from abusing the power by making excessive payments to themselves.

Section 248: Minutes of directors' meetings

462.   This section, together with section 249, replaces the provisions of section 382 of the 1985 Act relating to records of meetings of directors. The requirements of section 382 of the 1985 Act relating to records of meetings of managers have not been retained. This section requires a company to record minutes of all meetings of its directors.

463.   *Subsection (2)* is new. The minutes must be kept for at least ten years.

464.   Failure to make and keep minutes as required by this section is a criminal offence, applying to every officer of the company who is in default. In a change from section 382 of the 1985 Act, liability for the offence will no longer fall on the company.

465.   Part 37 of the Act makes provision as to the form in which company records (including minutes) may be kept and imposes a duty to take precautions against falsification.

Section 249: Minutes as evidence

466.   This section makes provision in respect of the evidential value of the minutes of directors' meetings.

Section 250: "Director"

467.   This section restates the definition of "director" in section 741(1) of the 1985 Act.

Section 251: "Shadow director"

468.   This section restates the definition of "shadow director" in section 741(2) of the 1985 Act.

Section 252: Persons connected with a director

469.   This section sets out the definition of "connected person" which is used in many of the sections in this Part in relation to the regulation of directors. The persons who are "connected" for this purpose with a director include:

- certain family members (see section 253);

- certain companies with which the director is connected (see section 254);

- trustees of a trust under which the director or a relative mentioned in section 253 or a company with which the director is connected is a beneficiary (but not if the trust exists for the purposes of an employees' share scheme as defined in section 1166 or a pension scheme);

- certain partners; and

- certain firms with legal personality (such as a Scottish firm in which the director is a partner).

470.   This section, together with sections 253 to 255, replaces section 346 of the 1985 Act.

Section 253: Members of a director's family

471.   This section sets out those members of a director's family who fall within the definition of persons connected with the director. The list includes all those family members currently falling within the definition of connected person in section 346 of the 1985 Act, and in addition it covers:

- the director's parents;

- children or step-children of the director who are over 18 years old (those under 18 were already included under section 346 of the 1985 Act);

- persons with whom the director lives as partner in an enduring family relationship; and

- children or step-children of the director's unmarried partner if they live with the director and are under 18 years of age.

472.   This implements the Law Commissions' recommendation that the definition of connected person be extended so as to include cohabitants, infant children of the cohabitant if

they live with the director, adult children of the director and the director's parents. The recommendation that the definition be extended to siblings has not been implemented.

Section 254: Director "connected with" a body corporate

473.   This section determines whether a company or other body corporate is a person connected with a director. Broadly speaking, the director, together with any other person connected with him, must be interested in 20% of the equity share capital, or control (directly or indirectly through another body corporate controlled by them) more than 20% of the voting power exercisable at any general meeting.

474.   Schedule 1 contains the rules for determining whether a person is "interested in shares" for this purpose.

Section 255: Director "controlling" a body corporate

475.   This section defines the circumstances in which a director is deemed to control a body corporate for the purposes of section 254. These circumstances involve two cumulative hurdles. First, the director or any other person connected with him must be interested in the equity share capital or be entitled to control some part of the voting power exercisable at any general meeting. Secondly, the director, fellow directors and other persons connected with him must be interested in more than 50% of the equity share capital or be entitled to control more than 50% of the voting power exercisable at any general meeting.

476.   Schedule 1 contains the rules for determining whether a person is "interested in shares" for this purpose.

Section 256: Associated bodies corporate

477.   This section is a new provision. It explains what is meant by references in this Part to associated bodies corporate and associated companies. A holding company is associated with all its subsidiaries, and a subsidiary is associated with its holding company and all the other subsidiaries of its holding company.

Section 257: References to company's constitution

478.   This section is new. It makes provision as to the meaning of references to a company's constitution in this Part.

479.   The section is relevant to a number of provisions in this Part, including the duty to act within powers (section 171) and the duty to exercise independent judgment (section 173).

Section 258: Power to increase financial limits

480.   This section confers power on the Secretary of State by order to increase financial limits in this Part of the Act. All the financial limits appear in Chapter 4 (provisions regulating transactions with directors requiring approval of members). This section restates section 345 of the 1985 Act.

Section 259: Transactions under foreign law

481.   This section makes clear that the rules under this Part of the Act apply whether or not the proper law governing a transaction or arrangement is the law of the UK or a part of the UK.

482.   This provision is necessary to prevent parties seeking to avoid the application of the rules relating to approval of long-term service contracts, substantial property transactions and loans and similar transactions by choosing a foreign law. This section restates section 347 of the 1985 Act.

PART 11: DERIVATIVE CLAIMS AND PROCEEDINGS BY MEMBERS

483.   Section 170 provides that directors' general duties are owed to the company rather than to individual members (or third parties such as employees or pressure groups). It follows that, as now, only the company can enforce them. There are three main ways in which the company can take legal action against a director (or, more usually, a former director) for breach of duty:

- if the board of directors decides to commence proceedings;

- if the liquidator or administrator following the commencement of a formal insolvency procedure such as liquidation or administration decides to commence proceedings;

- through a derivative claim or action brought by one or more members to enforce a right which is vested not in himself but in the company.

This part of the Act is concerned with the third of these types of action.

EXISTING LAW

England and Wales or Northern Ireland

484.   In England and Wales, it is possible as a matter of common law for a member to bring an action, in certain circumstances, on behalf of the company of which he is a member. This is known as a derivative claim. As noted above, a member may bring such an action to enforce liability for a breach by one of the directors of his duties to the company.

485.   The law relating to the ability of a member to bring proceedings on behalf of the company is not written down in statute. The general principle – commonly known as the rule in *Foss v Harbottle* – is that it is for the company itself to bring proceedings where a wrong has been done to the company. However, where there has been conduct amounting to a "fraud on the minority", an exception may be made to the rule, so that a minority shareholder may bring an action to enforce the company's rights (for example, where there has been an expropriation of company property or dishonest behaviour by a director, and the company is improperly prevented from bringing proceedings against the director by the majority shareholders, perhaps because the wrongdoing director controls the majority of votes).

486.   Under the current law, if a wrong has been effectively ratified by the company, this will be a complete bar to a derivative claim. In addition, if a wrong is capable of being ratified, then even if there has been no formal ratification, it may not be possible for a minority shareholder to bring a derivative claim.

487.   The law in Northern Ireland in this area is the same as that in England and Wales.

Scotland

488.   Under Scots law, the member's right to raise an action is conferred by substantive law. Accordingly, a member has title as a matter of substantive law to raise proceedings in respect of a director's breach of duty to obtain a remedy for the company. The action is raised

in the name of the member but the remedy is obtained for the company and the rights which the member can enforce against a director or third party are those of the company.

489. The member's right arises where the action complained of is fraudulent or ultra vires and so cannot be validated by a majority of the members of the company. This remedy is not available if the majority of members acting in good faith have validated or may validate the act complained of.

490. Two rules of substantive law apply to actions brought by the member to protect the company's interests (as well as to actions brought to protect the shareholder's personal interests such as enforcement of rights in the articles of association). First, the directors of a company owe duties to the company and not to the members. Second, the court will not interfere in matters of internal management which may be sanctioned by a majority of the members. The effect of these rules is similar to the first two legs of the rule in *Foss v Harbottle*.

CHAPTER 1: DERIVATIVE CLAIMS IN ENGLAND AND WALES OR NORTHERN IRELAND

491. The sections in this Part do not formulate a substantive rule to replace the rule in *Foss v Harbottle*, but instead reflect the recommendation of the Law Commission that there should be a "new derivative procedure with more modern, flexible and accessible criteria for determining whether a shareholder can pursue an action" (*Shareholder Remedies*, paragraph 6.15). In line with the recommendations of the Law Commission, the derivative claim will be available for breach of the duty to exercise reasonable care, skill and diligence, even if the director has not benefited personally, and it will not be necessary for the applicant to show that the wrongdoing directors control the majority of the company's shares.

492. The sections in Chapter 1 of this Part introduce a two-stage procedure for permission to continue a derivative claim. At the first stage the applicant will be required to make a *prima facie* case for permission to continue a derivative claim and the court will be required to consider the issue on the basis of the evidence filed by the applicant only, without requiring evidence from the defendant. The courts must dismiss the application if the applicant cannot establish a *prima facie* case. At the second stage – but before the substantive action begins – the court may require evidence to be provided by the company. The sections set out a list of the matters which the court must take into account in considering whether to give permission and the circumstances in which the court is bound to refuse permission.

493. The sections will be supplemented by amended Civil Procedure Rules.

Section 260: Derivative claims

494. This section sets out the key aspects of a derivative claim.

- *Subsection (1)* defines what is meant by a derivative claim. There are three elements to this: the action is brought by a member of the company; the cause of action is vested in the company; and relief is sought on the company's behalf. (A "member" is defined in section 112. *Subsection (5)* provides that references to a member in this Chapter include a person who is not a member but to whom shares in the company have been transferred or transmitted by operation of law, for example where a trustee in bankruptcy or personal representative of a deceased member's estate acquires an interest in a share as a result of the bankruptcy or death of a member).

- *Subsection (2)* provides that the claim may only be brought either under this Chapter or in pursuance of an order of the court in proceedings under section 994 (proceedings for protection of members against unfair prejudice).

- *Subsection (3)* provides that a derivative claim "may be brought only in respect of a cause of action arising from an actual or proposed act or omission involving negligence, default, breach of duty or breach of trust by a director of the company". As such, a derivative claim may be brought in respect of an alleged breach of any of the general duties of directors in Chapter 2 of Part 10, including the duty to exercise reasonable care, skill and diligence (section 174).

- *Subsection (3)* also provides that the cause of action may be against the director or against a third party, or both. Derivative claims against third parties would be permitted only in very narrow circumstances, where the damage suffered by the company arose from an act involving a breach of duty etc on the part of the director (e.g. for knowing receipt of money or property transferred in breach of trust or for knowing assistance in a breach of trust).

- *Subsection (4)* provides that a derivative claim may be brought by a member in respect of wrongs committed prior to his becoming a member. This reflects the fact that the rights being enforced are those of the company rather than those of the member and is the position at common law.

- Under *subsection (5)*, the reference to a director in this Chapter includes a former director; and a shadow director is treated as a director.

Section 261: Application for permission to continue derivative claim

495.   This clause provides that, once proceedings have been brought, the member is required to apply to the court for permission to continue the claim. This reflects the current procedure in England and Wales under the Civil Procedure Rules. The applicant is required to establish a *prima facie* case for the grant of permission, and the court will consider the issue on the basis of his evidence alone without requiring evidence to be filed by the defendant. The court must dismiss the application at this stage if what is filed does not show a *prima facie* case, and it may make any consequential order that it considers appropriate (for example, a costs order or a civil restraint order against the applicant). If the application is not dismissed, the court may direct the company to provide evidence and, on hearing the application, may grant permission, refuse permission and dismiss the claim, or adjourn the proceedings and give such directions as it thinks fit. This will enable the courts to dismiss unmeritorious claims at an early stage without involving the defendants or the company.

Section 262: Application for permission to continue claim as a derivative claim

496.   This section addresses the possibility that, where a company has brought a claim and the cause of action on which the claim is based could be pursued by a member as a derivative action:

- the manner in which the company commenced or continued the claim may amount to an abuse of process (e.g. the company brought the claim with a view to preventing a member bringing a derivative claim);

- the company may fail to prosecute the claim diligently; and

- it may be appropriate for a member to continue the claim as a derivative claim;

497. The section provides that, in these circumstances, a member may apply to the court to continue the claim as a derivative action.

Section 263: Whether permission to be given

498. This section sets out the criteria which must be taken into account by the court in considering whether to give permission to continue a derivative claim.

499. *Subsection (2)* provides that the court must refuse leave to continue a derivative claim if it is satisfied that:

a) a person acting in accordance with the general duty of directors to promote the success of the company (section 172) would not seek to continue the claim; or

b) the act or omission giving rise to the cause of action has been authorised or ratified by the company. Section 180(4) preserves any rule of law enabling the company to give authority for anything that would otherwise be a breach of duty. Section 239 preserves the current law on ratification of acts of directors, but with one significant change. Any decision by a company to ratify conduct by a director amounting to negligence, default, breach of duty or breach of trust in relation to the company must be taken by the members, and without reliance on the votes in favour by the director or any connected person.)

500. *Subsection (3)* sets out the criteria which the court must, in particular, take into account in considering whether or not to grant permission for the derivative claim to be continued.

501. *Subsection (4)* provides that, in considering whether to give permission, the court must have particular regard to any evidence before it as to the views of independent members of the company i.e. members who have no personal interest, direct or indirect in the matter.

502. *Subsection (5)* confers on the Secretary of State a power to make regulations with regard to the criteria to which the court must have regard in determining whether to grant leave to continue a derivative claim and where leave of the court must be refused. *Subsection (6)* provides that, before making any such regulations, the Secretary of State must consult with such persons as he considers appropriate. The power reflects a recommendation by the Law Commission in its 1997 report on shareholder remedies in respect of analogous shareholder actions in Scotland. Under *subsection (7)*, the regulations will be subject to the affirmative resolution procedure.

Section 264: Application for permission to continue derivative claim brought by another member

503. This section addresses the possibility that, where the court has already decided that there is an appropriate case for a derivative claim and a member has commenced or continued a claim:

- the manner in which the member commenced or continued the claim may amount to an abuse of the court (e.g. the member brought the claim with a view to preventing another member from bringing the claim);

- the member may fail to prosecute the claim diligently;

- it may be appropriate for another member to continue the claim (e.g. because the member who brought the claim has become very ill).

504.   The section provides that, in these circumstances, another member may apply to the court to continue the claim as a derivative action.

CHAPTER 2: DERIVATIVE PROCEEDINGS IN SCOTLAND

505.   Sections 265 to 269 seek to ensure maximum consistency between the position in England and Wales and Northern Ireland and the position in Scotland (although the clauses reflect the different procedural requirements which apply where proceedings are commenced in the Scottish courts, in particular the fact that the leave of court must be obtained before derivative proceedings may be raised). In view of this, they also put the rights of the member to raise actions on behalf of the company on a statutory footing.

506.   Section 265 differs from section 260 in its approach in that it confers the right to bring the proceedings in the first place, and then, in the clauses which follow, regulate the proceedings. (By contrast, the sections relating to proceedings in England and Wales and Northern Ireland assume that there is already a right to bring such proceedings in England and Wales and Northern Ireland; they therefore regulate the proceedings rather than confer the right to bring them.)

507.   *Subsections (4) to (6)* of section 268 confer on the Secretary of State a parallel power to that in section 263 to make regulations with regard to the criteria to which the court must have regard in determining whether to grant leave to continue a derivative claim and where leave of the court must be refused.

PART 12: COMPANY SECRETARIES

Section 270: Private company not required to have secretary

508.   This section replaces section 283(1) of the 1985 Act insofar as it applies to private companies. It implements the CLR recommendation (Final Report, paragraph 4.7) that the requirement for a private company to have a secretary be abolished. It defines a private company "without a secretary" for the purposes of the Act as a company which has taken advantage of the exemption provided by *subsection (1)* as opposed to one which normally has a secretary but for some reason (for example the death of the office holder) is without a secretary at a given time. *Subsection (3)* makes provision for private companies without a secretary.

Section 271: Public company required to have secretary

509.   This section replaces section 283(1) of the 1985 Act insofar as it applies to public companies. It retains the requirement that a public company must have a secretary. The secretary may also be one of the directors.

Section 272: Direction requiring public company to appoint secretary

510.   This section is a new provision, enabling enforcement of the continuing requirement for a public company to have a secretary. It does not apply to private companies. Where it appears that a public company does not have a secretary, the Secretary of State may give a direction to the company. The company must comply with the direction (by making the

appropriate appointment and giving notice of it) within the period specified in the direction. The section provides for an offence for failure to comply with a direction.

Section 273: Qualifications of secretaries of public companies

511.   This section updates section 286 of the 1985 Act. It makes it the duty of the directors of a public company to ensure that the secretary has both the necessary knowledge and experience and one of the qualifications listed in *subsection (2)*. The qualifications specified in this section are the same as in the 1985 Act except that:

- they do not include the qualification of having held the office of the company's secretary (or assistant or deputy secretary) on 22 December 1980;

- in *subsection (3)(f)*, "Chartered Institute of Management Accountants" replaces "Institute of Cost and Management Accountants" as the Institute changed its name in 1986.

There is no requirement for the company secretary to be a natural person. (Compare the requirement in section 155 that a company must have at least one director who is a natural person.)

Section 274: Discharge of functions where office vacant or secretary unable to act

512.   This section replaces section 283(3) of the 1985 Act. It provides for the situation where the office of secretary is vacant or there is no secretary capable of acting for any other reason. In these circumstances, if the company has an assistant or deputy secretary, then that person may fill the position of secretary; if not, any person authorised by the directors may do so. This section differs from section 283(3) of the 1985 Act by permitting the directors to authorise any person to act as secretary, rather than only an officer of the company.

Section 275: Duty to keep register of secretaries

513.   This section replaces the requirement in section 288 of 1985 Act. It requires every company to keep a register of its secretaries containing specified details. *Subsection (3)* provides that the register must be kept available for inspection either at the company's registered office or at a place specified in regulations made under section 1136. *Subsections (5) to (8)* retain the public right of inspection, sanctions and means of enforcement of the right of inspection.

Section 276: Duty to notify registrar of changes

514.   This section replaces the requirement in section 288(2) of the 1985 Act. It requires notification to the registrar within 14 days of any change in the company's secretary or any change in the particulars contained in the register of secretaries. The consent of the person having become a secretary or joint secretary of a company must accompany the notice. The section retains the existing sanction and ensures that the public record is kept up to date as regards the secretary of every company.

Section 277: Particulars of secretaries to be registered: individuals

515.   This section replaces section 290 of the 1985 Act insofar as it applies to secretaries who are individuals. It requires a company to enter in its register of secretaries the name and address of any individual who is its secretary. The definition of name is the same as for directors (see section 163): in particular, the register must include any name used or in use for

business purposes since the age of 16. The section retains an exception relating to the former names of peers but, as recommended by the CLR, not that for the former names of married women. The address to be registered is a service address: this implements the CLR recommendation (Final Report, paragraph 11.46) that the requirement for home addresses for company secretaries be abolished.

Section 278: Particulars of secretaries to be registered: corporate secretaries and firms

516.   This section replaces section 290 of the 1985 Act insofar as it applies to secretaries who are not individuals. It sets out the details which must be registered where the secretary of a company is either a body corporate or a firm which is a legal person under the law by which it is governed. The requirements that apply in the case of an EEA company follow the recommendations of the CLR (Final Report, paragraph 11.39).

517.   The section also makes provision about the details which must be registered where all the partners in a firm are joint secretaries.

Section 279: Particulars of secretaries to be registered: power to make regulations

518.   This section is a new provision. It provides a power for the Secretary of State to make regulations that add or remove items from the particulars that have to be entered in a company's register of secretaries. A similar power is provided by section 166 for directors' particulars.

Section 280: Acts done by person in dual capacity

519.   This section replaces section 284 of the 1985 Act. It provides that where a provision requires or authorises a thing to be done by or to both a director and a secretary of a company it will not be not be satisfied if done by the same person acting in both capacities.

PART 13: RESOLUTIONS AND MEETINGS

520.   The provisions in this Part replace most of Chapter 4 of Part 11 of the 1985 Act on meetings and resolutions. The changes in the law derive principally from the CLR's consultation on "Company General Meetings and Shareholder Communications" and recommendations from Chapters 2, 6 and 7 of their "Final Report", together with two subsequent consultations; the Modernising Company Law White Paper of July 2002 and the Company Law Reform White Paper of March 2005.

521.   In addition to implementing detailed policy changes, Part 13 implements two general changes.

- First, the law makes the current "elective" regime the default for private companies. This means, for instance, that private companies will no longer need to "elect" to dispense with the Annual General Meeting (AGM): they will not be required to hold an AGM in the first place.

- Second, the current law is drafted on the basis that the main way in which shareholder decisions are taken is in general meetings. The new provisions proceed on the basis that in future this will not be the case for many private companies. Private companies will not be required in future to hold general meetings; instead provision is made for new procedures for decisions to be taken by written resolution.

522.   The law relating to decisions has been restated in a way that deals first with private companies. Additional layers of requirements for public and quoted companies holding general meetings follow in subsequent provisions. There are provisions at the end of the Part about record keeping. In general, where this Part imposes an obligation or confers a power, it will apply notwithstanding anything in the articles unless otherwise indicated.

CHAPTER 1: GENERAL PROVISIONS ABOUT RESOLUTIONS

Section 281: Resolutions

523.   This section provides that members' resolutions can only be passed in accordance with the provisions of this Part. There is no equivalent in the current legislation. *Subsection (1)* allows a private company to pass a resolution either as a written resolution or at a meeting of the members. *Subsection (2)* allows a public company to pass a resolution only at a meeting of the members. *Subsection (3)* ensures that where a resolution is required but the type of resolution is not specified, the default will be an ordinary resolution unless the articles require a higher majority. When a provision specifies that an ordinary resolution is required, the articles will not be able to specify a higher majority. *Subsection (4)* preserves the common law unanimous consent rule.

Section 282: Ordinary resolutions

524.   This section provides a definition of an ordinary resolution, whether of the members generally or of a class of the members and whether as a written resolution or as a resolution passed at a meeting. A simple majority – that is, over 50% – is required.

Section 283: Special resolutions

525.   This section provides a definition of a special resolution, whether of the members generally or of a class of the members and whether as a written resolution or as a resolution passed at a meeting. A 75% majority is required. If a resolution is proposed as a special resolution, there is a requirement to say so, either in the written resolution text or in the meeting notice. Where a resolution is proposed as a special resolution, it can only be passed as such. The main difference from the existing definition in section 378(2) of the 1985 Act is that there is no longer a requirement for 21 days' notice where a special resolution is to be passed at a meeting. The subject matter of section 378(3) of the 1985 Act is now dealt with *in* section 307(4) to (6) (notice required of general meeting), while the subject matter of section 378(4) and (6) is dealt with in sections 320 and 301 respectively.

Section 284: Votes: general rules

526.   This section sets out the general rules on votes of members taken by written resolution, on a show of hands at a meeting or on a poll taken at a meeting. These are adapted from section 370 of the 1985 Act and the default regulations in Table A. *Subsection (4)* allows these general rules to be varied by the company's articles.

Section 285: Votes: specific requirements

527.   This section sets out specific requirements on votes of members, which the company's articles may not override. *Subsections (1) and (2)* provide for entitlement to vote where proxies have been appointed and ensure that the articles do not disadvantage a member voting by proxy or proxies. *Subsection (3)* makes new provision for voting rights on written resolutions, reflecting the fact that they will no longer need to be passed unanimously. A

member will have the same number of votes whether passing a resolution on a poll in general meeting or on a written resolution.

Section 286: Votes of joint holders of shares

528. This section puts on a statutory footing what was a default regulation under article 55 of Table A on votes of joint holders of shares. The person whose vote counts is the "senior" holder, the joint holder whose name appears first in the register of members

Section 287: Saving for provisions of articles as to determination of entitlement to vote

529. This section makes new provision to preserve the right for a company to require objections to votes to be made in accordance with procedures in their articles. If an objection is overruled, the decision will be final except in cases of fraud and certain other kinds of misconduct detailed in case law where a court may intervene. This provision preserves the current law. The provision ensures, on the one hand, certainty for company by enabling the chairman to settle matters relating to the admissibility of votes in accordance with the articles and, on the other hand, sufficient remedies for members to challenge a decision if they have suffered unfair prejudice.

CHAPTER 2: WRITTEN RESOLUTIONS

530. The provisions of this Chapter replace the present rules on written resolutions of private companies. A key change (apparent from sections 282 and 283) is that where the statutory procedure under the 1985 Act requires unanimity, the procedure in this Act does not. Consequently, the sections are more detailed than sections 381A to 381C of the 1985 Act and set out the procedures for decisions taken outside of a general meeting framework. The use of the expression "written resolution" does not mean that there is a requirement for "writing" in the sense of hard copy.

General provision about written resolutions

Section 288: Written resolutions of private companies

531. This section introduces the written resolution provisions of this Chapter. They apply to private companies only. *Subsection (2)(a) and (b)* reproduce the two exceptions currently provided for in Part 1 of Schedule 15A to the 1985 Act: a resolution to remove a director or an auditor before the expiration of his term of office may not be passed as a written resolution. These are the only two exceptions to a private company's right to pass resolutions using the written resolution procedure.

Section 289: Eligible members

532. The eligibility of members to vote on a written resolution is fixed on the day the resolution is circulated. *Subsection (2)* ensures that the same shares cannot be voted more than once on the same written resolution. If the person entitled to vote changes during the course of that day, the eligible member is the person entitled to vote at the time that the first copy of the resolution is sent or submitted to a member for his agreement.

Circulation of written resolutions

Section 290: Circulation date

533. This section provides that the circulation date of a written resolution means the date on which copies are sent or submitted to members (or if copies are sent on different days, the first of those days.

Section 291: Circulation of written resolutions proposed by directors

534. This section provides for the circulation of written resolutions by directors of the company. A company must circulate a written resolution either by sending it to all eligible members at the same time or, if it can be done without undue delay, submitting the same copy of the resolution to each eligible member in turn or a combination of these. The latter two options allow companies to pass round a document or email rather than sending out several copies.

Section 292: Members' power to require circulation of written resolution

535. This section enables members to require a written resolution to be circulated. They may also require circulation of a statement about its subject matter. Like the members' right to require a resolution to be moved at an AGM, the percentage needed is 5% of the total voting rights (or lower if specified in the company's articles). *Subsection (2)* specifies some limits on the kind of resolution that may be circulated in this way, designed to stop the power being abused.

Section 293: Circulation of written resolution proposed by members

536. This section specifies what a company has to do when it is required under section 292 to circulate a resolution and accompanying statement. It must circulate the resolution and statement by sending it to all eligible members at the same time or, if it can be done without undue delay, by submitting the same copy of the resolution and statement to each eligible member in turn or a combination of these. The latter two options would allow companies to pass round a document or email rather than sending out several copies. *Subsection (3)* requires that the members' written resolution be circulated within 21 days of the company being requested to do so by those members, except that if the written resolution is circulated to members on different days, then the *first* copy should be dispatched not more than 21 days after the request to circulate the resolution.

Section 294: Expenses of circulation

537. This section provides that the expenses of complying with section 293 are to be paid by the members who requested the circulation of the resolution unless the company resolves otherwise. The company can require the deposit of a sum to meet its expenses before it circulates the resolution, again subject to any resolution to the contrary.

Section 295: Application not to circulate members' statement

538. This section enables the court, on application by the company or other aggrieved person, to relieve the company of an obligation to circulate a members' statement under section 293 if in the court's view the right to require circulation is being abused. This mirrors section 317 in the context of general meetings.

Agreeing to written resolutions

Section 296: Procedure for signifying agreement to written resolution

539.   Under this section, a member may signify agreement to a written resolution in hard copy or electronic form, although if the company does not permit electronic form communications, or is not deemed to do so by virtue of section 298, the member will have to signify his consent in hard copy (see paragraph 6 (conditions for use of communications in electronic form) of Schedule 4 (documents and information sent or supplied to a company). Once a member has signified agreement to a written resolution, he cannot withdraw his agreement. This provides certainty for the company as to when the required majority of eligible members needed to agree the resolution has been reached.

Section 297: Period for agreeing to written resolution

540.   This section puts a time limit of 28 days for passing a written resolution, unless the company's articles specify a different period. This means that there will be a definite point when the company can say that a resolution with insufficient support has not been passed.

Supplementary

Section 298: Sending documents relating to written resolutions by electronic means

541.   This clause needs to be read together with the provisions about electronic communications to companies in Part 3 (communications in electronic form) of Schedule 4. Taken together, these provisions allow a member to communicate with the company by electronic means where the company has given an electronic address in a document containing or accompanying a proposed written resolution.

Section 299: Publication of written resolution on website

542.   This section should be read in conjunction with the provisions about communications by means of a website by a company other than a traded company in Part 4 (communications by means of a website) of Schedule 5 (communications by a company). This clause, together with those provisions, allow a company, provided certain conditions are met, to publish a written resolution on a website rather than send it to a member individually.

Section 300: Relationship between this Chapter and provisions of company's articles

543.   This section ensures that the company's articles cannot remove the ability of a private company and its members to propose and pass a statutory resolution using the statutory written resolutions procedures of this Chapter.

CHAPTER 3: RESOLUTIONS AT MEETINGS

544.   This Chapter replaces sections 368 to 377, 379 and 381 of the 1985 Act and makes provision about resolutions passed in general meeting. The provisions apply equally to private and public companies. The new provisions reflect the fact that private companies will no longer have to hold AGMs. For example, the provisions about circulation of statements in sections 376 and 377 of the 1985 Act have been separated from the provisions on circulation of resolutions prior to an AGM – which are in Chapter 4. The Act repeals section 367 of the 1985 Act which gives the Secretary of State a power to call a meeting where there is no AGM.

General provisions about resolutions at meetings

Section 301: Resolutions at general meetings

545.   This is a general provision about the circumstances in which resolutions at meetings are validly passed. It extends to all resolutions the principle in section 378(6) of the 1985 Act relating to special resolutions: that passing a resolution in a meeting is not just a question of obtaining the right majority but of using the correct procedures. An important difference from the position under section 378(6) is that, under this section, a resolution must be passed in accordance with the relevant provisions of the Bill and any additional requirements imposed by the company's articles. So, where there are mandatory provisions in the Bill (like those about proxies' rights to vote) these cannot be avoided by making alternative provision in the articles; and where provision is made about meetings in a company's articles, these must also be complied with.

Calling meetings

Section 302: Directors' power to call general meetings

546.   This section puts into statute part of the default regulation at article 37 of Table A which allows the directors to call a general meeting. The company's articles will set out how the directors act collectively.

Section 303: Members' power to require directors to call general meeting

547.   This section, together with sections 304 and 305 make provision similar to that in section 368 of the 1985 Act requiring the directors to call a general meeting if requested by the members. There are three main changes.

548.   First, there is a change in the threshold required for a meeting request. For public companies this remains members with voting rights holding at least 10% of the paid-up capital. For private companies the threshold is 5% or 10% of the paid-up capital (or, in a company with no share capital, 5% or 10% of the total voting rights) depending on when there was last a meeting in advance of which members had a right – equivalent to the right under this clause (see below) – to circulate resolutions. The threshold is lower if there has been no such meeting in the last twelve months. Second, as indicated above, *subsection (4)(b)* extends the provisions of the 1985 Act by enabling members to include the text of a resolution to be moved at the requested meeting. *Subsection (5)* defines what type of resolution may be properly moved. For example, if the resolution would have no effect, then it cannot be properly moved. Third, requests in electronic form are permitted.

Section 304: Directors' duty to call meetings required by members

549.   This section sets time limits within which the directors must call and hold a meeting required by members. *Subsection (2)* requires that if the members' request identifies a resolution to be moved at the meeting, notice of this resolution should be included in the notice of the meeting.

Section 305: Power of members to call meeting at company's expense

550.   This section enables the members to call a meeting at the company's expense in the event that the directors fail to call a meeting on the members' request. *Subsections (6) and (7)* provide for members to be reimbursed appropriately and that the directors are penalised directly by the reimbursement being taken out of the fees or other remuneration due to them.

Section 306: Power of court to order meeting

551.   This section reproduces the effect of section 371 of the 1985 Act and gives the court power to order a meeting of the company and to direct the manner in which that meeting is called, held and conducted.

Notice of meetings

Section 307: Notice required of general meeting

552.   This section replaces part of section 369 of the 1985 Act. It retains the current minimum notice period requirement of 21 days for public company AGMs, with 14 days' notice required for all other general meetings (whether public or private company general meetings). A general meeting may be called on shorter notice if the requisite majority of members agree. The key substantive change from the position under existing legislation is that the requisite majority required to agree a short notice period has been reduced for private companies from 95% to 90% of the voting rights, although the articles may specify up to 95% if the company wishes. For public companies, the majority required to agree a short notice period remains at 95% of the voting rights.

Section 308: Manner in which notice to be given

553.   This section should be read in conjunction with the general requirements for companies in sending and supplying information as set out in Part 37 and Schedule 5.

Section 309: Publication of notice of meeting on website

554.   This section contains some specific provisions on communications by means of a website and needs to be read with the general provisions on communications referred to above. The overall effect is similar to that of the website provisions in the current section 369 of the 1985 Act.

Section 310: Persons entitled to receive notice of meetings

555.   This section puts into statute part of article 38 of Table A. The new provision ensures that notice of meetings must be sent to all members, directors and any person entitled to a share as a consequence of the death or bankruptcy (or the equivalent in Scots insolvency law) of a member. The provision is subject to any enactment and to any provision in the articles. This means that a company may, for example, make provision in its articles to stop sending notice of meeting to members for whom the company no longer has a valid address.

Section 311: Contents of notices of meetings

556.   This section puts into statute another part of article 38 of Table A. The new provision ensures that the notice of meeting must include the time, date and place of the meeting and, subject to the articles, the general nature of the business to be conducted at the meeting.

Section 312: Resolution requiring special notice

557.   This section replaces section 379 of the 1985 Act setting out the requirements for special notice resolutions. It makes provision only in relation to resolutions passed at meetings. This is because the resolutions for which special notice is required are either resolutions that are not capable of being passed as written resolutions (in the case of sections 168 and 510) or in relation to which written resolutions have their own special procedure (see sections 514 and 515).

558.   There is no change from the existing law whereby at least 28 days' notice must be given to the company of the intention to move a resolution requiring special notice. Where it is not practicable for the company to give members notice of such a resolution at the same time as it gives notice of the meeting at which the resolution is to be moved, the company must in future give at least 14 days' notice either by newspaper advertisement or by any other manner allowed by the articles.

Section 313: Accidental failure to give notice of resolution or meeting

559.   This section expands on article 39 of Table A. It contains the rule that an accidental failure to give notice of a resolution or a general meeting is generally disregarded. Under *subsection (2)*, this rule can be altered by the articles in some but not all cases.

Members' statements

Section 314: Members' power to require circulation of statements

560.   This section, together with section 315, replaces sections 376 and 377 of the 1985 Act and provides a right for members to require the company to circulate a statement of up to 1,000 words. The key policy change is that where the statement relates to a resolution or other matter to be dealt with at a public company's AGM and is received before the company's financial year-end, the shareholders are not required to cover the costs of circulating the statement. There are two other notable changes. The first is that the shares relied on to trigger the circulation of a statement must in each case carry rights to vote on the relevant resolution rather than just at the meeting. The second is that requests in electronic form are permitted.

Section 315: Company's duty to circulate members' statement

561.   This section replaces the remainder of sections 376 and 377 of the 1985 Act and specifies what the company is to do when it is required to circulate a members' statement. The statement must be circulated in the same manner as notice of the meeting and at the same time, or as soon as reasonably practicable, after the company gives notice of the meeting. Where the company fails to comply with the provisions of this section an offence is committed by every officer of the company who is in default.

Section 316: Expenses of circulating members' statement

562.   This section provides that the expenses of complying with section 315 need not be paid by the members if the meeting to which the request relates is a public company AGM and a sufficient number of requests are received before the company's year-end. Otherwise the company's expenses will have to be met by the members who requested the circulation of the statement unless the company resolves otherwise. In this case, the members requesting the statement must deposit a sum to cover the company's costs (unless the company has resolved otherwise).

Section 317: Application not to circulate members' statement

563.   This section replaces section 377(3) of the 1985 Act. It enables the court on application to relieve the company of an obligation to circulate a members' statement if in its opinion the right to require circulation is being abused.

Procedure at meetings

Section 318: Quorum at meetings

564.   This section replaces sections 370(4) and 370A of the 1985 Act. It sets a quorum for a meeting of one "qualifying person" in the case of a single member company and – as a default – two "qualifying persons" in any other case. *Subsections (2) and (3)* ensure that a member, corporate representative or proxy present at the meeting may all be "qualifying persons", but excludes the possibility of two or more corporate representatives or proxies of the same member comprising a quorum. Under these provisions, proxies and corporate representatives do not count towards a quorum in companies with more than one member.

Section 319: Chairman of meeting

565.   This section reproduces the effect of section 370(5) of the 1985 Act and provides a default provision where the company's articles are silent, allowing any member to be elected as chairman of a general meeting by a resolution of the company passed at the meeting.

Section 320: Declaration by chairman on a show of hands

566.   This section replaces section 378(4) of the 1985 Act and part of article 47 of Table A. This provision ensures that the chairman's declaration of a vote taken on a show of hands is conclusive evidence of the resolution being passed or lost without further proof being provided, unless a poll is demanded on the resolution. There are two main differences from section 378(4), both of which are drawn from Table A. First, if the demand for a poll is withdrawn, then the chairman's declaration will stand. Second, the minutes of the meeting also provide conclusive evidence of the chairman's declaration. This section is intended to provide certainty by preventing members from challenging a declaration of the chairman as to the votes cast on a resolution at a meeting otherwise than by calling a poll.

Section 321: Right to demand a poll

567.   This section replaces section 373 of the 1985 Act. It restricts companies' ability, through their articles, to exclude members' rights to call a poll. However, it allows articles to exclude the right to a poll on the election of the chairman of the meeting and the adjournment of the meeting. The section provides for three effective types of demands for a poll, including a demand made by at least 5 members with a right to vote on the resolution.

Section 322: Voting on a poll

568.   This section replaces section 374 of the 1985 Act. This provision recognises that a member may hold shares on behalf of third parties and allows the member to cast votes in different ways according to instructions from his clients. The reference to class meetings in section 374 is dealt with by section 334.

Section 323: Representation of corporations at meetings

569.   This section replaces section 375 of the 1985 Act. The section expressly provides for the appointment of multiple corporate representatives. This is possible under section 375 of the 1985 Act, although the effect of appointing multiple representatives under the existing law is in some cases unclear. The new section spells out the position. Any one of the corporate representatives will be entitled to vote and exercise other powers on behalf of the member at meetings, but in the event that representatives' votes or other powers conflict, the corporation is deemed to have abstained from exercising its vote or power. If a corporation

wishes to appoint people with different voting intentions or with authority to vote different blocks of shares, they should appoint proxies.

Proxies

Section 324: Rights to appoint proxies

570.   This section sets out new provisions for the appointment of proxies, expanding on the existing rights given under section 372 of the 1985 Act and Table A. It puts on a statutory footing certain rights that under the 1985 Act are subject to the articles. In future, members of both private and public companies will have the right to appoint more than one proxy. All proxies will be able to attend, to speak and to vote at a meeting. As to the voting rights of a proxy on a show of hands, see sections 284(2)(b) and 285. The effect of those sections is that the default position will be that, where a member appoints more than one proxy, each proxy will have a vote. The articles will be capable of restricting the number of votes of the proxies, provided that they still have at least one vote between them.

Section 325: Notice of meeting to contain statement of rights

571.   This section replaces sections 372(3) and 372(4) of the 1985 Act with changes consequential on the extended rights to appoint proxies under section 324. The new provision requires every notice calling a meeting to contain a statement informing the member of his rights to appoint one or more proxies and any more extensive rights conferred by the company's articles. Failure to include such a statement will not invalidate the meeting, but is an offence attracting a fine for every officer of the company found in default.

Section 326: Company-sponsored invitations to appoint proxies

572.   This section reproduces the effect of section 372(6) of the 1985 Act and requires a company to ensure that if it invites members to appoint a particular person or persons as proxy, such an invitation must be issued to all members entitled to vote at the meeting. *Subsection (2)* lists two exceptions to the requirement. Failure to comply attracts a fine for every officer in default.

Section 327: Notice required of appointment of proxy etc

573.   This section replaces section 372(5) of the 1985 Act. There are two changes. The first relates to the timing required for a notice of proxy appointment. The new provision ensures that weekends, Christmas Day, Good Friday and any bank holiday are excluded from the time counting towards the minimum 48 hour notice required to appoint proxies. This means, for example, that for a meeting to be held at 3.00 pm on a Tuesday after a bank holiday Monday, the cut-off point for proxy appointment will be 3.00 pm the previous Thursday, not 3.00 pm on Sunday as under the 1985 Act. The second is that polls which are not taken immediately are covered by the rules as well as meetings and adjourned meetings.

Section 328: Chairing meetings

574.   This section provides as a default rule, subject to the articles, that a proxy may be elected as chairman of a general meeting by resolution of the company passed at the meeting.

Section 329: Right of proxy to demand a poll

575.   This section sets out the way in which a proxy may participate in a demand for a poll.

Section 330: Notice required of termination of proxy's authority

576.   This section provides a default regulation to replace article 63 of Table A. This ensures that, subject to the articles, an appointed proxy's actions at a meeting are valid unless notice of termination of the proxy's authority is given before the meeting starts. The company's articles may specify a longer advance notice period but this cannot be more than 48 hours in advance of the meeting (excluding weekends, Christmas Day, Good Friday and bank holidays).

Section 331: Saving for more extensive rights conferred by articles

577.   This section makes clear that the company's articles may confer more extensive rights than are provided for under the provisions of the Bill on members and their proxies.

Adjourned meetings

Section 332: Resolution passed at adjourned meeting

578.   This section reproduces the effect of part of section 381 of the 1985 Act as it applies to members' meetings. It ensures that a resolution of the members of the company passed at an adjourned meeting is treated as passed on that date and not on any earlier date. The reference to class meetings in section 381 is dealt with by section 334.

Electronic communications

Section 333: Sending documents relating to meetings etc in electronic form

579.   This section needs to be read together with the provisions about electronic communications to companies in Part 3 of Schedule 4. Taken together these provisions allow a member to communicate with the company by electronic means where the company has given an electronic address in a notice calling a meeting or in an instrument of proxy or proxy invitation.

Application to class meetings

Section 334: Application to class meetings

580.   This section applies the provisions of this Chapter with some modifications to meetings of holders of a class of shares in companies having a share capital.

Section 335: Application to class meetings: companies without a share capital

581.   This section applies the provisions of this Chapter with some modifications to meetings of classes of members of companies without a share capital.

CHAPTER 4: PUBLIC COMPANIES: ADDITIONAL REQUIREMENTS FOR AGMS

582.   The requirements for public companies relating to annual general meetings are set out in this Chapter. The main substantive changes to the 1985 Act are, as the CLR recommended, that:

- private companies will no longer be required to hold an AGM. The provisions of this Chapter therefore do not apply to private companies; and

- public company AGMs must be held within six months of their financial year-end.

Section 336: Public companies: annual general meeting

583.   This section replaces section 366 of the 1985 Act but will apply only to public companies since private companies are no longer to be required to hold an AGM. Where section 366 required an AGM to be held each year and not more than 15 months after the previous AGM, a public company will now be required to hold an AGM within 6 months of its financial year-end. This new requirement is intended to ensure that shareholders have a more timely opportunity to hold the directors of a public company to account.

Section 337: Public companies: notice of AGM

584.   This section reproduces the effect of parts of section 369 of the 1985 Act relating to the AGM notice. The minimum notice period for calling a public company AGM is 21 days as set out in subsection (2) of section 307 or longer if provided for in the company's articles. An AGM may be called at shorter notice if all members of the company agree.

Section 338: Public companies: members' power to require circulation of resolutions for AGMs

585.   This section, with section 339, replaces sections 376 and 377 of the 1985 Act (to the extent that they relate to resolutions proposed by members to be moved at an AGM). Members holding at least 5% voting rights or at least 100 members holding on average £100 paid-up capital have the right to propose a resolution for the AGM agenda and to require the company to circulate details of the resolution to all members. A change from the existing legislation is that the shares must in each case carry rights to vote on the relevant resolution. The key policy change is that, if the members' request is received before the financial year-end, then the members are not required to cover the costs of circulation.

Section 339: Public companies: company's duty to circulate members' resolutions for AGMs

586.   This section replaces the remaining parts of sections 376 and 377 of the 1985 Act (to the extent that they relate to resolutions proposed by members to be moved at an AGM). It specifies what a company has to do when it is required to circulate a members' resolution for an AGM.

Section 340: Public companies: expenses of circulating members' resolutions for AGM

587.   This section provides that the expenses of complying with section 339 need not be paid by the members who requested the circulation of the resolution if requests sufficient to require the company to circulate it are received before the company's year-end. Otherwise the company's expenses will have to be met by the members who requested the circulation of the resolution unless the company resolves otherwise. In this case, the members requesting the statement must deposit a sum to cover the company's costs (unless the company has resolved otherwise).

CHAPTER 5: ADDITIONAL REQUIREMENTS FOR QUOTED COMPANIES

588.   This Chapter imposes new requirements on quoted companies relating to the disclosure on a website of the results of polls at general meetings, and an independent report on a poll if a sufficient number of members demand one. These two measures were recommended by the CLR (Final Report, paragraph 6.39(ii) and (iv)).

Website publication of poll results

Section 341: Results of poll to be made available on website

589.   This section requires quoted companies to disclose on a website the results of all polls taken at a general meeting. *Subsection (1)* sets out the minimum information that must be disclosed. Companies may disclose additional information about the poll results if they wish. *Subsection (4)* imposes a penalty on every officer in default for non-compliance. Non-compliance however does not invalidate the poll, the resolution or other business to which the poll relates. Section 353(requirements as to website availability) sets out the requirements relating to the website on which the poll results must be published.

Independent report on poll

Section 342: Members' power to require independent report on poll

590.   This section gives members of a quoted company the right to require an independent report of any poll taken, or to be taken, at a general meeting. The minimum threshold required for the demand is the same as that for requiring the circulation of a resolution – that is members holding 5% of the voting rights or 100 members holding on average £100 of paid-up capital. The members' request must be made within one week of the meeting where the poll is taken. This allows members to decide after a poll is taken whether they wish to require an independent report, for example on a controversial resolution or where there appears to be a problem relating to voting procedures. Members may make their request in advance of the meeting if they wish, but unless the company's articles already require all votes to be taken on a poll, members may need to take steps to ensure that a poll is called.

Section 343: Appointment of independent assessor

591.   The appointment of an independent assessor must be made within one week of the members' request. This means that the appointment could be made either before or after the meeting depending on when the members' request is made. The independent assessor must be independent (see section 344) and must not be someone already involved in the voting process for the company.

Section 344: Independence requirement

592.   This section prevents a person acting as an independent assessor on a poll if he is too closely connected to the company or an associated undertaking of the company. The independence requirements are set out in *subsection (1)*. They correspond to the independence requirements for a statutory auditor (see section 1214). *Subsection (2)* allows, but does not require, an auditor to be appointed as an assessor.

Section 345: Meaning of "associate"

593.   This section defines "associate" for the purposes of the independence requirements in section 344.

Section 346: Effect of appointment of a partnership

594.   This section provides for where a partnership that is not a legal person is appointed as an independent assessor on a poll.

Section 347: The independent assessor's report

595.   This section sets out the minimum information the independent assessor's report must contain.

Section 348: Rights of independent assessor: right to attend meeting etc

596.   This section gives the independent assessor rights to attend the meeting at which the poll or polls may be taken and to be provided with information relating to the meeting. He is to exercise these rights only to the extent he considers necessary for the preparation of his report.

Section 349: Rights of independent assessor: right to information

597.   This section gives the independent assessor the right to access company records relating to any poll on which he is to report and to the meeting at which the poll or polls may be taken.

Section 350: Offences relating to provision of information

598.   This section imposes a penalty on any person listed in subsection (2) of section 349 who fails to comply with the requirement to provide information or explanation relating to the poll on which the independent assessor is preparing a report.

Section 351: Information to be made available on website

599.   This section requires the company to publish on a website the independent assessor's report of the poll or polls and sets out the minimum information relating to the assessor's appointment, his identity, the text of the resolution and the assessor's report that must be made available. *Subsections (3) and (4)* impose a penalty on every officer in default for non-compliance with this requirement. Failure to comply, however, does not invalidate the poll or the resolution or other business to which the poll relates. Section 353 sets out the requirements relating to the website on which the independent report must be published.

Supplementary

Section 352: Application of provisions to class meetings

600.   This section applies the provisions of this Chapter to meetings of holders of a class of shares of a quoted company.

Section 353: Requirements as to website availability

601.   This section sets out the minimum requirements that should apply to information to be published on a quoted company's website under section 341 and section 351. The website on which the information is made available must be maintained by or on behalf of the quoted company and must identify the company in question. This provides flexibility as to whether a website is the company's own or one operated by a website service provider. Information published on a website must be kept available for a minimum of two years. *Subsection (5)* provides a let-out when a company's failure to make the information available on a website for part of the period is wholly attributable to circumstances beyond the company's control.

Section 354: Power to limit or extend the types of company to which provisions of this Chapter apply

602.   At present the provisions of this Chapter apply to quoted companies as defined in section 385, which replaces the definition of "quoted company" in section 262 of the 1985 Act. This section confers on the Secretary of State a power to make regulations to limit or extend the types of company to which the provisions of this Chapter apply. The Parliamentary procedure that will apply to such regulations depends on whether they extend or limit the application of the Chapter.

CHAPTER 6: RECORDS OF RESOLUTIONS AND MEETINGS

603.   The following provisions replace sections 382, 382A, 382B and 383 of the 1985 Act relating to the records of company proceedings. They should be read in conjunction with the provisions on company records in Part 31. The main changes are the ten year minimum period for keeping records (the 1985 Act envisaged that records would be retained forever); that meetings of directors are dealt with elsewhere (in Part 10 of the Act); and that the new provisions apply to class meetings.

Section 355: Records of resolutions and meetings etc

604.   This section requires all companies to maintain records comprising: copies of all resolutions passed otherwise than at general meetings (which would include all written resolutions), minutes of all proceedings of general meetings, and details of decisions of a sole member taken in accordance with section 357. All records must be kept for a minimum of 10 years. *Subsections (3) and (4)* impose a penalty on every officer in default for non-compliance.

Section 356: Records as evidence of resolutions etc

605.   This section ensures that all records of resolutions or written resolutions and minutes of meetings, where signed off by a director or a company secretary or by the chairman in the case of a general meeting, are evidence of the passing of a resolution or the proceedings at the meeting. In legal proceedings, a litigant will have to accept that the records are accurate unless he can prove that they are not.

Section 357: Records of decisions by sole member

606.   This section makes provision for the recording of decisions of a company with only one member.

Section 358: Inspection of records of resolutions and meetings

607.   This section requires every company to keep its records available for inspection by members for 10 years. *Subsection (5)* enables a member to seek a court order to compel the company to make the records available for inspection or to provide copies of the records.

Section 359: Records of resolutions and meetings of class of members

608.   This section applies the provisions of this Chapter to resolutions and meetings of holders of a class of shares in the case of a company with share capital or to classes of members in the case of a company without a share capital.

CHAPTER 7: SUPPLEMENTARY PROVISIONS

Section 360: Computation of periods of notice etc: clear day rule

609.   This is a new provision to ensure clarity and consistency in the calculation of time periods in relation to meetings and resolutions under Part 13. The section provides that in calculating periods of notice, or periods before a meeting by which a request must be received or sum deposited or tendered, the following are to be excluded –

- the day of the meeting,

- the day on which notice is given,

- the day on which the request is received or the sum is deposited or tendered.

Section 361: Meaning of "quoted company"

610.   This section provides that the definition for "quoted company" is as stated in Part 15 (Accounts and reports) of the Act.

PART 14: CONTROL OF POLITICAL DONATIONS AND EXPENDITURE

Background and summary

611.   In October 1998 the Committee on Standards in Public Life presented to the Prime Minister its report on the funding of political parties in the UK. The Report recommended that any company intending to make a donation (whether in cash or in kind, and including any sponsorship, or loans or transactions at a favourable rate) to a political party or organisation should be required to have the prior authority of its shareholders. The Government accepted this recommendation, and implemented it through the Political Parties, Elections and Referendums Act 2000 ("the PPERA"). The new regime for control of political donations and expenditure is in Part 10A of the 1985 Act, as inserted by section 139 of and Schedule 19 to the PPERA.

612.   Part 14 of the Act restates the existing provisions in a style consistent with the other sections, but most of the key elements of the framework established by the PPERA remain. In particular:

- companies will continue to be prohibited from making a donation to a political party or other political organisation or from incurring political expenditure unless the donation or the expenditure has been authorised, in a typical case by the members of the company;

- a "political donation" will continue to be defined by reference to sections 50 to 52 of the PPERA, and for this purpose amendments made to the PPERA by the Electoral Administration Act 2006 (which remove from the definition of "donations" loans made otherwise than on commercial terms) will be disregarded;

- an approval resolution may authorise the making of donations and incurring of expenditure for a period of not more than four years commencing with the date of the passing of the resolution up to a value specified in the resolution;

- donations or expenditure by a subsidiary must, in general, be authorised by resolutions of the members of the subsidiary and of the holding company; and the directors of such a holding company will continue to be liable for unauthorised donations by the subsidiary company;

- a company need not seek prior shareholder consent for a donation to a political party or organisation unless the aggregate amount of the donation together with any other relevant donations made by the company and other companies in the group of which it is a member in the previous 12 months exceeds £5,000;

- there are no criminal sanctions in relation to the making of unauthorised donations or the incurring of unauthorised political expenditure;

- civil remedies are available to a company in the event of breach of the prohibitions and may be pursued in the normal manner by the company. There will continue to be available an action under which shareholders may enforce on behalf of the company any of the remedies available to a company.

613.   The main changes from Part 10A of the 1985 Act are that:

- in line with the general approach in the Act, references to the general meeting are removed to make it clearer that private companies can authorise donations and/or expenditure by written resolution;

- a holding company must authorise a donation or expenditure by a subsidiary company only if it is a "relevant holding company" (that is, the ultimate holding company or, where such a company is not a "UK-registered company", the holding company highest up the chain which is a "UK-registered company");

- a holding company is permitted to seek authorisation of donations and expenditure in respect of both the holding company itself and one or more subsidiaries (including wholly-owned subsidiaries) through a single approval resolution (section 367(1));

- companies are permitted to table separate approval resolutions in respect of donations to political parties and donations to other political organisations (section 367(3));

- companies are required to seek authorisation for donations to independent candidates at any election to public office held in the UK or other EU member state and for expenditure by the company relating to independent election candidates;

- the sections provide greater clarity for companies about the provision of facilities (for example, meeting rooms) for trade union officials by introducing a specific exemption for donations to trade unions (section 374). The Act does not introduce a specific exemption in relation to paid leave for local councillors because this does not constitute a political donation or political expenditure under Part 10A of the 1985 Act or this Act;

- there are important changes to the rules on ratification and liability in cases of unauthorised donations or expenditure;

- the special rules in respect of the parent company of a non-GB subsidiary undertaking (sections 347E and 347G of the 1985 Act) are not reproduced;

- The new provisions apply to Northern Ireland.

COMMENTARY

Section 362: Introductory

614.   This section explains that this Part relates to political expenditure and to political donations made by companies to political parties, political organisations and independent election candidates.

Section 363: Political parties, organisations etc to which this Part applies

615.   This section establishes the general scope of the provisions of this Part and introduces the concepts of:

- political parties;

- political organisations other than political parties;

- independent election candidates at any election to public office.

Section 364: Meaning of "political donation"

616.   This section defines a "political donation" for the purposes of this Part by reference to sections 50 to 52 of the Political Parties, Elections and Referendums Act 2000. For this purpose, amendments made to the 2000 Act by the Electoral Administration Act 2006 (which remove from the definition of "donation" loans made otherwise than on commercial terms) are disregarded. This section reproduces the effect of section 347A(4) of the 1985 Act, except that it includes donations to independent election candidates.

Section 365: Meaning of "political expenditure"

617.   This section defines "political expenditure" for the purposes of this Part.

618.   It reproduces the effect of section 347A(5) of the 1985 Act, except that it extends the definition to expenditure incurred by the company in relation to independent election candidates.

Section 366: Authorisation required for donations or expenditure

619.   This section prohibits a company from making a donation or incurring political expenditure unless the transaction or the expenditure is authorised by a resolution of the members of the company. If the company is a subsidiary of another company, a resolution may instead, or in addition, be required from the members of the holding company. Sections 1159, 1160 and Schedule 6 provide the definition of "subsidiary". This section reproduces the effect of section 347C(1) and (6) and section 347D of the 1985 Act, except that:

- in line with the general approach in the Act, the section does not refer to the general meeting, to make it clear that private companies can authorise donations and/or expenditure by written resolution;

- a donation or expenditure by a subsidiary company must be authorised by the members of the company and by members of a "relevant holding company" (rather than by the members of each holding company within a group). A "relevant holding company" is the ultimate holding company or, where such a company is not a "UK-registered company", the holding company highest up the chain which is a "UK-registered company";

- a resolution is not required on the part of a company that is a wholly-owned subsidiary of a "UK-registered company" (rather than of any holding company, as in section 347D of the 1985 Act);

- the section does not reproduce the prohibition (in section 347C(5) of the 1985 Act) on retrospective ratification of breaches of the rules.

Section 367: Form of authorising resolution

620.   This section provides that an authorising resolution may identify the subsidiaries, the heads of donations or expenditure, and the amounts that it authorises. The section reproduces the effect of the 1985 Act, but with the following changes:

- under *subsection (1) and (2)*, a holding company may seek authorisation of donations and expenditure in respect of both itself and one or more of its subsidiaries (including wholly-owned subsidiaries) in a single approval resolution. The subsidiaries do not need to be named in the resolution if it applies to all of a holding company's subsidiaries;

- under *subsection (3)*, a company may pass separate approval resolutions in respect of donations to political parties and donations to other political organisations.

Section 368: Period for which resolution has effect

621.   This section provides that an approval resolution may seek authorisation for the making of donations and incurring of expenditure having effect over a period of not more than four years. It reproduces the effect of the 1985 Act.

Section 369: Liability of directors in case of unauthorised donation or expenditure

622.   This section imposes civil liability on directors where unauthorised donations are made or unauthorised political expenditure is incurred. The liabilities are owed to the company and may be pursued in the normal manner by the company; that is they may be pursued by the directors in the exercise of the management powers conferred by the articles of association. The directors will be subject to the general duties set out in Chapter 2 of Part 10 in the conduct of the company's business. In addition, section 370 provides for enforcement by shareholder action.

623.   The section largely reproduces the effect of section 347F of the 1985 Act, but:

- only a director of the company and of a "relevant holding company" may be liable in respect of an unauthorised donation or unauthorised expenditure. This reflects the new rules relating to the authorisation of donations or expenditure by subsidiaries in section 366;

- directors of the "relevant holding company" will not be liable for an unauthorised political donation or unauthorised political expenditure by a subsidiary if they took "all reasonable steps to prevent the donation being made or the expenditure being incurred".

624.   The conditions under which directors may be exempted from liability (currently set out in section 347H of the 1985 Act) are not reproduced in the new regime.

Section 370: Enforcement of directors' liabilities by shareholder action

625.   This section provides a mechanism by which an authorised group of shareholders may enforce on behalf of the company any liability under section 369. In the case of a company limited by shares, an action may be brought by a group of shareholders if they are at least 50 in number, or hold at least 5% of the issued share capital. This section reproduces the effect of section 347I of the 1985 Act, except that, in a case where liability is owed by directors of a holding company in relation to a donation made by a subsidiary, the action may be brought by shareholders of the subsidiary or of the holding company.

Section 371: Enforcement of directors' liabilities by shareholder action: supplementary

626.   This section makes further provision in relation to proceedings brought under section 370. It reproduces the effect of section 347I of the 1985 Act. The group of shareholders wanting to take action under section 370 must give written notice to the company at least 28 days in advance of bringing the proceedings. Any director of the company has the right to apply to the court within 28 days of when the notice was given to request that the proceedings not be brought.

627.   This section also provides that if the liability is already being pursued with due diligence by the company, the court may direct that the proceedings brought by the group of shareholders are either discontinued or brought on such terms and conditions as the court sees fit.

Section 372: Costs of shareholder action

628.   This section provides that the authorised group of members are not entitled as of right to have the cost of the shareholder action met from the funds of the company, but have the right to apply to the court for an indemnity out of the company's assets in respect of costs incurred or to be incurred in a shareholder action. The court would have full discretion to grant such an indemnity on such terms as it thinks fit. The section reproduces the effect of section 347J of the 1985 Act.

Section 373: Information for purposes of shareholder action

629.   This section provides that the authorised group of members is entitled, once the action is commenced, to be provided by the company in whose name it is brought with all information possessed by the company, or in its control or obtainable by it, relating to the subject matter of the action. It reproduces the effect of section 347K of the 1985 Act.

Sections 374 to 378: Exemptions

630.   These sections set out five exemptions from the requirement for prior shareholder authorisation:

- section 374 creates a new exemption in relation to donations to trade unions (including trade unions in countries other than the UK). The exemption covers donations such as the provision of company rooms for trade union meetings, the use of company vehicles by trade union officials and paid time off for trade union officials. However, a donation to a trade union's political fund is not covered by the exemption;

- section 375 restates the exemption in section 347B of the 1985 Act in respect of subscriptions paid to a trade association for membership of the association, except that it is not restricted to trade associations which carry out their activities mainly in the EU;

- section 376 restates the exemption in section 347B of the 1985 Act in respect of donations to all-party parliamentary groups;

- section 377 restates the exemption in section 347B of the 1985 Act for political expenditure that is exempt by virtue of an order by the Secretary of State. An order made by statutory instrument under this clause may confer an exemption on companies or expenditure of any description or category specified in the order. The parallel power in section 347B(8) to (11) of the 1985 Act was used in 2001 to exempt business activities such as the publication of newspapers which, by their very nature, involve the publication or dissemination of material which seeks to influence the views of members of the public;

- section 378 restates the exemption in section 347B of the 1985 Act under which authorisation for donations is not required unless the donation or aggregate amount of the donations by the company exceeds £5,000 in a 12 month period. Donations by other group companies (including subsidiaries) must be taken into account in calculating whether the £5,000 threshold has been exceeded.

Section 379: Minor definitions

631.   This section contains minor definitions for this Part.

PART 15: ACCOUNTS AND REPORTS

632.   The provisions of this Part replace the provisions of Part 7 of the 1985 Act relating to accounts and reports. The provisions of Part 7 of the 1985 Act relating to audit are replaced by provisions in Part 16 of the Act.

633.   The provisions have been reordered and redrafted to make it easier for companies of whatever size to find the requirements relevant to them. In Part 7 of the 1985 Act the provisions applying to small companies are generally expressed as modifications of the provisions applying to large companies. These sections proceed on the opposite basis: where provisions do not apply to all kinds of company, provisions applying to small companies appear before the provisions applying to other companies.

634.   A further change is to enable the Secretary of State to replace the detailed Schedules to Part 7 of the 1985 Act by regulations. This will give more flexibility to arrange the material currently in Schedules to make it easier to follow for different types of company. It is unnecessary and undesirable to have parallel and duplicative regimes on the detail for different types of company in primary legislation, but this could be done in parallel sets of regulations for different sizes and types of company.

635.   The main substantive changes in this Part are:

- a reduction in the time limit for private companies to file their accounts from ten months to nine months after the year end (section 442);

- a reduction in the time limit for public companies to lay full financial statements before the company in general meeting and file them from 7 months to 6 months after the year end (section 442);

- new requirements for quoted companies to publish their annual accounts and reports on a website (section 430); and

- replacement of the general power of the Secretary of State to alter accounting requirements in section 257 of the 1985 Act by a general power of amendment by regulations (section 468) and more specific powers in relation to specific sections.

CHAPTER 1: INTRODUCTION

Section 380: Scheme of this Part

636.   This introductory section indicates the main way in which the structure of this Part differs from that of Part 7 of the 1985 Act: provisions relating to small companies are set out before provisions relating to larger companies; provisions applying to private companies appear before those applying to public companies; and provisions applying to quoted companies appear after those applying to other companies.

Companies subject to the small companies regime

Section 381: Companies subject to the small companies regime

Section 382: Companies qualifying as small: general

Section 383: Companies qualifying as small: parent companies

Section 384: Companies excluded from the small companies regime

637.   These sections set out which companies, parent companies or groups fall within the small companies regime – that is, those that qualify as small companies or groups and are not excluded from the regime for one of the reasons set out in section 384. With two small changes, the conditions for qualification as a small company are unchanged from the current regime (sections 247, 247A and 249 of the 1985 Act). Firstly, section 382(5) now contains a generalised definition of balance sheet total for both Companies Act and IAS individual accounts. Secondly, whereas section 247A(2) of the 1985 Act provides that a group is ineligible if any of its members is a body corporate having power to offer its shares or debentures to the public, the reference in section 384(2)(b) is now to a body corporate whose securities are admitted to trading on a regulated market in an EEA state. The definition of "regulated market" is to be found in section 1173. This reflects changes made by the Accounts Modernisation Directive (2003/51/EEC).

Section 385: Quoted and unquoted companies

638.   The definitions of quoted and unquoted company in this section are equivalent to the definition of "quoted company" in section 262 of the 1985 Act. A power is conferred to amend the definition of "quoted company" by regulations. If the regulations extend the application of this Part then they will be subject to affirmative resolution procedure. Otherwise they are subject to negative resolution procedure.

CHAPTER 2: ACCOUNTING RECORDS

Sections 386 to 389: Accounting records

639.   These sections set out the general duty to keep accounting records and specify where and for how long records are to be kept. They replace equivalent provisions in sections 221 and 222 of the 1985 Act. Their purpose is to ensure that businesses record transactions to

enable them to show the company's financial position and to prepare accounts which comply with the Companies Act and, where relevant, with International Accounting Standards. "Accounting records" is a broad term and there is no specific definition as the records may differ depending on the nature and complexity of the business. For a simple business these may include, for example, bank statements, purchase orders, sales and purchase invoices, whilst a more sophisticated business may have integrated records, which it holds electronically.

640.   Section 387 creates a criminal offence for every officer of a company who is in default, where the company has failed to keep adequate accounting records under section 386. The section replicates the existing penalties under section 221(5) and (6) of the 1985 Act (imprisonment or a fine).

641.   Section 389 makes similar provision in relation to failure to comply with section 388, replacing section 222(4) and (6) of the 1985 Act.

CHAPTER 3: A COMPANY'S FINANCIAL YEAR

Section 390: A company's financial year

642.   This section replaces section 223 of the 1985 Act. A company's financial year is the period for which its accounts and reports must be prepared. A company's financial year is the same as its accounting reference period (see section 391), subject to the directors' decision to alter the last day of the period by plus or minus seven days.

Section 391: Accounting reference periods and accounting reference date

Section 392: Alteration of accounting reference date

643.   These sections replace sections 224 and 225 of the 1985 Act.

644.   Section 391(2) and (3) preserve the accounting reference dates of companies incorporated before 1st April 1996 (in the case of GB companies), and before 22nd August 1997 (in the case of Northern Irish companies). Otherwise, a company's accounting reference date is the last day of the month in which the anniversary of its incorporation falls. Its first accounting reference period is a period of more than six months but not more than eighteen months beginning with the date of incorporation and ending with the accounting reference date unless the company changes its accounting reference date (the date on which the accounting reference period ends), in accordance with section 392. Subsequent accounting reference periods (financial years) are successive periods of 12 months, again subject to any alteration of the accounting reference date.

645.   Section 392(4) provides that a company cannot change its accounting reference date if the period allowed for delivering accounts and reports to the registrar for that period has already expired. Under the corresponding provision in the 1985 Act, the company cannot change the date "if the period allowed for laying and delivering accounts and reports in relation to that period has already expired." Under the Act only public companies are obliged to lay their accounts at a general meeting (section 437).

CHAPTER 4: ANNUAL ACCOUNTS

Section 393: Accounts to give true and fair view

646.   *Subsection (1)* introduces an overarching obligation on directors (the preparers of accounts) not to approve accounts unless they give a true and fair view of the financial position of the company and, in the case of group accounts, the group. This provision reflects the underlying legal duty already expressed in Community law.

647.   *Subsection (2)* in addition places a requirement on auditors to take this overarching duty to give a true and fair view into consideration when giving an opinion on the accounts. This requirement supplements the functions of an auditor set out in section 485.

Individual accounts

648.   Sections 394 to 397, which replace sections 226, 226A and 226B of the 1985 Act, concern the duty of the directors to prepare individual accounts. The individual accounts may either be prepared under the Act (Companies Act individual accounts) or (unless the company is a charity) in accordance with international accounting standards adopted under the IAS Regulation (IAS individual accounts). The terms "IAS Regulation" and "international accounting standards" are defined in section 474. Once a company has switched to IAS individual accounts all subsequent individual accounts must be prepared in accordance with IAS unless there is a relevant change of circumstance (see section 395(3) to (5)). The provisions concerning the form and content of Companies Act accounts to be found in the Schedules to Part 7 of the 1985 Act will in future be contained in regulations to be made by the Secretary of State (section 396(3)). The Parliamentary procedure for such regulations is set out in section 473.

Group accounts: small companies

Section 398: Option to prepare group accounts

649.   This section provides that a company that is subject to the small companies regime and is a parent company is not obliged to prepare group accounts in addition to its individual accounts, (restating section 248 of the 1985 Act), but it may opt to do so. The current exemption in section 248 of the 1985 Act from preparation of group accounts by parent companies heading medium sized groups has been abolished, following the substantial increase in the financial thresholds for medium sized groups in 2004.

Group accounts: other companies

Sections 399 to 402: group accounts: other companies

650.   The sections relating to group accounts have been reorganised to make them easier to follow.

651.   Sections 399 to 402 re-enact sections 227(1) and (8), 228, 228A and 229(5) of the 1985 Act. Section 399 concerns the requirements and exemptions from requirements in relation to group accounts. Parent companies not subject to the small companies regime have the duty to prepare consolidated accounts unless exempt from having to do so under sections 400 to 402. Section 400 provides an exemption from preparing group accounts for companies included in EEA group accounts of a larger group. Section 401 provides such an exemption for companies included in non-EEA group accounts of a larger group, and section 402

provides an exemption when all the company's subsidiary undertakings could be excluded from consolidation in Companies Act group accounts (see section 405).

Group accounts: general

Section 403: Group accounts: applicable accounting framework

652.   This section replaces section 227(2) to (7) of the 1985 Act. Parent companies whose securities are publicly traded must prepare group accounts in accordance with the IAS Regulation. Other parent companies (with the exception of charitable companies) have the choice whether to prepare group accounts under the Companies Act (Companies Act group accounts) or in accordance with adopted international accounting standards (IAS group accounts). Once a company has switched to IAS group accounts all subsequent group accounts must be prepared in accordance with IAS unless there is a relevant change of circumstance (see *subsections (4) to (6)*).

Section 404: Companies Act group accounts

653.   For companies preparing Companies Act group accounts, this section gives the Secretary of State power to make provision by regulations as to the form and content of the consolidated balance sheet and consolidated profit and loss account and additional information to be provided by way of notes to the accounts. The regulations will replace the current requirements contained in Schedule 4A to the 1985 Act. These regulations are subject to the Parliamentary procedure in section 473.

Section 405: Companies Act group accounts: subsidiary undertakings included in the consolidation

654.   This section replaces section 229 of the 1985 Act. It requires all subsidiary undertakings to be included in the consolidated accounts subject to certain permitted exclusions.

Section 406: IAS group accounts

655.   This section re-enacts section 227B of the 1985 Act. A company may opt or may be required to prepare group accounts in accordance with international accounting standards. This section provides that where it does so, this must be stated in the notes to the accounts.

Section 407: Consistency of financial reporting within group

656.   This section re-enacts section 227C of the 1985 Act. If the parent company prepares both consolidated and individual accounts under IAS, it is not required to ensure that all its subsidiary undertakings also use IAS. However, it must otherwise ensure that its individual accounts and those of all its subsidiary undertakings use the same financial reporting framework, unless there are good reasons for not doing so.

Section 408: Individual profit and loss account where group accounts prepared

657.   This section replaces section 230 of the 1985 Act. A parent company that prepares group accounts and that meets the criteria in *subsection (1)(a) and (b)* may, subject to the profit and loss account being approved by the directors, dispense with the inclusion of a profit and loss account in the company's accounts, for example when delivered to the registrar. The profit and loss account may also omit the information on employee numbers and costs required by section 411. The exemption currently provided for in section 230(2) of the 1985

Act for certain information required by provisions of Schedule 4 to the 1985 Act, will be provided for in regulations under section 396.

Information to be given in notes to the accounts

Section 409: Information about related undertakings

658.   This section replaces section 231(1) to (4) of the 1985 Act. The requirement to disclose information about related undertakings in the notes to a company's annual accounts applies whether or not the company has to produce group accounts but there are different disclosure requirements in each case. This section gives the Secretary of State a new power to make regulations requiring information about related undertakings to be given in notes to a company's annual accounts. These regulations are subject to the Parliamentary procedure in section 473. The regulations will replace the provisions of Schedule 5 to the 1985 Act.

659.   *Subsection (3)* enables regulations under the section to make provision corresponding to section 231(3) of the 1985 Act authorising the omission from the notes to the accounts of information in respect of undertakings established outside the UK, or carrying on business outside the UK where the directors consider that disclosure would be seriously prejudicial to the business of that undertaking, or to the business of the company or any of its subsidiary undertakings. The Secretary of State must agree to the omission. This exemption is sought by a very small number of companies each year.

Section 410: Information about related undertakings: alternative compliance

660.   This section replaces section 231(5) to (7) of the 1985 Act. Where there are numerous related undertakings and the directors believe that full disclosure would result in information of excessive length in the notes to the accounts, they may give more limited information. As a minimum this must include information in *subsection (2)(a) and (b)*. *Subsection (3)* provides that the full information on the related undertakings must be submitted with the next annual return.

Section 411: Information about employee numbers and costs

661.   This section replaces section 231A of the 1985 Act concerning particulars of staff. Section 231A was inserted by the 1985 Act (International Accounting Standards and Other Accounting Amendments) Regulations 2004 (S.I. 2004/2947) re-enacting provisions previously in the Schedules to Part 7 of the 1985 Act so that they continued to apply both to companies preparing Companies Act accounts and to those preparing IAS accounts.

Section 412: Information about directors' benefits: remuneration

662.   This section, together with section 413, replaces section 232 of the 1985 Act. Section 232 of the 1985 Act, with Schedules 6 and 7A, provides for disclosure of specified information on directors' remuneration in notes to a company's annual accounts. Section 412 of the 2006 Act instead gives the Secretary of State a new power to make provision by regulations requiring information about directors' remuneration to be given in notes to a company's annual accounts. Regulations under this section are subject to the Parliamentary procedure in section 473.

Section 413: Information about directors' benefits: advances, credit and guarantees

663.   This section replaces section 232 of the 1985 Act as regards the disclosure of advances, credit and guarantees. Under section 232 of the 1985 Act, information on the following areas must be given in notes to a company's annual accounts:

- details of loans, quasi-loans, credit transactions and related guarantees and security between a company and its directors or persons connected with its directors;

- details of any other transactions or arrangements in which a director, indirectly or directly, has a material interest.

This can be seen as an extension of the internal disclosure of directors' interests required by section 317 of the 1985 Act.

664.   Section 413 sets out the new disclosure requirements in respect of (a) advances and credits granted by the company to its directors, and (b) guarantees of any kind entered into by the company on behalf of its directors. The wording of section 413 is much closer to that of articles 43(1)(13) and 34(13) of the Fourth (78/660/EEC) and Seventh (83/349/EEC) Company Law Directives.

665.   The powers under section 396(3)(b) (Companies Act individual accounts) and section 404(3)(b) (Companies Act group accounts) will be used to require the disclosure of information about certain related party transactions in the notes to Companies Act accounts. Companies will no longer be required to disclose transactions made between the company and officers other than directors.

666.   Under section 413(8) banks and the holding companies of credit institutions need only state (a) the amount of an advance or credit, and (b) in relation to a guarantee, the amount of the maximum liability that may be incurred by the company (or its subsidiary). In the light of the simplified disclosure regime for advances, credit and guarantees, sections 343 and 344 of the 1985 Act, which make special provision for financial institutions, are repealed.

Section 414: Approval and signing of accounts

667.   This section replaces section 233 of the 1985 Act. It provides that a company's annual accounts (its individual accounts and any group accounts) must be approved by the board of directors and the balance sheet must be signed. *Subsection (3)*, which requires the balance sheet of accounts prepared in accordance with the small companies regime to carry a statement to that effect, re-enacts section 246(8) of the 1985 Act. *Subsections (4) and (5)* re-enact the criminal offence in section 233 of the 1985 Act for approval of accounts that do not comply with the requirements of the Companies Act or, where applicable, of Article 4 of the IAS Regulation. Section 233 (4) of the 1985 Act, which required that a director of the company should sign the copy of the balance sheet delivered to the registrar, has not been reproduced. This requirement would have hampered developments in the electronic delivery of accounts.

CHAPTER 5: DIRECTORS' REPORT

Sections 415 to 419: Directors' report

668.   These sections concern the duty to prepare a directors' report, its content, approval and signature. They replace sections 234, 234ZZA, 234ZZB, 234ZA, 234A, 246(4)(a) and 246A(2A) and 246(8) of the 1985 Act.

669.   Section 416(4) gives the Secretary of State power to make provisions by regulations as to other matters that must be disclosed in the directors' report. These regulations replace the provision formerly made by Schedule 7 to the 1985 Act. The regulations are subject to the Parliamentary procedure in section 473.

670.   Section 417 provides for what must be contained in the business review element of the directors' report. All companies, other than small companies, will need to produce a business review, as required by the EU Accounts Modernisation Directive (2003/51/EEC). *Subsection (2)* sets out the purpose of the review, that is, to inform members of the company and help them assess how the directors have performed their duty under section 172 (duty to promote the success of the company). *Subsections (3), (4), (6) and (8)* specify the content of the review. *Subsection (5)* specifies information that quoted companies in particular must include in their review where necessary for an understanding of the company's business. Where directors of quoted companies have nothing to report on environmental, employee, social and community matters or essential contractual or other arrangements, their review must say so. *Subsection (7)* exempts medium-sized companies from reporting non-financial key performance indicators – an exemption allowed by the EU directive. *Subsection (9)* provides that where the directors' report is a group report, all references in section 417 to the company are to be read as references to the company and its consolidated subsidiary undertakings. *Subsection (10)* enables directors to omit from the business review information about impending developments or matters in the course of negotiation where in their opinion disclosure would be seriously prejudicial to the interests of the company. *Subsection (11)* enables directors to omit from the business review information about a third party otherwise required by subsection (5)(c) (essential contractual or other arrangements) where in the directors' opinion it would be seriously prejudicial to that third party and contrary to the public interest.

CHAPTER 6: QUOTED COMPANIES: DIRECTORS' REMUNERATION REPORT

Sections 420 to 422: Quoted companies: directors' remuneration report

671.   These sections replace sections 234B and 234C of the 1985 Act. Those sections, which were inserted into the Act by the Directors' Remuneration Report Regulations 2002 (S.I. 2002/1986), require quoted companies to:

- publish a report on directors' remuneration as part of the company's annual reporting cycle; and

- disclose within the report details of individual directors' remuneration packages, the company's remuneration policy, and the role of the board and remuneration committee in this area.

672.   Section 421 gives the Secretary of State power to make provision by regulations as to the information that must be contained in a directors' remuneration report and how it should

be set out. These matters are currently set out in Schedule 7A to the 1985 Act, and regulations made under section 421 will replace the provisions in Schedule 7A. The regulations will also specify the extent to which the directors' remuneration report should be subject to audit. Regulations under section 421 are subject to the Parliamentary procedure in section 473.

CHAPTER 7: PUBLICATION OF ACCOUNTS AND REPORTS

Section 423: Duty to circulate copies of annual accounts and reports

673.   This section replaces section 238 of the 1985 Act. *Subsection (1)* provides that a company must send a copy of its annual accounts and reports (as defined in section 471 and including any relevant auditor's report) to specified persons. *Subsection (2)* restricts the general obligation of companies to send copies of accounts and reports. The obligation will in future be to send the accounts and reports only to persons for whom the company has a current address. This is to avoid companies having to send copies of the annual accounts and reports to addresses from which correspondence has previously been returned marked not known at this address (or its electronic equivalent). General provisions about how to supply copies to joint holders are in Part 6 of Schedule 5 (Communications by a company).

Section 424: Time allowed for sending out copies of accounts and reports

674.   This section makes changes to the time for distributing accounts and reports for both private and public companies. Private companies (unless they opted out of the requirement) were previously required to lay their accounts at a general meeting and to send their accounts and reports to members 21 days before that meeting. They are no longer required to hold any general meeting and the requirement now is to send out their accounts and reports no later than the earlier of the date of actual delivery to the registrar or the deadline for delivery (see section 442 for the time limits for filing). Public companies must still send the annual accounts and reports out at least 21 days before the general meeting at which the accounts and reports are to be laid (defined as the "relevant accounts meeting").

Section 425: Default in sending out copies of accounts and reports: offences

675.   There is no change to these offences (in section 238(5) of the 1985 Act).

Sections 426 to 429: Option to provide summary financial statement

676.   These sections restate section 251 of the 1985 Act. All companies have the option under section 426 to provide summary financial statements instead of copies of the full accounts and reports. This section reproduces the existing power for the Secretary of State to make provision by regulations:

- as to the circumstances in which a company may send out summary financial statements; and

- as to the manner in which it is to be ascertained whether a person wishes to receive a copy of the (full) accounts and reports.

It also makes new provision for persons nominated to enjoy information rights under section 146 (indirect investors) to be able to be provided with summary financial statements rather than the full accounts and reports.

677.   Section 427 sets out the form and content requirements for summary financial statements prepared by unquoted companies, whilst section 428 sets out the form and content requirements for summary financial statements prepared by quoted companies. In both cases, the Secretary of State may make regulations as to the form and content of summary financial statements. There is also a new power for regulations to provide that any specified material be sent separately at the same time as the summary financial statement instead of being included in it. This is to cover the requirements of the Takeovers Directive as to necessary explanatory material (see section 992). As in the 1985 Act, these powers are subject to the negative resolution procedure. Section 429 restates the existing offences in section 251(6) of the 1985 Act.

Section 430: Quoted companies: requirements as to website publication

678.   This section introduces a new requirement on quoted companies (as defined in section 385) to put the full annual accounts and reports on a website. A quoted company will still have to send the full accounts and reports to its members under section 423.

679.   The annual accounts and reports must be made available as soon as is reasonably practicable on a website that is maintained by or on behalf of the company, and that identifies the company in question. Access to the website must be available to all members of the public and not just to members, and there must be continuous access to the website without charge. Access to the information on the website and the ability to obtain a hard copy of the information from the website, may be restricted by the company where necessary to comply with any statutory or regulatory requirement (e.g. of an overseas regulator).

680.   The annual accounts and reports for a financial year must remain available until the accounts and reports for the next financial year are published on the website. Right of member or debenture holder to demand copies of accounts and reports

Sections 431 and 432: Right of member or debenture holder to demand copies of accounts and reports

681.   These sections re-enact section 239 of the 1985 Act and entitle a member or debenture holder to demand a copy of the company's last annual accounts and reports without charge. Section 431 lists the documents to which members or debenture holders of unquoted companies are entitled, while section 432 lists those to which members or debenture holders of quoted companies are entitled. The company must comply with a demand within seven days of receipt of the request by the company.

Sections 433 to 436: Requirements in connection with publication of accounts and reports

682.   Section 433 brings together provisions scattered throughout Part 7 of the 1985 Act (in sections 233(3) and (6)(a), 234A(2) and (4)(a) and 234C(2) and (4)(a)) concerning statements of the name of the signatory in published accounts and reports. In the case of unquoted companies, every copy of the balance sheet and directors' report that is published by or on behalf of the company must state the name of the director who signed it on behalf of the board. For quoted companies this applies to copies of the balance sheet, directors' remuneration report and directors' report.

683.   Sections 434 and 435 re-enact section 240 of the 1985 Act concerning requirements in connection with the publication of statutory or non-statutory accounts.

684.   "Publication" is defined in section 436.

CHAPTER 8: PUBLIC COMPANIES: LAYING OF ACCOUNTS AND REPORTS BEFORE GENERAL MEETING

Section 437: Public companies: laying of accounts and reports before general meeting

Section 438: Public companies: offence of failure to lay accounts and reports

685.   These sections re-enact section 241 of the 1985 Act on the laying of accounts and reports before the company in general meeting, but restrict its application to public companies. Under the Act, private companies are under no statutory obligation to hold an AGM or to lay accounts and reports in general meetings. There is therefore no statutory link for them between the accounts and AGMs (although such a link might be provided for in the company's articles). Any AGM that a private company may hold pursuant to its articles will not be a statutory meeting. Public companies will still be required to hold AGMs and they must now hold them within 6 months of the end of the accounting reference period.

CHAPTER 9: QUOTED COMPANIES: MEMBERS' APPROVAL OF DIRECTORS' REMUNERATION REPORT

Section 439: Quoted companies: members' approval of directors' remuneration report

Section 440: Quoted companies: offences in connection with procedure for approval

686.   These sections restate the requirement under section 241A of the 1985 Act that a quoted company circulate a resolution approving the directors' remuneration report for the preceding financial year to its shareholders prior to its annual general meeting. The vote is advisory: as such, it does not require directors to amend contractual entitlements, nor to amend their remuneration policy, but the result of the vote will send a very strong signal to directors about the level of support among shareholders for the board's remuneration policy. In practice, directors will wish to take notice of the views of the company's members, and to respond appropriately. All "existing directors" (that is, every person who, immediately before the general meeting, is a director of the company) have a responsibility to ensure that the resolution is put to the vote of the meeting. As such, the requirement does not apply to past directors (even if they served on the board or as members of the remuneration committee in the current financial year), but it does apply to "existing directors" who were, for whatever reason, not present at the general meeting.

CHAPTER 10: FILING OF ACCOUNTS AND REPORTS

Sections 441 to 443: Duty to file accounts and reports

687.   These sections cover the general duty to file accounts and reports with the registrar of companies and the period allowed for filing accounts.

688.   Section 442 reduces the period for filing accounts from ten months to nine months for private companies and from seven months to six months for public companies. These periods are calculated from the end of the relevant accounting reference period. The timetable for delivering accounts to the registrar was last amended in 1976. The periods have been reduced to reflect improvements in technology and the increased rate at which information becomes out of date. Filing timescales in other countries are generally less generous than in the UK. Under subsection (6), whether a company is private or public for the purpose of its filing

obligations is determined by its status immediately before the end of the relevant accounting reference period.

689.   Section 443 is a new provision defining how to calculate the periods allowed for filing accounts and reports. In general this is the same date the relevant number of months later. So, for example, if the end of the accounting reference period is 5th June, 6 months from then is 5th December. However, as months are of unequal length, there can be confusion as to whether 6 months from say 30th June is 30th December (exactly 6 months later) or 31st December (the end of the sixth month). Under the rule laid down in this section, 6 months from 30th June will be 31st December. This reverses the "corresponding date rule" laid down by the House of Lords in *Dodds v Walker* [1981] 1 WLR 1027.

Sections 444 to 448: Filing obligations of different descriptions of company

690.   These sections concern the filing obligations of different sizes of company. They restructure the provisions in sections 242, 246, 246A and 254 of the 1985 Act to make clearer what companies have to do.

691.   Section 444 concerns the filing obligations of companies subject to the small companies regime. Such companies may file abbreviated accounts and this section gives the Secretary of State the power to make regulations concerning abbreviated accounts for such companies. Under *subsection (5)*, small companies filing a full balance sheet with the registrar (whether prepared in accordance with international accounting standards or under the Act), but omitting a copy of the profit and loss account and/or the directors' report, must include a statement on the balance sheet that they are delivered in accordance with the small companies regime. *Subsection (7)* requires the filed copy of the audit report to state the name of the auditor and, if there is one, of the senior statutory auditor, unless they are taking advantage of the exemption in section 506, in which case they must state that they are doing so.

692.   Section 445 restates provisions in section 246A of the 1985 Act permitting medium-sized companies (as defined in section 465) to file abbreviated accounts and gives the Secretary of State the power to make regulations concerning abbreviated accounts for such companies.

693.   Section 446 concerns the filing obligations of unquoted companies.

694.   Section 447 concerns the filing obligations of quoted companies. This is a restatement of section 242 of the 1985 Act. *Subsection (3)* provides for the copies of the filed documents including the balance sheet to state the name of the person who signed the documents.

695.   Section 448 replaces section 254 of the 1985 Act. It exempts unlimited companies from the obligation to file accounts. There are limitations on the exemption set out in *subsections (2) and (3)*.

Sections 449 and 450: Requirements where abbreviated accounts delivered

696.   Section 449 replaces the provision in section 247B of the 1985 Act. It requires a special auditor's report in place of the auditor's report required by section 495 where a company delivers abbreviated accounts to the registrar of companies. There is no requirement for the special auditor's report where the company is entitled to exemption from audit and has taken advantage of that exemption.

697. Section 450 replaces sections 246(7) and (8) and 246A(4) of the 1985 Act concerning the approval and signing of abbreviated accounts.

Sections 451 to 453: Failure to file accounts and reports

698. Sections 451 and 452 re-enact sanctions in section 242(2) to (5) of the 1985 Act for failing to file accounts and reports within the required periods.

699. Section 453, which provides a civil penalty for failure to file accounts, restates section 242A of the 1985 Act with one change. Rather than setting out the table of penalties in the legislation, *subsection (2)* provides for the Secretary of State to make regulations specifying both the relevant periods and the amounts of the penalties. Regulations that have the effect of increasing the penalty will be subject to the affirmative resolution procedure. Otherwise, they will be subject to the negative resolution procedure.

CHAPTER 11: REVISION OF DEFECTIVE ACCOUNTS AND REPORTS

Section 454: Voluntary revision of accounts etc

700. This section restates section 245 of the 1985 Act providing for the voluntary revision of defective accounts and reports and summary financial statements. It replicates the existing power for the Secretary of State to make provision in regulations as to the application of the provisions of this Act to revised annual accounts and reports and summary financial statements. Regulations under this section are subject to the negative resolution procedure, which is consistent with the existing powers.

Section 455: Secretary of State's notice in respect of accounts or reports

701. This section re-enacts section 245A of the 1985 Act. It concerns the Secretary of State's giving notice to the directors of a company if there is or may be a question as to whether the annual accounts or directors' report comply with the requirements of the Act or the IAS Regulation (Regulation (EC) 1606/2002 on the application of international accounting standards).

Sections 456 to 458: Application to court

702. Sections 456 and 457 concern applications to the court in respect of defective accounts or reports. They re-enact sections 245B and 245C of the 1985 Act. Section 457 gives the Secretary of State the power to authorise a person for the purposes of section 456 to apply to the courts to require the directors of companies to prepare revised accounts and reports where the original accounts or reports were defective. Authorisation is subject to the negative resolution procedure, which corresponds to the existing provision. The Financial Reporting Review Panel (FRRP) is the only authorised person under this provision to date (the Companies (Defective Accounts) (Authorised Person) Order 2005: SI 2005/699).

703. Section 458 re-enacts sections 245D and 245E of the 1985 Act. It provides for the disclosure of information by the Commissioners for Her Majesty's Revenue and Customs to a person authorised under section 457 (currently the FRRP) to apply to the court in respect of defective accounts and reports. The provision contains important limitations, including criminal offences for use or disclosure of the information other than for permitted purposes. Section 458(5)(b)(ii) increases the term of imprisonment from three months to six months for a person convicted on summary conviction in Scotland or Northern Ireland for an offence of

unlawful disclosure. *Subsection (2)* provides that personal data may not be disclosed in contravention of the Data Protection Act 1998.

Section 459: Power of authorised person to require documents, information and explanations

704.   This section re-enacts section 245F of the 1985 Act. *Subsections (1) to (3)* provide the FRRP (as the person authorised under section 457) with a statutory power to require a company and its officers, employees and auditors to provide documents and information. Where a person refuses to provide information or documents to the FRRP, the FRRP may apply to the court for an order. The court may make an order requiring disclosure. Failure to comply with such an order would be contempt of court.

Section 460: Restrictions on disclosure of information obtained under compulsory powers

705.   This section re-enacts section 245G of the 1985 Act. It ensures that information obtained by the FRRP under the powers in section 459 is subject to restrictions on onward disclosure. Information relating to the private affairs of an individual or to any particular business may not be disclosed by the FRRP without the consent of the individual or business in question, except for the purposes of carrying out the FRRP's functions, or unless it is disclosed to specified persons or for specified purposes set out in section 461.

Section 461: Permitted disclosure of information obtained under compulsory powers

706.   This section restates section 245G(3) of, and Schedule 7B to, the 1985 Act with modifications. It sets out the disclosures of information obtained by the authorised person under section 459 that are permitted. *Subsection (3)* lists the specified persons to whom disclosures are permitted and *subsection (4)* lists the specified purposes for which disclosure may be made. *Subsections (5) and (6)* set out the circumstances in which a disclosure to an overseas regulatory authority is permitted. *Subsection (7)* provides that nothing in the section authorises a disclosure in contravention of the Data Protection Act 1998.

Section 462: Power to amend categories of permitted disclosure

707.   This section re-enacts section 245G(4) to (6) of the 1985 Act. It gives the Secretary of State power to amend the disclosure provisions relating to information obtained by the authorised person. As under the current law, an order under the section is subject to the negative resolution procedure.

CHAPTER 12: SUPPLEMENTARY PROVISIONS

Section 463: Liability for false or misleading statements in reports

708.   This section is concerned with the extent of directors' liability in relation to the statutory narrative reporting requirements under this Part of the Act (accounts and reports). *Subsection (1)* specifies that the liability provision applies to statements made in the directors' report (which includes the business review under section 417), the directors' remuneration report (under section 420) or summary financial statements derived from them. *Subsection (2)* limits the directors' liability to the company only in respect of loss suffered by it as a result of any untrue or misleading statement in a report, or the omission from a report of anything required to be included. *Subsection (3)* specifies that a director will only be liable in certain circumstances – that is, if an untrue or misleading statement is made deliberately or

recklessly, or an omission amounts to dishonest concealment of a material fact. *Subsection (4)* ensures that third parties, such as auditors, will remain liable only to the company for negligence in preparing their own report. *Subsection (6)* ensures that these liability provisions do not affect any liability for a civil penalty or for a criminal offence.

Section 464: Accounting standards

709.   This section re-enacts section 256 of the 1985 Act.

Sections 465 to 467: Companies qualifying as medium-sized

710.   Medium-sized companies benefit from certain limited accounting and reporting exemptions. For example, section 417(7) exempts medium-sized companies from disclosing certain non-financial information in their directors' reports.

711.   Sections 465 to 467 set out which companies or parent companies qualify as medium-sized. The conditions for qualification as a medium sized company have been separated from those relating to small companies to make them easier to follow but are otherwise unchanged from the current regime (sections 247, 247A and 249 of the 1985 Act), save that, as in the case of the definition of small companies, the definition of balance sheet total in section 465(5) has been generalised.

Section 468: General power to make further provision about accounts and reports

712.   This section gives the Secretary of State a general power to amend Part 15 by regulations in the areas specified in *subsection (1)(a) to (d)*. This power, together with a number of specific powers in Part 15 to enable the form and contents of accounts and reports to be prescribed by regulations, replaces the wider general power in section 257 of the 1985 Act. *Subsection (3)* provides that the general power may not be used to amend the provisions of section 393 (accounts to give true and fair view) or Chapter 11 (revision of defective accounts and reports) other than consequentially. *Subsections (4) and (5)* enable regulations under the section to create criminal offences or provide for civil penalties in circumstances corresponding to those in Part 15. The regulations are subject to the Parliamentary procedure in section 473.

Section 469: Preparation and filing of accounts in euros

713.   This section re-enacts section 242B of the 1985 Act, replacing references to ECUs with references to euros. It enables companies to show the amounts in their annual accounts additionally in euros, and to deliver to the registrar an additional copy of their accounts translated into euros.

Section 470: Power to apply provisions to banking partnerships

714.   This section re-enacts section 255D of the 1985 Act. It gives the Secretary of State the power to apply the accounting and reporting provisions of this Act that apply to banking companies to banking partnerships. As under the current law, the regulations are subject to the affirmative resolution procedure.

Section 471: Meaning of "annual accounts" and related expressions

715.   This section provides definitions of the terms "annual accounts" and "annual accounts and reports" for the purpose of this Part, the meaning being different for unquoted and quoted companies.

Section 472: Notes to the accounts

716.   This section re-enacts section 261 of the 1985 Act. It concerns the notes to a company's accounts.

Section 473: Parliamentary procedure for certain regulations under this Part

717.   This section specifies the Parliamentary procedure that must be followed in connection with regulations made under the various provisions of this Part which replace the requirements as to the form and content of accounts and reports currently contained in Schedules to Part 7 of the 1985 Act, and in relation to the general regulation-making power in section 468. This section follows section 257 of the 1985 Act in requiring affirmative resolution procedure for regulations which add to the documents required to be prepared by companies, restrict the exemptions available to particular classes or types of company, add to the information to be included in any particular document or otherwise make the requirements more onerous. Other regulations are subject to negative resolution procedure.

Section 474: Minor definitions

718.   This section contains other definitions for the purposes of this Part.

PART 16: AUDIT

719.   This Part brings together various provisions on the audit of companies from the 1985 Act. It also introduces a number of significant changes to the law on auditing. Much of the law in this area reflects EU Company Law Directives, including parts of the Fourth (78/660/EEC), Seventh (83/349/EEC) and Eighth (84/253/EEC) Company Law Directives, and of the new Audit Directive (2006/43/EC), which will replace the Eighth.

CHAPTER 1: REQUIREMENT FOR AUDITED ACCOUNTS

720.   This Chapter restates the existing requirement for company accounts to be audited, currently in section 235 of the 1985 Act, and the existing exemptions (except for the special provisions about charities).

721.   The only changes from the existing law in this Chapter are the removal of special rules for the audit of the accounts of small charitable companies (see note on section 1175), and new provisions disapplying the requirement for audit in relation to certain companies in the public sector audited by public sector auditors.

Section 475: Requirement for audited accounts

722.   This section restates the basic requirement for accounts to be audited, unless they are exempt. The obligation is now expressed as a duty on the company to have its accounts audited, whereas section 235 of the 1985 Act expressed it as a duty on the auditor to audit the accounts.

723.   Directors must state in the balance sheet if they are taking advantage of an exemption. Unless the company is subject to a public sector audit, the statement must say that the members have not required an audit, and that the directors take responsibility for producing compliant accounts.

Section 476: Right of members to require audit

724.   This section restates the right of members to require an audit, even if the company qualifies for one of the audit exemptions.

Sections 477 to 479: Exemption from audit: small companies

725.   These sections restate the exemption from audit for small companies. Section 477 provides that a company must not only meet the general small company criteria in section 382, but its turnover and balance sheet totals must also fall below £5.6 million and £2.8 million respectively.

726.   Section 478 excludes from the exemption various categories of company including public companies and some financial services companies. Section 479 sets out the conditions for qualification for the small company exemption of a company which is in a group.

Sections 480 and 481: Exemption from audit: dormant companies

727.   These two sections restate the exemption from audit available to dormant companies. "Dormant" is defined in section 1169. Certain financial services companies are excluded from using the exemption even if they are dormant.

Sections 482 and 483: Companies subject to public sector audit

728.   These two sections, the only wholly new provisions in this Chapter, are intended to ensure that certain non-commercial, public sector bodies constituted as companies that are audited by a public sector auditor are not required to be audited under the Act.

729.   Section 482 exempts from Companies Act audit any non-departmental public body that is a company and is non-profit-making, if it is subject to public sector audit.

730.   A UK body may be subject to public sector audit by virtue of an order under the Government Resources and Accounts Act 2000 The body in question will then be audited by the National Audit Office on behalf of the UK Comptroller and Auditor General. Under the Audit and Accountability (Northern Ireland) Order 2003, an order can make a body subject to audit by the Comptroller and Auditor General for Northern Ireland. Alternatively, a body may be subject to audit by the Auditor General for Wales under section 96 of the Government of Wales Act 1998, or an order under section 144 of that Act.

731.   Some Scottish bodies are subject to public sector audit by the Auditor General for Scotland (AGS) under the Public Finance and Accountability (Scotland) Act 2000.

732.   The companies exempted by this section are not subject to the Fourth Company Law Directive: the Directive is based on Article 44(2)(g) of the EC Treaty (formerly 54(3)(g) of the EEC Treaty), and Article 48 of the Treaty excludes from the scope of Article 44 undertakings that are non-profit-making. That is why *subsection (3)* gives "non-profit-making" the same meaning as in the Treaty.

733.   *Subsection (2)* provides that a group company can benefit from this exemption only if every company in the group is non-profit-making. The effect of *subsection (4)* is that the exemption is not available unless the balance sheet contains a statement that the company is entitled to it.

734.   Section 483 confers a new power on Scottish Ministers to provide that a company should have its accounts audited by the Auditor General for Scotland (AGS). This is available

for companies depending on their functions or their funding. The Scottish Ministers can designate a company under this power if its functions are public functions that are all covered by the Scottish Parliament's responsibilities, or if the company receives all or most of its funding from a public body already audited by the AGS. In the latter case, the funding body may be audited by the AGS because it is covered by the Public Finance and Accountability (Scotland) Act 2000, or because it is itself a company that Scottish Ministers have made auditable by the AGS by a previous order under this section.

735.   If an order is made under this section providing that a company should have a public sector audit by the AGS, and if that company is non-profit-making, then it will benefit from the exemption from audit in the preceding section.

Section 484: General power of amendment by regulations

736.   This section provides a power for the Secretary of State to amend the provisions of this Chapter. Taken together with section 468, it broadly restates the power in section 257 of the 1985 Act. *Subsection (2)* enables the regulations to make consequential changes to other legislation. The power is subject to affirmative resolution if it is extending the requirement for audit, or otherwise making requirements more onerous; and to negative resolution otherwise.

CHAPTER 2: APPOINTMENT OF AUDITORS

737.   This Chapter broadly restates the existing law in sections 384 to 388A of the 1985 Act on the way in which shareholders appoint a company's auditors, with some minor changes (as explained below). The provisions are reorganised to deal with private and public companies separately. The Chapter also restates the rules in sections 390A and 390B of the 1985 Act on auditors' remuneration and the disclosure required of services provided by auditors and introduces a new power for the Secretary of State to require disclosure of the terms of audit appointments.

Private companies

738.   Sections 485 to 488 restate the law on appointment of auditors of private companies, providing that auditors are generally to be appointed by shareholders by ordinary resolution. For any financial year other than the first, this will generally be done within 28 days of the circulation to a company's shareholders of the accounts for the previous year.

739.   There are two changes: firstly, an auditor's term of office will typically run from the end of the 28 day period following circulation of the accounts until the end of the corresponding period the following year. This will apply even if the auditor is appointed at a meeting where the company's accounts are laid. The second change is that an auditor is now deemed to be re-appointed unless the company decides otherwise.

Section 485: Appointment of auditors of private company: general

740.   This section provides for a private company's obligation to appoint an auditor, unless it is taking advantage of an exemption from audit. The appointment is to be made by the shareholders by ordinary resolution, except that the directors can appoint the company's first auditor (or the first after a period of audit exemption), and can fill a casual vacancy.

Section 486: Appointment of auditors of private company: default power of Secretary of State

741.   This section requires a company to inform the Secretary of State if it has failed to appoint an auditor within 28 days of circulation of its accounts. The Secretary of State has power to appoint an auditor in those circumstances.

Section 487: Term of office of auditors of private company

742.   This section provides that the end of the term of office of the auditor of a private company is to be the end of the next period for appointing auditors. At the end of his term an auditor will automatically be deemed to be re-appointed except in five cases:

- if he was appointed by the directors;

- if the company's articles require actual re-appointment;

- if enough members have given notice to the company under section 488;

- if there has been a resolution that the auditor should not be reappointed; or

- if the directors decide that they do not need auditors for the following year.

743.   When there is a change of auditor the term of office of the incoming auditor does not begin before the end of the previous auditor's term. This means that a new auditor's term will typically begin immediately after the end of the 28-day period for appointing auditors.

Section 488: Prevention by members of deemed re-appointment of auditor

744.   This section enables members with at least 5% of the voting rights in a private company to prevent an auditor being automatically re-appointed by giving notice to the company. The company's articles can enable members to do this with less than 5% of the voting rights, but cannot increase the required percentage.

745.   *Subsection (3)* provides that the deadline for a notice preventing the deemed reappointment of an auditor is the end of the financial year for the accounts he is auditing.

Public companies

746.   Sections 489 to 491 restate the law on appointment of auditors of public companies, providing that auditors are generally to be appointed by shareholders by ordinary resolution in the general meeting before which the company's accounts are laid.

Section 489: Appointment of auditors of public company: general

747.   This section restates a public company's obligation to appoint auditors, unless it is taking advantage of exemption from audit. This is to be done by the shareholders by ordinary resolution, normally at the general meeting at which the accounts are laid. The directors can appoint the company's first auditors (or the first after a period of audit exemption), and can fill a casual vacancy.

Section 490: Appointment of auditors of public company: default power of Secretary of State

748.   This section restates the obligation of a company to inform the Secretary of State if it has failed to appoint an auditor at the general meeting that considers the previous year's accounts. The Secretary of State has power to appoint an auditor in those circumstances.

Section 491: Term of office of auditors of public company

749.   This section restates the rule that an auditor of a public company holds office until the end of the meeting at which the accounts are laid, unless re-appointed. Where there is a change of auditor, the term of office of the incoming auditor does not begin before the end of the previous auditor's term. This means that a new auditor's term will typically begin immediately after the end of the accounts meeting.

General provisions

750.   These sections apply to both private and public companies.

Section 492: Fixing of auditor's remuneration

751.   This section restates the rule that it is the members of a company, by ordinary resolution, who determine the auditor's remuneration, or decide the method by which it should be determined. If the auditor was appointed by someone other than the members, then it will be the directors or the Secretary of State as appropriate who will determine his remuneration.

Section 493: Disclosure of terms of audit appointment

752.   This section creates a new power for the Secretary of State to require companies to disclose information about the terms on which they engage their auditors. *Subsection (2)* provides some examples of the detailed requirements that the Secretary of State could specify in regulations. *Subsection (3)* provides that regulations can require disclosure of changes in terms as well as the terms at the time of appointment. *Subsection (4)* specifies that the regulations are to be made by affirmative resolution procedure.

Section 494: Disclosure of services provided by auditor or associates and related remuneration

753.   This section restates the existing power of the Secretary of State, in section 390B of the 1985 Act, to require disclosure of details of all the services supplied to a company by its auditor, and the remuneration involved. *Subsections (2) to (4)* give the detailed requirements that the Secretary of State can specify in regulations: subsection (2) relates to the level of disaggregation of different services and remunerations, and between the auditor and his associates; subsection (3) makes provision for some of the definitional issues that can be covered in regulations; and subsection (4) provides for where the information should be disclosed.

754.   Under subsection (4), the regulations might require disclosure in a document compiled by the company rather than the auditor. *Subsection (5)* provides that, if so, the regulations can require the auditor to supply the directors with the information to be disclosed e.g. about the auditor's associates. *Subsection (6)* specifies that the regulations are to be made by negative resolution procedure.

CHAPTER 3: FUNCTIONS OF AUDITORS

Sections 495 to 497: Auditor's report

755.   These sections restate, with modifications, the provisions of section 235 of the 1985 Act as to what the auditor should include in his report on the accounts.

756.   Section 495 imposes the basic duty to produce an audit report and requires that it should set out the way the auditor has approached the audit. Subsection (3) requires the auditor in his report to state his opinion on three matters: (i) whether the accounts provide a true and fair view, (ii) whether they comply with the appropriate reporting framework, and (iii) whether the accounts comply with the requirements in Part 15 of the Act (and, where applicable, with article 4 of the IAS Regulation (Regulation (EC) 1606/2002 on the application of international accounting standards)). *Subsection (4)* requires the audit report to be either qualified or unqualified, though it is open to the auditor to draw attention to aspects of his audit without qualifying the report.

757.   Sections 496 and 497 restate the law on what the auditor should include in relation to the directors' report and the directors' remuneration report.

Sections 498 to 502: Duties and rights of auditors

758.   These sections bring together and restate the existing law on the auditor's duties (currently in section 237 of the 1985 Act) in investigating, forming an opinion, and making his report; and on the auditor's rights (sections 389A to 390 of that Act) to be provided with appropriate information.

759.   Section 498 lists areas where an auditor must investigate and report on any problems: the company's accounting records, and whether there is consistency between these and (i) the accounts and (ii) – where there is one – the appropriate part of the directors' remuneration report. The auditor is also to report if he has not been able to get all the information he needs. If possible, he is to make good any gaps in the information relating to payments to directors. And he is to report if he believes that the company is taking advantage of the small companies accounts regime without being entitled to do so.

760.   Section 499 restates the auditor's rights to obtain information and explanations from the company and its UK subsidiaries, and from appropriate associated individuals. Section 500 sets out the corresponding right to require the company to obtain information or explanations from any subsidiaries that are not incorporated in the UK.

761.   Section 501 sets out offences for those who supply inaccurate information to auditors or fail to respond to auditors' requests for information without delay.

762.   Section 502 requires a private company to send to its auditor all the information about any written resolutions that it sends to its shareholders. It also gives the auditor of any company – public or private – the right to attend any general meetings it may have, and to be allowed to speak on anything relevant to the audit. The auditor must also receive all communications relating to general meetings.

Section 503: Signature of auditor's report

763.   This section specifies who must sign the audit report submitted to a company by its auditor. The report must state the name of the audit firm, or if an individual has been appointed as auditor, his name. This is as currently required by section 236 of the 1985 Act.

764.   For cases where the auditor is a firm, the section makes a change from the 1985 Act by requiring the senior statutory auditor, as defined in section 504, to sign the report in his own name on behalf of the firm. This implements a requirement of the Audit Directive (2006/43/EC). If the auditor is an individual, he must sign as under the 1985 Act.

Section 504: Senior statutory auditor

765.   This section defines a new term – "the senior statutory auditor" – for the individual who will be asked to sign his name to an audit report carried out by a firm. The firm will identify this individual according to standards to be issued by the European Commission, or if there are no standards, to guidance issued either by the Secretary of State or by a body appointed by him by order subject to negative resolution. *Subsection (2)* specifies that to be identified as a senior statutory auditor of a company, an individual must be eligible himself to be appointed as auditor of the company. *Subsection (3)* ensures that for an individual to be nominated as senior statutory auditor will not affect his exposure to liability in any way.

Section 505: Names to be stated in published copies of auditor's report

766.   This section requires a company to ensure that the copies of its auditor's report it sends out include the name of the auditor and of the senior statutory auditor if there is one, or to say that it is taking advantage of the exemption in the following section. *Subsection (2)* provides that this includes copies circulated to shareholders, as well as any others that would be expected to be seen by members of the public. It does not, however, cover copies sent to the registrar: these are dealt with by sections 444(7), 445(6), 446(4) and 447(4). *Subsections (3) and (4)* restate the offence, currently in section 236 of the 1985 Act, of not including the auditor's name – and now also the senior statutory auditor's name – as required.

Section 506: Circumstances in which names may be omitted

767.   This section provides an exemption from the requirements to include the names of the auditor in both the published and filed copies of the audit report. This is available if the company passes a resolution not to reveal the names because it considers on reasonable grounds that revealing them would lead to a serious risk of violence or intimidation. It is also a condition of using the exemption that the company must inform the Secretary of State, giving details of the name of the auditor, and of the senior statutory auditor if there is one.

Section 507: Offences in connection with auditors' report

768.   This section creates a new criminal offence in relation to inaccurate auditors' reports. The offence consists of knowingly or recklessly causing a report to include anything that is misleading, false or deceptive, or omitting a required statement of a problem with the accounts or audit.

769.   *Subsection (1)* sets out the offence of commission, and *subsection (2)* that of omission. The items whose omission can be an offence are listed in paragraphs (a) to (c) of subsection (2): statements about accounting records not being properly reflected in the accounts, about the auditor having been unable to obtain all necessary information and explanations, and about the directors wrongly claiming the company is exempt from the requirement for group accounts.

770.   *Subsection (3)* defines the individuals potentially caught by the offence as the auditor, if a sole practitioner, and his employees and agents; and the directors, members, employees and agents of an audit firm. But the offence only applies to such an individual if he is an accountant who would be qualified to act as auditor of the company in his own right. *Subsection (4)* sets out the maximum penalty as an unlimited fine.

Section 508: Guidance for regulatory and prosecuting authorities: England, Wales and Northern Ireland

771.   This section enables the Secretary of State to issue guidance about handling matters where the same behaviour by an auditor could give rise both to disciplinary proceedings by a regulatory body, and to prosecution for the new offence. *Subsection (2)* requires the Secretary of State to obtain the Attorney's General agreement to any guidance. *Subsection (3)* lists the regulatory and prosecuting authorities the guidance would be intended to help. The list comprises the accountancy supervisory bodies, recipients of grants under section 16 of the Companies (Audit, Investigations and Community Enterprise) Act 2004) (currently the Financial Reporting Council and its subsidiaries), the Director of the Serious Fraud Office and the Director of Public Prosecutions, as well as the Secretary of State himself. Under *subsection (4)*, the Secretary of State's guidance is limited to England, Wales and Northern Ireland.

772.   It is likely that one of the most important aspects of the guidance would be to enable prosecutors to decide not to prosecute in a particular case that would be better handled through disciplinary proceedings.

Section 509: Guidance for regulatory authorities: Scotland

773.   This section enables the Lord Advocate to issue guidance about handling matters in Scotland where the same auditor's report could give rise both to disciplinary proceedings by a regulatory body, and to prosecution for the new offence. *Subsection (2)* requires the Lord Advocate to consult the Secretary of State before issuing guidance. *Subsection (3)* lists the regulatory bodies the guidance is intended to help. The list comprises the accountancy supervisory bodies, recipients of grants under section 16 of the C(AICE) Act 2004) (currently the Financial Reporting Council and its subsidiaries) and the Secretary of State.

CHAPTER 4: REMOVAL, RESIGNATION, ETC OF AUDITORS

774.   This Chapter restates the law on the ways in which auditors can cease to hold office. The current provisions are in section 388 and sections 391 to 394A of the 1985 Act. There are some changes to the existing law resulting from the changes elsewhere in the Act relating to written resolutions of private companies. There are also changes in the requirements when auditors leave office: increasing the range of cases in which there is a requirement for a statement explaining why they are leaving, and for copies of any statement to be sent to shareholders and to appropriate regulators.

Section 510: Resolution removing auditor from office

775.   This section restates the rule that the shareholders in a company always have the right to dismiss its auditor by ordinary resolution. As at present, to remove the auditor before the end of his term of office, even a private company will need to hold a general meeting to pass such a resolution.

776.   *Subsection (2)* requires special notice of the resolution (see note on section 511). *Subsection (3)* provides that shareholders' right provided by this section does not prevent the auditor being entitled to being compensated for termination of his appointment. *Subsection (4)* specifies that the resolution described here is the only way in which an auditor can be removed before the end of his term of office.

Section 511: Special notice required for resolution removing auditor from office

777.   This section restates the requirement that a resolution to dismiss an auditor needs special notice (i.e. 28 days before the general meeting, as provided in section 312). The company must send a copy to the auditor it is proposed to dismiss, and he has the right to make a statement of his case. The company then has to circulate his statement to the shareholders (or if time does not allow, the statement can be read out at the meeting).

778.   *Subsection (6)* provides protection if the auditor it is proposed to dismiss is using the provision to have a statement circulated to secure needless publicity for defamatory material. It enables the company, or anyone else who is aggrieved by the statement, to apply to the court, and the court can then determine whether the auditor is using the provision in that way, in which case the company is not obliged to circulate the statement. The court can order the auditor to pay some or all of the costs of the proceedings.

Section 512: Notice to registrar of resolution removing auditor from office

779.   This section restates the obligation on a company that has decided to dismiss its auditor to inform the registrar within 14 days.

Section 513: Rights of auditor who has been removed from office

780.   This section restates the right of a dismissed auditor to attend certain meetings, namely, any meeting at which his term of office would have expired (i.e. a public company's accounts meeting) and any meeting at which it is proposed to replace him.

Section 514: Failure to re-appoint auditor: special procedure required for written resolution

781.   This section sets out the procedure for changing auditor from one financial year to the next by written resolution (a procedure only available to private companies). This may be done (i) during the term of office of the outgoing auditor, or (ii) afterwards, if no replacement has been appointed. But case (ii) will arise only if there is no automatic deemed reappointment for one of the five reasons in section 487(2).

782.   *Subsection (3)* provides that the company must send a copy of the proposed resolution both to the outgoing auditor and to his proposed replacement; and *subsection (4)* provides that the former then has 14 days to make a statement setting out his views. *Subsection (5)* then provides that the company must send, to its shareholders, the resolution together with any statement from the outgoing auditor. *Subsection (6)* specifies how the general rules on written resolutions are to apply in this case.

783.   *Subsection (7)* provides protection if the outgoing auditor is using the provision to have a statement circulated to secure needless publicity for defamatory material. It enables the company, or anyone else who is aggrieved by the statement, to apply to the court, and the court can then determine whether the auditor is using the provision in that way, in which case the company is not obliged to circulate the auditor's representations. The court can order the auditor to pay some or all of the costs of the proceedings.

784.   *Subsection (8)* provides that failure to comply with the rules in this section will make the resolution ineffective.

Section 515: Failure to re-appoint auditor: special notice required for resolution at general meeting

785.   This section sets out the procedure for changing auditor between one financial year and the next at a general meeting. This may be done by resolution at the meeting, but special notice is required if no deadline for appointing auditors has passed since the outgoing auditor left, or if the deadline has passed when an auditor should have been appointed without one being appointed. So, for example, if a public company intends not to re-appoint an auditor at its accounts meeting, it would need to give special notice of the meeting to be able to appoint replacement auditors.

786.   *Subsection (3)* provides that immediately it receives a proposed resolution for changing auditor, the company should send a copy of it both to the outgoing auditor and to his proposed replacement; and *subsection (4)* provides that the former may then send the company a written statement setting out his views. *Subsections (5) and (6)* provide that the company must send its shareholders any statement from the outgoing auditor, and that if it is received to late for this it should be read out at the meeting.

787.   *Subsection (7)* provides protection if the outgoing auditor is using the provision to have a statement circulated to secure needless publicity for defamatory material. It enables the company, or anyone else who is aggrieved by the statement, to apply to the court, and the court can then determine whether the auditor is using the provision in that way, in which case the company is not obliged to circulate the auditor's representations, nor need they be read out at the meeting. The court can order the auditor to pay some or all of the costs of the proceedings.

Section 516: Resignation of auditor

788.   This section restates the right of an auditor to resign by written notice to the company. His resignation is effective from the date it is delivered to the company's registered office, or from a later date specified in it. To be effective it must be accompanied by the statement required by section 519.

Section 517: Notice to registrar of resignation of auditor

789.   This section restates the obligation on a company whose auditor resigns to inform the registrar. Default in complying is an offence.

Section 518: Rights of resigning auditor

790.   This section restates the right of an auditor who resigns to require the directors to convene a general meeting of the company so that it can consider his explanation of the circumstances that led to his decision to resign. The auditor can ask the company to send out a written explanation either in advance of that meeting if he has requested one, or before the next appropriate general meeting. The directors have 21 days to send out a notice convening a meeting once a resigning auditor has asked for it, and it must then be held within 28 days of the notice.

791.   *Subsection (9)* provides protection if the resigning auditor is using the provision to have a statement circulated to secure needless publicity for defamatory material. It enables the company, or anyone else who is aggrieved by the statement, to apply to the court, and the court can then determine whether the auditor is using the provision in that way, in which case

the company is not obliged to circulate the statement. The court can order the auditor to pay some or all of the costs of the proceedings.

Section 519: Statement by auditor to be deposited with company

792.   This section requires a departing auditor to make a statement when he stops being the auditor of a company and to deposit it with the company. For quoted companies, this statement should explain the circumstances surrounding his departure. For other public companies and all private companies, it should explain the circumstances unless the auditor thinks that there is no need for them to be brought to the attention of the shareholders or creditors. In that case, the statement should state that there are no such circumstances.

793.   This changes the position under section 394 of the 1985 Act, where auditors were only required to make a statement if they considered there were relevant circumstances: auditors leaving quoted companies will now always be required to make a statement of the circumstances; and auditors leaving other companies must make a statement unless they think that there are no relevant circumstances.

794.   *Subsection (4)* sets out the deadline for depositing such a statement with the company, namely:

- if the auditor is resigning, the statement should accompany the resignation letter;

- if the auditor is deciding not to seek re-appointment, the statement should be deposited at least 14 days before the end of the time allowed for appointing the next auditor; or

- in any other case, no more than 14 days after the date on which he stops being the auditor.

Section 520: Company's duties in relation to statement

795.   Unless the departing auditor's statement says that there are no circumstances to be brought to the attention of shareholders and creditors, this section obliges the company to circulate the statement to everyone to whom it needs to send the annual accounts. The company must do this within 14 days of receiving it.

796.   If the company does not want to circulate the statement, it can apply to the court, and if the court decides that the departing auditor is trying to secure needless publicity for defamatory material, then the company need not circulate the statement, but instead must send an account of the court decision to those to whom it would have sent the statement. In the event of a successful application, the court can order the auditor to pay some or all of the costs. In the event of an unsuccessful application, the company must circulate the statement within 14 days of the end of the court proceedings.

Section 521: Copy of statement to be sent to registrar

797.   This section provides that the departing auditor must send a copy of his statement to the registrar, unless within 21 days of depositing it he hears that the company has applied to the court. If he does not hear of an application to the court within that time, he must send the statement to the registrar within the next seven days; and if an application is made and the company lets him know that it was unsuccessful, he must send the statement to the registrar within seven days of being told.

Section 522: Duty of auditor to notify appropriate audit authority

798.   This section introduces a new obligation on departing auditors to send copies of their leaving statements to an appropriate audit authority as defined in section 525. It contains different rules depending on whether the company the auditor is leaving is classified as a "major audit" as defined in section 525.

799.   In relation to major audits, the departing auditor should always send a copy of his statement to the appropriate audit authority. He should do this as the same time as he deposits his statement with the company under section 519. In relation to other audits, the departing auditor is required to send his statement to the appropriate audit authority only if he is leaving before the end of his term of office, meaning only if he has resigned or has been dismissed; and he must do so at the time required by the authority.

800.   *Subsection (3)* provides that where the auditor's statement to the company said that there were no circumstances that needed to be brought to the attention of shareholders or creditors, that statement must have attached to it a statement of the auditor's reasons for leaving when sending it to the audit authority.

801.   *Subsections (5) to (8)* set out the offence of failure to comply with these requirements, and the maximum penalties.

Section 523: Duty of company to notify appropriate audit authority

802.   This section introduces a new duty on a company to notify the appropriate audit authority whenever an auditor leaves office before the end of his term, that is when he has resigned or is dismissed. The company has the choice of sending in the statement of circumstances made by the auditor under section 519, or of sending in its own statement of the reasons. *Subsection (3)* sets the deadline for notification as 14 days after the auditor has deposited his statement with the company. *Subsections (4) to (6)* set out the offence of failure to comply with this requirement, and the maximum penalties.

Section 524: Information to be given to accounting authorities

803.   This section sets out the duty of the audit authorities to give the accounting authorities information about auditors' departure, and the power, if they think it right to do so, to pass on the statements which they receive from departing auditors under the section 522 or from companies under section 523. The accounting authorities are the Secretary of State and anyone the Secretary of State has authorised under Part 15 to apply to the court in respect of the revision of defective accounts. At present this is the Financial Reporting Review Panel, part of the Financial Reporting Council organisation.

804.   *Subsection (3)* deals with the situation where the same body is both an audit authority and an accounting authority. If an accounting authority receives a statement that the court has determined need not be circulated to members, then *subsection (4)* provides that it must treat the statement as confidential, in the same way that authorities have to treat information obtained under compulsory powers under Part 15.

Section 525: Meaning of "appropriate audit authority" and "major audit"

805.   This section defines two terms used in connection with the duty to inform the audit authority when an auditor leaves office, namely *appropriate audit authority* and *major audit*. The former means the Secretary of State, or the body to whom he has delegated functions in

relation to the supervision of statutory auditors under Part 42, currently the Professional Oversight Board, part of the Financial Reporting Council organisation.

806.   A major audit is defined as meaning the audit of a listed company, or of any other company where there is a major public interest. Whether there is a major public interest is to be determined by reference to guidance issued by any of the audit authorities. In practice, this will generally be guidance issued by the Financial Reporting Council.

Section 526: Effect of casual vacancies

807.   This section applies when one out of two or more joint auditors ceases to be an auditor of the company. It enables the remaining auditors to continue in office. It restates section 388(2) of the 1985 Act.

CHAPTER 5: QUOTED COMPANIES: RIGHT OF MEMBERS TO RAISE AUDIT CONCERNS AT ACCOUNTS MEETING

808.   This Chapter introduces a new right for members of a quoted company to raise questions about the work of the auditors (all shareholders in a company limited by shares are members).

Section 527: Members' power to require website publication of audit concerns

809.   This section creates a new right for members of a quoted company – if they have a large enough holding in the company, or there are enough of them – to ask the company to publish on a website a statement raising questions about the accounts, or about the departure of an auditor, that they propose to bring up at the next meeting where the accounts are to be discussed.

810.   *Subsection (2)* specifies the thresholds the members have to meet, which are the same as for shareholders who want to ask a company to circulate a statement under section 314: they must either have 5% of the total voting rights, or there must be at least 100 of them, holding shares on which there has been paid up an average sum per member of at least £100. *Subsection (4)* sets out the mechanics of transmitting the request to the company: it may be in hard copy or electronic.

811.   *Subsection (5)* protects the company if members abuse the new right, e.g. by requesting a defamatory statement to be published. It enables the company, or someone else such as the auditor or a director, to apply to the court, and the court can then determine whether the right is being abused, in which case the company is not obliged to publish the statement. *Subsection (6)* provides that the court can order the shareholders who requested publication to pay some or all of the costs of the proceedings.

Section 528: Requirements as to website availability

812.   This section sets out the requirements which the company must meet in making the shareholders' statements available on a website, in the same way as section 353. *Subsection (4)* requires the company to get the statement onto a website within three days of receiving it, and to keep it available at least until after the meeting to which it relates.

Section 529: Website publication: company's supplementary duties

813.   This section requires quoted companies to draw attention to the possibility of a website statement in the notice of the accounts meeting. It also specifies the costs of

publication are to be borne by the company. *Subsection (3)* requires the company to forward the statement to the auditor at the same time as it puts it on a website. *Subsection (4)* provides that a statement under this chapter can be dealt with at the accounts meeting.

Section 530: Website publication: offences

814.   This section provides for offences when a company fails to comply with either of the preceding two sections, with maximum penalties of an unlimited fine.

Section 531: Meaning of "quoted company"

815.   This section defines the phrase "quoted company" for the purposes of Chapter 5 of Part 16 as being the same as the definition in section 385 in Part 15, and that the power in Part 15 to amend the definition also applies in this Chapter.

CHAPTER 6: AUDITORS' LIABILITY

816.   This Chapter makes it possible for auditors to limit their liability by agreement with a company, but the agreement will be effective only to the extent that it is fair and reasonable.

817.   It achieves this by defining a "liability limitation agreement" – a contractual limitation of an auditor's liability to a company, requiring member agreement – as a new exception to the general prohibition, restated here, on a company indemnifying its auditor. The court will be able to substitute its own limitation if the agreement purports to limit liability to an amount that is not fair and reasonable in all the circumstances.

Section 532: Voidness of provisions protecting auditors from liability

818.   This section restates the existing general prohibition, currently in section 310 of the 1985 Act, against a company indemnifying its auditor against claims by the company in the case of negligence or other default. Any such indemnities are void and unenforceable except where permitted by sections 533 to 536.

Section 533: Indemnity for costs of successfully defending proceedings

819.   This section contains the current exception from the prohibition in section 532 allowing the company to indemnify the auditor against the costs of successfully defending himself against a claim, though it does not repeat the current exception that allows the company to buy insurance for its auditor.

Section 534: Liability limitation agreements

820.   This section defines a "liability limitation agreement" as an agreement that seeks to limit the liability of an auditor to a company whose accounts he audits. The agreement can cover liability for negligence, default, breach of duty or breach of trust by the auditor.

821.   *Subsection (2)* provides that such an agreement is excepted from the general voidness of such agreements under section 532, provided that the agreement complies with the rules in section 535, and that it has been authorised by the members of the company in the way specified in section 536. *Subsection (3)* provides that the agreement's effect is limited by section 537, which contains the test of fairness and reasonableness, and that certain provisions of the Unfair Contracts Terms Act 1977 do not apply.

Section 535: Terms of liability limitation agreement

822.   This section contains rules about the terms of a liability limitation agreement. An agreement must relate to the audit of a specified financial year, and the limitation may be expressed in any terms, not necessarily as a fixed financial amount or a formula.

823.   *Subsection (2)* confers on the Secretary of State a power to make regulations (subject to negative resolution) prescribing or proscribing specified provisions or descriptions of provisions; and *subsection (3)* provides that the power may be used to prevent adverse effects on competition.

Section 536: Authorisation of agreement by members of the company

824.   This section specifies the way in which members of a company are to give their approval to a liability limitation agreement, without which approval the agreement will not be effective. The members of a private company can pass a resolution waiving the need for approval. The members in a private or a public company can pass a resolution before an agreement is signed approving its principal terms, or can approve the agreement after it is signed. The resolution may be an ordinary resolution, unless a higher threshold is set in the company's articles.

825.   *Subsection (5)* specifies what the principal terms of a liability limitation agreement are for this purpose, namely the terms that specify, or enable one to determine, (i) the sorts of faults by the auditor that are covered, (ii) the financial year in relation to which those faults are covered, and (iii) the limit on the auditor's liability.

826.   *Subsection (6)* provides that members, by passing an ordinary resolution, can withdraw their approval of a liability limitation agreement at any time before the agreement is entered into. If the company has already entered into the agreement, approval can be withdrawn, by ordinary resolution, only before the start of the financial year to which the agreement relates.

Section 537: Effect of liability limitation agreement

827.   This section provides that a liability limitation agreement will not be effective to limit an auditor's liability if the limitation would result in the company recovering an amount that was less that what was fair and reasonable, in all the circumstances of the case, having regard in particular to the auditor's responsibilities, the auditor's contractual obligations, and the standards expected of the auditor. If a court decides that a liability limitation agreement would limit the auditor's liability to an excessive degree, the agreement will have effect as if it limited liability to the amount that the court determines is fair and reasonable.

828.   *Subsection (3)* provides that in assessing what is fair and reasonable, the court should not take into account circumstances arising after the loss or damage in question has been incurred. Nor should it take into account the chances of the company successfully claiming compensation from any other people responsible for the loss or damage.

Section 538: Disclosure of agreement by company

829.   This section requires companies to disclose any liability limitation agreement they have made with their auditor in accordance with any regulations made by the Secretary of State subject to negative resolution. *Subsection (2)* provides that the regulations may require

this disclosure to be in a company's annual accounts (or in any other manner in the case of group accounts), or in the directors' report.

CHAPTER 7: SUPPLEMENTARY PROVISIONS

Section 539: Minor definitions

830.   This section defines a number of terms used in this Part.

PART 17: A COMPANY'S SHARE CAPITAL

831.   This Part of the Act deals with various matters relating to a company's share capital. It replaces Part 4 and (in part) Part 5 of the 1985 Act and contains a mixture of new sections which replace corresponding provisions in the 1985 Act and sections which restate corresponding provisions in that Act. Sections 541, 543 to 544, 547 to 548, 552 to 553, 558, 561, 563 to 568, 570 to 572, 574 to 577, 579 to 582, 584 to 588, 590 to 605, 607 to 609, 611 to 616, 645 to 648 and 655 to 656 restate various provisions in the 1985 Act but do not make any changes to those provisions.

CHAPTER 1: SHARES AND SHARE CAPITAL OF A COMPANY

Section 540: Shares

832.   As now, generally speaking, references to a "share" in the Companies Acts (defined in section 2) includes stock. However, as recommended by the CLR, in future it will no longer be possible for a company to convert its shares into stock (see *subsection (2)*) but a company that has stock at the date that this provision comes into force will be able to reconvert its stock back into shares (see note on section 620).

Section 542: Nominal value of shares

833.   This is a new provision, which is required as a result of the changes to the requirements with respect to the memorandum (see note on section 8).

834.   Currently, section 2(5)(a) of the 1985 Act (requirements with respect to memorandum) requires that, in the case of a company having a share capital, the memorandum of a limited company must state the amount of the share capital with which the company proposes to be registered and the division of that share capital into shares of a fixed amount. This capital figure as stated in the memorandum (known as the "authorised share capital") acts as a ceiling on the amount of shares that a company may issue. Such authorised share capital may, however, be increased by ordinary resolution under section 121 of that Act. The CLR recommended that the requirement for a company to have an authorised share capital should be abolished (Final Report, paragraph 10.6), and so the Act does not require a company to state in its memorandum the amount of its authorised share capital.

835.   This section is required as a consequence of the repeal of this requirement. It does two key things:

- it makes it clear that the shares in a limited company having a share capital must have a fixed nominal value, e.g. 1p, £1, $1 or 1 euro and therefore prevents a company from issuing shares of no par value (thereby implementing for public companies, Article 8 of the Second Company Law Directive (77/91/EEC)); and

- it places in statute the common law rule that shares may be denominated in any currency and that different classes of shares may be denominated in different currencies. However, this is subject to the requirement in section 765 that a public company may only satisfy its initial authorised minimum share capital requirement if its shares are denominated in either sterling or euros.

836. Where a company purports to allot shares without a fixed nominal value, every officer of the company who is in default commits an offence and is liable to a fine (see *subsections (4) and (5)*). Moreover, such a purported allotment is void (see *subsection (2)*).

837. This section needs to be read alongside section 9, which requires the application for registration of a company that is to be formed with a share capital to include a "statement of capital and initial shareholdings". The contents of this statement are prescribed in section 10 and this includes a requirement to set out the total number of shares and the aggregate nominal value of the shares which are to be taken by the subscribers to the memorandum on formation.

Section 545: Companies having a share capital

838. Section 545 is a new provision which makes it clear that references in the Companies Acts (defined in section 2) to a company having a share capital are to company that has power under its constitution to issue shares.

Section 546: Issued and allotted share capital

839. Section 546 is a new provision which makes it clear that references in the Companies Acts (defined in section 2) to issued or allotted shares include the shares taken by the subscribers to the memorandum on the formation of a company.

CHAPTER 2: ALLOTMENT OF SHARES: GENERAL PROVISIONS

840. Generally speaking, the directors of a company may currently only allot shares (or grant rights to subscribe for shares or to convert any security into shares) if they are authorised to do so by ordinary resolution of the company's members or by the articles.

841. Such an authority may be general or specific (that is, it may, for example, be restricted to a specified allotment, an allotment of shares up to a specified value, or an allotment of shares of a particular class). In either case, the authority must state the "maximum amount of relevant securities that may be allotted under it" and the date when the authority will expire, (which must not be more than five years from the date on which the authority is given). The authority may be renewed for further periods not exceeding five years.

842. There is a relaxation for private companies from the requirement to state the date on which the authority will expire and so such companies may, by elective resolution under section 379A of the 1985 Act, give such authority either for an indefinite period or a fixed period of the company's choice.

843. The Act removes for private companies the requirement for prior authorisation in certain circumstances (described in section 550). It also abolishes the concept of authorised share capital (see note on section 542) and a company's constitution will therefore no longer have to contain a ceiling on the number of shares that the directors are authorised to allot.

Section 549: Exercise by directors of power to allot shares etc

844.   This section replaces section 80(1), (2), (9) and (10) of the 1985 Act. It provides that the directors may not allot shares (or grant rights to subscribe for shares or to convert any security into shares) except in accordance with one of the following two sections.

845.   *Subsection (2)* of this section provides that directors may allot shares in pursuance of an employees' share scheme without having to comply with one of the following two sections. This mirrors the current position (see section 80(2) of the 1985 Act).

846.   Similarly, where a right to subscribe for, or to convert any security into, shares already exists, then the directors may allot shares pursuant to that right without having to comply with one of the following two sections (see *subsection 3*).

847.   A director who knowingly allots shares in contravention of the requirements imposed by this section commits an offence. Such an allotment is not, however, invalid.

Section 550: Power of directors to allot shares etc: private company with only one class of shares

848.   In line with the recommendations of the CLR (Final Report, paragraph 4.5), this is a new provision which empowers the directors to allot shares (or to grant rights to subscribe for or convert any security into shares) where the company is a private company which will have only one class of shares after the proposed allotment and removes the current requirement, contained in section 80 of the 1985 Act, for the directors to have prior authority from the company's members for such an allotment of shares. In addition, it provides that the members may, if they wish, restrict or prohibit this power through the articles. The definition of "class of shares" is contained in section 629.

Section 551: Power of directors to allot shares etc: authorisation by company

849.   This section replaces section 80(1) and (3) to (8) of the 1985 Act and applies both to private companies which will have more than one class of shares after a proposed allotment and to public companies. It provides that the directors may only allot shares (or grant rights to subscribe for shares or to convert any security into shares) if they have been given prior authorisation for the proposed allotment by ordinary resolution of the company's members or by the articles.

850.   *Subsections (2) to (5)* set out details of the way in which prior authorisation (or a renewal of such authorisation) may be given and, in particular, provides that the authority may not be given for a period of more than five years. An authority given to the directors under this section, and any resolution of the company renewing such an authority, must state "the maximum amount of shares" to be allotted pursuant to the authority. This mirrors the formulation of words used in section 80 of the 1985 Act and enables the members to limit the authority to a specific number of shares or shares up to a given maximum nominal value.

851.   *Subsection (8)* makes it clear that an ordinary resolution of the company's members will suffice for the purposes of giving authority to the directors, even where the effect of the resolution is to alter the company's articles of association (which would normally require a special resolution of the company's members).

Section 554: Registration of allotment

852.   This is a new provision which requires the directors to register an allotment of shares as soon as practicable (but in any event within two months of the date of allotment). Whereas the 1985 Act imposes a duty on the company to issue certificates within two months after the allotment of its shares it does not stipulate a timescale relating to the step which is anterior to this, namely the registration of the allotment.

853.   *Subsection (2)* makes it clear that the requirement to register an allotment of shares does not apply if the company has issued a share warrant in respect of the shares in question (see section 779).

854.   Where a company fails to comply with this section, the company and every officer of the company who is in default commits an offence. The penalty for this offence is set out in *subsection (4)*.

Section 555: Return of allotment by limited company

855.   This section replaces section 88 of the 1985 Act. As now, within one month of an allotment of new shares in a limited company, the company is required to make a return of allotments to the registrar. This return must contain *"prescribed information"* relating to the allotment (that is, prescribed by the Secretary of State by order or by regulations made under the Act).

856.   A return of allotments made under this section must be accompanied by a statement of capital. A statement of capital is in essence a "snapshot" of a company's total subscribed capital at a particular point in time (in this context, the date to which the return of allotments is made up).

857.   The requirement for a statement of capital when an allotment of new shares is made is new. It is based on a recommendation by the CLR (Final Report, paragraph 7.30) and for public companies, this implements a requirement in the Second Company Law Directive (77/91/EEC) which states:

> "the statutes or instruments of incorporation of the company shall always give at least the following information…(c) when the company has no authorized capital, the amount of the subscribed capital….".

"Statutes" and "instruments of incorporation" equate to the articles and memorandum and the need to disclose information pertaining to the aggregate of a company's subscribed capital flows from the abolition of the requirement for a company to have an authorised share capital (see note on section 542).

858.   Whilst this Directive only applies to public companies, the requirement to provide a statement of capital, here and elsewhere in the Act, has been extended to private companies limited by shares (and in certain cases to unlimited companies having a share capital, for example, where such companies make their annual return to the registrar). This will mean that the public register will contain up-to-date information on a company's share capital (the requirement for a statement of capital supplements existing provisions which require a company to give notice to the registrar when it amends its share capital in any way).

859.   The information which will in future be set out in the statement of capital includes prescribed particulars of the rights attached to each class of shares. Again this information will be prescribed in regulations or by order made under the Act. Such information is currently required to be filed under either section 123 of the 1985 Act (which relates to

increases in authorised share capital) or section 128(1) and (2) of that Act (which relates to allotments of a new class of shares).

860.   Currently, if shares are allotted as fully or partly paid up otherwise than in cash, the company must deliver the contract that it has with the allottee (or details of this contract if it is not in writing) to the registrar. Such a contract may contain commercially sensitive information which the company would not normally want to disclose. This section does not reproduce this requirement. It should be noted, however, that, in prescribing the information which must be included in the return of allotments, the Secretary of State may require details of any consideration received in respect of shares which are allotted as fully or partly paid up otherwise than in cash.

Section 556: Return of allotment by unlimited company allotting new class of shares

861.   This section requires unlimited companies to make a return of allotments to the registrar where the directors allot a new class of shares. This carries forward the provisions of section 128(1) and (2) of the 1985 Act as they apply to unlimited companies. The return must contain "prescribed particulars of the rights attached to the shares", that is such information as may be prescribed by the Secretary of State in regulations or by order made under the Act.

Section 557: Offence of failure to make return

862.   This section replaces section 88(5) and (insofar as it relates to a requirement for an unlimited company to register particulars of an allotment of a new class of shares) section 128(5) of the 1985 Act. Where a company fails to comply with the requirements to make a return of allotments to the registrar, every officer of the company who is in default commits an offence.

863.   As now under section 88(6), where there is a default in making a return of allotments within the specified time (one month after the allotment) a person who is liable for the default may apply to the court for relief (see *subsection (3)* which extends the right to apply for relief to a person liable under section 556).

Section 559: Provisions about allotment not applicable to shares taken on formation

864.   This provision replicates the effect of section 80(2)(a) of the 1985 act and provides that the allotment provisions in Chapter 2 of this Part do not apply to the shares taken by the subscribers to the memorandum on the formation of a company. Such persons become members of the company in respect of the shares that are taken by them on formation by virtue of section 16 and the provisions of the Act on share allotments do not apply to them.

CHAPTER 3: ALLOTMENT OF EQUITY SECURITIES: EXISTING SHAREHOLDERS' RIGHT OF PRE-EMPTION

Section 560: Meaning of "equity securities" and related expressions

865.   This section sets out a definition of "equity securities" for the purposes of Chapter 3 of this Part (which is concerned with the allotment of equity securities and existing shareholders' right of pre-emption). It partially restates section 94(2), (3), (3A) and (5) of the 1985 Act. The exception for shares taken by a subscriber to the memorandum and for bonus shares provided in section 94(2) of the 1985 Act is contained in sections 577 and 564. The exclusion of the allotment of shares pursuant to the grant of a right to subscribe for such shares contained in section 93(3) of the 1985 Act is contained in section 561(3).

Section 561: Existing shareholders' right of pre-emption

866.   Subject to some exceptions, under section 89(1) of the 1985 Act, a company that is proposing to allot equity securities (defined in section 560) must offer them to existing shareholders first (that is, on a pre-emptive basis). The basic principle (which is unchanged by the Act) is that a shareholder should be able to protect his proportion of the total equity of a company by having the opportunity to subscribe for any new issue of equity securities. This is subject to various exceptions and *subsection (5)* provides a pointer to these exceptions.

Section 562: Communication of pre-emption offers to shareholders

867.   This section replaces section 90(1), (5) and (6) of the 1985 Act. Section 90(6) of the 1985 Act provides that where a company communicates a pre-emption offer to its existing shareholders the offer must state a period of not less than 21 days during which it may be accepted and it may not be withdrawn before the end of that period. This section contains a new provision which gives the Secretary of State the power to vary, in regulations made under the Act, the period of 21 days (but not so as to reduce it to fewer than 14 days) – see *subsection (6)*.

868.   It also updates the 1985 Act provision to ensure that the communications of pre-emption offers to shareholders continue to be compatible with EU law: in particular, in future companies will be required to give individual notice (which may be in hard copy or electronic form) to all shareholders who have a registered address in the EEA or who have given an address for service of notices in the EEA (under the 1985 Act, a company is only required to give individual notice to shareholders who have given a service address in the UK). As now, where no relevant address for service has been provided, the company may discharge its obligation by causing notice of the offer to be published in the London, Edinburgh or Belfast Gazette as appropriate.

Sections 569 to 573: Disapplication of pre-emption rights

869.   This group of sections deals with the circumstances in which the statutory pre-emption requirements may be disapplied or modified by a power under the articles or by special resolution in accordance with the detailed rules in these sections. The rules replace or restate equivalent provisions in section 95 of the 1985 Act.

870.   Section 569 is a new provision which sets out how members of a private company with only one class of shares may authorise the directors to allot shares without complying with the statutory pre-emption provisions.

871.   Section 573 is concerned with the disapplication of pre-emption rights in connection with a sale of treasury shares. Generally speaking, where a company buys back its own shares, it is normally required to cancel those shares (see section 706(b)). Certain companies (principally those which are listed or those whose shares are traded on the Alternative Investment Market and equivalent companies in the EEA) may however elect not to cancel shares which have been bought back but may hold the shares "in treasury". A share which is held in treasury may be sold at a future point in time and this facility enables such companies to raise capital more quickly than they would otherwise be able to do, as the directors do not have to obtain prior authority from the company's members before selling treasury shares. However, the provisions of section 561 do apply to sales of treasury shares as they apply to allotments of shares (see section 560(2)(b)).

872.   This section applies to a sale of shares which have been held in treasury by the company. It replaces section 95(2A) of the 1985 Act and reproduces the effect of that section by enabling a company's members to give a general power to the directors (through the company's articles or by special resolution of the company's members) to sell such shares as if statutory pre-emption rights did not apply, or applied with modifications.

873.   This section also permits the members to confer upon the directors (by special resolution) a specific power which enables them to sell treasury shares as if statutory pre-emption rights did not apply to a specified sale, or applied with modifications.

CHAPTER 4: PUBLIC COMPANIES: ALLOTMENT WHERE ISSUE NOT FULLY SUBSCRIBED

Section 578: Public companies: allotment where issue not fully subscribed

874.   The provisions of this section restate section 84 of the 1985 Act and relate to the allotment of shares by public companies, and apply where not all the shares offered are taken up. A public company must not allot shares following an offer to subscribe for shares unless all the shares offered are taken up or the offer is made on the basis that it will go ahead even if all the shares offered are not taken up or if other conditions specified in the offer are met. It is not possible for the terms of the offer to override the requirements of this section (*subsection 6*)).

875.   The purpose of this rule is to protect persons who apply for shares, by ensuring that if the increase in capital is not fully subscribed, the capital will be increased by the amount of the subscriptions received only if the conditions of the issue so provide (Article 28 of the Second Company Law Directive (77/91/EEC)).

876.   If 40 days after first making the offer, the offer is unsuccessful because not enough shares have been applied for under the offer, any money or other consideration received from those that did apply for shares under the offer must be repaid or returned (*subsection (2)*). Interest becomes payable after the expiration of the 48th day after the offer was first made (*subsection (3)*). The rate of interest will be as specified at the time under section 17 of the Judgments Act 1838 (currently 8%). This is a change from section 84(3) of the 1985 Act which sets the interest rate at 5% per annum.

877.   The 40 day and 48 day time limits imposed by subsections (2) and (3) now run from the making of the offer rather than from the issue of any prospectus (as was the case under section 84 of the 1985 Act) given that the requirement or otherwise for a prospectus is a matter of securities law.

878.   The regulation of public offers, especially requirements relating to prospectuses, is generally a matter of securities law. Sections 82 and 83 of the 1985 Act are, therefore, not restated in this Act.

Section 583: Meaning of payment in cash

879.   This section replaces section 738(2) to (4) of the 1985 Act. It provides a definition of "payment in cash" for the purposes of the Companies Acts and is relevant to a number of provisions (for example section 593 requires public companies to obtain an independent valuation of any non-cash consideration where it allots shares otherwise than for cash).

880.   *Subsection (3)* provides a definition of "cash consideration" which lists the items currently contained in section 738(2) of the 1985 Act. It is generally accepted that certain forms of payment, in addition to those listed in subsection (3), constitute "payment in cash" where shares in a company are deemed to be paid up or allotted for cash, for example an assured payment obligation under the CREST assured payment system, but this matter is not beyond doubt. (An assured payment obligation is the creation of an obligation to make payment to or for the account of the company in accordance with the rules and practices of the operator of a relevant system as defined by regulation 2(1) of the Uncertificated Securities Regulations 2001). The power contained in *subsection (4)* will enable the Secretary of State to make provision for other forms of payment to be regarded as falling within the definition of "payment in cash". This will eradicate the uncertainty which currently surrounds certain forms of payment and will also "future proof" the current definition should other settlement systems be developed in the future (or should other settlement systems within the EU be identified).

Section 589: Power of court to grant relief

881.   Section 589 restates section 113(1) to (7) of the 1985 Act. It enables the court to grant relief, to the applicant, from a liability to the company which has arisen as a result of a contravention of section 585, 587(2) or (4) or 588. There is a minor change in the restatement insofar as the matters to which the court must have regard in applying the just and equitable test in *subsection (3)* also apply where the liability relates to the payment of interest (under section 113 (2)(b)) of the 1985 Act the court is not required to have regard to those matters in applying the just and equitable test).

Section 606: Power of court to grant relief

882.   Section 606 restates section 113(1) to (8) of the 1985 Act. It enables the court to grant relief, to the applicant, from a liability to the company which has arisen (under any provision of Chapter 6) in relation to payment in respect of shares in a company or an undertaking given to the company in, or in connection with, payment for any shares in it. There is a minor change in the restatement insofar as the matters to which the court must have regard in applying the just and equitable test in *subsection (2)* also apply where the liability relates to the payment of interest (under section 113 (2)(b)) of the 1985 Act the court is not required to have regard to those matters in applying the just and equitable test).

CHAPTER 7: SHARE PREMIUMS

883.   Under section 130 of the 1985 Act, where shares in a company are issued at a premium, (that is, at a price which is greater than their nominal value), an amount equal to the premium paid on those shares must be transferred to a non-distributable reserve: the share premium account. This account can only be used in a limited number of circumstances described in section 130.

Section 610: Application of share premiums

884.   In line with the recommendations of the CLR (Completing the Structure, paragraph 7.8), this section further restricts the application of the share premium account and in the future, companies will not be able to use the share premium account to write off preliminary expenses (that is, expenses incurred in connection with the company's formation). Companies will continue to be able to use the share premium account to write off any

expenses incurred, or commission paid, in connection with an issue of shares but the application of the share premium account in these circumstances will be limited so that the company will only be able to use the share premium account arising on a particular issue of shares to write off expenses incurred or commission paid in respect of that issue. As now, companies will also be able to use the share premium account to pay up new shares to be allotted to existing members as fully paid bonus shares.

885.   A further change is that in future companies will not be able to use the share premium account to write off any expenses incurred, commission paid or discount allowed in respect of an issue of debentures or in providing for the premium payable on a redemption of debentures.

CHAPTER 8: ALTERATION OF SHARE CAPITAL

Section 617: Alteration of share capital of limited company

886.   This section prohibits a limited company from altering its share capital except in the ways permitted under the Act. It includes a signpost to a new provision which will enable companies limited by shares easily to convert (or "redenominate") their share capital from one currency to another (see section 622).

Section 618: Sub-division or consolidation of shares

887.   Consolidation of a company's share capital involves combining a number of shares into a new share of commensurate nominal value: for example, ten £1 shares may be combined to make one £10 share. Sub-division of a company's share capital involves dividing a share into a number of new shares with a smaller nominal value: for example, a £10 share may be sub-divided into ten £1 shares.

888.   Section 618 replaces section 121(2)(b) and (d) of the 1985 Act. It sets out the circumstances and manner in which a limited company may consolidate or sub-divide its share capital. Where shares in a company are sub-divided or consolidated, the proportion between the amount paid and the amount unpaid (if any) on the original share(s) must remain the same in relation to the share(s) resulting from the sub-division or consolidation. If, for example, £2 is unpaid on a £10 share that is subsequently sub-divided into ten £1 shares, there will now be 20p unpaid on each of those ten shares.

889.   A company may exercise a power conferred on it under this section only if the members have passed a resolution authorising it to do so, which may be an ordinary resolution or a resolution requiring a higher majority (as the articles may require). Such a resolution may authorise a company to exercise more than one of the powers conferred on it under this section, for example, the resolution may authorise a sub-division of one class of the company's shares and a consolidation of another. It may also authorise the company to exercise a power conferred on it under this section on more than one occasion or at a specified time or in specified circumstances. This avoids the directors having to obtain authorisation from the company's members on each and every occasion that a company alters its share capital under this section (which may be inconvenient to the directors and members alike or impractical due to timing constraints).

890.   The flexibility to pass a conditional resolution (that is, a resolution that will only take effect if certain conditions are met) given in *subsection (4)(c)* is necessary as a sub-division or consolidation of share capital (or any class of it) may form part of a wider re-organisation

of a company's share capital, for example, a reduction of share capital following a redenomination of share capital. It may, therefore, not be appropriate, or necessary, for a company's share capital to be altered in this way if the reorganisation of share capital that the sub-division or consolidation is linked to does not go ahead.

891.   Under the 1985 Act a company may only sub-divide or consolidate its share capital if it is authorised to do so by the company's articles (see section 121 of that Act). This restriction has not been retained.

Section 619: Notice to registrar of sub-division or consolidation

892.   The section replaces a similar requirement to notify the registrar contained in section 122(1)(a) and (d) of the 1985 Act. Where a company sub-divides or consolidates its share capital under section 618, it will continue to be required to give notice of this alteration to its share capital to the registrar within one month. However, there is a new requirement to file a statement of capital (see *subsections (2) and (3)*), which is in essence a "snap-shot" of the company's total share capital at a particular point in time: in this case following the consolidation/sub-division.

893.   For public companies, the requirement for a statement of capital is linked to the abolition of authorised share capital: it implements Article 2 of the Second Company Law Directive (77/91/EEC) which states:

> "the statutes or instruments of incorporation of the company shall always give at least the following information…(c) when the company has no authorized capital, the amount of the subscribed capital…".

894.   The statement of capital will require the following information to be provided:

- the total number of shares of the company,

- the aggregate nominal value of those shares,

- for each class of shares, prescribed particulars of the rights attached to the shares, the total number of shares of that class and the aggregate nominal value of shares of that class, and

- the amount paid up and the amount (if any) unpaid on each share (whether on account of the nominal value of the share or by way of premium).

895.   Whilst this Directive applies only to public companies it is important that the information on the public register is up-to-date. A statement of capital will, therefore, be required where it is proposed that a company formed under the Act will have a share capital on formation and, with limited exceptions (in particular, where there has been a variation of class rights which does not affect the company's aggregate subscribed capital) whenever a limited company makes an alteration to its share capital. A statement of capital is also called for in certain circumstances where an unlimited company having a share capital makes a return to the registrar (see, section 856).

896.   In making a statement of capital, a company is required to provide "prescribed particulars of the rights attached to the shares". Here, and elsewhere in the Act where a statement of capital is called for, "prescribed" means prescribed by the Secretary of State in regulations or by order made under the Act.

897.   The power conferred on the Secretary of State under this section enables the Secretary of State to specify the particular detail of the information which he requires to be filed with

the registrar by a company. A statutory instrument made pursuant to this power will not be subject to any form of Parliamentary scrutiny.

898.   Criminal liability for any failure to comply with the procedural requirements as to notice is retained (see *subsection (4)*). The penalty for this offence is set out in *subsection (5)*.

Section 620: Re-conversion of stock into shares

899.   Stock cannot be issued directly by a company but arises from a conversion of fully paid up shares into stock under section 121(2)(c) of the 1985 Act. This ability to convert shares into stock has not been retained. A company that currently has stock may, however, wish to re-convert this stock back into fully paid shares, and this is permitted by the following section.

900.   Section 620 replaces section 121(2)(c) of the 1985 Act. It retains the ability to re-convert stock back into fully paid shares but removes the requirement for prior authorisation in the articles (currently a company may only re-convert stock back into shares if provision for this is made in its articles).

901.   A re-conversion of stock into shares will require an ordinary resolution of the company's members. Such a resolution may give the directors power to convert stock into fully paid shares on more than one occasion; at a specified time; or only if certain conditions are met (see *subsection (3)*). The flexibility to pass a conditional resolution (that is, a resolution that will only take effect if certain conditions are met) is necessary as a re-conversion of stock into shares may form part of a wider re-organisation of a company's share capital.

Section 621: Notice to registrar of reconversion of stock into shares

902.   Where a company re-converts stock into shares it must give notice of the alteration to its share capital to the registrar under the provisions in section 621. This requirement replaces a similar provision in section 122(1)(c) of the 1985 Act.

903.   A statement of capital is required (see note on section 619).

904.   Criminal liability for any failure to comply with the procedural requirements as to notice is retained (see *subsection (4)*). The penalty for this offence is set out in *subsection (5)*.

Section 622: Redenomination of share capital

905.   Where a public company applies for a trading certificate under section 117 of the 1985 Act it must satisfy a minimum share capital requirement (known as the "authorised minimum"). There is a similar requirement where a private company re-registers as a public company under section 43 of that Act. The authorised minimum is currently set at £50,000 and must be expressed in sterling. This implements Article 6 of the Second Company Law Directive (77/91/EEC) which requires that, in order that a company may be incorporated or obtain authorisation to commence business, a minimum capital shall be subscribed the amount of which shall be not less than 25000 ECU (expressed in the domestic currency of the Member State). Under section 763, in future the authorised minimum will be capable of being satisfied in sterling (£50,000) or the euro equivalent to the sterling amount. Subject to this change, the Act retains the effect of the 1985 Act provisions on the authorised minimum (see, for example, section 91, section 650 and section 761).

906.   Subject to the above qualification (and any restriction in a company's articles) a company is free to allot shares in any currency that it wishes (see section 542(3)). It may also have its share capital made up of shares of a mixture of denominations, for example, one class of a company's shares may be denominated in sterling, whereas another class may be denominated in dollars, euros or some other currency of the company's choosing. What a company cannot currently do is easily redenominate its share capital (or any class of it) from one currency to another, for example, from dollars to sterling or vice versa. The current procedure involves cancelling existing shares under the court approved procedure for capital reductions set out in section 135 of the 1985 Act or, in the case of private companies only, buying back or redeeming shares out of capital under section 171 of that Act, and then issuing new shares in the desired currency.

907.   Section 622 introduces a new procedure that will allow a company limited by shares to redenominate its share capital easily. This requires a resolution of the company's members. (Unlimited companies having a share capital are already free to redenominate their share capital as they see fit and no change to the legislation is required in respect of such companies).

908.   *Subsection (2)* of this section provides that the spot rate used when converting a company's share capital from one currency to another must be specified in the resolution to redenominate the company's share capital. There is a choice of spot rates and this is set out in *subsection (3)*.

909.   A company is free to pass a conditional resolution under this section (see *subsection (4)*). A resolution will, however, lapse if the redenomination of share capital has not taken effect within 28 days of the date on which the resolution is passed (see *subsection (6)*). Where a resolution lapses, the company will not be able to redenominate its capital unless it passes a new resolution and the redenomination is effected in accordance with the new resolution.

910.   *Subsection (7)* makes it clear that, if it wishes, a company may restrict or prohibit a redenomination of its share capital by incorporating a provision to this effect in the company's articles.

911.   It should be noted that this section does not make provision for the authorised minimum to continue to be denominated in sterling (or the euro equivalent). This means that once a public company has obtained a trading certificate under section 761 (or previously under section 117 of the 1985 Act) or where a private company has re-registered as a public company, such a company is free, if it wishes, to redenominate all of its share capital, including the authorised minimum into any currency of its choosing.

Section 623: Calculation of new nominal values

912.   This section explains how the new nominal value of a share which has been redenominated from one currency to another should be calculated.

Section 624: Effect of redenomination

913.   This section makes it clear that a redenomination of a company's share capital (or any class of it) does not affect any rights or obligations that the members may have under the company's constitution or any restrictions affecting members under the company's constitution. In particular, it does not affect entitlement to dividends, voting rights or any

liability in respect of amounts unpaid on shares. If, for example, a dividend of 20p was declared on a £1 share prior to a redenomination of that share, and that £1 share is subsequently converted into a $1.5 share, the member who now owns a $1.5 share in the company will still be entitled to a 20p dividend (albeit that the company and the member in question may agree that the 20p dividend can be paid in cents – or indeed in some other currency). Similarly, where a company has issued partly paid shares, the member's liability to the company will remain in the currency in which the share was originally denominated.

Section 625: Notice to registrar of redenomination

914.   This section sets out the requirements as to notice where a company redenominates its share capital (or any class of it). Notice must be given to the registrar in accordance with *subsections (1) and (2)* of this section and there is a requirement for a statement of capital (see note on section 619).

915.   A copy of the resolution to redenominate the company's share capital must be forwarded to the registrar within 15 days after it is passed notwithstanding that it may be an ordinary resolution (see section 622(8) which provides that Chapter 3 of Part 3 applies to the resolution and in particular section 30)

916.   If a company fails to comply with the procedural requirements as to notice the company and every officer of the company commits an offence. The penalty for this offence is set out in *subsection (5)*.

Section 626: Reduction of capital in connection with redenomination

917.   Following a redenomination of a company's share capital, it is likely that the company will be left with shares expressed in awkward fractions of the new currency, for example, 0.997 dollars or 1.01 euros. The company may therefore wish to renominalise the value of the shares affected (that is, alter the nominal value of these shares) to obtain share values in whole units of the new currency. It can do this in one of two ways: if the company has distributable reserves it may capitalise those reserves to increase the nominal value of the shares affected; alternatively, it may reduce its share capital using the procedure set out in section 626.

918.   This section enables a company to renominalise the value of its shares by cancelling part of its share capital. A special resolution of the company's members is required but there is no need for the directors to make a solvency statement or for the company to go to court (as required where a company reduces its share capital under Chapter 10 of this Part).

919.   Under *subsection (3)*, a resolution to reduce capital in connection with a redenomination must be passed within 3 months of the resolution to redenominate the company's share capital.

920.   *Subsection (4)* provides that the amount by which a company can reduce its share capital using this new provision is capped at 10% of the nominal value of the company's share capital immediately after the reduction. This 10% cap is required by the Second Company Law Directive (77/91/EEC) and applies to any reduction of capital in a public company which is not approved by the court.

921.   Where a company reduces its share capital under this section, the amount by which the company's share capital is reduced must be transferred to a new non-distributable reserve (see section 628).

Section 627: Notice to registrar of reduction of capital in connection with redenomination

922.   This section sets out the requirements as to notice where a company reduces its share capital in connection with a redenomination of its share capital (that is, to renominalise the value of its shares). Notice must be given to the registrar in accordance with *subsection (1)* of this section. This notice must be accompanied by a statement of capital (see note on section 619).

923.   The resolution to reduce the share capital must be filed with the registrar in accordance with section 30.

924.   The reduction of capital will not take effect until the documents that are required to be delivered to the registrar under *subsections (1) and (2)* are registered by the registrar (see *subsection (5)*).

925.   In addition to delivering the above documents to the registrar, within 15 days of the date that a resolution to reduce capital in connection with a redenomination is passed, under *subsection (6)* the company must also deliver to the registrar a statement made by the directors confirming that the reduction of share capital was made in accordance with *subsection (4)* of section 626.

926.   If a company fails to comply with the procedural requirements as to notice the company and every officer of the company commits an offence. The penalty for this offence is set out in *subsection (8)*. In addition, where the statement made by the directors under *subsection (6)* is misleading, false or deceptive in a material particular, the directors are liable to an offence under section 1112.

Section 628: Redenomination reserve

927.   Where a company reduces its share capital under section 626 it must transfer an amount equal to the value of the reduction to a non-distributable reserve known as the redenomination reserve.

928.   This section provides that amounts transferred to the redenomination reserve may be used by the company in paying up shares to be allotted to existing members as fully paid bonus shares. Subject to this, the provisions of the Companies Acts relating to the reduction of a company's share capital, apply to the redenomination reserve as if it were paid-up share capital. These provisions mirror those contained in section 733 (which restates section 170 of the 1985 Act).

CHAPTER 9: CLASSES OF SHARES AND CLASS RIGHTS

929.   "Classes of shares" (or "class rights") is not defined in the 1985 Act but at common law this term is normally used where the rights that attach to a particular share relate to matters such as voting rights, a right to dividends and a right to a return of capital when a company is wound-up. Rights attach to a particular class of shares if the holders of shares in that class enjoy rights that are not enjoyed by the holders of shares in another class.

Section 629: Classes of shares

930.   This section provides that for the purposes of the Act, shares are of one class if the rights attached to them are in all respects uniform. It reproduces the provision in section

128(2) of the 1985 Act. It is particularly relevant to the provisions of section 550 and section 569. This definition of "classes of shares" also applies in determining the extent to which shares constitute different classes for the purposes of the statement of capital required to be filed under various provisions of the Bill (see note on section 619).

Section 630: Variation of class rights: companies having a share capital

931.   On variation of class rights the CLR recommended (Final Report, paragraph 7.28) that the current provisions should be retained with some simplification, and extended to companies without a share capital (see section 631).

932.   Section 630 replaces section 125 of the 1985 Act. It is concerned with the manner in which rights attached to a class of shares may be varied. Class rights typically cover matters such as voting rights, rights to dividends and rights to a return of capital on a winding up.

933.   Currently class rights may be set out in the memorandum or articles or elsewhere, and provision may or may not be made for their alteration. Under the Act it will not be possible for class rights to be set out in the memorandum (see section 8) and where class rights attaching to shares in an existing company are specified in the memorandum these will be deemed, by virtue of section 28, to be a provision in the company's articles.

934.   Class rights are "attached to a class of shares" (see *subsection (1)*). Where all the shares in a company fall within the one class, there are no class rights, only shareholder rights. What amounts to a class is not defined either in the current law or the Act (other than in section 629) and remains a matter for case law.

935.   The current requirement for an extraordinary resolution where a company is proposing to vary the rights attached to a class of its shares is replaced with a requirement for a special resolution (see *subsection (4)(b)*). The Act abolishes the concept of an extraordinary resolution. Special resolution is defined in section 283.

936.   *Subsections (2) and (4)* provide that rights may be varied in accordance with the company's articles or, where the articles make no provision for a variation of class rights, if the holders of at least three-quarters in nominal value of the issued shares of that class consent in writing or a special resolution passed by the holders of that class sanctions the variation. This means that the articles may specify a less demanding procedure for a variation of class rights than the statutory scheme (for example, that the holders of 51% by nominal value of the class consent in writing), or may permit a simple majority of the class at a class meeting.

937.   The provisions of section 630 are expressed to be without prejudice to any other restriction on the variation of rights (see *subsection (3)*). This has two important effects. First, if and to the extent that the company has adopted a more onerous regime in its articles for the variation of class rights, for example requiring a higher percentage than the statutory minimum, the company must comply with the more onerous regime. Second, if and to the extent that the company has protected class rights by making provision for the entrenchment of those rights in its articles (see section 22), that protection cannot be circumvented by changing the rights attached to a class of shares under this section.

Section 631: Variation of class rights: companies without a share capital

938.   This section extends the statutory provisions on variation of class rights to companies without a share capital. Companies limited by guarantee (which since December 1980 cannot

be formed with a share capital) may, for example, have different classes of members with different voting rights.

939.　At present the question of how members' rights may be varied will depend to a large extent on whether provision has been made, either in the memorandum or articles, for their variation. Under the Act class rights may also be varied in accordance with this section, which contains new provisions, comparable to those for companies with a share capital. Thus there is a minimum requirement that class rights may be varied if three-quarters of that class consent in writing or a special resolution of those members sanctions the variation, unless the company has made provision for a less onerous regime to apply in its articles. Again, a company may also make provision, in its articles, for a more onerous regime to apply than that provided in this section and where they do the company must comply with the regime set out in the articles.

Section 632: Variation of class rights: saving for court's power under other provisions

940.　This section preserves the court's powers under various other provisions of the Act and substantially restates section 126 of the 1985 Act.

Sections 633 and 634: Right to object to variation

941.　Section 633 replaces section 127 (which confers a right on shareholders to object to a variation of class rights). It sets out the procedure that must be followed where there is an objection to a variation of the rights attached to a class of a company's shares and enables shareholders holding not less in aggregate than 15% of the issued shares of the class in question (being persons who did not consent to or vote in favour of the resolution approving the variation) to apply to the court for the variation to be cancelled.

942.　Section 634 makes similar provision in respect of a variation of class rights in companies not having a share capital. This is a new provision which enables members, amounting to not less than 15% of the members of the class affected (being persons who did not consent to or vote in favour of the resolution approving the variation), to apply to the court to have the variation cancelled and gives the court the power to confirm the variation, or disallow it if the court is satisfied that it would unfairly prejudice the members in that class.

Section 635: Copy of court order to be forwarded to the registrar

943.　Section 635 sets out the procedural requirements as to notice where the court has made an order on an application under section 633 or 634. Where the court has made an order on application under these sections, the company must forward a copy of that order to the registrar within 15 days of the date on which the order is made. Where a company fails to comply with the provisions of this section, the company, and every officer of the company who is in default, commits an offence (see *subsections (2) and (3)*).

Section 636 to 640: Matters to be notified to the registrar

944.　These sections replace various provisions in sections 128 and 129 of the 1985 Act which are concerned with notification to the registrar of the creation of, and variations to, rights attached to a class of a company's shares (section 128 of the 1985 Act) or class rights of members (section 129 of that Act).

945.   Under the Act, where a limited company creates a new class of shares, it will be required to provide details of the rights attached to the shares in the return of allotment and statement of capital required under section 555. There is a similar requirement in section 556 where an unlimited company allots a new class of share. Those provisions replace section 128(1) and (2) of the 1985 Act.

946.   In addition, where a company <u>varies</u> the rights attached to any of its shares (or assigns a name or other designation, or a new name or other designation to any class or description of its shares) it will in future be required to register particulars of the rights affected under section 637 (or 636) irrespective of how the variation in rights was achieved. Currently companies are not required to provide this information if the rights attached to a particular share or class of shares are varied by an amendment to the company's memorandum or articles or by special resolution or agreement of the company's members which is required to be filed under section 380 of the 1985 Act. Sections 638 to 640 make similar changes to the disclosure requirements which apply to companies limited by guarantee not having a share capital and unlimited companies not having a share capital which may, nevertheless, have different classes of members.

947.   It should be noted, that, in contrast to other alterations to a company's share capital, there is no requirement in section 637 for a statement of capital (see note on section 619). Such a requirement would be superfluous, as a variation of class rights will not result in a change to the aggregate amount of a company's subscribed capital.

CHAPTER 10: REDUCTION OF SHARE CAPITAL

948.   Section 135 of the 1985 Act lays down a statutory procedure under which a limited company may, if authorised by its articles, reduce its share capital. This requires a special resolution of the company's members and the reduction must be confirmed by the court. Companies limited by shares may also reduce their share capital under section 171 (private company redemption or purchase of own shares out of capital) and sections 146 to 147 of the 1985 Act (which require a public company which acquires shares in any of the specified ways, for example, through forfeiture for failure to pay up, to cancel those shares within a specified period), the provisions of both of which are carried forward by the Act. A reduction of capital may also occur as a result of the court making an order for the purchase by a company of its members' shares.

949.   A company may wish to reduce its share capital for a variety of reasons, for example, where its capital is in excess of the company's wants or where the value of the company's net assets has fallen below the amount of its capital (as stated in the company's accounts) and the position is likely to be permanent.

Section 641: Circumstances in which a company may reduce its share capital

950.   This section replaces section 135(1) and (2) of the 1985 Act. It sets out the circumstances and manner in which a company limited by shares may reduce its share capital. As recommended by the CLR (Final Report, paragraph 10.6), in future a private company limited by shares will be able to reduce its share capital using a new solvency statement procedure for capital reductions (see section 642).

951.   A company may only reduce its share capital under section 135 of the 1985 Act if it is authorised to do so by its articles. In line with the recommendations of the CLR (Completing the Structure, paragraph 2.15), the requirement for prior authorisation in the articles has not been retained but, if it wishes, a company may restrict or prohibit a reduction of capital by making provision to this effect in its articles (see *subsection (6)*).

952.   *Subsection (1)(a)* contains a signpost to a new provision, which will enable a private company limited by shares to reduce its share capital using the new solvency statement procedure (see above). In addition, private companies and public companies alike will continue to be able to use the current court approved procedure for capital reductions – which is retained in *subsection (1)(b)*.

953.   In the case of a private company limited by shares which is proposing to use the new solvency statement procedure to effect a reduction of capital, the company may only reduce its share capital under *subsection (1)(a)* if it will have at least one member remaining after the proposed reduction (see *subsection (2)*). That member need only hold one share in the company but that share must not be a redeemable share. The principle behind this requirement is that a private company limited by shares should not be capable of reducing its share capital to zero unless the reduction of capital is sanctioned by the court. This mirrors the existing equivalent provision in section 162(3) of the 1985 Act – which applies to a purchase of own shares.

954.   Both the solvency statement procedure for capital reductions and the court-approved procedure require a special resolution of the company's members. Under *subsection (5)* a special resolution to reduce a company's share capital may not provide for the proposed reduction to take effect on a date later than the date on which the resolution to reduce capital takes effect. Under the solvency statement procedure a resolution to reduce capital will take effect when the documents referred to in section 644 have been registered by the registrar (see section 644(4)). This would operate to prevent a company passing a resolution on, say, 1st January stating that the reduction is to take effect on 1st October. Under the court approved procedure, the resolution will take effect on the registration of the court order and statement of capital or, in the context of a reduction forming part of a compromise or arrangement under Part 26, on delivery of those documents to the registrar (unless the court orders otherwise) (see section 649).

Section 642: Reduction of capital supported by solvency statement

955.   This section sets out the conditions that must be satisfied in order for a private company limited by shares to reduce its share capital using the new solvency statement procedure.

956.   The procedural requirements that the directors must follow when they propose a capital reduction using the solvency statement route are set out in *subsections (1) to (3)* which provides that the solvency statement made in connection with a reduction of capital by a private company cannot be made more than 15 days before the date on which the resolution to reduce capital is passed. It also provides that both the resolution and the solvency statement must be filed with the registrar in accordance with the provisions of section 644.

957.   The solvency statement must also be made available to the company's members when they vote on the resolution to reduce capital and the procedure for providing a copy of the solvency statement to the members varies according to whether the resolution to reduce

capital is proposed as a written resolution or at a meeting of the company's members (see *subsections (2) and (3)*). Whilst a failure to observe these procedural requirements will not affect the validity of the resolution to reduce capital, if a solvency statement which has not been provided to the company's members in accordance with the provision of this section is subsequently filed with the registrar, every officer of the company who is in default commits an offence (see section 644).

Section 643: Solvency statement

958.   A solvency statement made under section 643 must be made by all of the directors. If one or more of the directors is unable or unwilling to make this statement, the company will not be able to use the solvency statement procedure to effect a reduction of capital unless the dissenting director or directors resign (in which case the solvency statement must be made by all of the remaining directors).

959.   The solvency statement must be in the "prescribed form" and "prescribed" in this context means prescribed by the Secretary of State in regulations or by order made under the Act.

960.   The solvency statement must state the date on which it is made and the name of each director of the company but there is no requirement that the directors must all be in the same location when they make this statement. The registrar will be able to make rules under section 1068 as to the form of the solvency statement.

961.   In forming their opinions, the directors must take account of all the company's liabilities including contingent and prospective liabilities (see *subsection (2)*). So, in circumstances where a company holds redeemable preference shares which, for the purposes of the accounting standards that applied to the company on the date that the directors made the solvency statement, are treated as liabilities, a proposed redemption or purchase of these shares in the relevant period should be treated as a contingent or prospective liability.

962.   If the directors make a solvency statement without having reasonable grounds for the opinions expressed in it, and that statement is subsequently delivered to the registrar, every director who is in default commits an offence (see *subsection (4)*). The penalty for this offence is set out in *subsection (5)*.

Section 644: Registration of resolution and supporting documents

963.   This section sets out the requirements as to delivery of the solvency statement and other key documents to the registrar. The resolution to reduce capital itself must be filed with the registrar within the same time period as currently applies – that is, within 15 days of the date that it is passed (see section 30) and it will not take effect until the solvency statement and statement of capital (see *subsections (1)* and *(2)*) are registered by the registrar. As with all circumstances where the company makes an alteration to its subscribed capital, the company is required to deliver a statement of capital to the registrar (see note on section 619).

964.   In addition to making a solvency statement in accordance with section 643, the directors must also make a statement confirming that the solvency statement was made not more than 15 days before the date on which the resolution to reduce capital was passed and that this statement was provided to the company's members in accordance with section 642 – see *subsection (5)*.

965.   In addition to the new offences which are set out in sections 643(4) (directors making solvency statement without reasonable grounds for the opinion expressed in it) and *subsection (7)* (company delivering solvency statement that was not provided to members to registrar), where a company fails to comply with any of the filing requirements under section 644, an offence is committed by the company and every officer of the company who is in default (see *subsection (8)*). The penalty for this offence is set out *subsection (9)*.

Sections 645 to 649: Reduction of capital confirmed by the court

966.   These sections replace or restate various provisions in the 1985 Act that are concerned with reductions of capital confirmed by order of the court.

967.   Sections 645 and 646 restate section 136 of the 1985 Act which is concerned with the procedure for making an application to court to confirm a reduction of capital (including the creditors' right to object). If, on such an application, an officer of the company intentionally or recklessly conceals a creditor or misrepresents the nature or amount of a debt owed by the company, or is knowingly concerned in any such concealment or misrepresentation he commits an offence (see section 647). As now the court may make an order confirming the reduction of capital on such terms and conditions as it thinks fit (see section 648 which restates section 137 of the 1985 Act).

968.   Section 649 replaces section 138(1) to (4) of the 1985 Act. Under section 138 of that Act, a resolution to reduce capital using the existing court approved scheme takes effect when the court order confirming the reduction and minute of the reduction are registered by the registrar. The minute (which must be approved by the court) sets out key information regarding the company's share capital immediately after the reduction. Section 649 updates the 1985 Act provisions by replacing the current requirement for a minute of the reduction with a statement of capital (see note on section 619). Like the minute confirming the reduction, this statement must be approved by the court.

969.   In line with the CLR's recommendations (Final Report, paragraph 13.11), *subsection (3)(a)(i)* of this section provides that a reduction of capital that forms part of a compromise or arrangement under Part 26 of the Act will take effect at the same time as other aspects of that compromise or arrangement: namely on delivery of the court order confirming the reduction (and statement of capital approved by the court) to the registrar (unless the court orders that it should take effect on the registration of these documents) (see new *subsection (3)(a)(ii)*).

970.   In all other cases, that is, where the reduction of capital does not form part of a compromise or scheme of arrangement under Part 26, where a company reduces its share capital using the court approved procedure the reduction will, as now, take effect on registration of the court order confirming the reduction (and statement of capital) by the registrar. *Subsection (5)* requires the registrar to certify the registration of the order and statement of capital. *Subsection (6)* restates section 138(4) of the 1985 Act in relation to such certificate.

Section 651: Expedited procedure for re-registration as a private company

971.   This section, together with section 650, substantially restates section 139 of the 1985 Act and provides for the consequences where the court confirms the reduction by a public company of its share capital below the authorised minimum (defined in section 763): in particular they facilitate the re-registration of the company as private.

972. *Subsection (3)* replaces section 139(4) of the 1985 Act. It introduces a requirement to send a copy of the court's order (that is, the order authorising the company to be so re-registered without its having passed a special resolution) to the registrar, together with an application for re-registration. The current requirement for the application to be signed by a director (or secretary) has not been retained.

Sections 652 and 653: Effect of reduction of capital

973. These sections restate section 140 of the 1985 Act (with the exception of references to the "minute" being replaced with references to the statement of capital) which is concerned with the liability of a company's members in respect of any amounts unpaid on its shares following a reduction of capital. As now, there are special rules where a creditor was omitted from the list of creditors settled by the court.

CHAPTER 11: MISCELLANEOUS AND SUPPLEMENTARY PROVISIONS

Section 654: Treatment of reserve arising from reduction of capital

974. This is a new provision which enables the Secretary of State, by order, to specify the circumstances in which a reserve arising from a reduction of capital will be distributable.

975. Whilst there is no requirement in the Act (or indeed the 1985 Act) to create a statutory reserve following such a reduction, we understand that it is usual for companies to create an accounting reserve in these circumstances to "balance the books" (that is, the section relates to reserves that arise as a result of generally accepted accounting treatments). Currently, the question whether a reserve arising from a reduction of capital (which, for a limited company, may currently only be made pursuant to a court order) may be treated as a realised profit for the purposes of computing whether a company has sufficient distributable profits to make a distribution, is the subject of technical guidance issued by the Institutes of Chartered Accountants. The Act introduces a new procedure which enables private companies to reduce their share capital without going to court (see section 641) which is not on all fours with the court approved route (in particular there is no requirement to settle a list of creditors or to provide security for the company's debts) and in the circumstances it is desirable to deal with the question of when amounts credited to such a reserve should be treated as a realised profit in statute. Owing to the technical nature of the rules that will need to be made this issue will be dealt with in secondary legislation. An order made under section 654 will however be subject to the affirmative resolution procedure – that is, the regulations will need to be approved by both Houses of Parliament.

Section 656: Public companies: duty of directors to call meeting on serious loss of capital

976. Section 656 restates section 142(1) and (3) of the 1985 Act. It sets out the procedure that must be followed where the net assets of a public company fall below half (or less) of the company's called up share capital. *Subsection (4)* imposes liability on any director who knowingly authorised or permitted a failure to call a meeting as required by this section.

Section 657: General power to make further provision by regulations

977. This is a new provision which enables the Secretary of State, in regulations made under the Act, to modify various provisions in Part 17 of the Act (see *subsection (1)*).

978.   Regulations made under this section may amend or repeal any of the specified provisions or make such other provision as appears to the Secretary of State appropriate in place of those provisions. This will enable the Secretary of State to future-proof the specified provisions in this Part of the Act.

979.   Regulations made pursuant to the power in this section are subject to the affirmative resolution procedure.

PART 18: ACQUISITION BY LIMITED COMPANY OF ITS OWN SHARES

980.   This Part replaces various provisions in Chapters 6 and 7 of Part 5 of the 1985 Act and makes substantive changes to some of those provisions. Sections 658 to 659, 662, 666 to 677, 680 to 683, 687, 691, 693, 695 to 701, 704 to 706, 710 to 713, 716 to 719, 721 to 726, 728 to 729, 731 and 733 to 736 restate various provisions in the 1985 Act but do not make any changes to those provisions.

CHAPTER 1: GENERAL PROVISIONS

Sections 660 and 661: Shares held by company's nominee

981.   These sections restate sections 144 and 145(1) and (2) of the 1985 Act, but with the clarification that they apply to shares taken by a subscriber to the memorandum as nominee of the company.

Section 663: Notice of cancellation of shares

982.   This section restates section 122(1)(f) and (2) of the 1985 Act and Schedule 24 to that Act. *Subsections (2) and (3)* update the current notice requirements to require a company that has cancelled shares in order to comply with section 662 to provide the registrar with a statement of capital (see note on section 619) at the time of giving notice of the cancellation.

Section 664: Re-registration as private company in consequence of cancellation

983.   This section replaces section 147(2) and (3) of the 1985 Act. These provisions have been updated to reflect the fact that in future it will not be possible to alter the memorandum and that key information of a type which was previously in the memorandum will now be in the articles (see note on section 8). The resolution to re-register as a private company in consequence of a duty to cancel shares will however still need to be filed with the registrar under Chapter 3 of Part 3 of the Act.

984.   There is also a new requirement, in *subsection (3)*, for the application for re-registration to be accompanied by a statement of the company's proposed name on re-registration, *Subsections (5) and (6)* are also new. Consistent with the approach taken where a company is formed as a private company under the Act (see section 9), where a public company applies to re-register as private under this section the application for re-registration must be accompanied by a statement of compliance (see note on section 13).

Section 665: Issue of certificate of incorporation on re-registration

985.   This section replaces section 147(4)(a) of the 1985 Act and restates section 147(4) and (4)(b) of that Act. As with the previous section, the provision has been updated to reflect the fact that in future companies will not be capable of, and will not need to, alter their memoranda. *Subsection (3)* is new. Consistent with the approach taken in Part 7 of the Act, a certificate of incorporation issued on the re-registration of a company under section 664 will

need to specify that it is being issued on the re-registration of the company and the date on which it is issued.

CHAPTER 2: FINANCIAL ASSISTANCE FOR PURCHASE OF OWN SHARES

986.   The following sections replace Chapter 6 of Part 5 of the 1985 Act which contains a prohibition on the giving of financial assistance (broadly defined) by a company or any of its subsidiaries for the purpose of the acquisition of shares in itself. There are exceptions which apply to all companies, contained in section 153 of the 1985 Act, and a relaxation of the general rule for private companies in sections 155 to 158 of that Act.

987.   As recommended by the CLR (Final Report, paragraph 10.6), the Act abolishes the prohibition on private companies giving financial assistance for a purchase of own shares and, as a consequence, the relaxation for private companies (sometimes referred to as the "whitewash" procedure) is no longer required. The provisions in sections 155 to 158 have therefore been repealed and are not carried forward in the Act.

Section 678: Assistance for acquisition of shares in public company

988.   This section replaces section 151(1) and (2) of the 1985 Act and restates section 153(1) and (2) of that Act. The key change is that the prohibition on private companies providing financial assistance for a purchase of own shares is not carried forward.

989.   The general prohibition on the giving of financial assistance by a public company is required by the Second Company Law Directive (77/91/EEC) and this prohibition is retained in *subsection (1)*. As under the current law, the prohibition extends to post-acquisition assistance (see *subsection (3)*).

990.   The prohibition on the giving of post-acquisition assistance only applies if the company in which the shares were acquired is a public company at the time that the assistance is given (see subsection (3)). It follows that where a company has re-registered as a private company since the shares were acquired and is a private company at the time the post-acquisition assistance is given, the prohibition in this section will not apply. However, if at the time the shares were acquired the company was a private company, but at the time the post-acquisition assistance is given it has re-registered as a public company, the prohibition will apply.

991.   The provisions of section 153(1) and (2) of the 1985 Act are retained in *subsections (2) and (4)* which carry forward the current exemption from the prohibition on the giving of financial assistance: namely, that such assistance is not prohibited if the principal purpose of the assistance is not to give it for the purpose of an acquisition of shares, or where this assistance is incidental to some other larger purpose of the company and (in either case) where the assistance is given in good faith in the interests of the company. As now, in these circumstances no offence is committed by the company or its officers (see section 680). The changes introduced by section 678 also give statutory effect to the decision in *Arab Bank plc v. Mercantile Holdings Ltd* [1994] 2 All ER 74: namely, that the statutory prohibition on a company giving financial assistance for the purpose of acquiring its own shares or shares in its holding company does not apply to the giving of assistance by a subsidiary incorporated in an overseas jurisdiction.

992.   In the Arab Bank case, Millett J considered the geographical scope of section 151 of the 1985 Act and concluded that this had inadvertently been altered during the consolidation

of UK companies legislation in 1985. In particular, the 1985 Act appears to go further than the 1980 Act and, in interpreting the current provision, Millett J applied the presumption that, in the absence of a contrary intention, section 151 could not have extra-territorial effect. The difficulty with the 1985 Act provision arises as a result of how the prohibition is framed: in particular, the prohibition applies *"to the company or any of its subsidiaries"* and "subsidiary", as defined in section 736 of the 1985 Act, includes foreign companies. The prohibition in the Act is restricted to UK public companies and their UK subsidiaries as a result of the definition of "company" in section 1. Subsection (1) of that section makes it clear that, unless the context otherwise requires, "company" means a company which is formed and registered under the Act or a former UK Companies Act.

Section 679: Assistance by public company for acquisition of shares in its private holding company

993.   This section replaces sections 151(1) and (2) and 153(1) and (2) of the 1985 Act.

994.   Like section 678 this section does not carry forward the prohibition on private companies providing financial assistance for a purchase of own shares, but the current prohibition on the giving of financial assistance by a public company subsidiary for the purpose of an acquisition of shares in its private holding company is retained. Section 679 also retains the prohibition on the giving of post-acquisition assistance by a public company subsidiary.

CHAPTER 3: REDEEMABLE SHARES

995.   Under section 159 of the 1985 Act a company that is limited by shares, or limited by guarantee and having a share capital, may, if authorised to do so by its articles, issue shares which may be redeemed at a future point in time at the option of the company or the shareholder. The provisions of section 159 are carried forward in the following sections but there are changes to the ways in which companies may issue redeemable shares and redeem such shares (see below).

Section 684: Power of limited company to issue redeemable shares

996.   This section replaces section 159(1) of the 1985 Act and restates section 159(2) of that Act.

997.   For private companies only, it removes the requirement for prior authorisation in the company's articles for a proposed allotment of redeemable shares. If they wish, the members may, however, restrict or prohibit the authority given to a company by this section, by including a provision to this effect in the company's articles (see *subsection (2)*).

Section 685: Terms and manner of redemption

998.   This replaces section 160(3) of the 1985 Act (which provides that the terms and manner of redemption must be set out in the company's articles) and existing section 159A (also entitled "terms and manner of redemption"), which was inserted into the 1985 Act by section 133 of the Companies Act 1989 and remains uncommenced.

999.   As recommended by the CLR (Final Report, paragraph 4.5), this section enables the directors of both private and public companies alike to determine the terms, conditions and manner of a redemption of redeemable shares. The power conferred on the directors by this

section requires prior authorisation by the company's members, either by resolution of the company or through the articles (see *subsection (1)*). As recommended by the CLR (Final Report, paragraph 7.30) the terms and conditions of redemption will have to be stated in the statement of capital required to be filed under section 555. If the directors are not authorised to set the terms of the redemption, then they must be set out in the company's articles (see *subsection (4)*).

1000.   Where the directors exercise this power they must do so before the shares in question are allotted (see *subsection (3)*).

Section 686: Payment for redeemable shares

1001.   This section replaces section 159(3) of the 1985 Act (which requires that where a company issues redeemable shares, the terms of redemption must provide for payment on redemption). It removes the current requirement, in section 159(3), that the terms of redemption must provide for payment on redemption. This means that the terms of redemption may provide for the company and the holder of the shares to agree that payment may be made on a date later than the redemption date.

Section 688: Redeemed shares treated as cancelled

1002.   This section restates section 160(4) of the 1985 Act but with the exception of the reference to the impact of the redemption on the authorised share capital of the company – the concept of which is not replicated under the Act.

Section 689: Notice to registrar of redemption

1003.   This section restates section 122(1)(e) and 122(2) of the 1985 Act and Schedule 24 to that Act but there is a new requirement for a statement of capital where a company gives notice to the registrar of a redemption of redeemable shares (see *subsections (2) and (3)* and the note on section 619).

CHAPTER 4: PURCHASE OF OWN SHARES

1004.   Section 162 of the 1985 Act enables a company limited by shares or limited by guarantee and having a share capital to purchase its own shares, provided it is authorised to do so by the articles. It is common for the members to give authority for such a purchase of own shares through the articles, see, for example, regulation 35 of the Companies Act 1985, Table A.

Section 690: Power of limited company to purchase own shares

1005.   This section replaces section 162(1) of the 1985 Act and restates section 162(3) of that Act.

1006.   In line with the recommendations of the CLR (Completing the Structure, paragraph 2.15), section 690 removes the requirement for prior authorisation in a company's articles for a purchase of own shares (including any redeemable shares) by the company but makes it clear that, if they wish, the members may restrict or prohibit a purchase of own shares by including a provision to this effect in the company's articles.

Section 692: Financing of purchase of own shares

1007.   This section restates, the provisions of section 160(1) and (2) and 162(2) of the 1985 Act on a redemption of own shares which are applicable to a purchase of own shares, and makes such adaptations to those provisions as are necessary to ensure that the restated provisions work in this context.

Section 694: Authority for off-market purchase

1008. This section replaces sections 164(2) and 165(2) of the 1985 Act and restates sections 164(1), (3) and (4) and 165(1) of that Act.

1009. Under the 1985 Act a company may only enter into a contract for an off-market purchase of shares if the shareholders approve the contract by special resolution before the contract is entered into. An off-market purchase of shares is a purchase that is not conducted through a recognised investment exchange (for example, the London Stock Market).

1010. Section 694 enables a company to enter into a contract for an off-market purchase of its own shares conditional on the contract being approved by the shareholders. This will save companies valuable time as it will be possible for the directors to negotiate and agree the terms of a contract for an off-market purchase of shares ahead of seeking shareholder approval. If, however, the shareholders do not subsequently pass a special resolution approving the contract, the company may not purchase the shares in question and the contract will lapse.

Section 702: Copy of contract or memorandum to be available for inspection

1011. This section replaces section 169(4) and (9) of the 1985 Act. Under the 1985 Act, where a company enters into a contract for a purchase of own shares it must make available for inspection a copy of the relevant contract or a memorandum of its terms at the company's registered office for a period of 10 years. *Subsection (4)* alters the current requirements by providing that the contract may, alternatively, be kept available for inspection at a place specified in regulations made under section 1136. If the company is a private company, the contract must be available for inspection by any of its members; otherwise it must be open to inspection by anyone. If default is made an offence is committed by the company and every officer in default.

1012. *Subsection (5)* is a new provision which requires companies to give notice to the registrar of the place where the contract is kept available for inspection. This is consequential on the choice conferred on companies under subsection (4) as to where such documents are kept.

Section 703: Enforcement of right to inspect copy or memorandum

1013. This section replaces section 169(7) of the 1985 Act and Schedule 24 to that Act. It retains the existing offences for failing to keep available/allow inspection of the contract/memorandum as required under section 702, but with the addition of a new offence for failure to notify the registrar of the place where such documentation is kept. It also restates section 169(8) of the 1985 Act.

Section 707: Return to registrar of purchase of own shares

1014. This section replaces section 169(1), (1A) and (1B) and restates section 169(2), (3) and (6) of the 1985 Act and Schedule 24 to that Act. It requires a company to make a return to the registrar within 28 days of a purchase of own shares stating, amongst other things, the number and nominal value of the shares purchased. The return must indicate whether the shares are of a type which could be held in treasury (see section 724), and, if so, whether the shares were cancelled forthwith or whether they are being held in treasury.

Section 708: Notice to registrar of cancellation of shares

1015.   This section replaces sections 169(1), (1A) and (1B) and restates 169(6) of the 1985 Act and Schedule 24 to that Act. It updates the notice requirements so as to require that where shares are cancelled forthwith following a purchase (either in circumstances where the shares are treated as automatically cancelled or where treasury shares are cancelled) the company has to notify the registrar of such cancellation and provide the registrar with a statement of capital (see note on section 619).

1016.   As now, where a company fails to comply with the procedural requirements as to notice, the company, and every officer of the company who is in default, commits an offence (see *subsection (4)*).

CHAPTER 5: REDEMPTION OR PURCHASE BY PRIVATE COMPANY OUT OF CAPITAL

1017.   Sections 171 to 177 of the 1985 Act provide a statutory scheme for the redemption or purchase of own shares out of capital. This scheme is available to private companies only and the facility to redeem or purchase shares out of capital is carried forward in the following sections.

Section 709: Power of private limited company to redeem or purchase own shares out of capital

1018.   This section replaces section 171(1) of the 1985 Act and restates section 171(2) of that Act. It removes the current requirement for prior authorisation in the articles where a private company makes a payment out of capital in respect of a redemption or purchase of its own shares. If they wish, the members may, however, restrict or prohibit such a payment by including a provision to this effect in the company's articles.

Section 714: Directors' statement and auditor's report

1019.   This section replaces section 173(3) to (5) of the 1985 Act.

1020.   Currently, before a private company may make a payment out of capital in respect of a purchase of own shares, the directors must have made a full enquiry into the affairs and prospects of the company and are required, under section 173, to make a statutory declaration confirming that: as regards the company's situation immediately after the date on which the payment out of capital is made, there will be no grounds on which the company could then be found unable to pay its debts; and as regards the company's prospects for the year immediately following that date, the company will be able to continue to carry on business as a going concern and be able to pay its debts as they fall due in the year immediately following the date on which the payment out of capital is made. In forming their opinion on the company's solvency and prospects, the directors must take into account the same liabilities (including contingent and prospective liabilities) as would be relevant under section 122 of the Insolvency Act 1986 (winding up by the court) to the question whether a company is unable to pay its debts.

1021.   Consistent with the approach taken in respect of reductions of capital using the new solvency statement procedure (see sections 642 and 643 and in particular subsection (2) of section 643), this section requires a private company limited by shares that wishes to use this statutory scheme for a purchase or redemption of shares to take account of all contingent and prospective liabilities, not just those that are relevant for the purposes of section 122 of the Insolvency Act 1986 (see *subsection (4)).*

1022. Again, to achieve consistency with the approach taken elsewhere in the Act, the current requirement for a statutory declaration is replaced with a requirement for a simple statement. In contrast to a statutory declaration, the directors' statement does not need to be sworn before a solicitor or Commissioner of Oaths.

Section 715: Directors' statement: offence if no reasonable grounds for opinion

1023. This section restates section 173(6) of the 1985 Act and Schedule 24 to that Act (but substitutes the reference to "declaration" with "statement"). The offence that is currently contained in subsection (6) of section 173 (offence of making declaration without reasonable grounds) is replaced with an offence of making a statement under section 714 without having reasonable grounds for the opinion expressed in it. As now, the offence is committed by every director of the company who is in default.

Section 720: Directors' statement and auditor's report to be available for inspection

1024. This section replaces section 175(6)(a) and (7) and restates section 175(4), (6)(b), and (8) of the 1985 Act and Schedule 24 to that Act. *Subsection (2)* alters the current requirement, contained in section 175(6)(a), by providing that the directors' statement and auditor's report may, alternatively, be kept available for inspection at a place specified in regulations made under section 1136. There is a new requirement (in *subsection (3)*) for the company to give notice to the registrar of the place where the statement and report are kept available for inspection and of any change to that place. This change is consequential on the change introduced by subsection (2).

1025. *Subsection (5)* provides that if the company fails to give such notice to the registrar within 14 days or an inspection of the statement and report are refused, the company and every officer in default commit an offence.

CHAPTER 6: TREASURY SHARES

1026. Where a company buys back its own shares, it is normally required to cancel those shares. Certain companies (principally those which are listed or those which are traded on the Alternative Investment Market and equivalent companies in the EEA) may elect not to cancel shares which have been bought back but may hold the shares "in treasury". A share which is held in treasury may be sold at a future point in time and this facility enables such companies to raise capital more quickly than they would otherwise be able to, as the directors do not have to obtain prior authority from the company's members before selling treasury shares.

Section 727: Treasury shares: disposal

1027. This section replaces section 162D(2) of the 1985 Act and restates section 162D(1)(a) and (b) and 162D(3) of that Act. It defines (*in subsection (2)*) what is meant by "cash consideration" where treasury shares are sold and this mirrors, in part, the definition in section 583 (which restates section 738(2) to (4) of the 1985 Act and defines when a share is deemed to be paid up or allotted for cash).

1028. *Subsections (2)(e), (3) and (5) are new.* They enable the Secretary of State to specify, by order, what, in addition to the items specifically referred to in *subsection (2)*, constitutes "cash consideration" for the purposes of *subsection (1)(a)*.

1029. The power to make further provision in respect of what constitutes "cash consideration" for the purposes of a sale of treasury shares (that is, in addition to those already specified in subsection (2)) is intended to remove uncertainties surrounding other methods of settlement, for example, the CREST settlement system (see note on section 583) and will also act as a future proofing mechanism in the event that new methods of settlement are developed or identified.

Section 730: Treasury shares: notice of cancellation

1030. This section restates sections 169A(1)(b)(i), (2) to (4) of the 1985 Act and Schedule 24 to that Act. As now, where a company cancels shares which it has held in treasury it is required to give notice of this to the registrar within 28 days of the cancellation. The provision has, however, been updated to require companies to file a statement of capital in these circumstances (see note on section 619).

Section 732: Treasury shares: offences

1031. This section replaces section 162G of the 1985 Act. It renders both the company and every officer in default liable to an offence for any contravention of the provisions of this Chapter.

Section 737: General power to make further provision by regulations

1032. This section is a new provision which enables the Secretary of State, by regulations, to modify the provisions of Part 18 (see *subsection (1)*).

1033. Regulations made under this section may amend or repeal any of the provisions in this Part or make such other provision as appears to the Secretary of State appropriate in place of those provisions.

1034. The power to make regulations in this section will enable the Secretary of State to "future-proof" the provisions in Part 18 – which are primarily concerned with the maintenance of capital. This is desirable as many of these provisions are derived from EU law and may require amendment in the relatively near future (subject in part to the outcome of a fundamental study into alternatives to the current capital maintenance regime which is being carried out at EU level).

1035. Regulations made pursuant to the power in this section are subject to the affirmative resolution procedure, which means that they must be approved by both Houses of Parliament.

PART 19: DEBENTURES

1036. This part restates the provisions of the 1985 Act relating to debentures. Sections 738-740, 742 and 749-754 make no change to the law.

Section 741: Registration of allotment of debentures

1037. This is a new section which obliges a company to register an allotment of debentures as soon as practicable, but in any event within two months after their allotment. It completes the picture as regards the existing requirement in section 185(1) of the 1985 Act (which is restated in section 769(1)) which obliges a company to complete and deliver certificates for debentures within two months after their allotment.

Section 743: Register of debenture holders

1038. This section replaces section 190 of the 1985 Act. There is no requirement for a company to keep a register of debenture holders but if such a register is kept, then it (or any duplicate) must be kept available for inspection at either the company's registered office or a place permitted under regulations made under section 1136. (This is the same as for the obligatory registers of members, see section 114.)

Section 744: Register of debenture holders: right to inspect and require copy

1039. This section replaces part of section 191 of the 1985 Act. It modifies the existing right of public access to any register of debenture holders kept by a company. The changes mirror similar requirements in Part 8 relating to the register of members. *Subsections (3)* and *(4)* require those seeking to inspect or to be provided with a copy of the register to provide their names and addresses, the purpose for which the information will be used, and, if the access is sought on behalf of others, similar information for them.

Section 745: Register of debenture holders: response to request for inspection or copy

1040. This is a new provision. It provides a procedure by which the company can refer the matter to the court if it considers the request is not for a proper purpose. It specifies a 5-day period within which the company must either comply with the request or apply to the court for relief from the obligation. If the company opts for the latter, then *subsections (3), (4) and (5)* apply. Under *subsection (3)*, if the court is satisfied that the access to the register of debenture holders is not sought for a proper purpose, it will require the company not to comply with the obligation to meet the request and may require that the person who made the request pay the company's costs. Under subsection (4), the court may also require the company not to comply with other requests made for similar purposes. If the court does not make an order under subsection (3), or the proceedings are discontinued, then, under subsection (5), the company must immediately comply with the request.

Section 746: Register of debenture holders: refusal of inspection or default in providing copy

1041. This section retains the existing sanctions under section 191 of the 1985 Act for failure to comply with a request. They do not apply if the court has directed that the company need not comply with the request.

Section 747: Register of debenture holders: offences in connection with request for or disclosure of information

1042. This is a new provision. It creates two offences. First, in relation to the new requirement in section 744 to provide information in a request for access, it is an offence knowingly or recklessly to make a statement that is misleading, false or deceptive in a material particular. Second, it is an offence for a person having obtained information pursuant to an exercise of the rights in section 744 to do anything or fail to do anything which results in that information being disclosed to another person knowing or having reason to suspect that the other person may use the information for a purpose that is not a proper purpose.

Section 748: Time limit for claims arising from entry in register

1043. This section replaces section 191(7) of the 1985 Act. It amends the existing time limit for claims arising from errors in the register from twenty years to ten years. This mirrors equivalent provisions applicable to the register of members (see section 128).

PART 20: PRIVATE AND PUBLIC COMPANIES

1044. The provisions of this Part set out the two major differences between public and private companies.

1045. Chapter 1 replaces sections 58(3), 81 and 742A of the 1985 Act which provide that private companies are not allowed to offer their shares to the public.

1046. Chapter 2 replaces sections 117 and 118 of the 1985 Act which deal with the minimum share capital requirement for public companies (known as the "authorised minimum"). It contains new provisions that enable this requirement to be satisfied in euros as well as sterling. To facilitate this change it has been necessary to seek two new powers:-

a) a power to prescribe the amount in euros that is to be treated as equivalent to the sterling amount of the authorised minimum (see section 763); and

b) a power to prescribe how references to the authorised minimum in the Act are to be applied where a public company has shares denominated in more than one currency or redenominates its share capital (that is, converts its share capital from one currency to another) and to require that a company must re-register as a private company where the effect of redenomination is to bring the value of the company's share capital below the authorised minimum (see section 766).

1047. The authorised minimum is relevant to all public companies, not just those that are incorporated as such, see for example, section 91.

CHAPTER 1: PROHIBITION OF PUBLIC OFFERS BY PRIVATE COMPANIES

1048. The CLR considered the prohibition on private companies offering their shares to the public in paragraph 4.160 of Developing the Framework and then examined the dividing line between public and private companies in Chapter 2 of Completing the Structure. The CLR presented their conclusions in paragraphs 4.54 to 4.62 of the Final Report.

Section 755: Prohibition of public offers by private company

1049. *Subsection (1)* of this section continues the prohibition in section 81(1) of the 1985 Act on private companies offering their shares or debentures to the public, though the consequences of breaching the prohibition are changed. The prohibition applies only to private companies limited by shares or limited by guarantee and having a share capital. The prohibition does not apply to unlimited companies or to companies limited by guarantee and not having a share capital.

1050. Private companies are also prohibited from allotting their shares or debentures with the intention that they are offered to the public by someone else. *Subsection (2)* creates a presumption as to when shares or debentures have been allotted in this way. Similar provision was made in section 58(3) of the 1985 Act which this subsection replaces.

1051. A private company will no longer commit an offence if it offers its securities to the public. Instead, if a private company does breach the prohibition it will be compelled to re-register as a public company, unless it appears to the court that the company does not meet the requirements for re-registration and that it is impractical or undesirable to require it to take steps to do so, in which case the court may make a remedial order and/or an order for the compulsory winding up of the company.

1052. *Subsection (3)* contains an exemption to the prohibition on public offers. Where a private company intends to become a public company it will be able to make an offer before it has completed the formalities of re-registration as a public company. Acts done in good faith before allotment in anticipation of re-registration will not be treated as breaching the prohibition on offers to the public, even if the re-registration arrangements do not ultimately succeed. The exemption also applies if, as part of the terms of the offer, the company undertakes to re-register as a public company and then complies with that undertaking not later than 6 months after the day on which the offer is first made to the public.

Section 756: Meaning of "offer to the public"

1053. This section explains what is meant by "offer to the public" for the purposes of the prohibition on public offers contained in section 755. This section also sets out certain circumstances where an offer is not to be regarded as an offer to the public. It replaces section 742A of the 1985 Act.

1054. An offer will not be an offer to the public if it is not calculated to result in shares or debentures of the company becoming available to anyone other than those receiving the offer. An example would be where shares are offered to a particular person, with the intention that no one other than that particular person may take up the offer or acquire the shares as a result. Nor will an offer be an offer to the public if the offer is otherwise a private concern of the person receiving it and the person making it.

1055. *Subsection (4)* creates two further exemptions for offers to persons already connected with the company (as defined in *subsection (5)*) and for offers in respect of securities to be held under an employees' share scheme (as defined in section 1166). Such offers are presumed to be the private concern of those involved and so not an offer to the public if the conditions set out in subsection (4) are met.

1056. The range of persons already connected with the company for the purposes of subsection (4) has been expanded slightly from the current provision in section 742A of the 1985 Act. *Subsection (5)* now includes a trustee of a trust where the principal beneficiary is an existing debenture holder of the company or the widow or widower, or surviving civil partner of a person who was a member or employee of the company.

1057. *Subsection (6)* explains what is meant by a member of a person's family for the purposes of subsection (5).

Section 757: Enforcement of prohibition: order restraining proposed contravention

1058. This section enables members, creditors or the Secretary of State to apply to the court for an order restraining a private company from carrying out any proposed contravention of the prohibition on offering shares or debentures to the public. This is a new procedure which will enable the member, the creditor or the Secretary of State to prevent by civil action any further activity by the company towards making an offer in contravention of the public offer prohibition. The court must also make such an order if, in proceedings brought by a member under section 994 or by the Secretary of State under section 995, it appears to the court that the company is proposing to breach the public offer prohibition.

Section 758: Enforcement of prohibition: orders available to the court after contravention

1059. This section applies where a private company breaches the prohibition on offering securities to the public. It introduces a new enforcement procedure for breaches; it replaces the criminal offence currently imposed in section 81 of the 1985 Act with a civil enforcement procedure.

1060. If a company breaches the prohibition, certain members, certain creditors or the Secretary of State may apply to the court. In order to have standing to bring the application, the member or creditor must have been a member or a creditor at the time the offer was made in contravention of the public offer prohibition; in addition anyone who became a member as a result of the offer to the public may bring an application.

1061. On such an application, if the court decides the company has acted in contravention of the public offer prohibition then it must order the re-registration of the company as a public company, unless it appears to the court that the company does not meet the requirements for re-registration as a public company (see Part 7 of the Act), and it is impracticable or undesirable to require it to take steps to do so. If the court is unable to order re-registration for these reasons, it may instead make a remedial order or an order for the compulsory winding up of the company (see Chapter 6 of Part 4 of the Insolvency Act 1986). The court has discretion as to whether or not to make these orders. This might be appropriate for example where the company has breached the prohibition but has not allotted shares, and has withdrawn the offer and undertaken not to do it again.

Section 759: Enforcement of prohibition: remedial order

1062. A remedial order is an order for the purpose of putting anyone affected by the breach of the public offer prohibition back in the position they would have been in if the breach had not occurred. It may require any person knowingly concerned in the contravention, whether or not an officer of the company, to offer to purchase the shares or debentures that were the subject of the offer on such terms as the court thinks fit. The remedial order will override the terms of the company's constitution, but no one holding the securities will be obliged to accept the offer made to purchase them. It may be made whether or not the holder of the securities subject to the order is the person to whom the company allotted or agreed to allot them.

Section 760: Validity of allotment etc not affected

1063. This section makes clear that any allotment or sale of securities or any agreement to allot or sell securities is not made void simply because there has been a breach of the prohibition on offers to the public. Equivalent provision was made in section 81(3) of the 1985 Act.

CHAPTER 2: MINIMUM SHARE CAPITAL REQUIREMENT FOR PUBLIC COMPANIES

1064. Under the 1985 Act, a public company which is incorporated as such may not do business without first obtaining a trading certificate from the registrar. There is a minimum allotted share capital requirement, known as the "authorised minimum", which is currently set at £50,000 and which must be denominated in sterling. The same minimum share capital requirement applies where a private company re-registers as a public company under Part 7 of the Act.

1065. If a public company reduces its share capital below the authorised minimum it will no longer meet the minimum share capital requirement for a public company and must re-register as a private company.

1066. The requirement for public companies to have a minimum share capital is derived from EU law. Article 6 of the Second Company Law Directive (77/91/EEC) provides that:

> "The laws of member states shall require that in order that a company may be incorporated or obtain authorisation to commence business, a minimum share capital shall be subscribed the amount of which shall not be less than 25,000 euros."

1067. The Department's interpretation of this Directive is that it permits the authorised minimum to be denominated in euros, or the national currency of the Member State, but not in other currencies (so for example, the authorised minimum could not be satisfied in dollars).

1068. When this requirement was implemented in the Companies Act 1980 the amount of the authorised minimum was set at £50,000 (a figure considerably higher than the minimum required under the Directive). The CLR considered whether the authorised minimum should be maintained, increased or reduced. Their recommendation was to maintain it at £50,000.

Section 761: Public company: requirement as to minimum share capital

1069. This section replaces section 117(2) of the 1985 Act and restates section 117(1), (4) and (6) of that Act. Like the provisions of the 1985 Act, it only applies to public companies that are formed as such on their original incorporation (as opposed to companies that re-register from private limited to public under the provisions of Part 7 of the Act).

1070. The current requirement for a statutory declaration to be filed with an application for a trading certificate, contained in section 117(2) of the 1985 Act, has not been carried forward. This is replaced by a requirement for a statement of compliance (see section 762 and the note on section 13).

1071. As now, the registrar will only issue a trading certificate if she is satisfied that certain conditions are met: in particular the company must satisfy the minimum share capital requirement for public companies – known as the "authorised minimum" (see *subsection (2)*).

1072. A trading certificate has effect from the date that it is issued and is conclusive evidence that the company is entitled to do business as a public company.

Section 762: Procedure for obtaining certificate

1073. This section replaces section 117(3) of the 1985 Act. It prescribes the contents of the application for a trading certificate (see *subsection (1)*), which, amongst other things, must include a statement that the nominal value of the company's share capital is not less than the authorised minimum.

1074.   The current requirement for a statutory declaration (or "electronic statement") when an application is made for a trading certificate is replaced by a requirement to make a statement of compliance. This statement does not need to be witnessed and may be made in paper or electronic form. It will be for the registrar's rules to specify who may make this statement (and the form of it).

Section 763: The authorised minimum

1075.   This section replaces section 118(1) of the 1985 Act. Under section 118 the authorised minimum is £50,000. This implements Article 6 of the Second Company Law Directive which requires that in order that a public company may be incorporated or obtain authorisation to commence business, a minimum capital shall be subscribed (see above). As recommended by the CLR (Completing the Structure, paragraph 7.6), this section retains the authorised minimum at £50,000. In contrast to the 1985 Act provisions, the section also enables the minimum share capital requirement for public companies to be satisfied in sterling or the prescribed euro equivalent (see *subsection (1)*).

1076.   Once a company has obtained a trading certificate under section 762 or section 117 of the 1985 Act (in the case of companies that obtain a trading certificate before these provisions of the Act come into force), there is no requirement for the authorised minimum to remain denominated in sterling or euro, and if it wishes a public company may subsequently redenominate all of its share capital (including the authorised minimum) under the provisions of Chapter 8 of Part 17 of the Act (which contains new provisions which permit companies easily to redenominate or convert their share capital from one currency to another).

1077.   *Subsection (2)* of section 763 contains a new power which enables the Secretary of State, in regulations made under the Act, to prescribe the amount in euros that is for the time being to be treated as equivalent to the sterling amount of the authorised minimum. This is required in order to achieve parity between the prescribed sterling and euro amounts (which may become necessary due to exchange rate fluctuations). The amount prescribed will be determined by applying an appropriate spot rate of exchange to the prescribed sterling amount and rounding to the nearest 100 euros (see *subsection (4)*).

1078.   The power to alter the authorised minimum, contained in section 118 of the 1985 Act, is carried forward in section 764.

Section 764: Power to alter authorised minimum

1079.   This section replaces section 118(1) of the 1985 Act and restates section 118(2) and (3) of that Act. The power to alter the authorised minimum, contained in section 118, is carried forward but this has been updated to reflect the fact that in future companies will be able to satisfy the authorised minimum in sterling or the prescribed euro equivalent of the sterling amount (see section 763).

1080.   Section 764 also contains a new provision which enables the Secretary of State, in regulations made under the Act, to alter both the sterling amount of the authorised minimum and to make a corresponding alteration to the prescribed euro equivalent (which is to be determined by applying an appropriate spot rate of exchange to the sterling amount and rounding up to the nearest 100 euros – see *subsection (2)*).

1081.   As now, the power in this section will enable the Secretary of State to alter the sterling amount of the authorised minimum, for example from £50,000 to £60,000, (and the prescribed euro equivalent) should it become necessary to do so (for example, because of changes to the prescribed minimum capital requirement for public companies at EU level) or desirable (for example, if it was considered appropriate for business reasons to raise or lower the minimum share capital requirement for public companies within the limits permitted by the Second Company Law Directive).

Section 765: Authorised minimum: application of initial requirement

1082.   This section is a new provision which prescribes how the authorised minimum is to be met. Subsection (1) makes it clear that the authorised minimum may be satisfied by reference to allotted share capital denominated in sterling or euros (but not a combination of both).

1083.   Where a company has allotted sterling and euro shares, the question of whether the authorised minimum has been satisfied will be determined firstly by reference to the total sterling amount of the company's allotted share capital and then by reference to the company's euros shares (see *subsection (2)*). To take an example, if a company has allotted sterling shares to the total value of £25,000 and euro shares to the equivalent of £60,000, the authorised minimum will have been satisfied in euros. If the same company had allotted sterling shares to the total value of £10,000 and euro shares to the equivalent of £40,000 it would not have satisfied the minimum share capital requirement for a public company as the authorised minimum may be satisfied in sterling or euro but not partly in sterling and partly in euro.

Section 766: Authorised minimum: application where shares denominated in different currencies etc

1084.   This section is a new provision which enables the Secretary of State to prescribe, in regulations made under the Act, how references to the authorised minimum are to be applied where a public company has its share capital denominated in more than one currency, or where it redenominates (converts) its share capital from one currency to another (see section 622).

1085.   There are various provisions in the Act (for example where a public company applies to court to reduce its share capital) which provide that a company must re-register as a private company where the nominal value of its allotted share capital falls below the authorised minimum. It is therefore necessary to make provision for how references to the authorised minimum in the Act are to be applied where a public company has its shares denominated in different currencies, or currencies other than those in which the authorised minimum may be satisfied, and to require that a company must re-register as a private company where the effect of a redenomination of its share capital is to bring the value of the company's share capital below the authorised minimum.

1086.   To take an extreme example, the type of scenario that the power in this section is intended for is the situation where a public company incorporates with a share capital of £50,000 (expressed in sterling), allots additional dollar shares, subsequently redenominates part of its share capital into euros and then applies to the court to reduce its share capital. It will be necessary in such circumstances to determine what test should be applied to ascertain whether the company's allotted share capital has fallen below the authorised minimum (in other words what exchange rates must be applied, as at what date they should be applied and as between what currencies). Regulations made pursuant to this section will need to deal with this type of issue. They will be subject to the negative resolution procedure due to their highly technical nature.

Section 767: Consequences of doing business etc without a trading certificate

1087.   This section restates section 117 (7) and (8) of and Schedule 24 to the 1985 Act.

1088.   As now, where a public company which is required to have a trading certificate enters into a transaction without first obtaining such a certificate, the directors are jointly and severally liable for any loss or damage caused to the other party to the transaction as a result of the company failing to meet its obligations. A director will only be jointly and severally liable with the company if he was a director at the time that the transaction was entered into and if the company has failed to meet its obligations under the transaction in question within 21 days of being called on to do so (see *subsection (3)*).

1089.   Notwithstanding the fact that the company should not have entered into the transaction, the transaction itself is valid.

1090.   Where a public company that is formed under this section, or under section 117 of the 1985 Act, has not obtained a trading certificate within a year of its incorporation, it may be wound up by the court (see section 122(1)(b) of the Insolvency Act 1986).

PART 21: CERTIFICATION AND TRANSFER OF SECURITIES

CHAPTER 1: CERTIFICATION AND TRANSFER OF SECURITIES: GENERAL

1091.   Sections 768 to 770, 772 to 779 and 781 to 782 in this Chapter restate the provisions in Part 5 of the 1985 Act (sections 183 to 189) relating to the certification and transfer of shares and other securities.

Section 771: Procedure on transfer being lodged

1092.   Under section 183(5) of the 1985 Act, if a company refuses to register a transfer of shares (or debentures), it must, within two months of receipt of the transfer, send to the transferee notice of its refusal to register the transfer of shares. Such a refusal will not affect the transferee's beneficial interest in a share, for example, he will still be entitled to any dividend declared on that share, and a return of capital on winding-up, but the transferee will not be able to exercise all of the rights of a member of the company, for example, he may not vote at meetings, until such time as the transfer is registered and his name is entered in the register of members.

1093.   Section 771 is a new provision which amends the law on the registration of transfers. As recommended by the CLR, it requires the directors to either register a transfer of shares or debentures or provide the transferee with reasons for their refusal to register (see Final Report, paragraphs 7.44 and 7.45).

1094.   In either case, this must be done as soon as practicable, but in any event within two months of the transfer being lodged with the company.

1095.   Under *subsection (2)*, where the directors refuse to register the transfer of a share, the transferee is entitled to receive such information as he may reasonably require regarding the reasons for the directors' refusal to register the transfer. Such information does not extend to minutes of meetings of the directors.

1096. Where a company fails to comply with this section, the company and every officer of the company who is in default commits an offence (see *subsection (3)*).

1097. *Subsection (5)* makes it clear that this section does not apply to a transfer of shares if the company has issued a share warrant in respect of the shares under section 779 or in relation to a transmission of shares by operation of the law (for example, where a bankrupt member's trustee in bankruptcy or a deceased member's personal representative becomes entitled to shares).

Section 780: Duty of company as to issue of certificates on surrender of share warrant

1098. This provision is new and makes it clear that a company must issue a share certificate where a share warrant is subsequently surrendered for cancellation. It gives a company two months from the date of surrender to complete and have ready for delivery a certificate of the shares specified in the warrant and failure to do so is a criminal offence (see *subsection (3)*). This requirement is subject to any contrary provisions in the company's articles, which may give the company more or less time to deliver such certificates to the transferee (see *subsection (2)*).

CHAPTER 2: EVIDENCING AND TRANSFER OF TITLE TO SECURITIES WITHOUT WRITTEN INSTRUMENT

1099. This Chapter replaces the existing power under section 207 of the 1989 Act relating to transfer of securities without a written instrument but goes beyond it in that it can be used to require, as well as to permit, the paper-free holding and transfer of shares or other securities. The provisions that make changes to the power are in sections 784, 786, 787 and 789.

Section 784: Power to make regulations

1100. This section provides for the power to make regulations about the transfer of title to securities without written instrument to be exercisable by the Secretary of State or the Treasury. Responsibility for section 207 of the 1989 Act and the regulations made under it passed from the Department of Trade and Industry to HM Treasury by virtue of article 2(1) of the Transfer of Functions (Financial Services) Order 1992 (S.I. 1992/1315) as part of a general transfer of responsibility for financial services matters. Dual responsibility is considered more appropriate for the making of regulations under the new power as the extension of paperless holding and transfer to new classes of shares or other securities involve matters which are part of company law. Exercise of the power will continue to be subject to the affirmative procedure.

Section 786: Provision enabling or requiring arrangements to be adopted

1101. This section provides that regulations under this Chapter may require, as well as permit, the paper-free holding and transfer of securities. The effect of *subsections (1) and (2)* is that regulations made under section 207 may:

- enable members of companies, or of designated classes of company, by ordinary resolution, to adopt a new form of paperless holding and transfer of shares and abandon paper-based forms of holding and transfer in relation to all existing and new securities of that company, or to specified types of securities; or

- make the adoption of a form of paperless transfer and the abandonment of paper-based forms of transfer mandatory for all securities, or specified types of securities, issued by companies generally or by designated classes of company.

1102. Regulations do not need to make it obligatory both to hold and to transfer securities in a paper-free way: the new arrangements could relate just to holding or just to transfer.

1103. *Subsection (3)* is designed to protect the right of individual investors to continue to hold shares in their own names rather than through nominees. It ensures that the new arrangements prescribed in the regulations will not mean that:

- people who would have been entitled to have their names entered in the company's register of members will lose that entitlement; or

- people who are entitled to exercise rights in respect of securities will lose that right.

1104. *Subsection (4)* provides that the regulations will be able to:

- prohibit the issue of share certificates or certificates for other types of security. Holders of securities to which any such prohibition applies will lose the option of continuing to hold certificates and transfer their shares by paper-based methods;

- ensure that such holders of securities are sent periodic statements of their holdings;

- make provision about the evidential value of certificates or statements.

Section 787: Provision enabling or requiring arrangements to be adopted: order-making powers

1105. This section provides additional flexibility by enabling Ministers to designate, by order (subject to negative resolution procedure), companies or classes of company to which the regulations are to apply, or to modify the effect of the regulations (or disapply them) in relation to a designated class of companies or specified companies.

Section 789: Duty to consult

1106. Ministers will be obliged to consult such persons as they consider appropriate before making regulations or designating a class of companies by order under the new powers. This obligation reflects the breadth of the proposed new powers, as well as the technical nature of some of the regulations which could be made under it.

PART 22: INFORMATION ABOUT INTERESTS IN COMPANY'S SHARES

BACKGROUND

1107. The provisions of this Part concern a public company's right to investigate who has an interest in its shares. They replace equivalent provisions in Part 6 of the 1985 Act. These are purely domestic provisions, and are not required by European Community Law.

1108. The automatic disclosure obligations currently contained in sections 198 to 211 of Part 6 of the 1985 Act will be replaced by regulations under the Financial Services and Markets Act 2000, as amended by Part 43 of this Act, in implementation of the Transparency Obligations Directive. In the regulations, a different concept of "interest in voting rights" will be adopted in order to implement the Transparency Obligations Directive.

1109. This Part re-enacts, with certain modifications, the disclosure obligations pursuant to a notice issued by the company contained in sections 212 to 219 of the 1985 Act. There is no change to the definition of "interest in shares" for this purpose.

1110. The main changes to section 212 of the 1985 Act and related provisions are:

- making clear that notices are not required to be in hard copy, and therefore can be given in electronic form (section 793 read in conjunction with the provisions in Part 37 on the sending or supplying of documents or information);

- providing for how information is to be entered on the register of interests disclosed when the name of the present holder of the shares is not known or there is no present holder (section 808);

- removing the requirement on the company to verify third party information supplied in response to a section 793 notice before putting it on the register (section 817);

- requiring a company to refuse a request to inspect the register if it is not satisfied that the request is made for a proper purpose (section 812);

- removing the requirement for a company to keep information on the register in relation to entries made more than six years previously (section 816).

Section 791: Companies to which this Part applies

1111. This section provides that this Part only applies to public companies (as section 212 of the 1985 Act provides currently).

Section 792: Shares to which this Part applies

1112. This section re-enacts in part the definition in section 198(2) of the 1985 Act of the type of shares concerning which a section 793 notice may be issued, namely shares carrying rights to vote in all circumstances at general meetings. However, shares held by a company "in treasury" following a purchase of its own shares (as an alternative to cancelling such shares on purchase) are now included in the definition.

Section 793: Notice by company requiring information about interests in its shares

1113. This section re-enacts section 212(1) to (4) of the 1985 Act. It allows a public company to issue a notice requiring a person it knows, or has reasonable cause to believe, has an interest in its shares (or to have had an interest in the previous three years) to confirm or deny the fact, and, if the former, to disclose certain information about the interest, including information about any other person with an interest in the shares.

1114. *Subsections (3) and (4)* enable the company to require details to be given of a person's past or present interests and to provide details of any other interest subsisting in the shares of which he is aware. This provision allows the company to pursue information through a chain of nominees by requiring each in the chain to disclose the person for whom they are acting. Under *subsection (6)*, where the addressee's interest is a past one, a company can ask for information concerning any person by whom the interest was acquired immediately subsequent to their interest. Particulars may also be required of any share acquisition agreements, or any agreement or arrangement as to how the rights attaching to those shares should be exercised (sections 824 and 825).

1115. This section serves a different purpose to the automatic disclosure obligations currently contained in sections 198 to 211 of Part 6 of the 1985 Act. It enables companies to discover the identity of those with voting rights (direct or indirect) that fall below the thresholds for automatic disclosure, and it also enables companies (and members of the company) to ascertain the underlying beneficial owners of shares.

1116. The notice is not required to be in hard copy (see the general provisions on sending or supplying documents or information in Part 37 of the Bill). Notices, and responses thereto, may be given in electronic form. A response must be given in a reasonable time. What is reasonable has not been defined so as to allow flexibility according to the circumstances, but if the time given is not reasonable, the company will not have served a valid notice.

Sections 794 and 795: Notice requiring information: order imposing restrictions on shares and offences

1117. These sections re-enact section 216(1) to (4) of the 1985 Act. They specify the penalties for failure to provide information within the specified time when served with a notice under section 793. There are criminal penalties (although a person does not commit an offence if he can show that the requirement to give information was frivolous or vexatious).

1118. Additionally, application may be made to the court for a direction that the shares in question are to be subject to the restrictions specified in section 797.

Section 796: Notice requiring information: persons exempted from obligation to comply

1119. This section re-enacts section 216(5) of the 1985 Act. It provides that the Secretary of State may exempt a person from complying with a notice. The Secretary of State must consult the Governor of the Bank of England, and must be satisfied that there are special reasons for exempting the person (taking account of any undertaking given).

Sections 797 to 802: Orders imposing restrictions on shares

1120. These sections restate Part 15 of the 1985 Act without substantive change in so far as its provisions apply in relation to Part 22 of this Act. They set out the effect of a court order made under section 794 imposing restrictions on shares, and the penalties for attempted evasion of the restrictions. They also make provision for the relaxation or removal of restrictions, or for an order for the sale of shares.

Section 803: Power of members to require company to act

1121. This section re-enacts section 214(1) and (2) of the 1985 Act. It requires a company to exercise its powers under section 793 on the request of members holding at least 10% of such of the paid up capital of the company as carries the right to vote at general meetings (other than voting rights attached to shares held in treasury). This provision, which has rarely been used under the 1985 Act, recognises that members of a company may have a legitimate reason for wanting the company to exercise its statutory powers to demand information even if the management does not want to. For example, the members might want to act where they suspect that the directors are involved in building a holding from behind the shelter of nominees.

1122. Provision is made as to the form and the procedure in relation to requests. In contrast to section 214, the 10% threshold may be met by a series of requests from members that the company act, rather than one collective request. Those making a request must not only specify the manner in which they require the powers to be exercised, but must also give reasonable grounds for requiring the company to exercise the powers in the manner specified (*subsection (3)(b)(ii) and (iii)*).

Section 804: Duty of company to comply with requirement

1123.   This section re-enacts section 214(4) and (5) of the 1985 Act. It specifies the criminal penalties arising if the company fails to act as required. In contrast to section 214, every officer in default is liable to a fine, but the company itself is not.

Section 805: Report to members on outcome of investigation

1124.   This section re-enacts section 215 of the 1985 Act. It specifies that on the conclusion of an investigation required by members it is the duty of the company to prepare a report of the information received. The report must be available within a reasonable period (not exceeding 15 days) after the conclusion of the investigation. Where the company's investigation exceeds three months, it must make interim reports available at three monthly intervals. Those making the request must be notified of reports being available. In contrast to section 215, the report may be kept at the company's registered office or at a place specified in regulations made under section 1136.

Section 806: Report to members: offences

1125.   This section re-enacts section 215(8) of the 1985 Act. It specifies the criminal penalties arising if the company fails to report as required on the outcome of the investigation or to keep the report under section 805. Unlike section 215, every officer in default is liable to a fine for a failure to report, but the company itself is not.

Section 807: Right to inspect and request copy of reports

1126.   This section re-enacts provisions in section 219 of the 1985 Act. It requires the company to allow reports to members to be inspected by anyone without charge. Any person can request a copy of a report, on payment of the prescribed fee. *Subsections (3) to (5)* specify the criminal penalties arising if the company fails to disclose a report as required and make provision for the courts to compel disclosure.

Section 808: Register of interests disclosed

1127.   The register required to be kept by section 211 of the 1985 Act covers all interests notified, whether under the automatic disclosure rules or in response to a notice served under section 212 of that Act (company investigations). The latter are kept as a separate part of the register of interests in shares. In future it will be for regulations made under the Financial Services and Markets Act 2000 (as amended by Part 43 of this Act) to make provision as to how interests notified under the automatic disclosure rules will be made public.

1128.   This section provides that if, as a result of a section 793 investigation, the company receives information relating to interests held by any person in relevant shares, it must within three days enter in a register of interests disclosed:

- the fact that the requirement (to disclose information under the notice) was imposed and the date on which it was imposed; and

- the information received in response to the notice under section 793.

1129. The section provides that the information must be entered either against the name of the present holder of the shares in question (as under the 1985 Act), or if the present holder is not known or there is no present holder, then against the name of the person holding the interest. *Subsections (5) and (6)* provide for criminal penalties for any default in complying with this section. *Subsection (7)* makes clear that information that a company receives under this Part does not mean that the company needs to be concerned with the existence of any trust over the shares.

Sections 809 and 810: Register to be kept available for inspection; and associated index

1130. These sections re-enact section 211(6) and (8) (as applied by section 213(3)) of the 1985 Act. Section 809 provides that the register of interests disclosed must be kept available for inspection at the company's registered office or at a place specified in regulations made under section 1136. The company must advise the registrar where the register is kept (unless it has always been kept at the registered office). *Subsections (4) and (5)* provide for criminal penalties for any default in complying with this section.

1131. Section 810 provides that the register should have an index unless it is in a form that itself constitutes an index (for example a searchable database).

Section 811: Right to inspect and require copy of entries

1132. This section re-enacts section 219 of the 1985 Act. It provides that the register and index must be open to inspection by any person without charge. For a prescribed fee, any person is entitled to a copy of any entry on the register. A person seeking access to the register under this section must provide the information specified in *subsection (4)*, including his name and address and the purpose for which the information is to be used.

Section 812: Court supervision of purpose for which rights may be exercised

1133. This section provides that the company must only allow the inspection of the register or provide the copy requested if satisfied that it is for a proper purpose. If it refuses, the person concerned may apply to the court for it to allow the inspection or require the copy to be provided. If an application to the court is made, the person must notify the company, and the company must use its best endeavours to notify any persons whose details might be disclosed.

Section 813 Register of interests disclosed: refusal of inspection or default in providing copy

1134. This section provides for court enforcement and criminal penalties for any default in complying with section 811.

Section 814 Register of interests disclosed: offences in connection with request for or disclosure of information

1135. This section provides for criminal penalties for misleading, false or deceptive statements given when making a request under section 811. It also makes it a criminal offence for the person who receives information under section 811 to disclose it to another person, if he knows or has reason to suspect that it may be used for an improper purpose.

Section 815: Entries not to be removed from register

1136. This section re-enacts section 218 of the 1985 Act. It provides that entries can only be removed from the register in accordance with sections 816 and 817, and if wrongly deleted must be restored as soon as reasonably practicable. *Subsections (3) and (4)* provide for criminal penalties for any default in complying with this section.

Section 816: Removal of entries from register: old entries

1137. Section 217(1) of the 1985 Act provides that a company may remove an entry against a person's name from the register of interests in shares if more than six years have elapsed since the date of the entry being made, and either:

- the entry recorded the fact that the person in question had ceased to have an interest notifiable under Part 6 in the company's relevant share capital (in which case the person's name may also be removed from the register); or

- the entry has been superseded by a later entry against the same person's name.

1138. By contrast, this section simply provides that a company is not required to keep information on the register if more than six years have elapsed since the entry was made.

Section 817: Removal of entries from register: incorrect entry relating to third party

1139. This section re-enacts in part section 217 of the 1985 Act but does not include the requirement for the company to verify information relating to third parties supplied in response to a section 793 notice. However, the third party retains the right to apply to have his name removed from the register if the information is incorrect. *Subsection (4)* provides for the courts to enforce removal of incorrect information.

Section 818: Adjustment of entry relating to share acquisition agreement

1140. This section re-enacts section 217(4) and (5) of the 1985 Act. It provides that a person identified in the register as being party to a section 824 share acquisition agreement (this may include a concert party agreement) may when he ceases to be party to the agreement, request that the register should be amended to record that information. Such entries may appear in several places on the register, as each member of the concert party is required in their individual notification to identify the other members of the concert party. If the company refuses an application, the court may order the company to comply if it thinks fit.

Section 819: Duty of company ceasing to be public company

1141. This section re-enacts provisions in section 211(7) and (10) (as applied by section 213(3)) of the 1985 Act. It provides that a company ceasing to be a public company must continue to keep any register it has kept under section 808 and any associated index for six years after it ceases to be a public company.

Section 820: Interest in shares: general

1142. This section re-enacts the definition of "interest in shares" in section 208 (as applied by section 212(5)) of the 1985 Act for the purposes of Part 22 of this Act. An "interest in shares" is widely defined as an interest of any kind whatsoever in the shares, and includes beneficial ownership as well as direct ownership. The courts have described this wide definition as being designed "to counter the limitless ingenuity of persons who prefer to conceal their interests behind trusts and corporate entities" (*re TR Technology Investment Trust plc* [1988] BCLC 256 at 261).

Section 821: Interest in shares: right to subscribe for shares

1143. This section re-enacts section 212(6) of the 1985 Act. It provides that a notice under section 793 applies in relation to rights to subscribe for shares.

Sections 822 and 823: Interest in shares: family and corporate interests

1144. These sections re-enact section 203 (as applied by section 212(5)) of the 1985 Act. They provides for certain family interests to be attributed to persons for the purpose of disclosure, as well as certain interests held indirectly through a corporate body.

Sections 824: Interest in shares: agreement to acquire interests in a particular company

1145. This section re-enacts section 204 (as applied by section 212(5)) of the 1985 Act concerning the obligation to give details of certain share acquisition arrangements in response to a notice under section 793. It covers any agreement or arrangement, whether or not legally binding, which involves undertakings, expectations or understandings that interests in shares will be acquired and that they will be subject to relevant restrictions while the agreement subsists. This may include groups of persons acting in concert to prepare the way for a takeover offer for the company or to support a pending takeover offer.

Section 825: Extent of obligation in case of share acquisition agreement

1146. This section re-enacts section 205 (as applied by section 212(5)) of the 1985 Act. It attributes interests in shares held by a party to a section 824 agreement to the other parties to the agreement.

Section 826: Information protected from wider disclosure

1147. This section re-enacts provisions in section 211(9) (as applied by section 213(3)) and 215(4) of the 1985 Act. Under section 409 the Secretary of State may make regulations exempting a company from the need to disclose information relating to related undertakings in notes to its accounts in certain circumstances. The Secretary of State must agree that the information need not be disclosed. Where advantage is taken of this exemption, the fact must be stated in the company's annual accounts. This section provides that this same information must not be included in a section 805 report, (though its omission must be noted in the report), and must not be available for inspection under section 811.

Section 827: Reckoning of periods for fulfilling obligations

1148. This provision re-enacts the provision of section 220(2) of the 1985 Act concerning the calculation of periods in the Part expressed as a number of working days (as defined in section 1173). In contrast to section 220(2), the definition of "working days" excludes bank holidays only in the part of the UK where the company is registered.

Section 828: Power to make further provision by regulations

1149. This section re-enacts section 210A of the 1985 Act. It confers power on the Secretary of State to make regulations to amend the definition of shares to which this Part applies (*subsection (1)(a)* re-enacting section 210A(1)(a)). Power is also conferred to amend the provisions in section 793 as to notice by a company requiring information about interests in its shares, *(subsection (1)(b)* re-enacting section 210A(1)(e)), and the provisions as to what is to be taken to be an interest in shares, *(subsection (1)(c)* re-enacting section 210A(1)(d)).

PART 23: DISTRIBUTIONS

1150. This Part restates the provisions on distributions in Part 8 of the 1985 Act. The only substantive change is to the rules on distributions in kind, and the new provisions are in sections 845, 846 and 851.

Sections 845 and 846: Distributions in kind

1151. In Capital Maintenance: Other Issues (paragraphs 24 to 43) the CLR explored the difficulties created by the decision in *Aveling Barford Ltd v. Perion Ltd* [1989] BCLC 626 and made a number of suggestions as to how these difficulties might be overcome. Section 845 is a new provision which removes doubts to which the decision in this case has given rise: in particular when a transfer of an asset to a member amounts to a distribution. The concern behind this section is that, following the decision in the *Aveling Barford* case, it is unclear when intra-group transfers of assets can be conducted by reference to the asset's book value rather than its market value (which will frequently be higher than the book value).

1152. The decision in *Aveling Barford* concerned the sale of a property by a company (which had no distributable profits) at a considerable undervalue to another company controlled by the company's ultimate sole beneficial shareholder. The transaction was held to be void as an unauthorised return of capital. Whilst this case decided nothing about the situation where a company that has distributable profits makes an intra-group transfer of assets at book value, there was a concern that, as such a transfer of an asset at book value may have an element of undervalue, the transaction would constitute a distribution thereby requiring the company to have distributable profits sufficient to cover the difference in value. The result has been that companies are often required either to abandon a transfer or to structure it in a more complex way, for example, having the assets revalued and then sold (or distributed under section 276 of the 1985 Act) so that the distributable reserves are increased by the "realised profit" arising on the sale/distribution followed by a capital contribution of the asset to the relevant group member.

1153. Section 845 does not disturb the position in the *Aveling Barford* case such that where a company which does not have distributable profits makes a distribution by way of a transfer of assets at an undervalue, this will be an unlawful distribution contrary to Part 23 of the Act.

1154. It clarifies, however, the position where a company does have distributable profits and provides that where the conditions referred to in *subsection (1)(a) and (b)* are met, the amount of any distribution consisting of or arising from the sale, transfer or other disposition by a company of a non-cash asset to a member of the company should be calculated by reference to the value at which that asset is included in the company's accounts, that is, its "book value". Thus, if an asset is transferred for a consideration not less than its book value, the amount of the distribution is zero, but if the asset is transferred for a consideration less than its book value, the amount of the distribution is equal to that shortfall (which will therefore need to be covered by distributable profits) – see *subsection (2)(a) and (b)*. This avoids the potential need for many companies to carry out asset revaluations requiring professional advice and incurring fees to advisors prior to making a distribution of a non-cash asset.

1155. The conditions that must be satisfied for subsection (2)(a) and (b) to apply are that at the time of the disposition of the asset, the company must have profits available for distribution and that if the amount of such a distribution were to be determined in accordance with this section, it could be made without contravening any of the provisions of this Part (for example, section 830 and section 831).

1156. Under *subsection (3)*, in determining whether it has profits available for distribution (as defined in section 830), a company may treat any profit that would arise on the proposed disposition of the non-cash asset (that is, the amount (if any) by which the consideration received exceeds the book value of the asset) as increasing its distributable profits.

1157. Section 846 replaces section 276 of the 1985 Act which applies where a company "*makes a distribution of or including a non-cash asset*" and allows a company which has revalued assets showing an unrealised profit in the accounts, to treat that profit as a realised profit where the distribution is one of, or including, a non-cash asset. Section 846 tracks the drafting of section 845 so that it applies not only where the company makes a distribution consisting of or including a non-cash asset, but also where a company makes a distribution arising from the sale, transfer or other disposition by it of a non-cash asset, in other words in the same circumstances that are described in section 845.

Section 851: Application of rules of law restricting distributions

1158. This section is a new provision which preserves the existing common law rules on unlawful distributions (see *subsection (1)*) – which continue to be an essential component in determining what amounts to an unlawful distribution.

1159. *Subsection (2)* makes an exception to this: in particular, it provides that the lawfulness and amount of distributions in kind are established by the statutory rules in sections 845 and 846 and not by any applicable common law rules.

PART 24: A COMPANY'S ANNUAL RETURN

1160. This Part restates Chapter 3 of Part 11 of the 1985 Act. It requires every company to deliver to Companies House an Annual Return with the specified information. The only significant difference from the 1985 provisions is that section 857 confers power on the Secretary of State not only to amend or repeal sections 855 and 856 but also, in *subsection (2)(b)*, to make exceptions from the requirements of those sections. (The comparable power in the 1985 Act is only to amend or repeal.)

PART 25: COMPANY CHARGES

CHAPTERS 1 AND 2: COMPANIES REGISTERED IN ENGLAND AND WALES OR IN NORTHERN IRELAND; AND COMPANIES REGISTERED IN SCOTLAND

1161. This Part of the Act provides a scheme for the registration of charges created by a company. Part 12 of the 1985 Act was prospectively repealed and replaced by the 1989 Act, but these amendments and repeals were never brought into force, and they are now themselves being repealed (see Schedule 16).

1162. Chapters 1 and 2 of Part 25 restate Part 12 of the 1985 Act, with a few changes. The principal differences between the restated provisions and those of the 1985 Act are described below.

- Changes have been made to provisions in this Part as a result of other provisions in the Act. So, for example, references to a statutory declaration in sections 403 and 419 of the 1985 Act are replaced by references to a statement in sections 872 and 887. Additionally changes have been made to sections 408 and 423 of the 1985 Act (now sections 877 and 892 respectively) to enable a company to keep its instruments creating charges and its register of charges in a place other than its registered office, bringing these provisions into line with provisions elsewhere in the Act relating to availability of documents for inspection.

- The provisions relating to charges created by an overseas company in sections 409 and 424 of the 1985 Act have not been restated. Instead section 1052 provides a new regulation-making power for the Secretary of State to make provision about the registration of charges over property in the United Kingdom of an overseas company that has registered its particulars with the registrar under section 1046.

- There are no longer to be daily default fines for the offences under this Part of failure to register a new charge under section 860 or 878 (compare sections 399 and 415 of the 1985 Act) and failure to register an existing charge over acquired property under section 862 or 880 (compare sections 400 and 416).

CHAPTER 3: POWERS OF THE SECRETARY OF STATE

Section 893: Power to make provision for effect of registration in special register

1163. This is a new provision, which provides power for the Secretary of State to make an order providing that, if a charge is registered in another register (for example, the register of floating charges to be established under the Bankruptcy and Diligence etc (Scotland) Bill), then the registrar may not register it, but it will be treated as if it had been registered in accordance with the requirements of Part 25. The power may only be exercised if appropriate information-sharing arrangements have been made between the registrar and the person responsible for the other register. This is to ensure that a person searching of the register will have access to information about charges registered in that other register.

Section 894: General power to make amendments to this Part

1164. This is a new provision providing the Secretary of State with a power to amend the provisions of Part 25.

PART 26: ARRANGEMENTS AND RECONSTRUCTIONS

1165. The provisions of this Part enable companies to apply to the court for an order sanctioning an arrangement or reconstruction agreed with a majority of members or creditors. They restate sections 425 to 427 of the 1985 Act. In addition to drafting changes resulting from the re-arrangement of the provisions, there are two changes of substance.

1166. Section 899(2) makes clear that the persons who may apply for a court order sanctioning a compromise or arrangement are the same as those who may apply to the court for an order for a meeting (under section 896(2));

1167. Section 901 requires a company to deliver to the registrar a court order that alters the company's constitution. It also requires that every copy of the company's articles subsequently issued must be accompanied by a copy of the order, unless the effect of the order has been incorporated into the articles by amendment. These changes are included for consistency with other provisions in the Act concerning such orders.

PART 27: MERGERS AND DIVISIONS OF PUBLIC COMPANIES

1168. The provisions of this Part enable a public company – under certain conditions – to apply to the court for an order under Part 26 sanctioning an arrangement or reconstruction which concerns the merger or division of a public company. They implement the Third Council Directive 78/855/EEC concerning mergers of public limited liability companies and the Sixth Council Directive 82/891/EEC concerning the division of public limited liability companies.

1169. The provisions of this Part restate section 427A and Schedule 15B to the 1985 Act. The opportunity has been taken to put the provisions in a form more closely corresponding to that of the Directives. Chapters 2 and 3 deal separately with mergers and divisions and the provisions within those Chapters broadly follow the order of the provisions of the relevant Directive.

1170. The independence requirements for experts and valuers in sections 936 and 937 are new and correspond to the new independence requirements for a statutory auditor (see section 1214). They include a new power for the Secretary of State to define a disallowed connection for the purposes of determining whether a person is sufficiently independent to be an expert or valuer under this Part. This is consistent with the approach taken in sections 344 and 1151 of the Act.

PART 28: TAKEOVERS ETC

Introduction

1171. This Part implements the European Directive on Takeover Bids (2004/25/EC, the "Takeovers Directive") which was adopted on 21 April 2004 and had to be implemented by 20 May 2006. It also contains a few minor amendments to the existing law not required by the Directive.

Summary and background

1172. With the exception of Chapter 3 which restates, with amendments, Part 13A of the 1985 Act, the provisions in Part 28 are new. The principal body of provisions emerged from the consultation document, "Company Law – Implementation of the European Directive on Takeover Bids" published by the DTI in January 2005. Additionally, the CLR considered issues related to "squeeze-out" and "sell-out" (concerning the problems of, and for, residual minority shareholders following a successful takeover bid) in Chapter 11 and Annex B of "Completing the Structure" and presented their conclusions in Chapter 13 of the Final Report. Certain provisions in this Part have been developed in the light of these conclusions.

Overview of the Part

1173. The Part is divided into 4 Chapters:

- Chapter 1 deals with matters related to the Takeover Panel and its takeover regulatory functions;

- Chapter 2 concerns matters related to barriers to takeovers;

- Chapter 3 contains provisions relating to "squeeze-out" and "sell-out" (concepts designed to address the problems of, and for, residual minority shareholders following a successful takeover bid); and

- Chapter 4 amends the provisions in Part 7 of the 1985 Act about the content of annual reports of companies traded on a regulated market.

Note: It is intended that certain provisions of Part 28 will be extended to unregistered companies with shares traded on a regulated market. This will be achieved by the regulation-making power at section 1043 of the Act. It is necessary to ensure compliance with the Takeovers Directive.

CHAPTER 1: THE TAKEOVER PANEL

SUMMARY AND BACKGROUND

1174. Since 1968, takeover regulation in the UK has been overseen by the Panel on Takeovers and Mergers ("the Panel") which administered rules and principles contained in the non-statutory City Code on Takeovers and Mergers. In order to bring UK takeover regulation within the requirements laid down in the Takeovers Directive, Chapter 1 places it within a statutory framework.

1175. The Panel will supervise takeover activity and similar types of transactions. The Panel will retain considerable autonomy to provide for its own constitution and appointment procedures. However, a minimum constitutional structure is laid down, providing for the Panel to make arrangements for carrying out its functions and, in particular, to function through committees, sub-committees, officers and members of staff. It is envisaged that the Panel will continue to carry out its day-to-day activities through its Executive. Provisions underpinning the funding of the Panel's regulatory activities are also included.

1176. Principally, the Panel is placed under an obligation to make statutory rules giving effect to certain Articles of the Directive. It is also given a statutory rule-making power to make rules in relation to takeover activity and similar types of transactions, reflecting the current field of activity over which the existing Code lays down rules.

1177. Sections 945, 951, 955, 956 and 961 of the Act are intended to limit litigation by: (a) channelling parties to seek decisions of the Panel (including the Panel's Hearings Committee and the independent Takeover Appeal Board) before having recourse to the courts; (b) excluding new rights of action for breach of statutory duty; (c) protecting concluded transactions from challenge for breach of the Panel's rules; and (d) exempting the Panel and its individual members, officers and staff from liability in damages for things done in, or in connection with, the discharge of the regulatory functions of the Panel.

1178. The Bill does not affect the availability of judicial review by the courts. In the takeovers field, in the Datafin case (*R v Panel on Takeovers, ex parte Datafin plc* [1987] QB 815) the Court of Appeal concluded that generally the courts should limit themselves only to reviewing the Panel's decision-making processes after the bid has been concluded.

1179. The Bill confers on the Panel powers to make rulings and directions and to enforce these through the courts, to obtain information and documents from those involved in regulated activities and to impose sanctions on those who transgress its rules.

The Panel and its rules

Section 942: The Panel

1180. This section confers on the Panel the takeover regulatory functions set out in Chapter 1. The Panel is empowered to do anything that it considers necessary or expedient in relation to its prescribed functions and it may also make arrangements for such functions to be carried out on its behalf by a committee or sub-committee of the Panel or an officer or member of staff of the Panel or a person acting as such.

1181. This Chapter does not confer on the Panel the status of a statutory body. The Panel will remain an unincorporated body, as constituted from time to time, and, as such, having rights and obligations under the common law. Those rights and obligations will be supplemented by the specific provisions set out in the Bill.

Sections 943 and 944: Rules; Further provisions about rules

1182. The Panel is given the power to make rules in relation to takeover regulation. The rule-making power is broadly drawn to ensure that the Panel can continue to make rules on the range of matters presently regulated by the City Code on Takeovers and Mergers. The following provisions are included:

a) The Panel is placed under an obligation to make rules as required by specified Articles of the Takeovers Directive. These are the general principles (Article 3.1 of the Directive), jurisdictional rules (Article 4.2), matters related to the protection of minority shareholders, mandatory bid and equitable price (Article 5), contents of the bid documentation (Article 6.1 to 6.3), time allowed for acceptance of a bid and publication of a bid (Articles 7 and 8), obligations of the management of the target company (Article 9) and other rules applicable to the conduct of bids (Article 13). In making rules in relation to these Articles, the Panel will be entitled to exercise Member State options where these are provided for in the Directive. The Panel's rules will not, however, deal with certain matters contained in the Directive such as barriers to takeovers (Article 11), squeeze-out and sell-out (Articles 15 and 16), and information to be published by companies in their annual reports (Article 10) which are more appropriately dealt with in company legislation (and are the subject of further provision at Chapters 2, 3 and 4 of this Part).

b) The Panel is permitted to make rules on takeover bids (including, but not limited to, those which are the subject of the Directive), mergers and other transactions affecting the ownership or control of companies. The power is designed to be broad enough to cover the existing scope of the Code and sufficiently flexible to take account of future market developments. Types of matters currently covered by the Code but not covered by the Directive include the takeovers of companies not traded on a regulated market and transactions involving a change of control of a like nature to takeovers.

1183. When making rules under this section, the Panel must do so by a committee of the Panel, except in the case of rules for fees and charges under section 957 which must be made either by a committee of the Panel or by the Panel itself.

1184. The further provisions about rules that may be made by the Panel under section 944 include the power to grant derogations and waivers, which by virtue of section 943(1) must respect the general principles laid down in Article 3.1 of the Directive.

1185. Section 944(2) to (7) makes provision as to the form, public availability and verification of rules made by the Panel.

Section 945: Rulings

1186. This section enables the Panel, including (by virtue of section 942(3)) its Executive, to make rulings on the interpretation, application or effect of the rules made by the Panel.

1187. To the extent and in the circumstances specified in the rules, a ruling of the Panel has binding effect unless reviewed by the Hearings Committee or successfully appealed to the Takeover Appeal Board in accordance with rules made under section 951. It is envisaged that rules made under sections 943 and 944 will address matters such as notice to parties and right of representation of persons who might be bound by a Panel ruling.

Section 946: Directions

1188. This section allows the Panel to make provision in its rules for it to give a direction preventing a person from breaching the rules (including a direction operating on an interim basis whilst a matter is awaiting determination by the Panel) or otherwise to ensure compliance with the rules.

Information

Section 947: Power to require documents and information

1189. The Panel has historically had no formal power to require those involved in takeover activity to provide it with the information the Panel requires to carry out its functions. Persons authorised under the Financial Services and Markets Act 2000 are required by the rules of the Financial Services Authority to provide information and assistance to the Panel. In relation to others, the Panel has relied on the voluntary co-operation of market participants to provide explanations and documents which are not publicly available.

1190. This section enables the Panel to require the production of such documents and information as it may reasonably require in the exercise of its functions. The Panel may also authorise a person to exercise the powers under the section on its behalf, for example, if the Panel were to appoint a law or accountancy firm to help it collect and analyse documents.

1191. *Subsection (7)* provides that a lien on a document is not affected by the production of that document in compliance with a requirement imposed by the Panel or someone authorised on its behalf. A lien is a legal right to keep possession of a document belonging to someone else until a claim is satisfied – for example, a claim for payment of professional fees. This subsection does not entitle a professional to refuse to hand over a document to the Panel but preserves his rights over those documents.

1192. The section provides that the Panel may require the production of information in hard copy where it is held in some other form (for instance, electronically on a floppy disk).

1193. The Panel may not compel the production of documents which would be protected from disclosure in legal proceedings on the grounds of legal professional privilege or confidentiality of communications.

Sections 948 and 949: Restrictions on disclosure; Offence of disclosure in contravention of section 948

1194. These sections provide that information obtained by the Panel in the course of exercising its functions will be subject to restrictions on onward disclosure. Aside from the desirability of such provisions, so that those providing information to the Panel can do so knowing that it will not be subject to improper further disclosure, these provisions also meet a requirement under Article 4.3 of the Directive that Member States shall ensure that information provided to those employed, or formerly employed, by takeover supervisory authorities shall not be further divulged: *"to any person or authority except under provisions laid down by law."* Section 948, accordingly, prescribes the conditions under which such information can be released.

1195. Information concerning the private affairs of an individual or a business provided to the Panel in connection with its functions may not be disclosed during the individual's lifetime or while the business is carried on without the consent of the individual or business in question except for the purposes of carrying out the Panel's functions or unless it is disclosed to a person or for a purpose set out in Schedule 2.

1196. Schedule 2 sets out the "gateways" for disclosure of information obtained by the Panel in the exercise of its functions which are permitted under section 948, including the circumstances in which a disclosure to an overseas regulatory authority is permitted. Under section 948(4) and (5), the Secretary of State has the power to amend the Schedule, but only to specify persons exercising functions of a public nature or descriptions of disclosure where the purpose for which the disclosure is permitted is likely to assist in the exercise of a function of a public nature.

1197. Section 948(6)(a) provides that certain authorities mentioned in *subsection (7)* are not bound by the restrictions on disclosure imposed by *subsection (2)*. These bodies are those other takeover supervisory authorities and financial services regulators with which the Panel has a duty to co-operate. *Subsection (6)(b)* provides that persons or bodies obtaining information from those authorities (whether directly or indirectly) are also not bound by the restrictions on disclosure imposed by subsection (2). These provisions are necessary to implement fully Article 4.4 of the Directive. Those bodies mentioned in subsection (7), and persons and bodies receiving information from them, will themselves be subject to restrictions on disclosure that will mirror those imposed by section 948, and so information originating from the Panel will still be protected from improper further disclosure.

1198. Section 949 makes it an offence to disclose information in contravention of section 948. A person guilty of such an offence is liable on conviction on indictment to two years' imprisonment or a fine or both; and on summary conviction to twelve months' imprisonment (six months in Scotland and Northern Ireland) or a fine or both. Section 949(1) provides a person with a defence if he can prove that he did not know, and had no reason to suspect, that the information in question had been provided to the Panel in the exercise of its functions; or that he took reasonable steps to prevent wrongful disclosure.

Co-operation

Section 950: Panel's duty of co-operation

1199. Article 4.4 of the Directive requires that takeover supervisory authorities and financial services regulators provide reasonable assistance to other such authorities within the EEA for the purposes of the Directive. This section is designed to give effect to this requirement by obliging the Panel to co-operate with overseas takeover and financial services regulatory authorities.

1200. The form and manner of co-operation will be as the Panel considers appropriate in the light of the circumstances (in particular, its power to require documents and information may be exercised to support such an authority) and may include sharing information which the Panel is not prevented from disclosing. The section mirrors similar co-operation obligations imposed on the Financial Services Authority by section 354 of the Financial Services and Markets Act 2000.

Hearings and Appeals

Section 951: Hearings and Appeals

1201. This section ensures that proper procedures for review of and appeal against decisions taken by the Panel in connection with its regulatory functions are provided. Section 951(1) requires that the rules made by the Panel provide for a decision of the Panel to be subject to review by a "Hearings Committee" when requested by affected persons specified in the rules. Section 951(3) provides that the rules must give a right of appeal to an independent tribunal (the "Takeover Appeal Board") against a decision of the Hearings Committee. The rules may make provision in relation to the Hearings Committee as to procedural matters, evidence and the powers of the Committee. Further, rules may contain provisions related to enforcement of decisions of the Hearings Committee and the Takeover Appeal Board.

1202. The section also requires the rules to provide that:

a) when appearing before the Hearings Committee or the Takeover Appeal Board, the Panel must act through an officer or member of staff of the Panel (who must not be a member of the rule-making committee referred to in section 943(5), the Hearings Committee or the Appeal Board); and

b) no person who is, or has been, a member of the rule-making committee can be a member of the Hearings Committee or the Takeover Appeal Board.

1203. The general rules of natural justice will preclude a person who had taken part in a decision from later considering a review or appeal in relation to that decision.

1204. This approach is designed to ensure a clear and transparent division of responsibilities between the various organs of the Panel in its executive, judicial and rule-making roles.

Contravention of rules, etc

Section 952: Sanctions

1205. This section confers on the Panel the power to make rules for imposing sanctions for breach of its rules or directions given under section 946. The Panel's current sanctions regime, which is set out in the Introduction to the City Code on Takeovers and Mergers and which it is envisaged will remain in place under the Act, provides for private and public statements of censure of persons in breach of the Code.

1206. Particularly flagrant breaches may lead to the Panel publishing a statement indicating that the offender is someone who is not likely to comply. The rules of the Financial Services Authority and certain professional organisations contain provisions obliging their members, in certain circumstances, not to act for a person named in such a statement. This is referred to as "cold-shouldering". The provisions in question cover transactions that are subject to the City Code on Takeovers and Mergers, such as transactions in relevant securities requiring disclosure under rule 8 of the Code. Under section 952, it will continue to be possible, in the case of transactions that are subject to the Panel rules, for the Panel to issue "cold-shouldering" statements in appropriate cases. (The Panel will also be able to pass information concerning breaches of rules to other regulatory authorities and professional bodies by virtue of the statutory "gateways" set out at section 948 and Schedule 2.)

1207. Should future rules made by the Panel confer a power on the Panel to impose a sanction of a kind not contained in the City Code on Takeovers and Mergers as it has effect immediately before the passing of the Act, the Panel must prepare a policy statement in respect of the sanction. The policy statement must set out the policy of the Panel with regard to imposition of the sanction and, for financial penalties, the penalty that may be imposed. An element of the policy must be that the Panel, in making a decision about any such matter, have regard to the seriousness of the breach or failure, the extent to which the breach or failure was deliberate or reckless and whether the person on whom the sanction is to be imposed is an individual.

Section 953: Failure to comply with rules about bid documentation

1208. This section creates new offences in relation to takeover bid documentation (i.e. offer documents prepared by the bidder and documents in response to the bid prepared by the board of the target company). Provisions related to bid documentation are laid down in particular by Articles 6.3 and 9.5 of the Directive which are to be implemented by rules which the Panel are obliged to make under section 943. Consequently, in each case an offence will be committed where the document in question does not comply with rules designated by the Panel as giving effect to those provisions. The offence relating to offer documents may be committed by the bidder and any of its directors, officers or members who caused the offer document to be published. The offence relating to response documents may be committed by directors or other officers of the target company. Where either offence is committed by a corporate body (for instance, a corporate director), provisions are also included dealing with liability of directors, officers or members of that body. In each case, an offence will be committed only where the relevant person knew that the document did not comply (or was reckless as to whether it did so) and failed to take all reasonable steps to ensure that it did comply.

1209. A person guilty of an offence under this provision is liable on conviction to a fine (on summary conviction limited to the statutory maximum).

Section 954: Compensation

1210. This section confers on the Panel the power to make rules providing for financial redress (together with interest (including compound interest)) in consequence of a breach of rules which require monetary payments to be made (for instance, a payment by the bidder to shareholders of any difference between the price actually paid and any higher price for shares that the bidder should have paid under the rules).

Section 955: Enforcement by the court

1211. This section provides a mechanism by which the Panel may, if necessary, apply to the court in order to enforce Panel rule-based requirements as well as requests for documents and information under section 947. The Panel may apply to the court either where there is reasonable likelihood that a person will contravene a requirement imposed by or under the rules or where a person has failed to comply with such a requirement or with a requirement imposed under section 947.

1212.   It is expected that in accordance with usual practice, the court will not, in exercising its jurisdiction under this section, rehear substantively the matter or examine the issues giving rise to the ruling or, as the case may be, the request for documents or information except on "judicial review principles", where there has been an error of law or procedure.

1213.   The court is given a broad discretion as to the order it may make to secure compliance with the requirement; but aside from the power granted to the Panel by this section, there is no right to seek an injunction (or interdict) to prevent a person contravening, or continuing to contravene, a rule-based requirement or disclosure requirement.

Section 956: No action for breach of statutory duty etc

1214.   Compliance with the rules made by the Panel is a matter solely for the Panel. This section does two things:

a) it excludes new rights of action for breach of statutory duty for contraventions of requirements imposed by or under rules or a requirement imposed under section 947; and

b) in order to ensure certainty, it provides that a contravention of a rule based requirement does not make a transaction void or unenforceable and (subject to any provision of the rules) does not affect the validity of any other thing. As currently, transactions will be capable of being set aside or unravelled in cases of, for example, misrepresentation or fraud.

Funding

Section 957: Fees and charges

1215.   This section enables the Panel to make rules for the payment of fees or charges to the Panel for the purposes of meeting the Panel's expenses incurred in exercising its functions. Such fees and charges may be imposed to meet expenses of the Takeover Appeal Board; the cost of repaying capital and paying interest on loans; and the cost of maintaining adequate reserves. The rules under this section must be made by the Panel itself or by a committee of the Panel (section 943(4)).

Section 958: Levy

1216.   This section gives the Secretary of State the power to make regulations imposing a levy for meeting the costs of the Panel. In determining the appropriate rate of the levy, the Secretary of State must take account of other income received, or expected to be received, by the Panel (which would include fees and charges under section 957) and may take account of estimated as well as actual costs of the Panel.

1217.   It is anticipated that a levy would only be imposed if the existing voluntary levy funding arrangements (contributions collected by member firms of the London Stock Exchange and Ofex currently set at a flat rate charge of £1 on contract notes on all chargeable transactions with a consideration in excess of £10,000) were no longer viable. The categories of persons or bodies to which the levy would apply may include only those capable of being directly affected by the exercise of the Panel's functions or otherwise having a substantial interest in the exercise of those functions.

1218. The first regulations made in respect of the levy power – and any further regulations which change the persons or bodies by whom, or the transactions on which, the levy is payable – will be subject to the affirmative resolution procedure in both Houses of Parliament. A draft of an instrument containing such regulations will not be treated as being hybrid even if otherwise it would be. Any other subsequent regulations will be subject to the negative resolution procedure.

Section 959: Recovery of fees, charges or levy

1219. This section provides that an amount payable by a person as a consequence of fees and charges imposed by the Panel under section 957 or as a result of any levy fixed by the Secretary of State under section 958 will constitute a debt owed by that person to the Panel and be recoverable by the Panel as a debt.

Miscellaneous and supplementary

Section 960: Panel as party to proceedings

1220. This section provides that, notwithstanding its unincorporated status, the Panel may in its own name bring proceedings under this Chapter and bring or defend other proceedings.

Section 961: Exemption from liability in damages

1221. This section confers limited immunity on the Panel and those involved in carrying out its regulatory activities. The immunity provisions are consistent with those recently extended to the Financial Services Authority and the Financial Reporting Council in the exercise of their duties under financial services and companies legislation.

1222. The section exempts the Panel, its members, officers and staff (which would include secondees), and persons authorised under section 947(5) by the Panel to exercise its powers in relation to requiring documents and information, from liability in damages for things done or omitted in relation to the Panel's regulatory activities. (The Takeover Appeal Board benefits from a common law immunity on account of its exercise of judicial functions.)

1223. Section 961(3) sets out the circumstances where the exemption will not apply – that is to say, where the act or omission was in bad faith or where it was unlawful under section 6(1) of the Human Rights Act 1998.

Section 962: Privilege against self-incrimination

1224. This section provides that a statement made by a person to the Panel, or a person authorised on its behalf, in compliance with a requirement to provide information under section 947 (or a court order made to secure compliance with such a requirement under section 955) cannot be used against that person in most types of criminal proceedings. Such statements can, however, be used in proceedings for offences of making false statements otherwise than on oath under section 5 of the Perjury Act 1911 and its Scottish and Northern Irish equivalents. These offences exist to deter and punish the making of false statements and it would not be possible to prosecute such offences if the false statements themselves could not be used in evidence against those by whom they were made.

Section 963: Annual reports

1225. As is the Panel's existing practice, the Panel will be required to publish an annual report containing annual accounts, setting out how the Panel's functions were discharged and including other matters considered by the Panel to be of relevance. Annual reports published by the Panel are available on the Panel's website.

Section 964: Amendments to Financial Services and Markets Act 2000

1226. This section repeals section 143 of the Financial Services and Markets Act *2000* ("FSMA") which, by endorsing the City Code on Takeovers and Mergers, presently provides a mechanism for the Financial Services Authority to bring disciplinary and enforcement action against authorised persons for misconduct in relation to the Code. Given that the Code will be replaced by rules which have legal force as a consequence of the Act, it is considered that there is no longer a need to maintain section 143.

1227. This will not, however, preclude the Panel from reporting breaches of the Code by authorised persons in relation to takeover bids to the Financial Services Authority, as at present, and any such breaches will still be taken into account by the FSA, for example, in assessing whether such persons are fit and proper to be authorised for business of that kind or have otherwise complied with their regulatory obligations (for example, whether they are meeting proper standards of market conduct).

1228. A consequential amendment is made by section 964(3) to preserve the definition of "consultation procedures" currently contained at section 143(7) for the purposes of the provisions in *section 144* of FSMA relating to price stabilising rules. Additionally, to ensure consistency with the requirements of Article 4.4 of the Directive as regards the duties of takeover regulatory and financial services authorities within the EU to co-operate with each other, the existing disclosure and regulatory co-operation obligations of the Financial Services Authority under sections 349 and 354 of FSMA are amended to include cooperation with relevant authorities referred to by the Directive and to remove restrictions on disclosure to such authorities. These duties reflect the disclosure and co-operation provisions in sections 948 and 950 (including provisions related to the rules on disclosure that apply where information is passed to other takeover supervisory authorities and financial services regulators described in relation to section 948(6)).

Sections 965 and 973: Power to extend to Isle of Man and Channel Islands

1229. These sections allow any provisions of Chapters 1 and 2 to be extended to the Isle of Man or any of the Channel Islands by Order in Council, with any specified modifications.

CHAPTER 2: IMPEDIMENTS TO TAKEOVERS

Summary and background

1230. Article 11 of the Takeovers Directive seeks to override, in certain circumstances relating to a takeover, a number of defensive devices that may be adopted by companies prior to the bid, such as: differential share structures under which minority shareholders may exercise disproportionate voting rights; restrictions on transfer of shares in the company articles or in contractual agreements; and limitations on share ownership.

1231. There are currently no restrictions on the way that UK companies which are admitted to trading on a regulated market can structure their share capital and control. However, market pressure brought to bear, in particular, by institutional investors has ensured that there are now few UK listed companies with differential voting structures.

1232. As permitted by Article 12 of the Directive, it has been decided not to apply the provisions of Article 11 in all cases but instead to include in the Act (sections 966 to 972) provision for companies with voting shares traded on a regulated market to opt in to its provisions should they choose to do so.

Sections 966, 967 and 970: Opting in and opting out; Further provision about opting-in and opting-out resolutions; Communication of decisions

1233. A company may pass a special resolution opting in to Article 11 (an "opting-in resolution") provided that three conditions are met:

a) it has voting shares admitted to trading on a regulated market (it is not considered necessary to extend this provision to other types of companies which are not covered by the Directive);

b) the company's articles of association do not contain restrictions of the kind mentioned in Article 11 (or other provisions which would be incompatible with Article 11) or, if they do contain such restrictions, the restrictions will not apply in circumstances related to a takeover bid as described by Article 11. Article 11 relates to both the takeover bid period and the time following the bid when the bidder has acquired 75% or more of the company's capital carrying voting rights. It provides that restrictions both on the rights to transfer shares and on voting rights that are contained in the articles of the company should not apply. It also provides that, in certain circumstances, shares carrying multiple voting rights shall only have one vote and extraordinary rights of shareholders concerning the appointment or removal of board members should be disapplied; and

c) no shares are held by a Minister conferring special rights in the company and no such special rights are provided for in law. The Directive expressly provides that Article 11 does not apply to shares held by Member States conferring special rights on the Member State which are compatible with the Treaty, or to special rights provided for in national law which are compatible with the Treaty. The UK Government holds a number of so-called "golden shares" in formerly publicly-owned businesses which have been privatised to ensure that essential public interest considerations are protected. This provision will exclude all such companies where the Government holds the beneficial ownership of a golden share (since holdings by nominees and subsidiaries are also covered). The concept of Minister is broadly defined in section 966(7) of the Act to include Scottish Ministers and Northern Ireland Ministers under section 7(3) of the Northern Ireland Act 1998. (As a result of the Government of Wales Act 2006, the definition of Minister will be changed to include Welsh Ministers). Under section 966(8), a power is provided to the Secretary of State by the negative resolution procedure to apply the provision in section 966(4) (Minister holding golden shares) to persons or bodies exercising functions of a public nature as it applies in relation to a Minister.

1234. Section 966(5) enables a company to revoke an opting-in resolution by means of a further special resolution (an "opting-out resolution").

1235. Section 967 sets down provisions relating to the date on which the opting-in and opting-out resolutions will take effect. Generally, this will be the date stated in the resolution.

1236. Section 970 requires companies, within 15 days of an opting-in or opting-out resolution being passed, to notify the Panel and any other takeover supervisory authority in a Member State in which the company has shares admitted to trading on a regulated market or has requested such admission. Where a company fails to comply with this requirement, the company and every officer in default will be guilty of an offence and be liable on summary conviction to a fine not exceeding level 3 on the standard scale (and to a daily default fine for continued contravention).

Section 968: Effect on contractual restrictions

1237. This section provides that agreements entered into between shareholders in the company on or after 21 April 2004 (the date on which the Takeovers Directive was adopted), and agreements entered into between a shareholder and the company before as well as on or after that date, are invalid in so far as they impose any of the restrictions set out in *subsection (2)*.

1238. Those restrictions relate both to the bid period and to the time following a takeover bid when the bidder holds 75% or more in value of all the voting shares in the company. Types of restrictions overridden are those imposing restrictions on the transfer of shares and on rights to vote at general meetings of the company to decide on action to frustrate the bid and at the first meeting to be held after the end of the offer period. For the purposes of determining when the bidder holds 75% or more in value of all the voting shares in the company, both debentures and shares which do not normally carry rights to vote at a general meeting (such as preference shares) held by the bidder are to be disregarded (see *subsection (8)*).

1239. The provisions related to the types of contractual agreements to which the override will apply (including the date at which such contracts were entered into) and the restrictions which are made invalid are designed to replicate the provisions of Article 11 of the Directive.

1240. Section 968(6) provides that a person who suffers loss as a result of a contractual agreement being overridden can apply to the court for compensation. It is expected that, in the first instance, such compensation will be offered by the bidder in making the takeover offer. Where, however, the compensation offered by the bidder is not acceptable to the person whose rights are being overridden, there is a right to apply to the court. The court will award compensation to the person who suffers loss on a just and equitable basis to be paid by any person (which could include the bidder or the other party to the contract which has been overridden) who would have been liable to him for committing or inducing the breach of contract which would have been committed had the restriction in question not been made invalid by this section.

Sections 969 and 972: Power of offeror to require general meeting to be called; Transitory provision

1241. Section 969 provides the bidder with the special right to require the directors of an opted-in company to call a general meeting of the company when he holds 75% in value of all the voting shares in the company (excluding debentures and shares that do not normally carry rights to vote at a general meeting (such as preference shares)). Section 969(3) applies sections 303 to 305 of the Act, which deal with the calling of meetings, to such a request (with the necessary modifications). But as those sections may not be in force at the time when section 969 comes into force, section 972 makes the same sort of adaptations in relation to the equivalent provisions of the 1985 Act. In particular, section 972(3) alters the application of section 378(2) so that a special resolution may still be passed at a general meeting called at only 14 days' notice (normally at least 21 days' notice would have to be given of the meeting for it to be able to pass a special resolution).

CHAPTER 3: "SQUEEZE-OUT" AND "SELL-OUT"

Summary and background

1242.   The concepts of "squeeze-out" and "sell-out" are designed to address the problems of, and for, residual minority shareholders following a successful takeover bid. Squeeze-out rights enable a successful bidder to compulsorily purchase the shares of remaining minority shareholders who have not accepted the bid. Sell-out rights enable minority shareholders, in the wake of such a bid, to require the majority shareholder to purchase their shares. Because they involve the compulsory purchase or acquisition of shares against the will of the holder of the shares or the acquirer, high thresholds apply to the exercising of such rights and there are protective rules on the price that must be paid for the shares concerned.

1243.   Squeeze-out and sell-out provisions have been a feature of national company law for many years (and were previously contained in Part 13A (Takeover Offers) of the 1985 Act). Articles 15 and 16 of the Takeovers Directive, however, introduce EU-wide rules requiring all Member States to put appropriate provisions in place for the first time. The provisions at sections 974 to 991 of the Act restate Part 13A of the 1985 Act in a clearer form. However, in doing so they also make important changes to reflect the need to ensure compliance with the Directive and the decision to accept some recommendations of the CLR. These are described below.

Detail of changes made to the operation of provisions previously contained in Part 13A of the 1985 Act

1244.   The rules laid down in the Directive in relation to squeeze-out and sell-out are broadly consistent with provisions of Part 13A (sections 428 to 430F) of the 1985 Act. The restated and amended provisions will apply equally to all companies and all bids within the ambit of Part 13A of the 1985 Act, regardless of whether or not the Directive is required to be applied to such companies and bids.

1245.   The following changes are made in implementation of the Directive:

- Calculation of Squeeze-out Threshold (section 979) – there is a dual test imposed: in order to acquire the minority shareholder's shares, the bidder must have acquired both 90% of the shares to which the offer relates, and 90% of the voting rights carried by those shares. Where the offer relates to shares of different classes, then, in order to acquire the remaining shares in a class, the bidder must have acquired 90% of the shares of that class to which the offer relates, and 90% of the voting rights carried by those shares. Under section 429 of the 1985 Act, in each case only the first limb of that test applied.

- Calculation of Sell-out Threshold (section 983) – mirroring the change to be made in relation to the squeeze-out threshold, a dual test is similarly imposed in relation to the sell-out threshold, so that a minority shareholder may force a bidder to acquire his shares (i) when the bidder holds 90% of the shares in the company, and 90% of the voting rights attached to those shares, or (ii) when the bidder holds 90% of the shares in the class to which the minority shareholder's shares belong, and 90% of the voting rights attached to those shares. Under section 430A of the 1985 Act, the test was that the bidder should have acquired 90% of all shares in the company (or in the class concerned).

- Revised Period during which Squeeze-Out and Sell-Out Rights may be Exercised (section 980(2)) – the Directive provides (Articles 15.4 and 16.3) that squeeze-out and sell-out rights must be exercisable within a three month period following the time allowed for acceptance of the bid. Section 429(3) of the 1985 Act provided that squeeze-out could be exercised within a period of four months beginning with the date of the offer and had to be exercised within two months of reaching the 90% threshold. Accordingly, the rule provided by the Directive is substituted for the rule in the 1985 Act. An exception to this rule is provided where takeover bids are not subject to the Directive, for instance takeovers of most private companies. In these cases, the squeeze-out notices must be given within six months of the date of the offer if this is earlier than the period ending three months after the end of the offer. This is intended to prevent offerors in such circumstances continually extending the offer period. A change is also made as regards the period during which sell-out may be exercisable so that this period is to be either three months from the end of the offer or, if later, three months from the notice given to the shareholder of his right to exercise sell-out rights (section 984(2)). An extended period during which the sell-out right can be exercised where notice of such a right is only given after the end of the offer period is consistent with provisions of the Directive allowing more stringent provisions to be put in place (in this case to ensure the proper protection of minority shareholders).

- The court will no longer be able to reduce the consideration in relation to squeeze-out or sell-out following a takeover bid to below the consideration offered in the bid (which the Takeovers Directive presumes to be fair in all cases). Again utilising provisions of the Directive which allow more stringent provisions to be included to protect minority shareholders, minority shareholders will continue to be able to apply to the court to request that consideration higher than that offered in the bid be paid in exceptional circumstances (section 986(4)).

1246. In most instances, it is considered that the first and second changes above will make no practical difference as the percentage of total capital carrying voting rights in a company (or class of shares) and the percentage of voting rights will normally be the same. The provisions about voting rights will not apply where the shares being squeezed out or sold out are non-voting shares.

1247. The CLR also considered the issue of squeeze-out and sell-out and the scope for improving the provisions in the 1985 Act. Its Final Report (chapter 13, pages 282 – 300), made a number of recommendations in relation to the reform of the squeeze-out and sell-out regime. Some of these recommendations are closely related to implementation of the Takeovers Directive. For instance, the CLR questioned whether, in calculating the relevant squeeze-out and sell-out thresholds, only shares that had been unconditionally acquired should be taken into account or whether shares acquired subject to contract should also be included.

1248.   In implementing the Takeovers Directive, the opportunity is being taken to adopt recommendations of the CLR, whether or not related to implementation of the Directive, except to the extent that they are not consistent with Articles 15 and 16 of the Directive or are no longer appropriate as a consequence of the Directive. The recommendations made by the CLR implemented by Chapter 3 of Part 28 are set out below:

Meaning of takeover offer and entitlement to dividends (sections 974 and 976)

1249.   In order to be a takeover offer for the purposes of Part 13A of the 1985 Act, an offer to acquire shares had to be on terms which were the same in relation to all the shares to which the offer related. One problem with the 1985 legislation was how to treat any variations in value between shares of the same class that were attributable to the fact that some of the shares, because they were allotted later, do not yet carry a dividend. Section 976(2) rectifies this problem by providing that, even if the offeror offers to pay more for shares that carry a dividend than for those in the same class which do not, the offer will be treated as being made on the same terms in relation to those shares.

Meaning of a takeover offer and communication of that offer (sections 974 and 978)

1250.   To deal with issues arising from an increasingly globalised market in shares and different legislative regimes outside the EEA, it is made clear that an offer is not prevented from being a takeover offer for the purposes of Chapter 3 of Part 28 merely because there are some offerees who will be unable to accept it (for instance, where the offeree cannot accept the offer because of restrictions on the cross-border transfer of cash or securities in the country in which the offeree resides). It is also provided that an offer can still be a takeover offer for the purposes of the squeeze-out and sell-out provisions if a shareholder has no registered address in the UK and the offer is not communicated to him to avoid contravening the law of another country as long as either the offer itself is published in the Gazette or a notice is published in the Gazette stating that a copy of the offer document can be obtained from a place in the EEA or on a website.

Shares that the offeror has "contracted to acquire" (section 975)

1251.   Clarificatory amendments are made on this issue. Section 428(5) of the 1985 Act dealt with the offeror's position at the start of the bid, for the purpose of determining which shares could not be counted towards the achievement of the 90% threshold (at which point shares may be compulsorily purchased). It was unclear as to whether the phrase "contracted to acquire" in section 428(5) covered conditional as well as unconditional contracts. It is, therefore, clarified that, in ascertaining the offeror's position at the start of the bid, the shares he has conditionally contracted to acquire (other than those subject to irrevocable undertakings (see below), as under the 1985 Act) should be treated as being shares already held by the offeror. This means that only shares that the offeror has either acquired or unconditionally contracted to acquire will count towards the 90% total needed to exercise squeeze-out. Consequential changes are also made to the provisions on joint offers and associates of the offeror to bring these into line with the above.

1252.   Under the 1985 Act, the registered holder of shares could give an irrevocable undertaking to accept a takeover bid, and if he did this for no consideration or only in exchange for a promise to make the bid, his shares were still treated for the purposes of squeeze-out as included within the offer. This is extended to include undertakings given for only negligible consideration and undertakings the effect of which is to require the registered holder to accept the offer (where the undertaking is given by a person who is not the registered holder of the shares but can contract to bind the registered holder, such as the manager of shares held by a bare nominee). ("Irrevocable undertakings" are contractual agreements entered into by a bidder usually with major shareholder(s) of a proposed target company. Such agreements aim to give the bidder certainty – he will know that support for the offer can be guaranteed from shareholders party to the contract – so that his bid has a greater prospect of success. Such undertakings would normally prevent the giver of the undertaking from selling their shares or exercising voting rights to prevent the takeover from becoming successful.)

Date of the offer (section 991(1))

1253. The "date of the offer" is defined to mean either the date of publication, or if the offer is not published or notice of the offer is sent out earlier, the date on which the offeror first sends notice of the offer to the offerees.

Right of offeror to buy out minority shareholders: treatment of options etc (section 979(5))

1254. Where an offeror makes an offer for all the target company's allotted shares and all or any shares subsequently allotted, it is provided that (a) in deciding whether the offeror has reached the 90% threshold for the purposes of section 979, the offeror need only bring into the calculation shares which are actually in issue (i.e. allotted) at the relevant time; (b) if the offeror serves squeeze-out notices and more shares are subsequently allotted which take the percentage of acceptances then received below 90%, that will not invalidate squeeze-out notices already served; and (c) if the offeror wishes to serve further squeeze-out notices, he must have at least 90% acceptances of shares (or shares in a class) then in issue and subject to the offer at the time he sends the notices out.

Consideration not exclusively in cash (section 981(5))

1255. It is clarified that where an offer of shares, or a mixture of shares and cash, is made, and it is no longer possible when the offeror exercises his right of squeeze-out to give the consideration in shares, the offeror should pay the cash equivalent irrespective of whether the shareholders had previously been offered a choice (i.e. whether the offer was "mix and match" or not). Parallel changes are made as regards sell-out (section 985(5)).

Shares that the offeror has "contracted to acquire" (section 983)

1256. It is clarified that, in addition to shares acquired by the offeror, shares subject to both conditional and unconditional contracts of acquisition are included in calculating whether the sell-out threshold has been reached. As a result of this change, there might be circumstances where the 90% threshold required for sell-out to be exercised was reached only because of shares which the offeror had conditionally contracted to acquire. However, if the conditions of such contracts were not fulfilled, the offeror could in fact find that he was being required to buy a minority shareholder's shares even though the offeror had not actually acquired 90% of the shares. So section 983 also provides that, if that is the case at the time when the minority shareholder exercises his right of sell-out, the offeror does not have to purchase the shares unless he has acquired or unconditionally contracted to acquire 90% or more of the shares by the time the period referred to in section 984(2) (the period within which shareholders can exercise sell-out rights) ends. (A corresponding change is made in section 979(6) and (7) to prevent minority shareholders in this situation who have to wait to see if they can exercise sell-out from being squeezed out in the meantime.)

Applications to the Court (section 986)

1257. This section provides that a shareholder receiving a squeeze-out notice may make an application to the court (within six weeks of receiving the notice) seeking to overturn an offeror's intention to purchase his shares compulsorily (or the terms of that purchase). A requirement that the offeror be promptly notified of such an application is now included (this was not previously required by section 430C of the 1985 Act). As a consequence of this requirement, it is also required that the offeror is obliged, at the earliest opportunity, to notify shareholders who are being squeezed out or who are exercising their rights of sell-out, and are not party to a section 986 application, that proceedings have been initiated.

CHAPTER 4: AMENDMENTS TO PART 7 OF THE COMPANIES ACT 1985

Section 992: Matters to be dealt with in directors' report

1258. This section implements Article 10 of the Takeovers Directive. Article 10.1 and 10.2 require companies admitted to trading on a regulated market to provide in their annual reports detailed information relating to matters such as the control and share structures of the company. It is, therefore, provided by amendment to Part 7 of the 1985 Act that the information required by the Directive must be set out in the directors' report.

1259. Additionally, Article 10.3 of the Directive requires boards of companies to present an explanatory report to shareholders on the issues referred to in Article 10.1 and 10.2 at the company's annual general meeting. This section requires this additional explanatory material to be contained in the directors' report submitted to the annual meeting of shareholders.

1260. Section 992(5) amends section 251 of the 1985 Act on summary financial statements. It provides for the explanatory material required by Article 10.3 of the Takeovers Directive either to be included in the summary financial statement or to accompany it.

1261. Failure to include either the information concerning control and share structures or explanatory material in the annual report will attract existing criminal sanctions under section 234(5) of the 1985 Act (directors responsible for the failure to comply with provisions related to the directors' report are to be liable to a fine).

1262. Section 992(6) provides that these new provisions will apply in relation to directors' reports for financial years beginning on or after 20 May 2006 (the date by which the Directive had to be implemented).

1263. These are general requirements designed to bring greater transparency to the market and apply to all relevant companies whether or not they are involved in a takeover. Accordingly, the requirements will apply to all companies registered in the UK which have voting shares traded on a regulated market, whether or not that includes an official listing on the London Stock Exchange.

Under Part 15 of the Act (section 416), the Secretary of State may in future make regulations as to the contents of the directors' report and those regulations will be able to incorporate the provisions introduced by section 992(2) to (4). Regulations under sections 427 and 428 will be able to make provision for the additional explanatory material when a summary financial statement is sent out rather than the full accounts and report.

PART 29: FRAUDULENT TRADING

Section 993: Offence of fraudulent trading

1264. This section restates section 458 of the 1985 Act, but in doing so increases the maximum sentence for the offence from seven years' imprisonment to ten years.

PART 30: PROTECTION OF MEMBERS AGAINST UNFAIR PREJUDICE

1265. Sections 994-998 restate sections 459, 460 and 461 of the 1985 Act, which provide a remedy where a company's affairs are being conducted in a manner which is unfairly prejudicial to the interests of its members.

Section 999: Supplementary provisions where company's constitution altered

1266. Section 999 is a new section which ensures that, if the court makes an order under Part 30 amending the company's articles, updated articles are registered and a copy of the court order is supplied with any copies of the articles that are issued by the company, unless they already incorporate the amendments.

PART 31: DISSOLUTION AND RESTORATION TO THE REGISTER

CHAPTERS 1 AND 2: STRIKING OFF AND PROPERTY OF DISSOLVED COMPANY

1267. These Chapters restate sections 652 to 654 and sections 656 to 658 of the 1985 Act with no changes of effect, except as described below for sections 1003 and 1013.

Section 1003: Striking off on applications by company

1268. Section 652A of the 1985 Act currently provides that, in certain circumstances, a company may apply to the registrar to be struck off the register. The provision is limited to private companies. This section, in restating that provision, no longer includes the limitation, with the effect that public companies too may now apply for voluntary strike-off.

Section 1013: Crown disclaimer of property vesting as bona vacantia

1269. Where a company is dissolved while still holding property, that property passes to the Crown. Section 656 of the 1985 Act provides that the Crown's title to the property may be disclaimed by means of a notice signed by the Crown representative.

1270. At present this disclaimer must generally be executed within 12 months of the date on which vesting of the property came to the notice of the Crown representative or within three years of the Crown representative receiving an application from an interested party. This section, in restating the relevant provisions, extends the 12-month period to three years, and provides that, if the ownership of the property is not established when the Crown representative first has notice that the property may have vested, that period runs from the end of the period reasonably necessary for the Crown representative to establish ownership.

1271. Section 656 of the 1985 Act also provides that a disclaimer may be made within three years of the Crown representative receiving an application from an interested party. This section changes this to 12 months.

CHAPTER 3: RESTORATION TO THE REGISTER

1272. Under the 1985 Act, where a company has been struck off the register, mechanisms are available (sections 651 and 653) by which the company may be restored to the register following a court order. The CLR (Final Report, pages 227 to 229) recommended that an alternative, administrative restoration procedure should be available in certain circumstances. Sections 1024 to 1028 make provision implementing that recommendation.

Section 1024: Application for administrative restoration to the register

1273. This section provides that an application may be made to restore a company that has been struck off under sections 1000 or 1001; that it can be made whether or not the company has also been dissolved; that the application must be made by a former director or former member of the company, and that it must be made within six years of the date of dissolution.

Section 1025: Requirements for administrative restoration

1274. This section sets out the requirements for restoration, including the conditions that the company was carrying on business or in operation at the time of its striking off; that the Crown representative has given any consent that may be necessary; and that the applicant has delivered any documents necessary to bring the registrar's records up to date and has paid any penalties due at the date of dissolution or striking off.

Section 1026: Application to be accompanied by statement of compliance

1275. This section provides that an application for restoration must be accompanied by a statement that the applicant has the necessary standing to make the application and that the requirements for administrative restoration have been met. The registrar may accept the statement of compliance as sufficient evidence of the matters stated in it.

Section 1027: Registrar's decision on application for administrative restoration

1276. This section provides that the registrar must give notice of her decision, and that (if the decision is that the company is restored) the restoration takes effect from the date that notice is sent. The section also sets out the consequential actions the registrar must take.

Section 1028: Effect of administrative restoration

1277. This section provides that the effect of restoration is that the company is deemed to have continued in existence as if it had not been struck off, and that application may be made to the court within three years of restoration for the court to make such directions as may be needed to place the company itself, and other persons, in the same position as they would have been had the company not been struck off.

Restoration to the register by the court

1278. These sections bring together what are currently two separate procedures for a company to be restored to the register by court order (under sections 651 and 653 of the 1985 Act). The CLR recommended (Final report pages 227 to 229) that the two separate procedures be replaced by a single new procedure, which should largely be based on the precedent of the procedure under section 653 of the 1985 Act.

Section 1029: Application to court for restoration to the register

1279. The section sets out that an application may be made for the restoration of companies which have been dissolved, are deemed to be dissolved, or have been struck off under the various provisions set out in *subsection (1)*. *Subsection (2)* sets out the persons who may make such an application.

Section 1030: When application to the court may be made

1280. At the moment, applications to the court under section 651 of the 1985 Act must be made within two years, and under section 653 within twenty years. This new section provides that the time limit for the new single procedure will generally be six years, although special provision is made (*subsection (5)*) for situations where an application for administrative restoration has been made and refused.

1281. *Subsection (1)* makes clear that there is no time limit where the application is for the purpose of bringing proceedings against the company for damages for personal injury.

Section 1031: Decision on application for restoration by the court

1282. This section sets out the circumstances in which the court may order restoration (including any case in which the court considers it just to do so) and provides that restoration takes effect when the court's order is delivered to the registrar. It also requires the registrar to give appropriate public notice of the restoration.

Section 1032: Effect of court order for restoration to the register

1283. This section provides that the effect of restoration is that the company is deemed to have continued in existence as if it had not been struck off, and that the court may make such directions as are needed to place the company itself, and other persons, in the same position as they would have been had the company not been struck off. The court may also make directions as to the issues set out in *subsection (4)* to do with the company's file at Companies House and costs.

Restoration to the register: supplementary provisions

Section 1033: Company's name on restoration

1284. This section establishes the fundamental position that a company is restored to the register with the name it had before it was struck off, but also makes new provision for circumstances where restoration of a company would have the effect that two companies with the same or very similar names would appear in the registrar's index. There is a procedure for the restored company to change its name.

Section 1034: Effect of restoration to the register where property has vested a bona vacantia

1285. This section replaces section 655 of the 1985 Act with little change of substance. However, it makes new provision (*subsection (3)*) that, where a company's property has passed to the Crown and been disposed of, the Crown, in reimbursing the newly restored company, may deduct the reasonable costs of sale which were incurred.

PART 32: COMPANY INVESTIGATIONS: AMENDMENTS

Powers to appoint inspectors

1286. The 1985 Act gives the Secretary of State the power to appoint competent inspectors to carry out inspections, and report the result to him, in a number of circumstances. There are three categories of inspections at present:

- investigations into the affairs of companies;

- investigations into the membership or control of companies; and

- investigations of dealings in share options by company directors and their families and failure to disclose interests in shares.

1287. Investigations by inspectors into the affairs of companies and certain other bodies corporate can be initiated under sections 431 and 432. Such inspections can be launched on the application of a company or a proportion of its members, or on the Secretary of State's own initiative, and must be carried out where the court orders it.

1288. Investigations by inspectors into the membership or control of companies can be initiated under section 442. The Secretary of State can launch such an inspection on his own initiative under section 442(1), and is obliged to do so where the requisite number of members of a company apply.

1289. Inspections in the third category, under section 446, relate to suspected contraventions of certain provisions of Part 10 of the 1985 Act. The 2006 Act repeals the relevant provisions of Part 10 (see section 1177) and section 446 is repealed in consequence.

1290. Two inspectors are generally appointed to carry out an inspection – usually a QC and a partner in one of the leading accountancy firms.

1291. Inspectors are appointed to investigate and to report the results of their investigations to the Secretary of State. At the end of an inspection, the inspectors generally have a duty to make a final report to the Secretary of State. The inspectors may also make interim reports during the course of the inspection, and the Secretary of State can direct them to do so.

1292. Unless the appointment was made under section 432 of the 1985 Act on terms that any report is not for publication (section 432(2A)) interim and final reports are publishable; the Secretary of State has discretion to publish an interim or final report under section 437(3). The availability of a published report is a crucial aspect of the inspection system.

Changes brought in by the 2006 Act

1293. The 2006 Act confers new powers on the Secretary of State to bring to an end an investigation when it is no longer in the public interest to continue with it, to revoke the appointment of an inspector and to issue directions about the scope of an investigation, its duration and certain other matters.

1294. The main purpose of these sections is to give the Secretary of State power to take appropriate action where an investigation appears to be taking too long. The sections also provide for situations not currently explicitly provided for, such as the resignation or death of inspectors, and the ability to appoint replacement inspectors.

1295. The details of these changes and the circumstances in which the changes will apply are set out below.

Section 1035: Powers of Secretary of State to give directions to inspectors

1296. *Subsection (1)* inserts new sections 446A and 446B into the 1985 Act, which provide new powers for the Secretary of State to give directions to inspectors with which they are obliged to comply (new sections 446A(1) and 446B(5)).

1297. The power in new section 446A(2) is exercisable by the Secretary of State in relation to inspectors appointed under sections 431, 432(2) and 442(1). Directions under new section 446A(2) can either relate to the investigation itself or the inspectors' reports of the results of their investigations. Regarding the former, such directions can take two forms:

- a direction as to the subject matter of an investigation (whether by reference to a specified area of a company's operation, a specified transaction, a period of time or otherwise); or

- a direction which requires an inspector to take or not to take a specified step in his investigation.

1298. As regards inspectors' reports the Secretary of State will have a power to secure that any report (new section 446A(3)):

- includes the inspector's views on a specified matter;

- does not include any reference to a specified matter;

- is made in a specified form or manner; or

- is made by a specified date.

1299. New section 446A(4) enables directions by the Secretary of State to be capable of being given on an inspector's appointment. It also provides that directions may vary or revoke a direction previously given and may be given at the request of an inspector.

1300. New section 446A(5) confirms that the scope of the term "investigation" will include any investigation undertaken under section 433(1) into the affairs of the company's holding company or subsidiary (or a subsidiary of its holding company or a holding company of its subsidiary).

1301. New section 446B(1) will give the Secretary of State power to direct an inspector to take no further steps in an investigation, and the inspector shall comply with any direction given to him under this section (new section 446B(5)). However, if the appointment of inspectors is one that the Secretary of State is obliged to make (either because a court orders that a company's affairs ought to be so investigated or because the requisite number of its members has applied for an investigation into its ownership), such a direction can only be given if matters have come to light in the course of the investigation which suggest that a criminal offence has been committed and those matters have been referred to the appropriate prosecuting authority (new section 446B(2)).

1302. Under new section 446B(3), any direction given to the inspector under section 437(1) to produce an interim report, and any direction under new section 446A(3) in relation such a report, shall cease to have effect.

1303. If the Secretary of State directs an inspector to take no further steps in an investigation then the inspector shall not make a final report to him unless:

- the requisite number of a company's members has applied for an investigation into its ownership, matters have come to light in the course of the investigation which suggest that a criminal offence has been committed, those matters have been referred to the appropriate prosecuting authority and the Secretary of State directs the inspectors to make a final report; or

- the inspector was appointed following a court order that a company's affairs ought to be investigated (new section 446B(4)).

1304. New section 446B(6) confirms that the scope of the term "investigation" will include any investigation undertaken under section 433(1) into the affairs of the company's holding company or subsidiary (or a subsidiary of its holding company or a holding company of its subsidiary).

1305. *Subsections (2) to (5)* concern consequential changes to other sections within the 1985 Act.

Section 1036: Resignation, removal and replacement of inspectors

1306. This section inserts new sections 446C and 446D which provide for the resignation or revocation of an inspector's appointment and the provision to replace an inspector.

1307. New section 446C(1) and (2) provides not only that an inspector may resign but also that the Secretary of State has the power to revoke his appointment.

1308. New section 446D(1) provides that, if an inspector resigns, dies or has his appointment revoked, the Secretary of State has the power to appoint a replacement inspector to continue the investigation. Any appointment which takes place under new *subsection (1)* will be treated as though it were made under the provision under which the former inspector were appointed (new section 446D(2)).

1309. The Secretary of State is obliged to ensure that at least one inspector continues the investigation (new section 446D(3)) unless such a step would be pointless because he could direct the termination of the investigation in circumstances which would result in a final report not being made (new section 446D(4)).

1310. New section 446D(5) confirms that the scope of the term "investigation" will include any investigation undertaken under section 433(1) into the affairs of the company's holding company or subsidiary (or a subsidiary of its holding company or a holding company of its subsidiary).

Section 1037: Power to obtain information from former inspectors etc

1311. *Subsection (1)* inserts new section 446E into the 1985 Act.

1312. New section 446E(1) provides that, where an inspector resigns or has his appointment revoked or is given a direction under section 446B (termination of an investigation) (new section 446E(2)), the Secretary of State can direct him to hand over documents that he has obtained or generated during the course of his investigation, either to the Secretary of State or to another inspector appointed under this Part (new section 446E(3)).

1313. A requirement under new *subsection (3)* includes the power to ensure that the production of a copy of the document is made in hard copy or in a form from which a hard copy can be obtained (new section 446E(4)). A document includes information recorded in any form (new section 446E(7)(b)). New section 446E(5) enables the Secretary of State to direct any person to whom this section applies to inform him of any matters that came to that person's attention as a result of the investigation. New section 446E(6) confirms that a person shall comply with any direction given to him under this section.

1314. New section 446E(7)(a) confirms that the scope of the term "investigation" will include any investigation undertaken under section 433(1) into the affairs of the company's holding company or subsidiary (or a subsidiary of its holding company or a holding company of its subsidiary).

1315. *Subsections (2) and (3)* concern consequential changes to other sections within the 1985 Act.

Section 1038: Power to require production of documents

1316. The 2006 Act introduces a new definition for documents in hard copy form, (see section 1135). This section ensures that there is a consistent approach in existing investigation provisions where there is a requirement to produce documents.

Section 1039: Disqualification orders: consequential amendments

1317. *Subsections (a) and (b)* extend the Company Directors Disqualification Act 1986 so that decisions on whether to take action to disqualify directors can be taken on the basis of information that was obtained or generated by an inspector (or came to his knowledge) as a result of his investigation, notwithstanding whether such information is or will be included in any formal report. In some cases this may speed up the ability to seek to disqualify directors.

PART 33: UK COMPANIES NOT FORMED UNDER COMPANIES LEGISLATION

1318. The CLR considered the position of unregistered companies in Chapter 9 of Completing the Structure and presented their recommendations in paragraphs 11.34 to 11.37 of the Final Report. The provisions in this Part have been developed with these recommendations in mind.

CHAPTER 1: COMPANIES NOT FORMED UNDER COMPANIES LEGISLATION BUT AUTHORISED TO REGISTER

Section 1040: Companies authorised to register under this Act

1319. This section replaces section 680 of the 1985 Act. It applies to companies incorporated within the UK but not formed under the Companies Acts (or certain earlier companies legislation). It enables such companies to register under the Act. The types of company that can take advantage of this provision are listed in *subsection (1)*. They include companies formed before 2 November 1862; companies formed by private Act of Parliament and companies incorporated by royal charter.

1320. The company may apply to register as a company limited by shares, a company limited by guarantee or as an unlimited company. *Subsections (4)* and *(5)* impose restrictions on this choice. So, a company with limited liability may not register as an unlimited company, and only a company with share capital may register as a company limited by shares.

1321. A company may wish to apply to register under the Act in order to take advantage of legislation applying to companies registered under the Companies Acts. *Subsection (6)* makes clear that a company may register even if it is in order to take advantage of certain provisions of the Insolvency Act 1986 not available to unregistered companies. For example, under section 221(4) of the Insolvency Act 1986, unregistered companies may not be wound up under that Act voluntarily (except in accordance with the EC regulation on insolvency proceedings).

Section 1041: Definition of "joint stock company"

1322. This section restates section 683 of the 1985 Act. It defines the joint stock companies that may register under section 1040.

Section 1042: Power to make provision by regulations

1323. This section is a new provision. It confers power on the Secretary of State to make regulations in connection with the registration of a company following an application under section 1040 (application by UK company not formed under the Companies Acts to register under the Companies Acts). Regulations made under this section will replace the provisions made by sections 681 to 682, 684 to 690 and Schedule 21 of the 1985 Act. The regulations will cover the procedural requirements for registration, the conditions to be satisfied before registration and the documents to be supplied on an application for registration. The regulations will also set out the consequences of registration, including the status of the company following registration and the application of the Companies Acts to such companies following registration. The regulations are subject to the negative resolution procedure.

CHAPTER 2: UNREGISTERED COMPANIES

Section 1043: Unregistered companies

1324. This section replaces section 718 of the 1985 Act. The section confers a power on the Secretary of State to apply provisions of the Companies Acts to certain unregistered companies. These are companies incorporated in the UK, and having their principal place of business in the UK, but not formed or registered under the Companies Acts or any other public general Act of Parliament. Examples include companies formed by letters patent or by private Act of Parliament. *Subsection (1)* exempts certain other companies from regulations under this section, including those exempted by direction of the Secretary of State.

1325. Regulations under this section will replace the provision made by Schedule 22 to the 1985 Act. The regulations may apply specified provisions of the Companies Acts to specified descriptions of unregistered company, and may make limitations, adaptations and modifications to the application of the Companies Acts to unregistered companies. The regulations are subject to the negative resolution procedure.

PART 34: OVERSEAS COMPANIES

1326. This Part applies to companies incorporated outside the UK ("overseas companies"). It enables various registration, reporting and disclosure requirements to be imposed on overseas companies.

1327. This Part, together with the regulations to be made under it, will replace the provisions made by Part 23 (including Schedules 21A to D) of the 1985 Act. Regulations made under this Part will continue to implement the requirements of the Eleventh Company Law Directive (89/666/EEC), which imposes disclosure requirements on overseas companies that set up branches in the UK.

1328. As originally enacted, Part 23 of the 1985 Act applied to companies incorporated outside Great Britain that established a place of business in Great Britain. Subsequently, the

Eleventh Company Law Directive imposed a different set of disclosure requirements on those overseas companies with branches in the UK. The branch disclosure requirements also differ depending on whether or not the overseas company is incorporated within another EEA State. The result is that there are at present effectively two parallel regimes that apply to overseas companies.

1329. The CLR set out their initial analysis of the rules for regulating companies formed abroad in Chapter 5.6 of the Strategic Framework and then put forward their provisional detailed conclusions in their consultation document of October 1999 entitled "Reforming the law concerning overseas companies." The CLR presented their conclusions in paragraphs 11.21 to 11.33 of the Final Report.

Section 1044: Overseas companies

1330. This section explains that for the purposes of the Companies Acts an "overseas company" means a company incorporated outside the UK. This is wider than the definition of "oversea company" in section 744 of the 1985 Act which it replaces. The definition in section 744 refers to companies incorporated outside Great Britain that establish a place of business in Great Britain. Under the Act the regulations will be able to specify the connection with the UK that gives rise to the various disclosure obligations imposed under this Part.

Section 1045: Company contracts and execution of documents by companies

1331. This section restates section 130(6) of the Companies Act 1989 (company contracts and execution of documents by companies).

Section 1046: Duty to register particulars

1332. This section confers on the Secretary of State a new power to make regulations to require overseas companies to register with the registrar of companies. The regulations may require particular information to be included in the registration. For example, an address for the company and details of its directors. The regulations may also require particular documents to be sent to the registrar, such as a copy of the company's constitution. *Subsection (2)* ensures that the regulations implement the requirements of the Eleventh Company Law Directive (89/666/EEC), under which an overseas company must register if the company opens a branch in the UK.

1333. Regulations may require the overseas company to inform the registrar of companies of any changes in the details or documents it has registered (*subsection (4)*). The regulations may set deadlines for sending the information to the registrar of companies. They may also determine whether the overseas company should register with the registrar for England and Wales, the registrar for Scotland or the registrar for Northern Ireland. For example, an overseas company that opens a branch in Scotland may be required to register with the registrar of companies for Scotland.

1334. The Eleventh Company Law Directive imposes different disclosure requirements depending on where the overseas company setting up the branch is incorporated. Different reporting requirements are imposed on credit and financial institutions. Therefore regulations under this section may make different provision according to the place where the company is incorporated and the activities carried on by it.

1335. Regulations made under this section will be subject to the affirmative resolution procedure.

Section 1047: Registered name of overseas company

1336. This section applies to overseas companies required to register with the registrar of companies by regulations made under section 1046 (duty to register particulars). Overseas companies registered under that section must be required to provide a name for registration. The name will be entered on the index of company names (see section 1099).

1337. The company may register its corporate name (by which is meant its registered or legal name in its place of incorporation) or another name. All companies are free to choose whether to register their corporate name or another name, subject to the restrictions imposed by *subsections (4) and (5)*. A name other than the corporate name can be registered only if it complies with the requirements imposed on the names of companies formed and registered under the Act. Likewise, unless the overseas company is incorporated in an EEA State, its corporate name can only be registered if it complies with these requirements. The only requirements of Chapters 1 to 4 of Part 5 (a company's name) that do not apply are the requirements for the names of certain types of company to end with certain words (sections 58 and 59). These rules are not appropriate for overseas companies as they are specific to the types of company formed under the Companies Acts.

1338. Where the overseas company is incorporated in an EEA State (defined in section 1170), it may always register its corporate name, even if it does not comply with the requirements imposed on the names of companies formed under the Act provided that it complies with the requirement relating to permitted characters (contained in section 57). This section, together with section 1048 (registration under alternative name) replaces section 694 of the 1985 Act.

Section 1048: Registration under alternative name

1339. This section enables an overseas company to be registered under a name other than its corporate name. It also enables an overseas company to change the name by which it is registered. To do so it must deliver a statement to the registrar of companies with its proposed new name for registration. As long as the proposed name complies with the requirements for registration (see section 1047) the registrar of companies will enter it on the index of company names in place of the name previously registered.

1340. The section also provides that whatever name an overseas company is registered under, whether its corporate name or another, it is treated as being its corporate name for the purposes of the law in the UK. The change of name will not affect any legal proceedings that are continued or commenced by or against the company.

Section 1049: Accounts and reports: general

1341. This section confers on the Secretary of State a power to make regulations requiring overseas companies to prepare accounts and directors' reports, and to obtain an auditor's report. The requirements must be like those imposed on companies formed and registered under the Act. The accounts, directors' report and auditor's report requirements applying to companies formed and registered under the Act appear in Part 15 (accounts and reports) and Part 16 (audit).

1342. Regulations under this section may require the overseas company to deliver to the registrar of companies copies of the accounts and reports prepared in accordance with the regulations; alternatively the overseas company may be required to deliver to the registrar a copy of the accounts and reports that it prepared and had audited in accordance with the law of the country in which it is incorporated. The registrar will place the accounts and reports on the public register.

1343. Regulations under this section will replace sections 699AA to 703 of, and Schedule 21D to, the 1985 Act. The regulations will be subject to the negative resolution procedure.

Section 1050: Accounts and reports: credit or financial institutions

1344. This section applies only to credit or financial institutions incorporated or formed outside the UK and Gibraltar, with their head office outside the UK and Gibraltar but having a branch in the UK (*subsection (1)*). This section confers on the Secretary of State a power to make regulations specifically in respect of accounts and directors' reports by these credit or financial institutions.

1345. Credit institution and financial institution are both defined in section 1173.

1346. Regulations under this section will implement requirements of the Bank Branches Directive 89/117/EEC of the Council of 13 February 1989. The definition of "branch" for the purposes of this section (*subsection (2)*) is based on Article 1.3 of Directive 2000/12/EC of the European Parliament and of the Council of 20 March 2000 relating to the taking up and pursuit of the business of credit institutions. The power to make regulations under this section is similar to that in under section 1049 (accounts and reports: general).

1347. The regulations will replace section 699A of, and Schedule 21C to, the 1985 Act. The regulations will be subject to the negative resolution procedure.

Section 1051: Trading disclosures

1348. This section confers on the Secretary of State a power to make regulations as to the information that overseas companies must display in specified locations, include in specified documents or communications, or provide to those who make a request in the course of business. Regulations made under this section will replace the provision made by section 693 of the 1985 Act. This section complements the similar power under section 82 to make regulations imposing trading disclosure obligations on companies formed and registered under the Companies Acts. Regulations under this section may require an overseas company carrying on business in the UK:

- to display particular information in particular places. For example, a sign with its name outside every branch;

- to include particular information in certain documents. For example, its name and country of incorporation on every invoice;

- to provide certain information, such as its name, to those who request it when doing business with the overseas company.

1349. They may also make provision, corresponding to that made in sections 83 and 84, in respect of a failure by a company formed and registered under the Companies Acts to comply with the trading disclosure requirements imposed on them by regulations under section 82.

1350. Regulations under this section, like those under section 82, are subject to the affirmative resolution procedure.

Section 1052: Company charges

1351. This section applies to overseas companies that are required to register particulars under section 1046. It confers on the Secretary of State a power to make regulations about the registration by those companies of charges they grant over property in the United Kingdom. *Subsection (2)* lists some of the matters that may be dealt with in such regulations, and *subsections (3) and (4)* enable the regime for overseas companies to mirror specified provisions in Part 25, with modifications. This section replaces sections 409 (charges on property in England and Wales created by an overseas company) and 424 (extension of Chapter 2) of the 1985 Act.

Section 1053: Other returns etc

1352. This section applies to overseas companies that are required to register particulars under section 1046. It confers on the Secretary of State a power to make regulations requiring those companies to deliver returns to the registrar if they are being wound up or subjected to insolvency proceedings. The regulations may also require the liquidator of such a company to deliver returns to the registrar. They may specify the circumstances in which a return is to be made to the registrar. For example, on termination of the winding-up. The regulations may specify the information to be included in the return and set deadlines for sending it to the registrar (*subsection (3)*). They may require notice to be given to the registrar of certain appointments (*subsections (4) and (5)*).

1353. The regulations will replace sections 703P and 703Q of the 1985 Act. The regulations will be subject to the affirmative resolution procedure.

Section 1054: Offences

1354. This section ensures that the regulations will be able to specify the person or persons who would be responsible for complying with any specified requirement of the regulations. It allows regulations to provide for offences, including who would be liable in the event of any contravention and what might be considered a defence should a charge be brought. The maximum level of penalty permissible under the regulations on indictment is an unlimited fine and on summary conviction a fine not exceeding level 5 on the standard scale, or for continued contravention, a daily default fine not exceeding one-tenth of that.

Section 1055: Disclosure of individual's residential address: protection from disclosure

1355. If the regulations under section 1046 require an overseas company to register an individual's usual residential address, then the regulations must also provide for its protection on the same basis as is provided for directors' residential addresses in Chapter 8 of Part 10.

Section 1056: Requirement to identify persons authorised to accept service of documents

1356. Every overseas company required by regulations under section 1046 to register with the registrar of companies must register particulars identifying every person resident in the UK who is authorised to accept service of documents on the company's behalf or make a statement that there is no such person.

1357. As to how a document may be served on a registered overseas company, see section 1139(2) and the company communications provisions (sections 1144 to 1148 and Schedules 4 and 5).

1358. This section replaces the provision made by section 691(1)(b)(ii) and paragraph 3(e) of Schedule 21A to the 1985 Act.

Section 1057: Registrar to whom returns, notices etc to be delivered

1359. This section makes provision for regulations in respect of overseas companies that are required to register, or have registered, particulars under section 1046 in more than one part of the United Kingdom. The regulations may set out what should happen, for example, if the overseas company has registered branches in Scotland and in Northern Ireland; the regulations may require the returns or notices to be delivered to each registrar with whom the company is registered, or to the registrar for such part or parts of the United Kingdom as the regulations may specify.

1360. Regulations made under this section will be subject to the negative resolution procedure.

Section 1058: Duty to give notice of ceasing to have registrable presence

1361. Where an overseas company has registered particulars with the registrar following the opening of a branch in the United Kingdom, this section will enable regulations to require the overseas company to give notice to the registrar if it subsequently closes that branch. In addition, an overseas company that has registered particulars in other circumstances specified by regulations under section 1046 may be required by regulations to give notice to the registrar if those circumstances cease to obtain.

1362. The regulations will require the notice to be delivered to the registrar for the part of the United Kingdom in which the overseas company was registered and may set deadlines for sending the information to the registrar.

1363. Regulations made under this section will be subject to negative resolution procedure.

Section 1059: Application of provisions in case of relocation of branch

1364. This section provides that the relocation of a branch from one part of the UK to another is to be treated as the closing of the branch in one part and the opening in another. For example, if an overseas company moves a branch from Scotland to Wales, it must tell the registrar for Scotland that it is closing the branch. It must also tell the registrar for England and Wales that it is opening a branch in Wales. This section replaces the provision made by section 695A(4) of the 1985 Act.

PART 35: THE REGISTRAR OF COMPANIES

1365. This Part largely replaces Part 24 of the 1985 Act, and sets out the basic functions of the registrar of companies (these functions are currently carried out by Companies House for England and Wales and in Scotland and by the equivalent registry in Northern Ireland). The new sections implement a number of recommendations of the CLR.

Sections 1060 and 1061: The registrar and the registrar's functions

1366. Section 1060 carries forward the approach of section 704 of the 1985 Act as to the appointment and status of the registrar of companies but omits some of the more antiquated parts of that provision. It specifies that there shall continue to be a registrar for England and Wales, for Scotland and for Northern Ireland.

1367.   Section 1061 the registrar continues to have the functions conferred by the Companies Acts and in other legislation as specified in the section. The Secretary of State also has power to confer functions on the registrar, in relation to the registration of companies or other matters.

Section 1062: The registrar's official seal

1368.   This section, replacing section 704(4) of the 1985 Act, provides that the registrar must have an official seal for the authentication of documents.

Section 1063: Fees payable to the registrar

1369.   This section gives the Secretary of State a power to set fees by regulations in relation to any function of the registrar and in relation to the provision of services and facilities incidental to the registrar's functions. It replaces section 708 of the 1985 Act, but is more specific about the types of things for which fees may be charged, although this list is not exhaustive.

1370.   As now, fees relating to the normal statutory obligations of companies under companies legislation are to be set by regulations made by the Secretary of State. It is also possible for fees to be charged for any *ad hoc* or bespoke services that Companies House provides. The 1985 Act (section 708(5)) provides that the registrar determines fees for services for which there is no direct legal obligation. *Subsection (6)* of this section replaces this with a more general power for the registrar to determine fees where no fee has been set in regulations by the Secretary of State. Such fees might relate for example to the introduction of new services (e.g. those made possible by new technologies) which could not have been anticipated when the Secretary of State last made fees regulations; or for services such as seminars and road shows which Companies House arranges.

Section 1064 to 1065: Certificates of incorporation

1371.   Section 1064 replaces section 711(1)(a) of the 1985 Act and provides for notice of the issue of certificates of incorporation to be published in the Gazette. The publication must include the company's registered number as well as its name. Section 1065 replaces section 710 of that Act and allows any person to obtain a certificate of incorporation of a company. These sections cover all certificates of incorporation (including, for example, certificates of incorporation on change of name).

Section 1066 and 1067: Registered numbers

1372.   Section 1066 replaces section 705 of the 1985 Act on companies' registered numbers, without change of substance. Section 1067 replaces the provisions of section 705A of that Act relating to registered numbers of branches of overseas companies.

Delivery of documents to the registrar

Section 1068: Registrar's requirements

1373.   This section gives the registrar power to make rules about form, authentication and manner of delivery of documents, including the physical form and means of communication, the format, and the address to which they are to be sent, and where appropriate, technical specification. The power conferred by this section does not authorise the registrar to require documents to be delivered in electronic form.

Section 1069: Power to require delivery by electronic means

1374. This section provides that the Secretary of State (not the registrar) has a new power to provide for electronic-only delivery of classes of document. The Secretary of State may only exercise this power in respect of classes of document which are authorised or required to be delivered and for which the registrar has published rules relating to electronic delivery (in other words where it is clear precisely what mechanism is to be used for the electronic communication).

Section 1070: Agreement for delivery by electronic means

1375. This section sets out the power of the registrar to make agreements with companies to deliver information only electronically. The agreements could cover all documents (to the extent that electronic means of filing are available) or just selected documents. It is envisaged that the agreements will be in a standard form and contain detailed provisions for communications between the registrar and the company (including possible use of codes and encryption). The agreements need not be available to be entered into by everyone in the same form or at all.

Section 1071: Document not delivered until received

1376. This section provides that "delivery" obligations go beyond an obligation simply to send or post information to the registrar, and that the registrar may make rules governing what it means for a document to be "received" (which might include, for example, setting out which offices of the registrar should receive a document).

Requirements for proper delivery

Section 1072: Requirements for proper delivery

1377. This section provides that, in order for a document to be properly delivered to the registrar, various conditions (specified in *subsection (1)(a) to (g)*) must be met. Where those conditions are not satisfied, and the document is therefore not "properly" delivered, it is not to be treated as having been delivered for the purposes of the underlying provision which authorises or requires it.

Section 1073: Power to accept documents not meeting requirements for proper delivery

1378. The registrar may still accept (and register) a document that does not comply with the requirements for proper delivery, although such acceptance does not (*subsection (4)*) exempt the filer from any consequence attaching to failure to comply with the original requirements for delivery.

Section 1074: Documents containing unnecessary material

1379. Documents are sometimes delivered to the registrar which contain "unnecessary" material, i.e. material for which there was no legal requirement or authorisation. Where the unnecessary material cannot readily be separated from the necessary material, then the document as a whole is treated as not properly delivered. Where it is separable, the registrar has the option of either registering the entire document as delivered, or excising the unnecessary material and registering the remainder.

Section 1075: Informal correction of document

1380. This is a new provision, giving the registrar power to correct information in a document by informal means (for example, by taking revisions or supplementary information from the company over the telephone) but only in very limited circumstances. It can be used as an alternative to rejecting or removing information:

- on the grounds that it is incomplete (e.g. empty fields within the document);

- on the grounds that it is internally inconsistent (e.g. the company number does not correspond to the company name);

1381. This ability to make informal corrections only applies where companies have informed the registrar that it should apply. The registrar needs to initiate the correction and be satisfied that the person is authorised to give the information sought. In order to be satisfied as to the authority of the person she is telephoning, the registrar may provide for identification numbers or other checks on identity.

Section 1076: Replacement of document not meeting requirements for proper delivery

1382. This section sets out how the registrar may accept a replacement document that was not properly delivered in the first place. In essence, the registrar must be satisfied that the replacement document is delivered by the original filer, or by the company to which the original document relates, and that the replacement is "properly delivered" (as defined in section 1072)). It also allows the registrar to impose requirements to ensure that the replacement can clearly be associated with a particular original.

Sections 1077 and 1078: Public notice of receipt of documents subject to Directive disclosure requirements

1383. These sections replace section 711 of the 1985 Act, which provides that certain notices must be published in the Gazette, and lists the documents to which that requirement relates. This list derives from Community legislation, principally the First Company Law Directive (68/151/EEC) as amended by Directive 2003/58/EC.

1384. Section 1077 provides that notice of receipt of these documents must be published either in the Gazette, or by some other means (as may be specified under section 1116). Section 1078 lists the documents subject to Directive disclosure requirements.

Section 1079: Effect of failure to give public notice

1385. This section effectively replaces section 42 of the 1985 Act. It sets out how a company, in its dealings with third parties, may not rely on the consequences of certain events (those which are set out in *subsection (2)*) unless notice of the event has duly appeared in the Gazette or been published in some other way provided for in section 1116.

The register

Section 1080: The register

1386. This section imposes an obligation on the registrar to keep a record of the material received. It gives a discretion as to the form in which the record is kept. *Subsection (3)* provides that this discretion is subject to the terms of the amended First Company Law Directive (68/151/EEC), Article 3.2 of which requires any documents and particulars it covers which are delivered on after 1 January 2007 to be retained in electronic form. The documents covered by this obligation are those set out in section 1078.

Section 1081: Annotation of the register

1387. It is important that the register is as useful and transparent a source of information as possible for users. Hence, this section sets out certain circumstances in which the registrar is obliged to annotate the information on the register to gloss it or provide supplementary information. Annotations must for example be provided to show the date of delivery of information; and the fact that information has been replaced, corrected or removed. This section responds to a recommendation of the CLR (summarised in their Final Report at paragraph 11.48). *Subsection (5)* provides that the court can dispense with the need for annotation in certain circumstances.

1388. The Secretary of State has power to make provision by regulations extending the circumstances where the registrar can or should make annotations.

Section 1082: Allocation of unique identifiers

1389. This section is a new provision. It gives the Secretary of State a power to make regulations so that unique identifiers can be allocated to company officers such as directors. This provision supports those that provide for the home addresses of directors no longer to be kept on the public record. The unique identifier enables searchers to distinguish between different persons of the same name.

Sections 1083 and 1084: Preservation of original documents and records relating to companies that have been dissolved etc

1390. Section 1083 replaces section 707A(2) of the 1985 Act. However, the obligation on the registrar to keep the originals of documents received now only applies for three years (as opposed to ten in the existing provision). This section also provides that the obligation to retain originals does not extend to an original document provided electronically (provided that the information itself has been placed on the register).

1391. Section 1084 replaces sections 707(3) and (4) of the 1985 Act, and provides that records may be transferred to the Public Records Office two years after a company has been dissolved. It also makes equivalent provision for certain overseas companies which, for example, by ceasing to have any connection with the UK, are no longer caught by UK regulatory requirements.

Inspection etc of the register

Section 1085: Inspection of the register

1392. This section provides that any person may inspect the register. Searchers however have a right to inspect the *original* of a hard copy document only where the registrar still retains it and where the public record kept by the registrar and derived from it is illegible or unavailable.

Section 1086: Right to copy of material on the register

1393. This section provides that any person is entitled to a copy of material on the register. Consistent with the provisions of the amended First Company Law Directive (68/151/EEC), *subsection (2)* provides that the fee for a copy may not exceed the administrative cost of providing the service.

Section 1087: Material not available for public inspection

1394. This section sets out a number of exceptions to the above rights to inspect and copy material on the register. These are listed in *subsection (1)(a) to (k)* and include, for example, "protected information", i.e. information about directors' home addresses. *Subsection (2)* provides that the fact that certain material (for example, an address), which has been placed on the register as a result of the filing of two or more different types of document, is confidential in one of those contexts, does not mean that it cannot be made public in its other context.

Section 1088: Application to registrar to make address unavailable for public inspection

1395. This section is a new provision. It confers power on the Secretary of State to make regulations providing for applications to remove addresses from the public record held by Companies House. The regulations may set out the details of who can apply and on what grounds and the procedure involved. They are subject to the affirmative resolution procedure.

Sections 1089 to 1091: Provision of copies of material on the register

1396. These sections enable the registrar to specify the form and manner in which applications for inspection of the register, or for copies of material on it, must be made, and to determine the form and manner in which copies are provided. They are subject to important exceptions, arising from the amended First Company Law Directive (68/151/EEC), in respect of the documents listed at section 1078.

1397. Section 1089 provides that applications must be capable of being submitted in hard copy or in electronic form, as the applicant chooses. Section 1090 similarly provides that the applicant is entitled to insist on receiving the copies themselves in hard copy or in electronic form (subject to an exception in respect of documents delivered before 1 January 2007).

1398. Section 1091, again responding to provisions of the amended First Company Law Directive (68/151/EEC), provides that, unless the applicant chooses otherwise, copies of information provided in hard copy must be certified as true copies but electronic copies must not be so certified. *Subsection (3)* provides for the evidential status of certified hard copies in legal proceedings. The Secretary of State has power to prescribe by regulations methods of certification for copies provided by electronic means.

Section 1092: Issue of process for production of records kept by the registrar

1399. This section restates section 709(5) of the 1985 Act and provides that no-one can take proceedings against the registrar for production of records without first obtaining the permission of the court.

Correction or removal of material on the register

Section 1093: Registrar's notice to resolve inconsistency on the register

1400. This section enables the registrar to notify a company of an apparent inconsistency in the information on the register. An example might be where a document is received notifying the removal of a director where there is no record of his appointment. In such circumstances, the registrar may give notice to the company requiring them to resolve the inconsistency within 14 days by providing additional or replacement documents. Failure to do so on the company's part is an offence (*subsection (3)*).

Section 1094: Administrative removal of material from the register

1401. The registrar has a power to remove from the register information that there was a power but no duty to enter. Under *subsection (4)*, the registrar will need to send a notice to the presenter of the information in question, or to the company to which the material relates, on or before removing the material.

1402. The registrar may not however remove information from the register where registration has had legal consequences for the company as regards certain key events, as set out in *subsection (3)*, including for example its formation or a change of registered office.

Section 1095: Rectification of register on application to registrar

1403. This section gives the Secretary of State a power to make regulations under which, following a successful application, the registrar may be required to remove certain kinds of material from the register. The procedure may only cover certain types of document. It may operate in respect of material that derives from something that is invalid or ineffective or from something that was done without the authority of the company (this would cover forms filed without authority); and material that is factually inaccurate or forged or derives from something that is factually inaccurate or forged.

1404. The registrar may only act as a result of an application, and regulations may provide for matters such as who may make the application and what information will need to be provided with it. Where the material removed is of a kind whose registration has had legal consequences, *subsection (5)* provides that interested parties have the right to go to court to obtain an order as to the material's legal effect.

Section 1096: Rectification of the register under court order

1405. The registrar is also required to remove material from the register where there is a court order to that effect. The court's rectification power operates in the same circumstances as the registrar's power following regulations made under section 1094. However, the court's power is of general application. For example, there is no limit on the types of document covered. The court may make an order to remove material from the register where its presence on the register has caused damage or may cause damage to the company and the company's interests in removing the material outweigh the interests of others in it continuing to be on the register. The court may make such consequential orders as appear just regarding the period that the information was on the register and the effect of the information being on the register during that period. The court's rectification power does not operate where the court has other rectification powers (e.g. in relation to accounts or charges).

Section 1097: Powers of court on ordering removal of material from the register

1406. This section provides that where a court decides that certain information should be removed from the public register, the court may also make directions as to annotations (removing notes that are already there or directing that now new notes appear as a result of its order – or that notes appear in a restricted form) and as to whether its own order should be available for public inspection.

Section 1098: Public notice of removal of certain material from the register

1407. Section 1077 provides for the registrar to give public notice that she has received certain documents relating to a company in the Gazette or through some other form of publication. This section creates a corresponding obligation for her to give notice where she removes such material.

Section 1099: The registrar's index of company names

1408. This section replaces section 714 of the 1985 Act with changes. It provides for the registrar of companies to keep an index of the names not only of companies incorporated under Companies Acts but also of business entities formed under other legislation and of overseas companies with a UK branch.

1409. The section provides power for regulations to update the categories of business entities that are included in the index. This power is subject to negative resolution procedure.

Section 1100: Right to inspect index

1410. This section retains the public right to inspect the index. (It can be searched online, without charge, at www.companieshouse.gov.uk.) The index of company names is important not only as the means of access to the information on the public record of companies incorporated in the United Kingdom but also as the list of names with which a proposed new name is compared to ensure that a new entity is not registered in a name that is the same or similar to that of an existing entity.

Section 1101: Power to amend enactments relating to bodies other than companies

1411. This section provides power for the Secretary of State to amend the rules for the names that can be adopted by other business entities on the index of company names. This power is subject to affirmative resolution procedure.

1412. Each category of business entity is subject to its own rules which include various safeguards to minimise the risk of public confusion. These rules differ from those that apply to companies in particular as regards the adoption of a name the same or similar to one already on the index. This lack of reciprocity is a weakness of the existing system which this section provides power to address.

Section 1102: Application of language requirements

Section 1103: Documents to be drawn up and delivered in English

1413. These sections set out language requirements. Section 1103 sets out the general rule that all documents must be in English (subject to the exceptions in the following sections). Section 1102 provides that this general rule, and its exceptions, apply automatically to documents required under the Companies Acts and Insolvency Act 1986 (and its Northern Ireland equivalent).

1414. There are however a variety of other pieces of legislation which may require companies in certain circumstances to supply material to the registrar. Depending on the nature of the particular requirement and its origin (for example, whether it responds to European Community law), it may or may not be appropriate to apply the language provisions of this Act unchanged to such material. *Subsection (2)* of section 1102 therefore enables the Secretary of State to make regulations to apply specified requirements to documents filed under other legislation.

Section 1104: Documents relating to Welsh companies

1415. This section provides an exception to the general rule in section 1103: documents relating to Welsh companies may be drawn up and filed in Welsh (and sometimes only in Welsh). It replaces, without any substantive change, section 710B of the 1985 Act.

Section 1105: Documents that may be drawn up and delivered in other languages

1416. This section sets out the circumstances in which documents may be drawn up and filed in other languages, but requires them to be accompanied by a certified translation into English. These documents are listed in *subsection (2)*: agreements affecting the company's constitution, documents relating to group accounts for companies in a group, and instruments relating to company charges. For some companies, documents of these sorts may well originate in languages other than English, and there may be an interest in ensuring that the original version is registered with the registrar. *Subsection (2)(d)* also allows the Secretary of State to extend the categories of documents to which this section applies.

Section 1106: Voluntary filing of translations

1417. The main purpose of this section is to implement aspects of the amended First Company Law Directive (68/151/EEC). It provides that companies may send the registrar certified translations of documents relating to the company. *Subsection (2)* enables the Secretary of State to set out in regulations the languages and documents in relation to which this facility is available. *Subsection (3)* provides that these regulations must as a minimum specify the official languages of the EU, and the documents covered by the amended First Company Law Directive (68/151/EEC) (see section 1078), to ensure compliance with that Directive. However, other languages (and categories of document) may be covered by the regulations.

Section 1107: Certified translations

1418. This section provides that a "certified translation" is one that has been certified in a manner prescribed by the registrar. It also provides that, where there is a discrepancy between an original and a translation, the company may not rely on the translation as against a third party, but the third party may rely on the translation (unless the company can show that the third party had knowledge of the original). This implements article 3a.4 of the amended First Company Law Directive (68/151/EEC).

Section 1108: Transliteration of names and addresses: permitted characters

1419. This section is a new provision. It deals with the possibility that the name and address of a director or of an overseas company may use a character set (for example, that of Urdu or Japanese) which is different from those with which the bulk of Companies House's users are familiar. This section restricts the characters that are permitted for names and addresses in a document delivered to the registrar to those specified in regulations. The regulations, which are subject to negative resolution procedure, may also provide for names and addresses to be delivered in their original form.

Section 1109: Transliteration of names and addresses: voluntary transliteration into Roman characters

1420. This section is a new provision. It provides for the possibility that the Regulations made under section 1108 may permit letters and characters that are not drawn from the Roman alphabet, for example Greek letters. This section permits these names to be transliterated provided that certain requirements are met.

Section 1110: Transliteration of names and addresses: certification

1421. This section is a new provision. It confers power on the Secretary of State to make regulations relating to the certification of the transliteration of names and addresses. The regulations, which are subject to negative resolution procedure, may distinguish between compulsory transliteration under section 1108 and voluntary transliteration under section 1109.

Section 1111: Registrar's requirements as to certification or verification

1422. Documents delivered to the registrar are sometimes required to be certified or verified in some way, for example to the effect that they are an accurate translation. This section allows the registrar to impose requirements as who must provide the relevant certification or verification. *Subsection (2)* provides that the registrar's general powers to specify requirements in relation to documents submitted to her (section 1068) extends to the certification or verification as if it were a separate document.

Section 1112: General false statement offence

1423. This section provides a new offence of knowingly or recklessly delivering to the registrar information which is misleading, false or deceptive in a material particular. It responds to a recommendation of the CLR (Final Report, paragraph 11.48). This new general offence makes it unnecessary to reproduce specific offences covering false information or false statements in respect of specific legislative requirements that were a feature of the 1985 Act.

Section 1113: Enforcement of company's filing obligations

1424. This section, which restates section 713 of the 1985 Act, provides the mechanism for ensuring that companies can be compelled to comply with their obligations to file documents or give notices to the registrar. Where a company has defaulted on an obligation, the registrar herself, any member of the company, or any creditor, may serve a notice on the company requiring it to file. If the company continues the breach after 14 days, the applicant may apply to the court for an order requiring the company, or any specified officer of it, to make good the default. The court may order that the costs of the proceedings are borne by the company or its officers. *Subsection (5)* provides that this process does not affect any offence or civil penalty arising from the company's failure to comply with the original requirement.

Section 1114: Application of provisions about documents and delivery

1425. This section, which replaces section 715A of the 1985 Act, provides that "document" means information recorded in any form, and that "delivering" a document includes forwarding, lodging, registering, producing or submitting it, or giving a notice. It also provides that requirements relating to documents also apply (unless otherwise provided for) to information passed to the registrar in some other way. This caters for the possibility that information may not be in documentary form, for example when it is sent via a link to a website.

Section 1115: Supplementary provisions relating to electronic communications

1426. This section, which replaces section 710A of the 1985 Act, allows the registrar to require those who choose to file electronically to accept electronic communications from the registrar. It also provides that, where a document is required to be signed by the registrar, or authenticated by seal, she may determine by rules how it is to be authenticated when it is sent by electronic means.

Section 1116: Alternative to publication in the Gazette

1427. The registrar is required under the 1985 Act to publish certain statutory notices in the Gazette. The objective of that requirement is to ensure that such notices are well-publicised and made available to all those who might wish to take notice of them. The Gazette is a long-established and well-understood mechanism for ensuring such publicity. However, it is possible that developments, in particular in electronic publishing, will mean over time that alternative mechanisms are equally or more appropriate as ways of meeting the underlying policy objective. The CLR envisaged that the registrar should be able to make use of such mechanisms (Final Report, paragraph 11.48). This section therefore provides a power for the Secretary of State to specify alternative means which the registrar may then approve for use. To ensure that any such change is itself well-publicised in advance, *subsection (5)* provides that the change must itself be announced in the Gazette.

Section 1117: Registrar's rules

1428. Other provisions in this Part enable the registrar to impose requirements in relation to certain matters. For example, section 1068 enables the registrar to specify the form, authentication and manner of delivery of documents to her; and section 1075 similarly enables her to determine the form and manner of any company instructions as to informal correction of the register. This section provides that the registrar may set out these requirements in registrar's rules. The rules can make different provision for different cases, and may allow the registrar to modify or disapply the rules. The registrar must publicise any rules in a way designed to make sure that those who will need to know about them get to hear of them (which might in practice, for example, be by using the Companies House website); and must make copies of the rules publicly available.

Section 1118: Payments into the Consolidated Fund

1429. This section ensures that nothing in this or other companies legislation affects the continued operation in relation to the registrar of the Government Trading Funds Act 1973. (Companies House is and remains a Trading Fund.)

Section 1119: Contracting out of registrar's functions

1430. This section largely restates subsections (7) and (8) of section 704 of the 1985 Act. The Deregulation and Contracting Out Act 1994 envisages that some of the registrar's functions may be contracted out. This section provides for this possibility by saying that where a contractor is processing documents the registrar can provide for them to be sent directly to the contractor.

1431. The Deregulation and Contracting Out Act 1994 does not permit the function of making subordinate legislation to be delegated. *Subsection (3)* provides that registrar's rules are not regarded as subordinate legislation for this purpose, permitting the contractor to make rules about form and manner of delivery, for example.

Section 1120: Application of Part to overseas companies

1432. This section provides that, except where the context otherwise requires, the provisions of this Part of the Act apply equally to overseas companies.

PART 36: OFFENCES UNDER THE COMPANIES ACTS

1433. The CLR sought to draw out the basis on which criminal liability for a breach of Companies Act requirements is allocated under existing legislation to companies and to officers of companies. It stated in its final report that a reformed Companies Act must be underpinned by effective and proportionate sanctions and enforcement.

1434. The key changes in the Act are:

- refinements to the "officer in default" provisions to make it clearer which individuals in which circumstances may be liable for a breach; and

- removal of criminal liability from the company itself in certain circumstances.

1435. The general principle adopted as to whether a company should be liable for a breach of requirements of the Companies Acts is that where the only victims of the offence are the company or its members, the company should not be liable for the offence. On the other hand, where other persons may be victims of the offence, then the company should be potentially liable for a breach, whether or not the offence may also harm the company or its members.

Section 1121: Liability of officer in default

1436. This section specifies which persons may be liable as an officer of a company for an offence committed by the company under the Act (or the other Companies Acts). It only applies where another provision expressly states that an offence is committed by every officer of a company who is in default.

1437. An "officer" of a company is defined as including a director, manager or (company) secretary, and any person who is to be treated as an officer of the company for the purposes of the provisions in question. An officer is liable for an offence when he is "in default", meaning he authorises or permits, participates in, or fails to take all reasonable steps to prevent the offence being committed.

Section 1122: Liability of company as officer in default

1438. Under this provision, where a company is an officer of another company, liability for an offence can be fixed upon the company as an officer in default only if one of its officers is in default.

Section 1123: Application to bodies other than companies

1439. This clause provides that section 1121 applies to persons in bodies other than companies where their role is equivalent to that of an officer of a company. It makes specific provision for bodies corporate, partnerships and unincorporated bodies.

Section 1124: Amendments of the Companies Act 1985

Schedule 3: Amendments of remaining provisions of the Companies Act 1985 relating to offences

1440.   Section 1124 introduces Schedule 3, which contains amendments to certain provisions relating to offences which remain in Parts 14 and 15 of the 1985 Act.

1441.   Many of these amendments are necessary due to the repeal by the Act of Schedule 24 to the 1985 Act. Schedule 24 set out the level of punishment for offences under the 1985 Act. The provisions in Parts 14 and 15 are amended so that the applicable punishments are now included alongside the description of the offence instead of in Schedule 24.

1442.   Schedule 3 also makes amendments to the offences provisions remaining in Parts 14 and 15 of the 1985 Act to reflect the (non-textual) changes made to that Act by the Criminal Justice Act 2003. Section 282 of the Criminal Justice Act increases from 6 months to 12 months the maximum term of imprisonment to which a person is liable on summary conviction of an offence triable either way, and section 154(1) of that Act gives power to magistrates to impose a 12 month term of imprisonment. The increased penalties only apply in England and Wales; in Scotland and Northern Ireland the maximum term of imprisonment that may be imposed on summary conviction remains 6 months. When the Act received Royal Assent, neither section 282 nor section 154(1) of the Criminal Justice Act 2003 had come into force (which is the reason for the transitory provision in section 1131).

1443.   A number of the amendments make reference to "the statutory maximum fine". This was set at £5,000 at the time the Act received Royal Assent.

1444.   Schedule 3 makes only one substantive change to the offence provisions in Parts 14 and 15. This is to include a daily default fine, of one-fiftieth of the statutory maximum, for continued contravention of section 444(3) (failure to provide information about interests in shares).

Section 1125: Meaning of "daily default fine"

1445.   This section defines "daily default fine". It replaces provision currently in section 730(4) of the 1985 Act.

Section 1126: Consents required for certain prosecutions

1446.   This section provides that certain proceedings can only be brought with the consent of specified persons. It replaces section 732(1) and (2) of the 1985 Act.

Section 1127: Summary proceedings: venue

1447.   This section restates section 731(1) of the 1985 Act. It specifies the possible venues for summary proceedings for any breach of Companies Acts requirements. For a body corporate the venue may be any place at which the body corporate has a place of business, and for any other person, it may be at any place that the person is.

Section 1128: Summary proceedings: time limit for proceedings

1448.   This section restates section 731(2) to (4) of the 1985 Act. It sets out time limits for summary proceedings. The prosecution must be commenced within three years of the offence being committed, and within one year of the prosecuting authorities receiving sufficient evidence to justify the prosecution.

Section 1129: Legal professional privilege

1449. This section restates section 732(3) of the 1985 Act and applies its provisions to all offences prosecuted under the Companies Acts, rather than just those instituted by the Director of Public Prosecutions or the Secretary of State. It provides that the Companies Acts provisions on offences are not to be read as requiring any person to disclose information that is protected by legal professional privilege.

Section 1130: Proceedings against unincorporated bodies

1450. This section restates section 734(1) to (4) of the 1985 Act. It provides for proceedings for offences under the Companies Acts committed by unincorporated bodies to be brought against such bodies as if they were corporate bodies.

Section 1131: Imprisonment on summary conviction in England and Wales: transitory provision

1451. This section provides for the period before the commencement of section 154(1) of the Criminal Justice Act 2003, which makes new provision about the powers of magistrates' courts in England and Wales to impose sentences of imprisonment on summary conviction. For offences committed before section 154(1) is brought into force, the maximum term of imprisonment in England and Wales for a person guilty of an offence on summary conviction under the Companies Acts is to be 6 months (as it is at present) instead of 12 months.

Section 1132: Production and inspection of documents where offence suspected

1452. This section restates section 721 of the 1985. It makes provision about orders for the production of documents where there is reasonable cause to believe that an offence has been committed.

Section 1133: Transitional provision

1453. This section provides that this Part of the Act (with the exception of section 1132) does not apply to offences committed before the commencement of the provision relevant to the offence.

PART 37: COMPANIES: SUPPLEMENTARY PROVISIONS

Sections 1134 and 1135: Company records

1454. These sections replace sections 722(1) and 723(1) and (2) of the 1985 Act and enable a company to use electronic storage or paper for its records provided that there can be paper printouts of electronic records. Section 1135(1) also enables the contents to be arranged as the directors see fit provided that it is adequately recorded. Section 1138 (duty to take precautions against falsification) also applies if the records are not kept in bound books.

Section 1136: Regulations about where certain company records to be kept available for inspection

1455. This section is a new provision. It provides power for the Secretary of State to make regulations to provide an alternative to the company's registered office as the location for inspection of specified records. The regulations are subject to negative resolution procedure.

Section 1137: Regulations about inspection of records and provision of copies

1456. This section replaces section 723A of the 1985 Act. It allows the Secretary of State to make regulations about the inspection and provision of copies of company records.

Section 1138: Duty to take precautions against falsification

1457. This section replaces section 722(2) and (3) of the 1985 Act. It makes it an offence not to take measures that protect records from falsification or help trace any falsification. This provision applies to records that are not kept in bound books, whether or not they are kept electronically, but does not apply either to companies' copies of the directors' service contracts or to copies of any qualifying third party indemnity provisions benefiting a director.

Section 1139: Service of documents on company

1458. This section replaces section 725 of the 1985 Act. It ensures that there is a place at which a document may be served on companies registered under the Act. It also applies to overseas companies registered in accordance with regulations made under section 1046. *Subsection (4)* enables court service on a company registered in Scotland or Northern Ireland at the company's principal place of business in England and Wales. (Since this is a provision about court service, the rules on companies registered in England and Wales carrying on business elsewhere in the UK will be found in the relevant legislation in those parts of the UK.) *Subsection (5)* makes clear that this section is supplemented by the "company communications provisions" referenced by section 1143.

Section 1140: Service of documents on directors, secretaries and others

1459. This section is a new provision. It ensures that the address on the public record for any director or secretary is effective for the service of documents on that person. *Subsection (3)* provides that the address is effective even if the document has no bearing on the person's responsibilities as director or secretary. This provision also applies to the address on the public record of various other persons for whom the Act requires an address on the public record. *Subsection (7)* similarly makes clear that this section is supplemented by the "company communications provisions" referenced by section 1143.

Section 1141: Service addresses

1460. This section defines "service address" for the purposes of the Companies Acts as an address at which documents may be effectively served and provides a power for regulations to specify conditions with which a service address must comply.

Section 1142: Requirement to give service address

1461. This section is a new provision. It qualifies requirements elsewhere to give an "address". Unless the requirement is for a particular kind of address (say, the usual residential address), the section makes clear that a service address (as defined in the previous Section) is what is required.

Section 1143: The company communications provisions

1462. Section 1143 introduces sections 1144 to 1148 and Schedules 4 and 5. These make new provision for communications with or from companies, typically with their members but also with debenture-holders and others.

1463. The Companies Act 1985 (Electronic Communications) Order 2000 facilitated the use of electronic and website communications in certain contexts, but there has been uncertainty as to whether other provisions under the 1985 Act for information to be communicated 'in writing' required the use of paper or could be satisfied by electronic communications. The Act makes new general provision about communications, including electronic and website communications for the Companies Acts as a whole.

1464. The general principle behind the company communications provisions is that companies should be able to use hard copy or electronic communications in all cases. However, these provisions are subject to anything in or under any other enactment, and, as regards communications between companies and Companies House, they are also subject to the provisions of Part 35 of the Act.

Section 1144: Sending or supplying documents or information

1465. This section introduces two Schedules, which apply irrespective of the company's articles:

- Schedule 4 deals with documents and information sent or supplied to a company;
- Schedule 5 deals with communications by a company and between companies

1466. Sections 1146 (requirement of authentication), 1148 (interpretation of company communications provisions) and 1168 (hard copy and electronic form and related expressions) contain provisions necessary for the interpretation of Schedules 4 and 5.

Schedule 4: Documents and information sent or supplied to a company

1467. This Schedule brings together the rules on communications to a company. In some cases a company will have other companies as members, debenture holders etc, and *paragraph 1(2)* of the Schedule makes clear that communications by such members etc is governed by Schedule 5.

1468. Part 2 of the Schedule sets out the position for communications sent or supplied in hard copy form. These are very similar to the present position. Part 3 sets out rules for communications in electronic form. Part 4 is a more general provision and means that unless the Companies Acts specify a means of communication, for example under section 291(3)(a) (circulation of written resolutions proposed by directors), then a communication to the company can be sent or supplied in any way agreed by the company.

Schedule 5: Communications by a company

1469. This Schedule sets out provisions on how companies are to communicate with their members, debenture holders etc. These rules are subject to, for example, additional rules which the FSA may require of companies traded on a regulated market.

1470. Part 2 of the Schedule sets out standard rules for communications in hard copy. *Paragraph 4* lists the addresses to which the company may send or supply documents or information. Where the company has no address for the intended recipient, the company may use the recipient's last known address. By virtue of section 310(4), this provision does not prevent a company making provision in its articles not to send notice of a general meeting to members for whom the company no longer has a valid address. Section 423(2) makes similar provision for the annual report and accounts.

1471. Part 3 of the Schedule relates to communications by e-mail or other electronic methods. *Paragraph 6* allows a company to send a document or information in electronic form to a person who has agreed (either generally for all communications or specifically for a particular document or piece of information) and where such person has not revoked that agreement.

1472. Part 4 deals with publication of documents or information on a website. *Paragraph 10* allows a company to pass a members' resolution or make provision in its articles about website communication. If it has done so, members (or their nominees) are taken to have agreed to receiving information from the company via a website if they have also been asked individually for their acceptance and have either agreed or not responded within 28 days of the company's request. Where a member has not agreed to communications in this way, the company may not ask the member again within a period of twelve months. In addition, section 1145 (right to hard copy version) gives a member the right to request a hard copy of the communication. *Paragraph 11* and section 1145 make equivalent provision for debenture holders. *Paragraph 13* requires companies to notify intended recipients each time material is published on a website. *Paragraph 15* enables the company and a member to agree alternative methods of communication, for example other than website communication where a company has defaulted to website communications.

Section 1145: Right to hard copy version

1473. This section provides individual members or debenture holders the right to require information to be sent in paper copy form. A company is required to send a paper copy of the document or information within 21 days of receiving a member's request at no charge to the member. *Subsections (4) and (5)* impose a penalty on every officer in default if the company fails to comply.

Section 1146: Requirement of authentication

1474. This section operates where provisions of the Companies Acts require information sent or supplied to a company to be authenticated. This is chiefly the case in the context of written resolutions and requests (formerly requisitions) for meetings, etc. The rule is that a signature on a document in hard copy form by the person sending it is always sufficient authentication. The company can make its own rules in respect of documents in electronic form (but there is a default where no such rules exist). *Subsection (4)* makes it clear that, where someone purports to authenticate a document on another's behalf, the company can require proof of the former's authority to do so.

Section 1147: Deemed delivery of documents and information

1475. This section sets out when communications from the company are deemed to have been delivered, but it can be excluded by contrary provision elsewhere (for example, in other legislation, in contracts or in the articles). *Subsection (5)* provides that the 48-hour period for deemed delivery is counted during normal working days only. For example, a document posted on a Friday at 3.00 pm is deemed to have been delivered the following Tuesday at 3.00 pm, unless it is a bank holiday weekend, in which case deemed delivery is the Wednesday at 3.00 pm.

Section 1148: Interpretation of company communications provisions

1476. This section sets out defined terms used in the company communications provisions and, in particular, makes clear that references in the Companies Acts to "sending" and "supplying" documents or information include all such similar expressions.

Sections 1149 to 1153: Requirements as to independent valuation

1477. These sections restate the requirements in sections 108 and 110 of the 1985 Act for the independent valuation of non-cash assets accepted by a public company. The independence requirements in sections 1151 and 1152 correspond to the independence requirements for a statutory auditor (see section 1214). They include a new specific power for the Secretary of State to define a disallowed connection for the purposes of determining whether a person is sufficiently independent to be a valuer. This is consistent with the approach taken in sections 344 and 936 of the Act.

Sections 1154 and 1155: Duty to notify registrar of certain appointments etc and failure to give such notice

1478. These sections are new provisions. The requirement to give notice of the appointment of a judicial factor (in Scotland) gives effect to a recommendation by the CLR (Final Report, paragraph 11.39). The section also requires the Charity Commissioners to notify their appointment of a receiver and manager and the regulator of community interest companies to give notice of the appointment of a manager. These officers displace directors. Section 1155 makes failure by a judicial factor to give notice an offence.

Section 1156: Meaning of "the court"

1479. This section defines the term "the court" for the purposes of the Companies Acts. The effect of this definition is that, except where an enactment or rule of law provides otherwise, cases under the Companies Acts can be heard either in the High Court or the county court in England and Wales, in the Court of Session or the sheriff court in Scotland, and, in Northern Ireland, in the High Court of Northern Ireland.

1480. The allocation of cases between the county court (or sheriff court) and the High Court (or Court of Session) will be determined partly by the courts' general powers and partly by subordinate legislation. The allocation of cases between county courts will, as now, be determined by orders made by the Lord Chancellor (see *subsection (3)*).

Section 1157: Power of court to grant relief in certain cases

1481. Under this section, which restates section 727 of the 1985 Act without substantive amendment, an officer of a company (such as a director) or a person employed by a company as auditor may apply to the court for relief from liability for negligence, default, breach of duty or breach of trust. A court may grant relief if it appears to the court that:

- the director (or other officer or auditor) has acted honestly and reasonably; and
- having regard to all the circumstances, he ought fairly to be excused.

PART 38: COMPANIES: INTERPRETATION

1482. This Part gives an interpretation of definitions used throughout the Act. Most are based on corresponding definitions in the 1985 Act. Those that are changed or new are described below.

Section 1158: Meaning of "UK-registered company"

1483. The expression "UK-registered company" is used as a drafting device to refer to any company registered under this Act. The expression includes companies treated as so registered (for instance, by virtue of having been registered under earlier legislation). It does not include an overseas company that is not itself registered in the UK but has registered particulars in the UK under section 1046.

Section 1168: Hard copy and electronic form and related expressions

1484. *Subsections (2) to (4)* of this section contain new definitions of the terms "hard copy", "electronic form" and related expressions for all purposes of the Companies Acts. *Subsection (5)* requires that documents or information be sent in electronic form must be in a form that is capable of being read and retained for future reference.

Section 1171: The former Companies Acts

1485. This section defines "former Companies Acts". The list includes the companies legislation listed in section 735 of the 1985 Act and the later enactments repealed by the Act.

Section 1172: References to requirements of this Act

1486. This section provides that requirements to be imposed *under* the Act (by regulations or orders to be made under a power contained in the Act) are included in references in the company law provisions of the Act to "the requirements of this Act".

Section 1173: Minor definitions: general

1487. The definitions in *subsection (1)* that are new or changed are as follows.

1488. The definitions of "body corporate" and "corporation", and of "firm", are new in part. They clarify the position of corporations sole and of partnerships that are legal persons but are not regarded as bodies corporate (as under Scots law).

1489. The definitions of "credit institution" and "regulated market" are changed to follow the definitions in more recent EU Directives. *Subsection (2)* makes provision to deal with the postponement of the Directive on markets in financial instruments and the fact that it may be implemented in different member States on different dates.

1490. The definition of "working day" is new. This expression replaces a variety of expressions in the existing legislation; there is no change of substance.

Section 1174 and Schedule 8: Index of defined expressions

1491. Section 1174 introduces Schedule 8 to the Act, which provides an index setting out where the definitions of terms used in the Companies Acts are to be found.

PART 39: COMPANIES: MINOR AMENDMENTS

Section 1175 and Schedule 9: Removal of special provisions about accounts and audit of charitable companies

1492. This section and Schedule remove from company law special rules about the audit of companies that are charities. Under section 249A of the 1985 Act, certain companies are subject to audit, or to an accountant's report, because they are charities, when they would be exempt as small companies if they were not charities.

1493. This section is part of achieving the objective of changing the treatment of small charitable companies so that, as far as their accounts scrutiny is concerned, they will be required to comply with the requirements of charity law rather than those of company law. The Charities Act 2006 introduced a power (section 77 of that Act) to enable the Office of the Third Sector to bring forward regulations, subject to the affirmative resolution procedure, applying charity law rules about scrutiny of financial records to charitable companies.

Section 1176: Power of Secretary of State to bring civil proceedings on company's behalf

1494. This section repeals the power of the Secretary of State, under section 438 of the 1985 Act, to bring civil proceedings on behalf of a company. *Subsections (2) and (3)* are consequential amendments to sections 439 and 453 of the 1985 Act respectively. This repeal does not affect any proceedings begun before this section comes into force.

Section 1177: Repeal of certain provisions about company directors

1495. This section repeals various provisions of Part 10 of the 1985 Act.

1496. Section 311 of the 1985 Act prohibits a company from paying director remuneration free of income tax. The Law Commissions recommended its repeal as the tax which the company agreed to pay is itself taxed as part of the emoluments of a director, and as the company is required to disclose in its annual accounts an estimate of the tax which it has undertaken to pay.

1497. Section 323 of the 1985 Act prohibits directors (including shadow directors) from buying "put" and "call" options in listed shares or debentures in the company or another in the same group. This prohibition is extended to spouses and minor children of directors by section 327 of the 1985 Act. The Law Commissions recommended its repeal.

1498. Sections 324 to 326 and 328 to 329 of, and Parts 2 to 4 of Schedule 13 to, the 1985 Act deal with the duty of a director to notify interests in shareholdings to his company and impose an obligation on the company to record those interests in a register and to disclose them to the relevant exchanges. They are repealed.

1499. Sections 343 and 344 of the 1985 Act make special provision for banking companies and the holding companies of credit institutions, allowing them to disclose in their annual accounts abbreviated particulars of loans, quasi-loans and credit transactions with directors or their connected persons. Section 413 of the Act, which replaces the annual accounts disclosure requirements of the 1985 Act in respect of loans, quasi-loans and credit transactions, makes its own special provision in *subsection (8)* of that section for banking companies and the holding companies of credit institutions.

Section 1178: Repeal of requirement that certain companies publish periodical statement

1500. This section repeals section 720 of, and the related Schedule 23 to, the 1985 Act. Section 720 requires certain insurers and deposit, provident or benefit societies to publish a periodical statement in the form set out in the Schedule. The statement contains basic information about certain liabilities and assets and, in the case of a company with shares, basic information about its share capital and issued shares. This general disclosure requirement has been superseded by specialised regulatory developments in particular fields of financial services. The application of the section is now very limited as it does not apply to any UK insurance company which is regulated by the FSA under FSMA and which complies with its rules as to the publication of annual accounts and balance sheet. Nor does it apply to any insurer authorised in any other EEA State carrying on business in the UK if it complies with equivalent rules of its home State.

Section 1179: Repeal of requirement that Secretary of State prepare annual report

1501. This section repeals the requirement, under section 729 of the 1985 Act, for the Secretary of State to cause a "general annual report on matters within the Companies Acts" to be prepared and laid before both Houses of Parliament.

Section 1180: Repeal of certain provisions about company charges

1502. This section repeals the provisions in Part 4 of the 1989 Act relating to company charges. These provisions have not been brought into force.

Section 1181: Access to constitutional documents of RTE and RTM companies

1503. This section enables the Secretary of State to make an order amending certain provisions of the Commonhold and Leasehold Reform Act 2002 and the Leasehold Reform, Housing and Urban Development Act 1993 so as to make it easier to ascertain the contents of the articles and other constitutional documents of Right To Manage ("RTM") and Right to Enfranchise ("RTE") companies (two new types of company provided for in the 2002 Act – in the case of RTE companies, by amendment to the 1993 Act).

1504. Under the Commonhold and Leasehold Reform Act 2002 and the Leasehold Reform, Housing and Urban Development Act 1993 as amended by it, the Secretary of State may make regulations prescribing model memoranda and articles of association for RTM and RTE companies, and the provisions of the model memoranda and articles so prescribed may have effect notwithstanding contrary provision in the memoranda and articles of such companies as registered at Companies House. As the legislation stands currently, a person consulting the Companies House record of an RTM or RTE company's memorandum or articles may not be aware of the company's RTM or RTE status, and therefore may also be unaware that its registered memorandum and articles have to be read in the light of any relevant regulations prescribing model memoranda and articles for RTM or RTE companies. Since the prescribed memoranda and articles may invalidate provisions of the registered documents and apply in place of them, this may cause problems.

1505. The RTM and RTE legislation is likely to be adjusted to reflect the new status of the memorandum under sections 8 and 28 in particular. Reference is made to "other constitutional documents" because it is possible that under the new constitutional arrangements, the RTM and RTE legislation should make provision about the contents of constitutional documents other than articles.

PART 40: COMPANY DIRECTORS: FOREIGN DISQUALIFICATION ETC

1506. Part 40 addresses a gap in the present law. Persons who have been disqualified from being a director, or from holding an equivalent position, or engaging in the management of a company in another State, are currently able to form a company in the UK, to appoint themselves a director of that company and then operate that company either in the UK or in the State where they have been disqualified. The provisions in this Part give the Secretary of

State a power to close the gap by making regulations to disqualify from being a director of a UK company, persons who have been disqualified in another State.

1507. Part 40 is the first Part which is outside the company law provisions of the Act. It does not, therefore, form part of the Companies Acts. This is due to the fact that the provisions in this Part are linked with those of the Company Directors' Disqualification Act 1986. That Act is not part of the Companies Acts because it has implications beyond companies to other bodies (such as NHS foundation trusts) and extends beyond persons covered by the Companies Acts to persons such as insolvency practitioners. The fact that Part 40 is not part of the Companies Acts has the consequence that the definitions in the earlier Parts of the Act do not apply – hence the need to define the term "the court" in section 1183. Similarly, the definitions for Part 40 are not listed in Schedule 8 to the Act.

Section 1182: Persons subject to foreign restrictions

1508. Section 1182 defines what is meant by "a person being subject to foreign restrictions." Only persons falling into this category may be disqualified by regulations made under this Part. This category is intended to include those who have been disqualified under (or otherwise fallen foul of) a foreign law equivalent to that in the Company Directors' Disqualification Act 1986.

Section 1183: Meaning of "the court" and "UK company"

1509. Section 1183 sets out the meaning of "the court" and "UK company" for the purposes of this Part.

Section 1184: Disqualification of persons subject to foreign restrictions

1510. Section 1184 provides a power for the Secretary of State to make regulations disqualifying a person subject to foreign restrictions from being the director of a UK company, acting as a receiver of a UK company's property, or, in any way, taking part in the promotion, formation or management of a UK company.

1511. The power is subject to affirmative resolution procedure.

Section 1185: Disqualification regulations: supplementary

1512. Section 1185 states that the regulations under section 1184 may make different provision for different types of case, and sets out some examples. If the regulations provide for application to the court (either by the Secretary of State for a disqualification order under section 1184(2)(b), or by a disqualified person seeking relief under section 1184(5)), the section requires the regulations to specify the grounds on which an application to the court may be made. It also allows the regulations to set out matters to which the court should have regard when considering an application.

Section 1186: Offence of breach of disqualification

1513. Section 1186 provides that regulations made under section 1184 may provide that a person disqualified under this Part who acts in breach of the disqualification commits an offence.

Section 1187: Personal liability for debts of company

1514. Section 1187 provides for the Secretary of State to make regulations to the effect that a person disqualified under this part who acts as a director of a UK company, or is involved in the management of a UK company is personally responsible for all debts and liabilities of the company incurred during the time that he or she is subject to foreign restrictions.

Section 1188: Statements from persons subject to foreign restrictions

1515. Section 1188 provides a power for the Secretary of State to make regulations providing that a person not disqualified under this Part but subject to foreign restrictions must send a statement to the registrar if he or she does anything that, if done by a person disqualified under this Part, would be a breach of the disqualification.

1516. The power is subject to affirmative resolution procedure.

Section 1189: Statements from persons disqualified

1517. Section 1189 provides a power for the Secretary of State to make provisions by regulation that would require a disqualified director to provide an additional statement where he or she has received approval from the court to act in a capacity that would otherwise be in breach of the disqualification.

1518. The power is subject to affirmative resolution procedure.

Section 1190: Statements: whether to be made public

1519. Section 1190 provides for regulations under sections 1188 and 1189 to state whether statements made under those regulations shall be on the public register, and the circumstances in which they may withheld from public inspection or removed from the register.

Section 1191: Offences

1520. Section 1191 provides for regulations to apply criminal sanctions for a failure to comply with any requirements on statements under sections 1188 and 1189.

PART 41: BUSINESS NAMES

1521. The provisions of this Part replace the Business Names Act 1985.

CHAPTER 1: RESTRICTED OR PROHIBITED NAMES

Section 1192: Application of this Chapter

1522. This section partly replaces section 1 of the Business Names Act 1985. It ensures that the restrictions on the use of names in the course of business apply to all persons carrying on business in the UK, other than certain individuals or partnerships (see below). In particular, the restrictions:

- apply to all companies (and not as in the Business Names Act, just to any company capable of being wound up under the Insolvency Act 1986 which trades under a name other than that under which it is registered); and

- apply to any partnership whose members include a company (and not, as in the Business Names Act, only if the name under which such a partnership does business includes names for the corporate partners other than those under which they are registered).

1523. As in the Business Names Act, the restrictions do not apply to individuals if they trade either alone or in partnership under their surnames augmented only by their forenames and/or initials. Sole traders and individuals carrying on business in partnership are also excluded from the scope of the Chapter if the only addition to their name shows the business's previous ownership

1524.   The main effect of the wider coverage is that controls apply to all overseas companies carrying on business in the UK. It also removes any uncertainty as to whether the controls apply to business entities other than companies incorporated under the Companies Acts.

Section 1193 to 1196: Sensitive words or expressions

1525.   Sections 1193 to 1195 replace sections 2, 3, 6 and 7 of the Business Names Act 1985. Section 1199 (see below) contains savings equivalent to those currently in section 2(2) of the Business Names Act.

1526.   These sections require prior approval for the use of any name for carrying on business for which a company would require approval before it could be registered under it. (Sections 54 to 56, replacing sections 26(2) and 29 of the 1985 Act, apply corresponding restrictions to company names.) The differences between the requirements under these sections and the requirements under the Business Names Act are:

- Section 1193(1)(a) requires prior approval for names likely to give the impression that the business is connected with Her Majesty's Government in Northern Ireland;

- Section 1193(1)(c) provides a power for the Secretary of State to specify in regulations the public authorities such that prior approval will be required for names likely to give the impression that the business is connected with it;

- The definition of local authority in section 1193(2) is brought up to date for Scotland and includes a district council in Northern Ireland;

- Section 1195(4) provides that the Secretary of State may refuse to consider an application for approval that is not compliant with the statutory requirements.

1527.   Section 1196 provides that approval for the use of a name may be withdrawn in appropriate circumstances.

Section 1197: Name containing inappropriate indication of company type or legal form

1528.   This section replaces sections 33, 34 and 34A of the 1985 Act. Rather than making it an offence on the face of the Act to use prohibited words, this section provides that the Secretary of State may by regulations make it an offence to carry on business under names using indicators of particular legal status, or similar words, unless entitled to do so. It complements sections 58 and 59, which control the use of statutory indicators of legal status (eg "ltd." and "p.l.c.") in companies' registered names.

Section 1198: Name giving misleading indication of activities

1529.   This section makes it an offence to use a business name that gives so misleading an indication of the nature of the activities of the business as to be likely to cause harm to the public. This section complements section 76 which gives the Secretary of State power to direct a company to change its registered name in these circumstances.

Section 1199: Savings for existing lawful business names

1530.   This section provides exemptions for those continuing to use a name that was lawful before the Act comes into force. The exemption is both from the requirement for prior approval and from using names that include a protected indicator of company status. It also retains the existing provision for when a business is transferred: providing the name was previously lawful, the business may continue under that name for 12 months even if otherwise it would not be lawful for whoever is now carrying on the business (see *subsection (3)*).

CHAPTER 2: DISCLOSURE REQUIRED IN CASE OF INDIVIDUAL OR PARTNERSHIP

1531. This Chapter re-enacts for individuals and partnerships the Business Names Act provisions relating to information which must be displayed at places of business and in correspondence. These sections ensure that a business's suppliers and customers can discover the legal identity of the person with whom they are doing business and can serve documents upon it. Section 1203 makes special provision for large partnerships so that not all the partners' names are required in all business documents, provided certain conditions are met.

Section 1200: Application of this Chapter

1532. This section partly replaces section 1 of the Business Names Act 1985. It provides that Chapter 2 applies to:

- sole traders if they trade under any name other than their true surnames augmented only by their forenames and/or initials. (Section 1208 defines initial to include any recognised abbreviation of a name);

- partnerships unless their name is the surnames of all its human partners (augmented only by their forenames and/or initials) and the registered names of its other partners.

1533. It also excludes sole traders and partnerships if the only addition to their name shows the business's previous ownership.

1534. This section ensures that the coverage of this Chapter is the same as the Business Names Act except that, unlike that Act, it does not apply to any companies. The comparable requirements for companies are in Part 5, Chapter 6.

Section 1201: Information required to be disclosed

1535. This section replaces section 4(1)(a)(i), (ii) and (iv) of the Business Names Act 1985. It specifies the information that is to be the subject of disclosure under this Chapter (ie names and addresses for service).

Sections 1202 to 1204: Disclosure requirements

1536. Sections 1202 and 1203 replace section 4(1)(a) and (2) to (7) of the Business Names Act 1985. They are designed to ensure that customers and suppliers:

- of sole traders know the true identity of the person with whom they are dealing and have an address for him/her which is effective for the service of documents relating to the business;

- of partnerships with 20 or fewer partners know the identity of every partner and the address which is effective for the service of documents relating to the business;

- of larger partnerships know the address which is effective for the service of documents relating to the business and either the identity of every partner or the address at which they can discover the identity of every partner.

1537. Large partnerships are not permitted to choose which partners' names are included in documents: they must either include the names of all the partners or none (except in the text or as a signatory) (see *subsection (2)(b)*).

1538. Section 1202 also provides power for regulations relating to the form of a notice giving the trader's or partners' name(s) and address in response to any person who asks for the information in the course of business. For companies' registered names, equivalent provision may be made in regulations under section 82.

1539. Section 1204 replaces section 4(1)(b) of the Business Names Act 1985 so far as it applies to sole traders and partnerships. It makes provision to enable customers and suppliers to discover the name(s) and the address for service of documents when visiting any business premises of the trader or partners.

Section 1205: Criminal consequences of failure to make required disclosure

1540. This section provides that certain provisions in Part 36 (offences under the Companies Acts) also apply to offences under this Part. It replaces and expands upon section 7 of the Business Names Act 1985 so far as it applies to sole traders and partnerships. It retains the existing offences of failure to comply with the requirements relating to disclosure of name and address in documents and notices.

Section 1206: Civil consequences of failure to make required disclosure

1541. This section replaces section 5 of the Business Names Act 1985 so far as it applies to sole traders and partnerships. It provides legal rights to anyone who has sustained losses as a result of failure to comply with this Chapter's requirements by a sole trader or partnership.

CHAPTER 3: SUPPLEMENTARY

Section 1207: Application of general provisions about offences

1542. This section replaces section 7(6) of the Business Names Act 1985.

Section 1208: Interpretation

1543. This section replaces section 8 of the Business Names Act 1985. In particular, the definition of "initial" means that the restrictions on names in Chapter 1 not only would not apply to James Alexander Scotland if he were to trade as "James Alexander Scotland" or "J. A. Scotland" but also if he were to trade as "Jimmy Scotland" or "Jim A. Scotland". However, the restrictions would apply if he were to trade as "Scotland Bakers" or "John Scotland".

PART 42: STATUTORY AUDITORS

1544. The provisions of this Part concern the regulation of auditors. The effects of this Part are:

- To replace Part 2 of the 1989 Act and equivalent Northern Ireland provisions, by restating those provisions with some modifications.

- To extend the category of auditors that are subject to regulation and to make provision for the registration and regulation of auditors (whether based in the UK or not) who audit companies which are incorporated outside the EU but listed in the UK;

- To provide that the Comptroller and Auditor General and the regional Auditors General are eligible to be appointed to perform statutory audits and provide a mechanism for the regulation and supervision of their functions as statutory auditor.

1545. Many of the provisions in this Part implement obligations contained in the Updated Eighth Company Law Directive on Audit (2006/43/EC) that was published on 9 June 2006. The provisions relating to Auditors General implement recommendations contained in Lord Sharman's report, "Holding to Account, The Review of Audit and Accountability for Central Government", published in 2001.

CHAPTER 1: INTRODUCTORY

Sections 1209 to 1211: Introductory

1546. Part 2 of the 1989 Act regulates only the auditors of companies. Section 1210(1) defines the meaning of statutory auditor more broadly. Persons within *subsection (1)(a) to (g)* are 'statutory auditors'. This list includes those persons who audit companies (as required under Part 16 of the Act) and those who audit building societies, insurers and banks. In addition, the Secretary of State has a power to add auditors of other persons to this list. Section 1211 cross-refers the eligibility for appointment as a statutory auditor to the requirements contained in Chapter 2 or Chapter 3 of this Part of the Act.

CHAPTER 2: INDIVIDUALS AND FIRMS

Sections 1212 and 1213: Eligibility for appointment

1547. These sections are restatements of sections 25 and 28 of the 1989 Act adapted so as to apply in relation to statutory auditors. The sections provide that for a person or firm (defined in section 1261) to be eligible for appointment as a statutory auditor, the person must be a member of a recognised supervisory body and be eligible for appointment under the rules of that body. Section 1217(2) clarifies that references to such members include references to persons who are not members but who are subject to the body's rules. (Section 1217 and Schedule 10 address the recognition of supervisory bodies, and lay down the requirements they must meet to be recognised.)

1548. Section 1213 provides that no person may act as a statutory auditor if he is ineligible. It specifies that, on becoming ineligible, the auditor must resign his office and give notice in writing. Failure to comply with this requirement is an offence, conviction of which can result in a fine (*subsections (3)* and *(4)*). If the auditor continues to act as a statutory auditor after conviction (*subsection (5)*), or continues to fail to give notice that he is ineligible for appointment as a statutory auditor (*subsection (6)*), he commits a further offence for which a daily fine may be imposed after conviction (*subsection (7)*). *Subsection (8)* provides a defence if the person did not know or had no reason to believe that he was, or had become, ineligible.

Section 1214: Independence requirement

1549. This section restates section 27 of the 1989 Act and indicates circumstances where a person may not act as a statutory auditor on grounds of lack of independence. Under *subsection (2)* this includes persons who are officers or employees of the audited entity, or the partner or employee of such a person. Under *subsection (3)*, this includes where the person is an officer or employee of a subsidiary of the audited entity. *Subsection (4)* allows the Secretary of State to make regulations regarding other connections between the audited entity and the statutory auditor by virtue of which a person will be regarded as lacking independence.

Section 1215: Effect of lack of independence

1550. This section sets out the consequences of the prohibition from acting as a statutory auditor on grounds of lack of independence, as defined in section 1214. They replicate the effect of ineligibility as explained for section 1213.

Section 1216: Effect of appointment of a partnership

1551. This section is a restatement of section 26 of the 1989 Act. The effect of the section is to ensure that when a partnership constituted in England and Wales, Northern Ireland, or any other country or territory in which a partnership is not a legal person, is appointed as a statutory auditor under this Part, the appointment may continue even if a partner leaves the partnership. For a partnership or other person to be considered as appropriate for the appointment to continue, they must be eligible for appointment as a statutory auditor and not be prohibited (as indicated in section 1214(1)). Without this provision, the appointment would cease every time the membership of the partnership changed.

Section 1217: Supervisory bodies

1552. This section restates section 30 of the 1989 Act and defines a supervisory body as a body established in the UK which maintains and enforces rules regarding the eligibility of persons appointed as statutory auditors and the conduct of statutory audit work. *Subsection (4)* introduces Schedule 10, which specifies the requirements supervisory bodies must meet in order to be recognised, and the process for doing so.

Schedule 10: Recognised supervisory bodies

Part 1: Grant and Revocation of recognition of a Supervisory Body

1553. This Schedule restates provisions in Schedule 11 to the 1989 Act. Paragraph 1 identifies the steps a body is required to take to become recognised by the Secretary of State. Paragraph 3 specifies the steps that the Secretary of State is required to take if the recognition of the body is revoked. Paragraph 5 provides that recognition (and revocation) orders are not statutory instruments. Paragraph 4 is a transitional provision that allows bodies recognised under the 1989 Act or the Companies (Northern Ireland) Order 1990 to continue to be recognised.

Part 2: Requirements for recognition of a supervisory body

1554. Paragraphs 6 and 7 require a recognised supervisory body to ensure that persons eligible for appointment as a statutory auditor hold appropriate qualifications (as defined in section 1219). They require a firm that is a statutory auditor to be controlled by qualified persons. Paragraphs 8 to 11 require the bodies to have rules and practices which ensure that

233

auditors are fit and proper persons, that professional integrity and independence is maintained, that technical standards for audits are assured and that there are procedures for maintaining appropriate levels of competence. Paragraphs 12 to 16 specify the requirements for monitoring, enforcement, discipline and investigation of complaints.

Part 3: Arrangements in which recognised supervisory bodies are required to participate

1555. Paragraphs 21 to 27 specify the arrangements with independent bodies that recognised supervisory bodies must enter into in order to meet the requirements of this Schedule described above.

Section 1218: Exemption from liability for damages

1556. This section is a restatement of section 48 of the 1989 Act. It sets out those bodies and individuals that are exempt from liability for damages arising from the discharge or claimed discharge of supervisory functions as specified in this Part of the Act (these include the effects of rules, practices, powers and arrangements of the body). It applies to recognised supervisory bodies (see sections 1217 and Schedule 10) and their officers, employees and members of their governing bodies. The exemption does not apply if they have acted in bad faith, or if it would prevent an award of damages because the act was unlawful under the Human Rights Act.

Section 1219: Appropriate qualifications

1557. This section restates section 31 of the 1989 Act. It provides that a person holds an appropriate audit qualification if he holds a professional qualification obtained in the UK which is recognised in accordance with section 1220 and Schedule 11. Qualifications recognised under Part 2 of the 1989 Act or the Companies (Northern Ireland) Order 1990 will continue to be recognised.

1558. Persons whose qualifications from other EU Member States are recognised under the European Communities (Recognition of Professional Qualifications) (First General System) Regulations 2005 to practise as statutory auditors are also considered to hold an appropriate qualification. So too are overseas qualifications from non-EU countries if approved under section 1221. *Subsection (2)* restates a transitional provision from the 1989 Act for those persons who began a course of study in accountancy before 1 January 1990 and obtained a qualification between 1 January 1990 and 1 January 1996, enabling them to apply to the Secretary of State for approval of their qualification. The transitional provisions contained in section 31(2) and (3) of the 1989 Act have not been restated.

Section 1220: Qualifying bodies and recognised professional qualifications

1559. This section is a restatement of section 32 of the 1989 Act. It defines the term "qualifying body" as a body that offers a professional qualification in accountancy and introduces Schedule 11 which sets out the requirements that qualifying bodies must impose. Only a qualification recognised in accordance with these provisions can be considered a recognised professional qualification within the meaning of section 1219(1)(a).

Schedule 11: Recognised Professional Qualifications

Part 1: Grant and revocation of recognition of a professional qualification

Paragraph 1: Application for recognition of professional qualification

1560. This Schedule restates provisions in Schedule 12 to the 1989 Act. *Paragraph 1* identifies the steps a body is required to take for a qualification it offers to be recognised by the Secretary of State. *Paragraph 3* specifies the steps that the Secretary of State is required to take if the recognition is revoked. *Paragraph 5* provides that recognition (and revocation) orders are not statutory instruments. *Paragraph 4* is a transitional provision that allows qualifications recognised under the 1989 Act or the Companies (Northern Ireland) Order 1990 to continue to be recognised.

Part 2: Requirements for recognition of a professional qualification

1561. *Paragraph 6* sets the minimum academic standards that a person must have attained before he can attempt to gain the professional qualification. *Paragraph 7* requires that the qualification is restricted to persons who have either completed a relevant academic course or have seven years' professional experience. *Paragraph 8* requires that an examination must be passed (part of which has to be in writing) for the person to achieve the qualification. This examination must be in subjects of theoretical knowledge prescribed by the Secretary of State; or a university or equivalent level examination; or by practical demonstration of knowledge to examination or diploma level that is recognised by the Secretary of State. *Paragraph 9* requires persons to carry out at least three years' practical training.

Section 1221: Approval of overseas qualifications

1562. This section restates section 33 of the 1989 Act as regards the approval of overseas qualifications from non-EU countries. It sets out the conditions that will need to be satisfied, relating to the assurance of professional competence. The section provides for approval of all those in a specified country who are qualified to audit accounts, or only those who hold specified qualifications in that country. In the case of the latter, the Secretary of State may specify any additional requirements to be satisfied. The section allows the Secretary of State to recognise an overseas qualification only if there is comparability of treatment of UK qualifications in the country in question.

Section 1222: Eligibility of individuals retaining only 1967 Act authorisation

1563. This section restates section 34 of the 1989 Act. Prior to 1967 auditors of an unquoted company were exempt from the statutory qualification requirements placed on other company auditors. The Companies Act 1967 abolished this exemption but allowed an auditor with sufficient practical experience to apply to the Secretary of State for authorisation to practise. Past authorisations will continue to be valid by virtue of the transitional provision in section 1219(1)(b). Section 1222 provides that auditors authorised under the 1967 Act may not be treated as statutory auditors for any purpose other than to perform the statutory audit of an unquoted company (as defined in section 385(2)).

Section 1223: Matters to be notified to the Secretary of State

1564. This section is a restatement of section 37 of the 1989 Act and allows the Secretary of State to identify events that must be notified to him if they occur. It requires that recognised supervisory and qualifying bodies must provide information, either in writing or some other specified manner, that is reasonably required for the Secretary of State to carry out his functions – this might include annual reports, or notification of rule or bye-law changes. This information might relate to specific time periods or specific occurrences.

Section 1224: The Secretary of State's power to call for information

1565. This section restates section 38 of the 1989 Act. It provides the Secretary of State with the power to require information from a recognised supervisory body, a recognised qualifying body or an individual statutory auditor. For example, as a result of a report provided under section 1223, the Secretary of State may request further information on a specific point to clarify if a recognised supervisory body is complying with the requirements in Schedule 10. The Secretary of State can specify the time period in which this information has to be provided.

Section 1225: Compliance orders

1566. This section is a restatement of section 39 of the 1989 Act. If a recognised supervisory or qualifying body fails to meet the requirements in Schedule 10 or 11, or it fails to comply with another requirement contained in this Part of the Act, then the Secretary of State may apply to the court for an order to make the body comply. The ultimate sanction for non-compliance by a body would be revocation of its status as a recognised body under Schedule 10 or 11.

CHAPTER 3: AUDITORS GENERAL

Section 1226: Auditors General: eligibility for appointment as a statutory auditor

1567. *Subsection (1)* defines an "Auditor General" for the purposes of this Part as the Comptroller and Auditor General, the Auditor General for Scotland, the Auditor General for Wales or the Comptroller and Auditor General for Northern Ireland. *Subsections (2) and (3)* explain that an Auditor General is eligible for appointment as a statutory auditor, unless his eligibility has been suspended by the Independent Supervisor under section 1234.

Section 1227: Individuals responsible for audit work on behalf of Auditors General

1568. This section provides that an Auditor General must ensure that the individuals within his charge, who are carrying out statutory audits on the Auditor General's behalf, are, in their own right, eligible for appointment as a statutory auditor by virtue of the qualifications and requirements that are set out in Chapter 2.

Section 1228: Appointment of the Independent Supervisor

1569. *Subsections (1) and (2)* provide that the Secretary of State must appoint a body to be the Independent Supervisor of Auditors General in respect of the exercise of statutory audit functions. *Subsection (3)* provides for the appointment of the Independent Supervisor to have the effect of making it subject to the obligations of the Freedom of Information Act 2000. *Subsections (4), (5) and (6)* provide that a body may be appointed as Independent Supervisor of an Auditor General if it is a corporate body or unincorporated association that is willing to carry out the function, that has arrangements in place that will ensure the supervision is carried out effectively, and that will exercise such functions and requirements that may be laid down in the Secretary of State's order appointing it. The appointed Independent Supervisor must perform its function on a UK-wide basis for all four Auditors General in accordance with section 1229(1).

Section 1229: Supervision of Auditors General by the Independent Supervisor

1570. This section sets the framework for the supervision arrangements to be carried out by the Independent Supervisor. *Subsection (2)* provides that the Independent Supervisor must establish arrangements with one or more third parties to carry out aspects of the supervisory function. *Subsection (3)* provides that the arrangements with a third party cover standards on professional integrity and independence, as well as the technical standards for statutory audit work; monitoring performance; investigating matters arising from that performance; and as necessary holding disciplinary hearings and deciding whether any disciplinary action should be taken. *Subsections (6) and (7)* make provisions relating to the payment of fines under the disciplinary arrangements.

Section 1230: Duties of Auditors General in relation to supervision arrangements

1571. *Subsection (1)* makes it a duty for each Auditor General to comply with the standards set by, as well as the monitoring arrangements and decisions of, the independent supervision arrangements. It also provides in *subsection (2)* for each Auditor General to pay the proportion of the costs of the independent supervisory arrangements that may be notified to the Auditor General in writing. *Subsection (3)* provides that the payment of such costs is to be regarded as expenditure of the National Audit Office in the case of the Comptroller and Auditor General, and as expenditure of the Northern Ireland Audit Office in the case of the Comptroller and Auditor General for Northern Ireland. In the case of the Auditor General for Scotland, under section 13 of the Public Finance and Accountability (Scotland) Act 2000 (asp 1) the expenses of the Auditor General are paid by Audit Scotland. In the case of the Auditor General for Wales, under section 93 of the Government of Wales Act 1998 the expenses of the Auditor General are met by the Assembly.

Section 1231: Reports by the Independent Supervisor

1572. This section provides that the Independent Supervisor must provide at least one report each calendar year to the Secretary of State and to the First Minister in Scotland, The First Minister and the Deputy First Minister in Northern Ireland and the Assembly First Minister in Wales. The Secretary of State must then lay the report before each House of Parliament.

Section 1232: Matters to be notified to the Independent Supervisor

1573. This section makes it a legal requirement for an Auditor General to notify the Independent Supervisor in writing of events that the Independent Supervisor may specify and is consistent with the requirement for other statutory auditors as contained in section 1223.

Section 1233: The Independent Supervisor's power to call for information

1574. This section makes provision enabling the Independent Supervisor to require an Auditor General to provide information. It enables the Independent Supervisor to specify the period within which the information must be provided and how the information must be verified. This section is consistent with the requirement for other statutory auditors as contained in section 1224.

Section 1234: Suspension notices

1575. This section provides the Independent Supervisor with the power to suspend an Auditor General's eligibility for appointment as a statutory auditor if, for example, he falls short of the standards laid down for performance of statutory audit work. It also sets out the provisions as to how the suspension will be effected, and the considerations pertaining to the decision to suspend. It provides for a process leading up to the issuing of a suspension notice, including the hearing of representations from the Auditor General in question.

Section 1235: Effect of suspension notices

1576. This section provides that an Auditor General must not act as a statutory auditor of a particular person if he is suspended in relation to that person. If the suspension starts during his term of office, the Auditor General must resign as a statutory auditor immediately, and tell the audited person that he has resigned. *Subsection (3)* makes it clear that the criminal offences in section 1213 (ineligibility for appointment as a statutory auditor) do not apply to an Auditor General who is ineligible by virtue of a suspension notice.

Section 1236: Compliance orders

1577. This section provides the power for the Independent Supervisor to take an Auditor General to court if he fails to comply with any obligation imposed by or by virtue of this Part of the Act. The court may direct the Auditor General to take such steps as it thinks fit to ensure compliance.

Section 1237: Proceedings involving the Independent Supervisor

1578. This section provides that where the Independent Supervisor is an unincorporated association it may take proceedings in the name of the body corporate under which it is constituted.

Section 1238: Grants to the Independent Supervisor

1579. This section amends section 16(2) of the C(AICE) Act 2004. The effect of the amendment is that the body that carries out the functions of the Independent Supervisor is eligible for grants from the Secretary of State under section 16 of that Act to meet the expenditure of the body and any subsidiary. It also means that the body may be exempt from liability in damages under section 18 of the Act.

CHAPTER 4: THE REGISTER OF AUDITORS ETC

Section 1239: The register of auditors

1580. This section restates section 35 of the 1989 Act but extends the provision to cover other statutory auditors (as defined in section 1210) and third country auditors (as defined in section 1241). It requires the Secretary of State to make regulations that require the keeping of a register of those persons eligible to be a statutory auditor and third country auditors. *Subsection (2)* sets out the information that must be included on the register and includes the person's name and address and the name of the relevant supervisory body for the person. If an individual statutory auditor works for a firm that is a statutory auditor, both must be entered separately on the register and cross-referenced. In *subsection (3)* additional information, namely the name and address of directors, members or partners, is required from bodies corporate (including limited liability partnerships), corporations sole and partnerships. The section allows for certain parts of the register to be kept by different persons, for example an oversight body may keep the information regarding third country auditors, whilst the recognised supervisory bodies may keep information regarding other statutory auditors. *Subsection (6)* confers a power to provide that information in the register, or a certified copy of it, is to be made available to the public upon request. A charge for access to this information is permitted. *Subsection (7)* allows the Secretary of State to disapply some or all of the requirements of *subsections (2)(e) and (3)* in relation to third country auditors (for example, if they are already subject to equivalent supervision in their home country).

Section 1240: Information to be made available to public

1581.   This new provision gives the Secretary of State the power to make regulations placing an obligation on statutory auditors to make information regarding their ownership, governance, internal controls with respect to quality and independence of audit work, turnover and names of persons for whom the person has acted as statutory auditor, available to the public. Any such obligations are additional to those referred to in section 1239.

CHAPTER 5: REGISTERED THIRD COUNTRY AUDITORS

Section 1241: Meaning of "third country auditor", "registered third country auditor" etc

1582.   This is a new provision that sets out the definition of a third country auditor and a registered third country auditor. The section provides that a third country auditor is an auditor (whether based in the UK or not) of the accounts of a company incorporated or formed in a non-EU country, whose shares are admitted for trading on a UK market such as the London Stock Exchange.

Section 1242: Duties of registered third country auditors

1583.   *Subsections (1) to (3)* require registered third country auditors to be subject to systems of independent monitoring and discipline in the UK in accordance with Schedule 12. These provisions are similar to supervision arrangements for statutory auditors contained in section 1212(1) (membership of a Recognised Supervisory Body) and section 1217 (Supervisory Bodies) and Schedule 10. *Subsection (4)* empowers the Secretary of State to disapply the requirements in subsections (1) to (3). For example, he may disapply the requirements if satisfied that the third country auditor is already subject to equivalent supervision arrangements in his home country.

Schedule 12: Arrangements in which registered third country auditors are required to participate

1584.   The requirements in this Schedule are new. They describe the independent monitoring and investigation arrangements which third country auditors must participate in.

Sections 1243 and 1244: Information

1585.   These sections replicate for registered third country auditors the requirements in section 1223 and 1224 for the notification of information to the Secretary of State. Third country auditors may be required to provide any information that might reasonably be required for the Secretary of State to carry out his functions.

Sections 1245 and 1246: Enforcement

1586.   The provisions in section 1245 enable the Secretary of State to apply to the court for an order to make a registered third country auditor comply with its obligations under the Part. The provisions in section 1246 empower the Secretary of State to make provision as to the removal of the third country auditors from the register of auditors in certain circumstances. In doing so, regard must be had to whether the third country auditor has complied with his obligations under this Part.

Section 1247: Grants to bodies concerned with arrangements under Schedule 12

1587. This section amends section 16(2) of the C(AICE) Act 2004. The effect of the amendment is that the body that carries out the monitoring and investigation functions in relation to third country auditors is eligible for grants from the Secretary of State under section 16 of that Act. It also means that the body may be exempt from liability in damages under section 18 of the Act.

CHAPTER 6: SUPPLEMENTARY AND GENERAL

Sections 1248 and 1249: Power to require second company audit

1588. These sections restate section 29 of the 1989 Act empowering the Secretary of State to require a second audit of a company in circumstances where the person appointed as statutory auditor was not eligible for appointment or was not independent of the company audited. *Subsection (2)* permits the Secretary of State to direct either that a second audit is performed or that a review of the first audit is carried out (which will inform whether a second audit is required). *Subsections (5) to (8)* set out the criminal sanctions on the company should it fail to comply with that order. Section 1249 allows the audited person to recover the costs of the second audit from the first auditor, if the first auditor knew when he acted that he was not eligible or not independent.

Section 1250: Misleading, false and deceptive statements

1589. This section is a restatement of the offences in section 41 of the 1989 Act but also extends these offences to third country auditors. *Subsection (1)* sets out offences in respect of persons who provide information that they know to be misleading, false or deceptive. *Subsection (2)* makes it an offence for a person to hold himself out as a registered auditor where he is not registered as such in accordance with section 1239. *Subsection (3)* makes a similar provision for third country auditors. *Subsection (4)* makes it an offence for either a supervisory or qualifying body to hold itself out as recognised when it is not so recognised. *Subsection (8)* provides a defence if the person took all reasonable precautions and exercised due diligence to avoid committing the offence.

Section 1251: Fees

1590. This provision is based on section 45 of the 1989 Act and extends the powers of the Secretary of State to make regulations to prescribe periodical fees which must be paid by the Auditors General and registered third country auditors as well as recognised supervisory bodies and recognised qualifying bodies.

Section 1252 and 1253: Delegation of Secretary of State's functions

1591. These provisions replace sections 46 and 46A of the 1989 Act and empower the Secretary of State to establish a body, or appoint an existing body, to exercise his functions relating to statutory auditors and the recognition of bodies that supervise auditors and/or provide professional qualifications. To do so, the Secretary of State must make a delegation order that is in accordance with Schedule 13. However, *subsection (6)* provides that some delegated functions must remain exercisable concurrently by the Secretary of State: namely the power to call for information (sections 1224 and 1244) and the power to issue directions to comply with international obligations (section 1254). *Subsection (7)* also provides that certain delegated functions concerning the approval of overseas qualifications (section 1221) can be exercised only with the consent of the Secretary of State. *Subsection (3)* provides for the delegation of the body to have the effect of making it subject to the obligations of the Freedom of Information Act 2000. The Professional Oversight Board is currently appointed under section 46 of the 1989 Act to exercise the Secretary of State's functions.

1592. Section 1253 specifies the conditions for delegating functions to an existing body. It ensures that an existing body is not precluded from exercising any delegated function on the basis of its involvement with the monitoring, investigation or disciplinary arrangements that are set out in Schedule 10.

Schedule 13: Supplementary provisions with respect to delegation order

1593. This Schedule restates the provisions of Schedule 13 to the 1989 Act. *Paragraph 2* provides that the delegated body is not to be regarded as acting on behalf of the Crown. *Paragraphs 7 to 9* provide for the delegated body to exercise any legislative functions by instrument in writing and not by statutory instrument. Instruments must be made available to the public and the Secretary of State may require the body to consult prior to the making of regulations. *Paragraph 10* requires the delegated body to report annually to the Secretary of State on the performance of its functions.

Section 1254: Directions to comply with international obligations

1594. This provision restates section 40 of the 1989 Act and empowers the Secretary of State to direct recognised supervisory or qualifying bodies, or any body delegated under section 1252, to comply with Community or other international obligations. If the body fails to comply with a direction, the Secretary of State can apply to the court for his direction to be enforced.

Section 1255: Offences by bodies corporate, partnerships and unincorporated associations

1595. This provision restates section 42 of the 1989 Act and deals with offences committed by bodies corporate, partnerships and other unincorporated associations. Where an offence committed by such a body is committed with the consent or connivance of, or is attributable to the neglect of, an officer (in the case of a body corporate), a partner (in the case of a partnership) or an officer or member (in the case of an unincorporated association), that officer, partner or member is also guilty of the offence.

Section 1256: Time limits for prosecution of offences

1596. This provision restates section 43 of the 1989 Act and sets a twelve-month time limit for the prosecution of offences within each of the jurisdictions. *Subsections (1) to (4)* identify that the date on which knowledge of sufficient evidence of the offence to justify prosecuting becomes known to either the Secretary of State or Director of Public Prosecutions (for England and Wales), the Lord Advocate (for Scotland) or Director of Public Prosecutions for Northern Ireland is taken as the date from which the twelve month time limit commences. In any event, the prosecution may not be commenced if three years have passed since the date on which the offence was committed.

Section 1257: Jurisdiction and procedure in respect of offences

1597. This provision restates section 44 of the 1989 Act and deals with the jurisdiction and procedure in respect of offences. It specifies that the jurisdiction is that in which a body corporate or unincorporated association has its place of business or, in the case of an individual, where he is located. It also provides for an unincorporated association to be treated in the same way as a body corporate.

Section 1258: Service of notices

1598. This provision restates section 49 of the 1989 Act and states how notices and other documents may be served under this Part of the Act on any person other than the Secretary of State. The three permitted methods of service are: delivery to the person, leaving the document at the person's address, or sending it by post to the person's address.

Section 1259: Documents in electronic form

1599. This is a new provision to allow delivery of notices, directions or other documents in electronic form. It allows the use of e-communications where existing provisions in this Part impose requirements on the giving or sending of notices, directions or other documents, provided the recipient indicates he is prepared to accept this form of delivery.

Section 1260: Meaning of "associate"

1600. This provision restates section 52 of the 1989 Act and defines the meaning of "associate". This definition is particularly relevant for the independence requirement for statutory auditors set out in section 1214.

Section 1261: Minor definitions

1601. This provision is a restatement of section 53 of the 1989 Act with certain extra definitions. *Subsection (3)* empowers the Secretary of State, by regulations, to make amendments to this Part which are needed in relation to the application of the Part to a "firm" (as defined by *subsection (1)*) which is not a partnership or body corporate.

Section 1262: Index of defined expressions

1602. This provision contains an index to the defined terms used in the Part.

Section 1263: Power to make provision in consequence of changes affecting accountancy bodies

1603. This provision restates section 51 of the 1989 Act. The provision empowers the Secretary of State to amend by regulation legislation (including this Act) that refers to accountancy bodies in the event of a name change, merger or transfer of engagements affecting the bodies.

Section 1264 and Schedule 14: Consequential amendments

1604. Section 1264 introduces Schedule 14, which contains amendments consequential on this Part to the C(AICE) Act 2004.

PART 43: TRANSPARENCY OBLIGATIONS AND RELATED MATTERS

Section 1265: The transparency obligations directive

1605. Section 1265 inserts a definition of the "transparency obligations directive" at the appropriate place in Part 6 of the Financial Services and Markets Act 2000("FSMA").

Section 1266: Transparency rules

1606. Section 1266 inserts seven new sections into Part 6 of FSMA: *sections 89A, 89B, 89C, 89D, 89E, 89F and 89G.* Part 6 of FSMA deals with certain aspects of the regulation of securities that are traded on regulated markets in the UK. These new sections make provision about rules that may be made by the "competent authority" (which is the Financial Services Authority ("the Authority")) for the purposes of the Transparency Directive (2004/109/EC)"transparency rules".

New Section 89A: Transparency rules

1607. *Subsection (1)* of new *section 89A* of FSMA enables the Authority to make transparency rules to implement the Transparency Directive in the UK. *Subsection (2)* enables the rules to include provision for any matter arising out of or related to the Directive provisions.

1608. The Transparency Directive itself covers issuers whose securities are traded on regulated markets and people who hold voting rights attached to shares in such issuers. The scope of the rule-making power allows the rules to address other matters arising from the Directive's implementation, for example, to ensure that secondary legislation adopted by the Commission can be incorporated into the transparency rules, and that optional aspects of the Directive can be implemented, where the Authority considers this appropriate.

1609. It is expected that rules made under *section 89A(1)* will implement the Transparency Directive by-

- requiring holders of votes attached to shares in issuers to make disclosure about their holdings at certain thresholds (see new *section 89B*);

- requiring issuers to make public their annual accounts and reports, prepared in accordance with the EU International Accounts Standards Regulation (Regulation (EC) 1606/2002), and, where appropriate, half-yearly and interim management statements about their business(see new *section 89C*);

- requiring issuers to make notification about voting rights held by themselves in respect of their own voting shares (see new *section 89D*);

- requiring issuers to notify the Authority and the market of any proposed change to their constitution (see new *section 89E*).

1610. *Subsection (3)(a)* enables the Authority to make rules about disclosures of voteholdings to UK markets that are not regulated markets (within the meaning of section 103(1) of FSMA) (such as the AIM). *Subsection (3)(b)* enables the Authority to make rules about disclosure in relation to certain comparable instruments in respect of voting shares. These are instruments that give the holder a level of economic, as opposed to legal, control over votes attached to shares. An example of the type of instrument that the rules could extend to cover is a contract for difference, known as a "CFD".

1611. *Subsection (4)* specifies further matters that the rules may cover. These include: how the proportion of voting rights held by an issuer is to be determined; when voting rights held by one person may be regarded as being held by another; the nature, form, timing and presentation of any notification; and the circumstances in which any of the requirements of *section 89A* may not apply.

New Section 89B: Provision of voteholder information

1612. New *section 89B* sets out provisions for notifications by voteholders under transparency rules. *Subsection (1)* specifies that notification can be required to be made to the issuer or to the public or to both. Under *subsection (2)*, rules may provide for such information to be notified at the same time to the Authority.

1613. *Subsection (5)* sets out the circumstances in which voteholders may be required to notify of a change in the proportion of voting rights (i.e. when a proportion crosses above or below, or reaches, a proportion designated in the rules).

New Section 89C: Provision of information by issuers of transferable securities

1614. New *section 89C* sets out provisions for issuers of transferable securities to provide information under transparency rules. *Subsection (1)* clarifies that information can be required to be given to the public or the Authority or both.

1615. The rules cover annual financial reports (both financial statements and management reports) and, for certain issuers, half-yearly financial reports and interim management statements, as required by the Transparency Directive. The rules can also require issuers to disclose certain other information relating to voteholder information, information about the different classes of share they have issued and the total number of voting rights attached to each class, their own voteholdings, their capital, and information about new loan issues.

New Section 89D: Notification of voting rights held by issuer

1616. New *section 89D* enables the rules to provide for issuers to make notification of the proportion of voting rights they hold in respect of their own voting shares. *Subsection (1)(a)* permits rules to set the initial notification period in accordance with the requirements of the Transparency Directive at Article 30.2. *Subsections (1)(b), (2) and (3)* set out the circumstances under which issuers of transferable securities must notify of a change in the proportion of voting rights (i.e. when a proportion crosses above or below, or reaches, a proportion designated in the rules).

New Section 89E: Notification of proposed amendment of issuer's constitution

1617. New *section 89E* enables the rules to provide that an issuer of transferable securities admitted to trading on a regulated market must notify a proposed amendment to its constitution to the Authority and the market.

New Section 89F: Transparency rules: interpretation etc

1618. New *section 89F* defines a number of terms used in the sections *89A to 89G*.

New Section 89G: Transparency rules: other supplementary provisions

1619. New *section 89G* sets out further supplementary provisions relating to the transparency rules. *Subsection (1)* enables the Authority to make rules imposing the same obligations on a person who has applied for the admission of transferable securities to trading on a regulated market without the issuer's consent as they impose on an issuer of transferable securities. *Subsection (2)* enables the Authority to make rules to allow it to make public information that voteholders or issuers are required to make public, where they fail to do so themselves. *Subsection (3)* will enable the Authority to make public information notified to it in accordance with transparency rules.

1620.   There is some overlap between notifications required by the Panel on Takeovers and Mergers in the rules made under Part 28, and notifications required by the Transparency Directive. Subsection (4) enables transparency rules to cross-refer to rules made by the Panel under Part 28, which will enable greater alignment between the two sets of rules.

Section 1267: Competent Authority's power to call for information

1621.   Section 1267 inserts three new sections into Part 6 of FSMA: *sections 89H to 89J*.

1622.   New *section 89H* permits the Authority to call for information from specified persons, set out in *subsection (2)*, including issuers of shares and their auditors and directors, and voteholders and their auditors, directors and persons controlling or controlled by voteholders.

1623.   *Subsection (3)* limits the Authority to requesting information and documents reasonably required in connection with the transparency rules. *Subsection (4)* enables the Authority to determine the timeframe for production and provision of information, and the location for the information to be provided. *Subsection (5)* makes it clear that the production of the material as required by this section does not affect any lien on a document.

1624.   New *section 89I* sets outs the requirements connected with the Authority's power to call for information. The Authority will be empowered to specify the form of the information or documents it calls for under *section 89H (1)*, and may require its authentication or verification (*subsection (2)*). The Authority is permitted, under *subsection (3)*, to take copies of and extracts from the documentation provided, and may also require the persons providing the information, or any "relevant person" within the meaning of *subsection (4)* (which includes directors, auditors, actuaries, accountants, lawyers and employees), to submit an explanation of any documentation produced.

1625.   If a person fails to comply with the requirement to produce a document, the Authority is permitted under *subsection (5)* to require a person to state where the document is.

1626.   New *section 89J* sets out the supplementary provisions in relation to the competent authority's power to call for information in *sections 89H and 89I*.

Section 1268: Powers exercisable in case of infringement of transparency obligation

1627.   Section 1268 inserts four new sections into Part 6 of FSMA: *sections 89K to 89N*.

1628.   The four new sections set out the Authority's powers in case of infringement of transparency obligations. *Section 89K* enables the Authority to make a public statement if an issuer is failing or has failed to comply with its obligations. It may only do so after it has issued a warning notice to the issuer (*subsection (2)*), and after any representations from the issuer, it has provided the issuer with a decision notice (*subsection (3)*). *Subsection (4)* requires the Authority to provide the issuer with notice that it has a right to refer the matter to the Tribunal.

1629.   New *section 89L* gives the Authority the power, in certain circumstances, to suspend or prohibit trading of securities admitted to trading on a regulated market, or to request the market operator to suspend or prohibit such trading. The powers are to be used where the Authority suspects (*subsections (2)* and *(3)*) or finds (*subsection 4*) applicable breaches of transparency obligations. The Authority's powers to request a market operator to prohibit trading could be used where and issuer whose home member State is the UK is listed in another EEA State.

1630. *Section 89M* sets out the procedures relating to the suspension and prohibition powers of the Authority set out in *section 89L*.

1631. New *section 89N* sets out the right for those who receive a decision notice or a notice under *section 89M* to refer matters to the Tribunal.

Section 1269: Corporate governance rules

1632. Section 1269 inserts new *section 89O* into FSMA which gives the Authority a power (under Part 6 of FSMA) to make rules implementing, enabling the implementation of or dealing with matters arising out of Community obligations on corporate governance of issuers on a regulated market.

1633. This rule-making power will enable the Authority to make corporate governance rules to cover issuers for whom the UK is the home member State, and whose securities are traded on a regulated market in the UK or elsewhere in the EEA.

1634. *Subsection (2)* sets out the type of corporate governance provision covered by this rule making power. These include:

- the nature, constitution or functions of the organs of issuers;
- the manner in which organs of the issuer conduct themselves;
- the requirements imposed on organs of the issuer;
- the relationship between the different organs of the issuer;
- the relationship between the organs of the issuer and the members of the issuer (or holders of the issuer's securities).

1635. *Subsection (3)* provides that greater burdens must not be imposed by corporate governance rules on issuers whose securities are traded outside the UK than those imposed by corporate governance rules or listing rules on issuers with securities on UK markets.

Section 1270: Liability for false or misleading statements in certain publications

1636. Section 1270 inserts *sections 90A and 90B* into FSMA and establishes a regime for civil liability to third parties by issuers admitted to trading on a regulated market in respect of disclosures made public in response to provisions implementing obligations imposed by the Transparency Directive.

1637. Although no issuer has been found liable in damages under English law in respect of statements made in narrative reports or financial statements, the law relating to financial markets and to the obligations of issuers to investors on those markets has been developing, in the light of increased regulation of both domestic and European origin. The Transparency Directive has continued that process and increased the level of uncertainty as to whether any actionable duty is owed by an issuer and its directors to investors.

1638. The Transparency Directive sets out the periodic financial disclosures that must be made by issuers admitted to trading on a regulated market. Articles 4 and 5 of the Transparency Directive provide for annual and half-yearly reports, including management statements, to be made public, and requires statements made by persons responsible within the issuer for these disclosures (the directors in the case of a public company) that these give a true and fair view, and that the management report includes a fair review of certain matters. Article 6 requires the disclosure of interim management statements.

1639. The Transparency Directive also sets out the minimum requirements for a liability regime that must be adopted by the UK at Article 7, and recital (17) states "Member States should remain free to determine the extent of the liability".

1640. These provisions give considerable flexibility to Member States in the liability regime they choose to adopt in respect of disclosures under the Directive. The Government has established an exhaustive regime in relation to ensuring the delivery and accuracy of these reports including criminal offences, administrative penalties and actions for civil damages. The provisions in this section relate only to the position in respect of the civil liability of issuers on regulated markets to investors in their securities. The liability regime does not cover issuers on exchange-regulated markets. Their position remains unchanged by implementation of the Transparency Directive.

1641. While it is intended that there be no additional liability under the Directive in respect of the disclosures to which it relates, the regime leaves undisturbed any other liability owed by directors to the issuer and to members of the company under UK and other national law, and any liability under other FSA rules. It also leaves undisturbed any liability of the issuer in respect of any loss or damage arising otherwise than as a result of acquiring securities in reliance on the relevant statement or report.

1642. The primary liability of directors and issuers for the accuracy of the required disclosures comprises criminal offences and administrative penalties under the provisions of Part 15 of this Act and Part 6 of FSMA. The provisions in Part 6 require compliance with FSA rules giving effect to the obligations in the Directive and provide for penalties in respect of failure to comply with the rules. In addition, restitution can potentially be ordered by the court, on application of the Authority or Secretary of State, under section 382 of FSMA or by the Authority directly under section 384 of FSMA.

1643. The Government's intention in developing a civil liability regime has been to provide certainty in an uncertain area and to ensure that the potential scope of liability is reasonable, in relation both to expectations and the likely state of the law after the implementation of the Transparency Directive. In particular, the Government was anxious not to extend unnecessarily the scope of any duties which might be owed to investors or wider classes of third parties, in order to protect the interests of company members, employees and creditors. However, as the state of the law after the implementation of the Transparency Directive is not certain, the Government has taken a power, at new *section 90B*, that will enable the provision introduced by section 1270 to be added to or amended if a wider or narrower civil liability regime is deemed appropriate.

New section 90A: Compensation for statements in certain publications

1644. *Subsection (1)(a)* of new *section 90A* provides that the civil liability regime set out in that section applies to those reports and statements required by provisions implementing

Articles 4 to 6 of the Transparency Directive. Depending on transparency rules, we would expect this to include annual and half yearly financial statements and management reports, the sign-off by directors or other responsible parties, as well as interim management statements.

1645. *Subsection (1)(b)* adds to the scope of the regime the information included in preliminary announcements of results made in advance of the reports and statements required by provision implementing Article 4 of the Transparency Directive, but only to the extent that it is intended that the information will appear in the final report or statement and be presented in substantially the same form as that in which it is presented in the preliminary announcement.

1646. *Subsection (2)* sets the scope of the civil liability regime to cover securities of all issuers for which the UK is the home Member State (whether the regulated market on which they are traded is situated in or outside the UK), as well as to cover those issuers whose securities are traded on a regulated market situated in the UK <u>and</u> for whom the UK is the host Member State. UK holders of securities of other issuers (i.e. those for whom the UK is neither a host nor a home State) will not be able to rely on the rights of action set out.

1647. *Subsection (3)* provides that issuers of such securities are liable to pay compensation to a person who has acquired those securities and has suffered loss in respect of them as a result of any untrue or misleading statement in a publication to which this section applies, or an omission of a required statement from such a statement. *Subsection (4)* however limits the liability of the issuer to circumstances where a "person discharging managerial responsibilities" in relation to the publication within the issuer (see *subsection (9)*) knows the statement to be untrue or misleading, or is reckless as to whether the statement is untrue or misleading, or, in the case of omissions, where it is known to be a dishonest concealment of a material fact.

1648. *Subsection (5)* provides that loss will not be regarded as having been suffered for the purposes of *subsection (3)* unless the person suffering it acquired the relevant securities in reliance on the information in the publication and at a time when and in circumstances where it was reasonable to rely on that publication.

1649. *Subsection (6)* limits the liability with regard to untrue or misleading statements, or omissions, in documents to which the section applies. It sets out that issuers are not liable for any liability other than that provided for by the section and that any person who is not the issuer is not liable, other than to the issuer.

1650. *Subsection (8)* clarifies that the section does not affect Part 6 of FSMA conferring liability for a civil penalty, liability for a criminal offence or the right to seek restitution.

1651. *Subsection (9)* sets out the persons who are to be considered as discharging managerial responsibilities for the purposes of the section. This is any director of the issuer, or where the issuer's affairs are managed by the members, a member of the issuer. In the case where the issuer does not have directors, or members, any senior executive with responsibilities in relation to the publication is considered as discharging managerial responsibilities.

New section 90B: Power to make further provision about liability for published information

1652. *Subsection (1)* of new *section 90B* establishes a power to make further provision about liability for published information. The new section allows the Treasury by regulations to amend any primary or subordinate legislation relating to the liability of issuers and others in respect of information, including the regime set out in new *section 90A* of FSMA. The exercise of the proposed power could, for example, result in that regime or some other appropriate regime applying to other classes of information, such as information that is required to be disclosed by issuers to shareholders or markets under the Market Abuse Directive (MAD).

1653. Regulations made under the section would be made using the affirmative procedure (see the amendment to section 429(2) of FSMA made by paragraph 12 of Schedule 15).

Section 1271: exercise of powers where UK is host member State

1654. Section 1271 inserts a new section into Part 6 of FSMA: section 100A.

1655. New *section 100A* sets out the Authority's ability to exercise powers in relation to infringements of prospectus rules and transparency rules or related provisions where issuers' home State is not the UK. *Subsection (2)* clarifies that the enforcement powers extend only to cover infringements required by the relevant directive. *Subsection (3)* sets out the process by which the Authority must engage with the home State competent authority when it finds there has been an infringement. *Subsection (4)* sets out limitations on the Authority's ability to act in those circumstances, but *subsection (5)* provides that, in the appropriate circumstances, it must take all appropriate measures to protect investors.

1656. *Subsection (6)* imposes an obligation on the Authority to inform the Commission where it takes action to protect investors.

Section 1272 and Schedule 15: Transparency obligations and related matters: minor and consequential amendments

1657. Section 1272 introduces Schedule 15, which makes minor and consequential amendments to FSMA related to the provision in sections 1265 to 1271. The Schedule also makes amendments to the C(AICE)Act 2004.

Part 1: Amendments of the Financial Services and Markets Act 2000

1658. Part 1 of Schedule 15 makes minor and consequential amendments to FSMA.

1659. *Paragraph 2* amends section 73 of FSMA to extend, for the purposes of the transparency rules (which can apply to non-regulated UK markets), the factors to which the Authority must have regard when making rules under Part 6 of FSMA, so that these extend to effects on markets other than regulated markets.

1660. *Paragraph 3* amends section 73A of FSMA to provide that transparency rules and corporate governance rules are "Part 6 rules" for the purposes of Part 6 of FSMA. But paragraph 3 also makes clear that these rules are distinct and separate from other Part 6 rules, such as the listing rules, disclosure rules, and prospectus rules. These different kinds of rules impose different, and sometimes overlapping, obligations on different groups of issuers.

1661. *Paragraph 6* amends the penalty regime for breaches of Part 6 rules in section 91 of FSMA, so that it applies also to non-compliance with transparency rules, provisions made under the Transparency Directive, and corporate governance rules.

1662.   *Paragraph 8* amends section 97 of FSMA to enable the Authority to appoint a person to carry out investigations into breaches of the transparency rules or related provisions or the corporate governance rules.

1663.   *Paragraph 9* amends section 99 of FSMA, which relates to fees, so as to enable the Authority to levy fees under the transparency rules.

1664.   *Paragraphs 10 and 11* amend two definitions in Part 6 of FSMA ("transferable securities" in *section 102A* and "regulated market" in *section 103*) to refer to the up–to-date Community legislation (i.e. the Markets in Financial Instruments Directive (2004/39)). These paragraphs also add definitions for the purposes of the provisions on transparency rules.

1665.   *Paragraph 12* adds regulations made under new section 90B of FSMA to the list of statutory instruments subject to the affirmative procedure in section 429(2) of FSMA.

Part 2: Amendments of Companies (Audit, Investigations and Community Enterprise) Act 2004

1666.   *Paragraphs 14 and 15* amend section 14 and 15 of the C(AICE) Act 2004. The amendments mean that periodic accounts and reports of issuers required under corporate governance rules or transparency rules may be examined by the FRRP.

Section 1273: Corporate governance regulations

1667.   Section 1273 provides the Secretary of State with a regulation-making power similar to the power given to the Authority in new *section 89O* of FSMA inserted by section 1269.

1668.   The Secretary of State may make regulations for the purposes of implementing, enabling the implementation of or dealing with matters arising out of Community obligations on corporate governance for UK companies whose securities are traded on a regulated market in the UK or elsewhere in the EEA.

1669.   *Subsection (3)(a)* allows for regulations to be made by reference to any code regulating corporate governance. This could include, for example, the Combined Code on Corporate Governance (issued by the Financial Reporting Council).

1670.   *Subsection (4)* specifies that any criminal offence created by the regulations may not impose a greater penalty than an unlimited fine.

1671.   *Subsection (5)* provides for regulations to be made by way of negative resolution. However, by virtue of section 1292(4), it will also be possible to make regulations under this power by affirmative procedure.

PART 44: MISCELLANEOUS PROVISIONS

Regulation of actuaries etc

1672.   These provisions are the first step in implementing the central recommendation of the Morris Review of the Actuarial Profession: that the Financial Reporting Council (the "FRC") take on a similar role in relation to the oversight of the actuarial profession to the one it currently exercises in relation to accountancy and the auditors' profession.

1673.   The Government announced in Budget 2005 its intention to legislate in due course to put the oversight regime onto a full statutory footing. It has not been possible to develop such a regime in time for inclusion in this Act. It was therefore agreed with the FRC and the

Institute and Faculty of Actuaries that, pending the introduction of a full statutory regime, the FRC would begin voluntary oversight of the actuarial profession at the earliest possible opportunity. The FRC assumed this responsibility for actuarial standards and oversight of the profession in April 2006.

1674. The aim of these provisions is to provide the minimum necessary statutory underpinning for a voluntary regime. They amend the C(AICE) Act 2004 in two ways:

- they extend the statutory immunity conferred on the FRC and its companion bodies so that it covers acts or omissions relating to oversight of the actuarial profession;

- they allow the Secretary of State, if necessary, to make regulations to require beneficiaries of the actuarial oversight to contribute towards the funding costs of the proposed regime.

1675. This latter is a reserve power. It is proposed, as is currently the case with accountancy and the auditors' professions, to fund this activity on a non-statutory basis by agreement with the insurance and pensions industries and the actuarial profession. The FRC published its final funding proposals in March 2006.

Section 1274: Grants to bodies concerned with actuarial standards etc

1676. This section amends section 16(2) of the C(AICE) Act 2004 so as to include in the list of matters carried on by bodies eligible for grants activities concerned with the setting of actuarial standards, compliance with those standards, oversight of the actuarial profession and related matters.

1677. A body to which a grant has been paid under section 16 is protected by section 18 of that Act from certain liabilities in connection with its section 16(2) activities.

Section 1275: Levy to pay expenses of bodies concerned with actuarial standards etc

1678. This section amends section 17 of the C(AICE) Act 2004 so as to include amongst those by whom a levy may be payable—

- the administrators of a public service pension scheme, and

- the trustees and managers of an occupational or personal pension scheme.

1679. The effect of the amendments is to enable the Secretary of State to make regulations specifying such persons as liable to pay a levy if he considers that the oversight activities of the FRC are relevant to them to a significant extent.

1680. *Subsection (4)* enables regulations under section 17 to make different provision for different cases so that, for example, they can provide for different rates of levy to be payable by different kinds of bodies or persons.

1681. *Subsection (5)* prevents the first regulations under section 17, and any other regulations under that section that would result in any change in the bodies or persons by whom the levy is payable, from being treated as hybrid instruments for the purposes of the standing orders of either House of Parliament. The effect is that such regulations are not subject to the special procedures in the House of Lords that apply to such instruments.

1682. *Subsection (7)* amends Schedule 3 to the Pensions Act 2004 to enable the Pensions Regulator to disclose restricted information to the Secretary of State to enable or assist him in the exercise of his functions under section 17 of the C(AICE) Act 2004.

Section 1276: Application of provisions to Scotland and Northern Ireland

1683. This section amends the C(AICE) Act 2004 as regards the application of certain provisions to Scotland and Northern Ireland.

1684. *Subsection (2)* amends section 16 of that Act so that paragraphs (a) to (t) of subsection (2) of that section, which list matters carried on by bodies eligible for grants, only apply to Scotland insofar as they relate to matters for which provision would be outside the legislative competence of the Scottish Parliament. This is necessary because, whilst section 16 and the provisions of this Act amending it extend to Scotland, some of the matters listed in paragraphs (a) to (t) are not reserved matters for the purposes of section 30 of the Scotland Act 1998 and are therefore within the legislative competence of the Scottish Parliament.

1685. *Subsections (3) to (5)* amend section 16(2) and (5) and section 66(2) of the C(AICE) Act 2004 so that sections 16 and 18, as well as section 17, of that Act extend to Northern Ireland.

Exercise of voting rights by institutional investors

1686. Institutional investors own and manage assets on behalf of and for the benefit of clients or members and have an obligation to manage those assets in their interests. In some cases there is a trustee-beneficiary relationship between the institution and the client, and in all cases there are contractual and regulatory requirements imposing duties of asset management on the institution. Voting is central to the exercise of ownership control. However, the ability of ultimate beneficiaries (e.g. members of a pension fund) to monitor the way in which institutional investors exercise voting rights is limited in practice.

1687. The CLR (Final Report, paragraph 6.39) concluded that disclosure of voting by institutional shareholders was a desirable objective. There has been a growing trend internationally to require disclosure. There has also been an increasing trend by UK fund managers towards voluntary disclosure.

Section 1277: Power to require information about exercise of voting rights

1688. This section confers a power on the Secretary of State and the Treasury to make regulations requiring certain categories of institutional investor to provide information about the exercise of their voting rights. The power is drawn intentionally widely to enable any mandatory disclosure regime to respond to varied corporate governance arrangements and to capture a range of institutions investing in different markets. Exercise of the power is subject to affirmative resolution procedure.

1689. *Subsection (4)* provides that the obligation imposed by regulations under this section is enforceable by civil proceedings brought either by the person to whom the information should have been provided or by a regulatory authority specified in the regulations (which could, for example, be the FSA).

Section 1278: Institutions to which information provisions apply

1690. This section lists the categories of institutions in relation to which the power conferred by section 1277 is exercisable. *Subsection (2)* enables the Treasury or Secretary of State to add to or amend the categories. *Subsection (3)* requires that the regulations specify by whom the duty imposed by the regulations is to be fulfilled.

Section 1279: Shares to which the information provisions apply

1691. This section confers power to specify by regulations the descriptions of shares in relation to which the information provisions apply. They will apply wherever a listed institution has an interest in such shares. *Subsections (2) to (4)* provide that an institution is taken to have an interest in shares in certain cases.

Section 1280: Obligations with respect to provision of information

1692. This section specifies the information that can be required. This covers the exercise or non-exercise of voting rights, instructions given by the institution and any delegation of a function related to the exercise or non-exercise of voting rights.

1693. *Subsection (1)* contains a power to require institutional investors to procure disclosure of voting or of any instructions given by any person acting on the institution's behalf. Institutional investors would need to make sure that their investment contracts required such information to be passed on to them or disclosed on their behalf.

1694. Under *subsection (4)*, the regulations may specify how and to whom the disclosure is to be made. This would allow the regulations to both specify the manner of disclosure and require disclosure to (for example) clients and members only, or to the public generally.

Disclosure of information under the Enterprise Act 2002

1695. Part 9 of the Enterprise Act applies to information which public authorities receive in connection with competition and consumer functions under certain Parts of the Enterprise Act 2002 and under other specified competition and consumer protection legislation. Information relating to the affairs of an individual or business must be kept confidential unless Part 9 permits its disclosure.

1696. This provision amends Part 9 so as to enable public authorities to disclose information for the purposes of civil proceedings or otherwise for the purpose of establishing, enforcing or defending legal rights.

Section 1281: Disclosure of information under the Enterprise Act 2002

1697. The new section 241A allows a public authority to disclose prescribed information to any person for the purposes of prescribed civil proceedings in the United Kingdom or elsewhere. *Prescribed* means prescribed by the Secretary of State by order. The new provision extends to prospective proceedings, taking legal advice about proceedings and other ways of establishing, enforcing or defending legal rights (such as alternative dispute resolution schemes).

1698. Information obtained by a public authority in connection with competition functions is excluded from the new provision.

Expenses of winding up

1699. The House of Lords decided in *Buchler and another v Talbot and others, in re Leyland Daf* [2004] UKHL 9 that property subject to a floating charge is not available to fund the general expenses of winding up. This provision is intended to reverse that decision.

Section 1282: Payment of expenses of winding up (England and Wales)

1700. *Subsection (1)* inserts a new section 176ZA in the Insolvency Act 1986 under which property subject to a floating charge may, where necessary, be used to fund the general expenses of winding up in priority to the floating charge holder and to any preferential creditors entitled to be paid out of that property. There is power to make provision by rules requiring the authorisation or approval of the floating charge holder, or any preferential creditors, or the court, in certain circumstances.

1701. *Subsection (2)* makes a corresponding amendment of the Insolvency (Northern Ireland) Order 1989 (S.I. 1989/2405 (N.I.19)).

Commonhold associations

1702. Commonhold associations are a new form of company limited by guarantee established under the Commonhold and Leasehold Reform Act 2002. Commonhold associations must register their memorandum and articles of association both with Companies House (on formation) and with HM Land Registry (on registration of the commonhold).

1703. At present paragraph 3(1) of Schedule 3 to the Commonhold and Leasehold Reform Act 2002 provides that an alteration of a commonhold association's memorandum or articles is of no effect if it is not registered with the Land Registry. The purpose of the provision is to ensure that the version of those documents held by the Land Registry is up to date. An unintended consequence of it, however, is that it effectively prohibits any change of an association's memorandum or articles before the land which the commonhold association is established to manage is registered as commonhold land or after it has stopped being commonhold land.

Section 1283: Amendment of memorandum or articles of commonhold association

1704. This section amends paragraph 3(1) of Schedule 3 to the Commonhold and Leasehold Reform Act 2002 so as to limit the application of the provision to alterations made at a time when the land the association is established to manage is commonhold land.

PART 45: NORTHERN IRELAND

1705. Companies Acts since 1929 have extended to Great Britain only. But Northern Ireland companies legislation has followed changes in GB companies legislation very closely. The principal piece of current Northern Irish companies legislation, the Companies (Northern Ireland) Order 1986, is effectively a copy of the 1985 Act, with only very minor modifications to fit the Northern Irish context.

1706. Following public consultation, it was decided that the new Act should extend directly to Northern Ireland, along with certain other closely related areas of law. Company law would remain in formal terms a transferred matter, and a future Northern Ireland Assembly could for example decide to enact separate Northern Ireland companies legislation if it considered it desirable. In the meantime, companies in Northern Ireland would experience the regulatory effects of new companies legislation at the same time as their GB counterparts. The Act gives effect to these arrangements.

Section 1284: Extension of Companies Acts to Northern Ireland

1707. This section provides that the Companies Acts extend Northern Ireland. The Companies Acts are defined in section 2 of the Act: in essence, they include the company law provisions of this Act, the remaining provisions of the 1985 Act, and Part 2 of the C(AICE) Act 2004 (which relates to community interest companies). Section 1284 also repeals the principal pieces of separate Northern Ireland companies legislation The other (non-company law) provisions of this Act extend to Northern Ireland by virtue of section 1299.

Sections 1285 to 1287: Extension of certain other GB enactments to Northern Ireland

1708. These sections similarly extend to Northern Ireland other GB legislation in various areas related to company law, and repeal the separate Northern Ireland legislation in these areas. This is the case in relation to:

- SEs (European Public Limited-Liability Companies);

- certain other forms of business organisation where the law is partly modelled on, and closely relates to, company law; namely limited liability partnerships, limited partnerships, open-ended investment companies, and European Economic Interest Groupings; and

- business names.

PART 46: GENERAL SUPPLEMENTARY PROVISIONS

Sections 1288 to 1292: Regulations and orders

1709. These sections provide how regulations and orders made under the Act are to be made.

1710. Section 1288 provides that, unless the provision in the Act creating the power states otherwise, all regulations and orders are to be made by statutory instrument.

1711. Most of the powers to make regulations or orders are exercisable by the Secretary of State and are to be made by statutory instrument. The Act also confers powers on the registrar of companies to make rules, which are not required to be made by statutory instrument (section 1117(3) requires appropriate publicity). Other non-statutory instrument powers are conferred on the Takeover Panel (see Part 28) and the Financial Services Authority (see Part 43, which inserts new sections into the FSMA).

1712. Virtually all the provisions of the Act conferring power to make regulations or orders by statutory instrument specify one or other of the following three types of Parliamentary procedure:

- negative resolution procedure (defined in section 1289): the statutory instrument containing the regulations or order is laid before Parliament and must be revoked if either House passes a resolution against it within 40 Parliamentary days. An instrument subject to the negative procedure is normally laid at least 21 days before it is to come into effect to ensure scrutiny of the instrument before its provisions come into force;

- affirmative resolution procedure (defined in section 1290): the statutory instrument containing the regulations or order is laid before Parliament in draft and can only be made when approved by affirmative resolution in each House. This means that they are always subject to debate in each House;

- approval after being made (defined in section 1291): the statutory instrument containing the regulations or order is laid before Parliament after being made. It ceases to have effect after 28 Parliamentary days unless it is approved by resolution of each House during the 28 day period. Should the regulations or order cease to have effect at the end of the 28 days, anything done under them during the period remains effective and new regulations or a new order may be made.

1713. Section 1292(1) provides that regulations or orders may make different provision for different cases or circumstances, may include supplementary, incidental and consequential provision, and may make transitional provision and savings.

1714. *Subsections (2) to (4)* of section 1292 enable orders or regulations to be made combining provisions in relation to which different procedural requirements apply. A power to make regulations can be exercised by making an order, and a power to make an order can be exercised by making regulations. Provisions subject to the affirmative resolution procedure, provisions subject to the negative resolution procedure and provisions subject to no Parliamentary procedure at all may be included in a single instrument, and subsections (3) and (4) clarify which procedure applies when powers are combined.

Section 1293: Meaning of "enactment"

1715. This clause explains what the term "enactment" includes, when used in the Act, to make it clear that it goes beyond the definition in the Interpretation Act 1978 (c.30). Unless the context in which it is used dictates otherwise, "enactment" includes:

- an enactment contained in subordinate legislation within the meaning of the Interpretation Act 1978 (c.30);

- an enactment contained in, or in an instrument made under, an Act of the Scottish Parliament;

- an enactment contained in, or in an instrument made under, Northern Ireland legislation within the meaning of the Interpretation Act 1978.

Section 1294: Power to make consequential amendments etc

1716. This section confers on the Secretary of State, and on the Treasury, order-making powers to amend enactments in consequence of any provision in the Act. Such amendments and repeals are additional to those made by any other provision of the Act. Orders under this section are subject to the affirmative resolution procedure.

1717. Orders may be made to amend, repeal or revoke any enactment that is:

- passed or made before the passing of the Act;

- contained in the Act or in subordinate legislation made under it;

- passed or made before the end of Parliamentary session 2006-7.

1718. In particular, orders may make provision corresponding to that made in the Act in relation to companies, and may extend provision to other forms of organisation. The provisions of the Act may be applied with any adaptations or other modifications that appear to be necessary or expedient.

Section 1295: Repeals

1719. This section introduces Schedule 16, the repeal Schedule. The repeals include, in addition to purely consequential repeals, repeals of the restated provisions of the 1985 Act and repeals of enactments that are no longer of practical utility.

1720. Schedule 16 repeals a number of Parts and/or sections of a number of pieces of legislation, including most of the 1985 Act, most of the Companies Act 1989 and the whole of the Business Names Act 1985.

Section 1296: Power to make transitional provision and savings

1721. This section gives the Secretary of State and the Treasury order-making powers to make transitional provision and savings in connection with the commencement of any provision made in the Act. Orders are subject to the negative resolution procedure.

Section 1297: Continuity of the law

1722. This section provides that things done under the provisions in the 1985 Act that are repealed and replaced by the Act will continue to be legally effective. Similarly, references to the repealed provisions in enactments, instruments or documents are to be construed as including references to the corresponding new provision.

1723. Articles of association, company resolutions and contracts are all likely to refer to provisions of the Companies Acts or to rely for their effect on the way in which those provisions work. Except where a change is intended, those articles, resolutions and contracts should continue to have effect, not only with old references converted into new but also with their legal effect capable of continuing despite verbal differences between the old and the new.

1724. The section applies automatically in all cases in which it is capable of applying. It is in addition to any more specific transitional provisions, which may be included in commencement orders by use of the power in section 1296.

PART 47: FINAL PROVISIONS

Section 1298: Short title

1725. This section sets out the short title of the Act.

Section 1299: Extent

1726. This section provides that, except where otherwise provided for or the context requires otherwise, the Act extends to the whole of the United Kingdom (in other words, including Northern Ireland, as provided for in Part 45 and discussed in the notes to that Part).

Section 1300: Commencement

1727. *Subsection (1)* provides for commencement on Royal Assent of Part 43 (except for a definition not yet in force) and of sections 1274 and 1276, so that the provisions on transparency obligations and related matters, those conferring a statutory immunity from liability in damages in relation to the oversight of the actuarial profession and those relating to the extension of provisions of the C(AICE) Act 2004 to Scotland and Northern Ireland came into force on that date (8 November 2006). It also provides for Parts 46 (general supplementary provisions) and this Part to come into force on Royal Assent, except for the repeals Schedule.

1728. *Subsection (2)* provides for the Secretary of State or the Treasury to appoint by order the timing of commencement of the other provisions of the Act.

COMMENCEMENT

1729. As explained in the note on section 1300 immediately above, certain provisions came into force on the day of Royal Assent. The other provisions will be the subject of commencement orders, and the Government has announced its intention to commence all parts of the Act by October 2008.

PARLIAMENTARY HISTORY

1730. The following table sets out the dates and Hansard references for each stage of this Act's passage through Parliament.

Stage	Date	Hansard reference
House of Lords		
First Reading	1 November 2005, HL Bill 34	Vol. 675, Col. 127
Second Reading	11 January 2006	Vol. 677, Cols. 180-249
Grand Committee	30 January, 1, 6, 9, 27 February, 1, 7, 14, 15, 20, 28, 30 March, 25 April 2006, reprinted HL Bill 98	Vol. 678, Cols. GC1-GC64, GC119-GC176, GC237-GC296, GC 321-GC382, Vol. 679, Cols. GC1-GC62, GC121-GC188, GC263-GC324, GC395-GC466, GC467-GC532, Vol. 680, Cols. GC1-GC70, GC285-GC356, GC357-GC440, Vol. 681, Cols. GC61-GC100
Report	9, 10, 16 May 2006, reprinted HL Bill 108	Vol. 681, Cols. 777-898, 912-1034, Vol. 682, Cols. 141-253
Third Reading	23 May 2006	Vol. 682, Cols. 709-797
House of Commons		
First Reading	24 May 2006, reprinted Bill 190	Votes and proceedings
Second Reading	6 June 2006	Vol. 447, Cols. 122-223
Committee	15, 20, 22, 27, 29 June, 4, 6, 11, 13, 18, 20 July 2006, reprinted Bill 218	Hansard Standing Committee D
Report and Third Reading	17, 18, 19 October 2006	Vol. 450, Cols. 743-838, 881-980, 1030-1108
House of Lords		
Consideration of Commons Amendments	3 November 2006, HL Bill 155	Vol. 686, Cols. 428-510
House of Commons		
Lords Reasons for insisting on certain of	6 November 2006, Bill 245	Vol. 451, Cols. 667-676

their amendments to which the Commons have disagreed, considered		

Royal Assent – 8 November 2006   House of Lords Hansard Vol 686 Col 750

House of Commons Hansard Vol 451 Col 825

ANNEX A: TRANSPOSITION NOTES

Part 28: Takeovers, etc. – Directive on Takeovers Bids (2004/25/EC)

The Takeovers Directive

1731.   *Part 28* of the Act implements Directive 2004/25 EC of the European Parliament and of the Council of 21 April 2004 on Takeover Bids (OJ L142, 30 April 2004).

1732.   The Takeovers Directive lays down, for the first time, minimum EU rules concerning the regulation of takeovers of companies whose shares are traded on a regulated market. The Directive was one of the measures adopted under the EU Financial Services Action Plan and aims to strengthen the Single Market in financial services by facilitating cross-border restructuring and enhancing minority shareholder protection.

1733.   The Takeovers Directive contains general principles that Member States must adhere to in regulating takeover activity and a framework relating to the functions and jurisdiction of takeover regulatory authorities. It also lays down provisions relating to the mandatory bid (a requirement whereby a party gaining control of a company must make an offer to all shareholders at an equitable price), takeover bid documentation, time allowed for acceptance of the bid, the obligations of the board of the offeree company and other matters related to the bid.

1734.   Additionally, the Takeovers Directive has provisions addressing barriers to takeovers (such as action that might be taken by a company or its board before or during a bid to prevent a takeover), requiring disclosure of certain information by companies traded on a regulated market and dealing with the problems of, and for, residual minority shareholders following a successful takeover bid (so-called 'squeeze-out' and 'sell-out' provisions).

The Takeovers Directive (Interim Implementation) Regulations 2006

1735.   In view of the fact that the Takeovers Directive was required to be implemented by 20 May 2006, by which date the Act had not completed Parliamentary passage and received Royal Assent, interim implementation provisions were introduced under section 2(2) of the European Communities Act 1972 (ECA 1972). These provisions are contained in The Takeovers Directive (Interim Implementation) Regulations 2006 (S.I. 2006 No.1183). A copy of those Regulations together with the accompanying Explanatory Memorandum, Regulatory Impact Assessment and Transposition Notes is available on the website of the Office of Public Sector Information (http://www.opsi.gov.uk/stat.htm). The Regulations will be repealed and replaced on commencement of Part 28 of the Act.

Part 28 – Takeovers etc

1736.   Since 1968, takeover regulation in the UK has been overseen by the Takeover Panel administering rules and principles contained in the "City Code on Takeovers and Mergers". In order to bring UK takeover regulation within the requirements laid down in the Directive,

Part 28 of the Act is designed to place it within a complete and coherent statutory framework.

1737. The detailed rules relating to takeover regulation in compliance with the Directive will be prescribed by the Panel in its Takeover Code, under a statutory rule-making obligation imposed upon the Panel by the Act (section 943(1)). The Takeover Code has already been revised with effect from 20 May 2006, on an interim basis under the 2006 Regulations, to make it wholly consistent with the requirements of the Takeovers Directive.

1738. 'Squeeze-out' and 'sell-out' provisions were previously prescribed by Part 13A of the 1985 Act. Chapter 3 of Part 28 of the Act replaces those provisions in their entirety with certain amendments which ensure they are wholly consistent with the Takeovers Directive requirements.

1739. Provisions related to disclosures by companies are contained in Part 7 of the 1985 Act and amendments to that Part are made in Chapter 4 of Part 28 to give effect to the additional disclosure requirements imposed by the Takeovers Directive on companies traded on a regulated market.

1740. Responsibility for the measures, described in this transposition note, taken to implement the Takeovers Directive lies with the Secretary of State for Trade and Industry.

1741. The table below describes the substantive provisions implementing the Takeovers Directive.

Part 24: Takeovers etc: Transposition Measures		
Article	**Objective**	**Implementation**
1	Defines the scope of Directive in terms of transactions and types of company to which it applies ("takeover bids for the securities of companies governed by the laws of Member States, where all or some of those securities are admitted to trading on a regulated market").	No specific implementing provision necessary.
2	Contains key definitions for the purposes of the Directive (such as, "takeover bid", "offeree company", and "securities").	No specific implementing provision necessary.
3.1	Lays down general principles which Member States shall ensure are adhered to for the purpose of implementing the Directive.	*Section 943(1)* requires that the Panel give effect to the general principles set out at Article 3.1 of the Directive in the exercise of their statutory rule-making duty.
3.2	Provides that Member States may, in ensuring that the minimum requirements laid down by the Directive are adhered to, lay down additional conditions and	No specific implementing provision necessary.

	provisions more stringent than those of the Directive.	
4.1	Requires Member States to designate supervisory authorities (which must act independently of parties to a bid).	This will be achieved by administrative designation of the Takeover Panel as supervisory authority for the purposes of the Directive.
4.2	Lays down jurisdictional rules in relation to takeover regulation	*Section 943(1)* requires that the Panel give effect to the jurisdictional provisions of the Directive in the exercise of their statutory rule-making duty.
4.3	Requires Member States to ensure that persons employed or formerly employed by takeover regulatory authorities are bound by professional secrecy (information covered by this obligation should not be disclosed other than under conditions laid down by national law).	*Section 949* makes it a criminal offence to disclose information provided to the Takeover Panel other than under the circumstances and gateways laid down in *section 948 and Schedule 2*.
4.4	Lays down cooperation obligations in relation to EU takeover and financial markets supervisory authorities.	*Section 950* requires the Takeover Panel to cooperate with EU takeover and financial services regulators. The existing cooperation duties of the Financial Services Authority under section 354 of the Financial Services and Markets Act 2000 are extended to include relevant authorities (section *964*).
4.5	Requires that takeover supervisory authorities be provided with all powers necessary for carrying out their duties and provides that Member States may, provided that the general principles are respected, permit derogation from the rules of the Directive in certain circumstances and grant supervisory authorities the power to grant waivers.	In addition to the rule-making duty at section *943(1)* and rule-making powers at section *943(2)*, the following powers are provided to the Takeover Panel: *Section 945* – power to make rulings *Section 946* – power to give directions *Section 947* – power to require documents and information *Section 952* – power to set down sanctions by rules *Section 954* – power to order compensation in certain circumstances *Section 955* – power to apply to the court for enforcement *Section 960* – power to bring and defend proceedings. *Section 944(1)* authorises the Takeover Panel to provide for derogations and waivers in certain circumstances from rules made under *section 943*.

4.6	Makes provision for certain Member States' powers to be unaffected by the Directive (for instance, designation of judicial or other authorities responsible for dealing with disputes, the circumstances in which parties may bring administrative or judicial proceedings, any capacity of the courts to decline to hear legal proceedings and the liability of supervisory authorities).	*Section 945(2)* provides that a ruling of the Takeover Panel is to have binding effect (subject to provisions in the Panel's rules and any review or appeal). *Section 951* provides for matters relating to reviews of and appeals from Takeover Panel decisions to be contained in the rules made by the Panel. *Section 956* provides that there shall be no action for breach of statutory duty, or any voidness or unenforceability of transactions, as a result of breach of rules made by the Panel. *Section 961* provides for exemption of the Takeover Panel (and those involved in its functions) from liability in damages in certain circumstances related to the regulatory activities of the Panel.
5	Requires that a "mandatory bid rule" is introduced requiring a person acquiring "control" of a company to make a bid to all holders of securities at an equitable price Contains rules related to the calculation of the equitable price.	*Section 943(1)* requires that the Panel give effect to the "mandatory bid" and "equitable price" provisions in the exercise of their statutory rule-making duty.
6	Requires that the decision to make a takeover bid is made public. Contains detailed provision related to the contents of the takeover offer document. Requires that the parties to a bid are obliged to provide supervisory authorities with information related to the bid.	*Section 943(1)* requires that the Panel give effect to the "bid" disclosure and documentation provisions in the exercise of its statutory rule-making duty. *Section 947* provides the Takeover Panel with power to require documents and information.
7	Lays down rules related to the time allowed for acceptance of the takeover bid.	*Section 943(1)* requires that the Panel give effect to the offer "acceptance" period provision in the exercise of its statutory rule-making duty.
8	Requires that takeover bids are made public so as to ensure market transparency. It also provides for the disclosure of bid documentation to shareholders and employees' representatives (or, where there are no such representatives, the employees directly).	*Section 943(1)* requires that the Panel give effect to the bid disclosure provisions in the exercise of their statutory rule-making duty.
9	Imposes obligations on the board of the offeree company, including the obligation not to take action to frustrate the bid without the approval of shareholders at the	*Section 943(1)* requires that the Panel give effect to the provisions relating to the obligations of the board of the offeree company in the exercise of their

	time of the bid and to draw up and make public a statement containing their views on the effects of implementation of the bid.	statutory rule-making duty.
10	Requires that companies shall publish detailed information on their share and control structures, etc. in their annual report and present an explanatory report on such matters to the annual general meeting of shareholders.	*Section 992* (amending Part 7 of the 1985 Act) requires that the relevant information, including necessary explanatory material, is set out in the annual report of companies.
11	"Breakthrough" – This provision overrides, in certain circumstances connected with a takeover, provisions in the articles of companies and contractual arrangements related to restrictions on transfer and voting rights of shares, etc. It does not apply to special shares held by Member States or to cooperatives. This provision may be made optional by Member States for companies under the provisions of article 12.	The right to make these provisions optional for companies is exercised in the implementing provisions. *Sections 966 and 967* define the types of companies, circumstances and mechanisms by which a company may opt-in to "breakthrough". *Section 968* lays down the effect on contractual restrictions overridden by "breakthrough".
12.1	Provides that Member States may make optional the provisions of articles 9(2) and (3) and/or Article 11.	Exercise of this option has been taken only in relation to the provisions of Article 11 (the relevant implementing provisions of which are described above).
12.2 (and 12.4)	Requires, where optional arrangements are in place, that companies have the right to voluntarily opt-in to the provisions of the relevant articles. Such a decision must be communicated to the supervisory authorities and be disclosed.	*Section 970* requires that any opting-in decision be communicated to the Takeover Panel without delay. The opting-in resolution passed by the company must be filed with the Registrar of Companies under section 30.
12.3 (and 12.5)	Permits Member States to provide that the effects of Articles 9(2) and (3) and/or Article 11 only apply on a "reciprocal" basis, i.e. where the takeover bid is made by a company also subject to the effects of the relevant articles. Such restrictions on the application of Articles 9(2) and (3) and Article 11 shall be subject to the authorisation of the general meeting of shareholders of the offeree company.	The Member State option to provide for "reciprocity" has not been exercised.
13	Requires that rules relating to the lapsing or revision of bids, competing bids, disclosure of results of bids and irrevocability of bids be put in place.	*Section 943(1)* requires that the Panel give effect to the requirement that such rules be put in place in the exercise of its statutory rule-making duty.
14	Provides that the Directive shall be without prejudice to various provisions relating to information and consultation of employees and their representatives.	No specific implementing provision necessary.

15	Requires Member States to put in place rules enabling a bidder to compulsorily purchase the shares of minority shareholders following a successful takeover bid ("squeeze-out" rights). The circumstances in which such a right must apply (including time periods and relevant thresholds) and relating to the price that must be paid are set out.	"Squeeze-out" rights were previously contained in the 1985 Act (Part 13A (sections 428-430F)). These have been replaced by Chapter 3 of Part 28 of the Act (necessary amendments to ensure these provisions are consistent with Article 15 have been made).
16	Requires Member States to put in place rules enabling minority shareholders to require a bidder to compulsorily purchase their shares following a successful takeover bid ("sell-out" rights). The circumstances in which such a rule must apply (including time periods and relevant thresholds) and relating to the price that must be paid are set out.	"Sell-out" rights were previously contained in the 1985 Act (Part 13A). These have been replaced by Chapter 3 of Part 28 of the Act (necessary amendments to ensure these provisions are consistent with article 16 have been made).
17	Requires that effective, proportionate and dissuasive sanctions be put in place.	*Sections 952 and 954* provide that the rules made by the Takeover Panel may confer power on the Panel to impose sanctions on those who transgress its rules or order compensation in certain circumstances. *Section 949* makes it an offence to contravene the provisions of section *948* (relating to the restrictions on disclosure of information provided to the Takeover Panel). *Section 953* provides an offence where takeover bid documentation does not comply with Panel rules giving effect to Articles 6.3 and 9.5 of the Directive. Misconduct in relation to takeover activity also needs to be viewed in the wider context of the overall regulatory framework and the protections available to shareholders and others. A robust market regulatory regime and company law framework is in place in the UK to investigate and pursue misconduct in relation to takeover activity (for instance, sanctions with stringent sanctions are already in place to deter fraudulent misrepresentation or market abuse).
18	Lays down a Committee procedure whereby the Commission may adopt rules related to the application of Article 6.3	No implementing provision necessary (no such rules have been adopted).

	(contents of takeover bid documentation).	
19	Requires the EU Commission to establish a Contact Committee to facilitate the harmonised application of the Directive and advise the Commission, if necessary, on any additions or amendments to the Directive.	No implementing provision necessary.
20	Provides for the review of the Directive by the EU Commission five years after its entry into force. Requires that Member States provide the Commission annually with certain information related to takeover bids.	No implementing provision necessary. Such information will be provided to the EU Commission as an administrative process.
21	Requires that the relevant provisions of the Directive be transposed no later than 20 May 2006. Details of transposition measures shall be communicated to the Commission.	No specific implementing provision necessary (NB paragraph 5 above regarding the Takeovers Directive (Interim Implementation) Regulations 2006 which came into force on 20th May 2006). Details of the transposition measures will be communicated to the EU Commission by administrative process.
22	Provides that the Directive enters into force on 20 May 2004	No implementing provision necessary.
23	Addresses the Directive to the Member States.	No implementing provision necessary.

Part 35: The Registrar of Companies – Directive 2003/58/EC (which amends Council Directive 68/151/EEC as regards disclosure requirements in respect of certain types of companies)

1742. Various provisions within *Part 35* of the Act serve to implement Directive 2003/58/EEC, which amends section I of the First Company Law Directive (68/151/EEC), primarily to enable companies to register certain documents electronically and searchers to access them electronically.

1743. Section I of the First Company Law Directive requires that basic company documents be disclosed via filing with a company registry, and by publication in the national gazette either of the full or partial text of the document or by reference to the document deposited in the company registry. It also requires that those documents be available for inspection. In addition, the First Company Law Directive specifies minimum information that companies must include on their letters and order forms. The First Company Law Directive assumes the use of paper documents. The amended directive reflects the use of information technology and electronic communications.

1744. In practice, the 1985 Act already allows the Registrar to accept electronic filing of all documents covered by the First Company Law Directive, although specific directions as to the form and manner of filing any particular document electronically have to be given by the Registrar. At present, the Registrar has mechanisms for the electronic filing of many of those documents.

1745. The 1985 Act also already allows the Registrar to keep documents in electronic form, and to provide for inspection by electronic means. Legislation is however necessary to impose formal obligations on the Registrar in relation to electronic filing, so as to transpose the amending Directive properly.

1746. Responsibility for the transposition of the amending Directive lies with the Secretary of State for Trade and Industry. The table below describes the substantive provisions in the Act which implement it.

Part 35: The Registrar of Companies		
Article	Objective	Implementation
2.	(Which amends Article 2.1(f) of the First Company Law Directive) requires certain accounting documents to be filed.	Part 35 of the Act contains the relevant filing requirements (which are restated from the current legislation).
3.	(So far as it amends Article 3.2.) Company Registries must allow companies to file electronically all basic documents (those specified in Article 2 of the First Company Law Directive, and those to which Article 3 of the First Company Law Directive is applied by other legislation).	Section 1078 lists the documents which are now subject to the Directive disclosure requirements under Article 2 of the First Company Law Directive as amended. Section 1068(5) provides that all such documents may be delivered to the Registrar in electronic form.
3.	(So far as it also amends Article 3.2.) Company Registries must allow requests for inspection of such documents to be made electronically.	Section 1089(2) provides that applications in respect of such documents may be submitted electronically.
3.	(So far as it also amends Article 3.2.) Company Registries must offer electronic copies of such documents to those inspecting the register (subject to a permitted derogation in respect of documents filed before 1 January 2007).	Section 1090(2) provides that copies of such documents must be provided in electronic form if the applicant so chooses (subject to section 1090(3) which takes advantage of the permitted derogation).
3.	(So far as it also amends Article 3.2.) Company Registries must keep all such documents (whether submitted electronically or in hard copy) in electronic form.	Section 1080(3) provides that information from such documents must be kept in electronic form.

3.	(So far as it amends Article 3.3) In the case of electronic copies, Company Registries need only provide certified copies if they are asked to do so. Member States need to take measures to ensure the authenticity of electronic certified copies.	Section 1091 contains provision about certifying copies and allows the Secretary of State to make regulations about how electronic copies are certified.
3.	(So far as it amends Article 3.4.) The option is provided to Members States of using an alternative to publication in the National Gazette as a means of publicising information received.	Section 1077 specifies that notices must be published either in the Gazette, or in accordance with section 1116. The latter section enables the Secretary of State to make regulations specifying alternative means of publication.
4.	(Which inserts a new Article 3a.) This provides that, while documents must be submitted in a language permitted by the language rules of the member state in question, voluntary translations in other Community languages must also be accepted.	Sections 1106 and 1107 provide that companies may deliver certified translations of documents. The languages and types of document in respect of which this facility is available will be specified in regulations made by the Secretary of State, but subsection (3) of section 1106 provides that these regulations must as a minimum cover the documents subject to the directive disclosure requirements and the official languages of the EU.
5.	(Which replaces the previous Article 4). This provides that certain information (already currently required on hard copy letters and order forms) must be stated in documents in any form and displayed on websites.	This will be implemented by regulations under section 82.
6.	This provides that that there must be appropriate penalties for breach of new Articles 2(1)(f) and 4 of the First Company Law Directive.	See entries for new Articles 2(1)(f) and 4 above.

Part 43: Transparency obligations and related matters – Transparency Directive (2004/109/EC)

1747. Sections 1265, 1266, 1267, 1268, 1270, 1271, and 1272 in Part 43 (Transparency obligations and related matters) of the Act implement Directive 2004/109/EC on the harmonisation of transparency requirements in relation to information about issuers whose securities are admitted to trading on a regulated market and amending Directive 2001/34/EC. Section 1266 inserts seven new sections into Part 6 of the Financial Services and Markets Act 2000; *sections 89A, 89B, 89C, 89D, 89E, 89F and 89G*. The new sections give power to the competent authority (at present the Financial Services Authority ("FSA")) to make rules for the purposes of the Transparency Directive (2004/109/EC) ("Transparency Directive") and connected regulatory purposes. Sections 1267 and 1268 insert three and four sections, respectively, into Part 6 of FSMA (*89H to 89N*) setting out the regulatory powers of the FSA in connection with the Directive. Section 1270 inserts new *sections 90A and 90B* into FSMA, which set out the issuers' liability in damages for disclosures required under the Transparency Directive, and section 1271 inserts a new *section 100A* into FSMA setting out provisions in relation to the exercise of the FSA's powers where the UK is a host member state.

1748. The Transparency Directive imposes minimum harmonisation requirements on the information to be provided to the public about issuers whose securities are traded on a regulated market and the control of votes attached to shares in those issuers. It permits Home Member States to impose more stringent requirements on entities that they regulate but Host Member States, i.e. those states in which the issuers securities are traded on a regulated market but whose competent authority are not responsible for primary oversight of that issuer, are not permitted to impose any requirements more stringent than those contained in the Transparency Directive.

1749.   There are three main categories of obligation that are imposed under the Transparency Directive and that the FSA's transparency rules will implement in respect of UK markets and issuers:

a) requirements for issuers to make public, at regular intervals, information about their financial position and the progress and management of the business of the issuer;

b) requirements for holders of votes attached to shares of issuers to notify the issuers when the number of votes they control reaches specified proportions of the total votes available; and

c) requirements for issuers to treat the holders of the same securities equally.

1750. The detailed and technical provisions about the required notifications, disclosures and treatment of security-holders will be prescribed in rules made by the FSA under the new rule-making power at *section 89A* of the Financial Services and Markets Act 2000. The FSA is required by that Act to carry out consultation and a cost benefit analysis when making any rules under this power.

1751. Having the power to make these rules will promote the harmonisation of practice with other EU jurisdictions, and help enhance investor confidence through increased transparency of the financial markets.

1752. Responsibility for the transposition of the Transparency Directive lies both with HM Treasury and with the FSA. The measures in the Companies Act that implement the Transparency Directive are the responsibility of HM Treasury.

1753. The table below describes the substantive provisions in the Act implementing the Transparency Directive.

Part 43: Transparency obligations and related matters		
Arti	**Objective**	**Implementation**

cle		
1.	Sets out scope of the Directive and two derogations from the requirements of the Directive. The Member States may apply the derogations in respect of securities issued by the government, local government or a state's national central bank.	Part 43 of the Act inserts new provisions into the Financial Services and Markets Act 2000 ("FSMA") to give the Financial Services Authority power to make Transparency Rules. Most provisions in the Transparency Directive will be implemented by the FSA's Transparency Rules. Other provisions in the Act or in FSMA implement the other requirements. If the derogations are to be implemented, the FSA's Transparency Rules will do this.
2.	Provides various definitions used in the Directive.	These will be applied in Transparency Rules, or apply in relation to the implementation of the Article to which they relate.
3.	Limits the circumstances in which Member States may impose more stringent requirements than those contained in the Directive on issuers of securities and holders of interests in those issuers' shares.	Transparency Rules and new FSMA *section 100A(2)* introduced by section 1271 of the Act.
4.	Requires issuers of securities which are traded on regulated markets to make public its annual financial report consisting of its audited financial statements and the management report.	Transparency Rules: see in particular new *sections 89A and 89C* of FSMA, inserted by section 1266 of the Act.
5.	Requires issuers of shares or debt securities which are traded on a regulated market to make public a half-yearly financial report.	Transparency Rules: see in particular new *sections 89A and 89C* of FSMA, inserted by section 1266 of the Act.
6.	Requires issuers whose shares are traded on a regulated market to make public an interim quarterly statement.	Transparency Rules: see in particular new *sections 89A and 89C* of FSMA, inserted by section 1266 of the Act.
7.	Requires Member States to ensure that responsibility for the information to be drawn up and made public in accordance with Articles 4, 5, 6 and 16 lies at least with the issuer or its administrative, management or supervisory bodies and to ensure that their laws, regulations and administrative provisions on liability apply to the issuers, the bodies referred to in this article or the persons responsible within the issuers.	Provisions relating to liability inserted into FSMA as new *sections 90A and 90B* by section 1270 of the Act.

8.	Provides various exemptions from the requirements of articles 4, 5 and 6 including to optional exemptions.	Transparency Rules.
9.	Provides that where a shareholder with a significant level of holding acquires or disposes of shares of an issuer whose shares are admitted to trading on a regulated market and to which voting rights are attached, such shareholder notifies the issuer of the proportion of voting rights in the issuer held by the shareholder as a result of the acquisition or disposal where that proportion reaches, exceeds or falls below the thresholds of 5%, 10%, 15%, 20%, 25%, 30%, 50% and 75%.	Transparency Rules: see in particular new *sections 89A and 89B* of FSMA, inserted by section 1266 of the Act.
10.	The notification requirements in Article 9 shall also apply to a natural person or legal entity to the extent it is entitled to acquire, to dispose of, or to exercise voting rights in any of the cases set out in the Article or a combination of them. (Voting rights acquired through agreement or interest).	Transparency Rules.
11.	Exempts shares provided to or by the members of the ESCB in certain circumstances from the notification requirements imposed by Articles 9 and 10.	Transparency Rules.
12.	Sets out the information that must be included in the notification under Articles 9 and 10 and includes provision on the timing of the notification and when aggregation of holdings required. Paragraph (6) requires the issuer to make public all information contained within a notification within 3 days.	Transparency Rules.
13.	Requires the holders of financial instruments, which are to be specified by the Commission, to notify the issuer of their control of votes in accordance with the requirements in Article 9.	Transparency Rules.
14.	Requires an issuer of shares admitted to trading on a regulated market to make public the proportion of its own shares that it holds when those proportions reach, exceed or fall below the thresholds of 5% or 10%.	Transparency Rules: see in particular new *sections 89A and 89C* of FSMA, inserted by section 1266 of the Act.

271

15.	Requires the Member State to ensure that an issuer of shares traded on a regulated market, makes public the total number of voting rights and capital at the end of each month during which the number changes.	Transparency Rules.
16.	Requires issuers of securities to make public information about any changes in the rights attached to their securities and any new loan issues and any guarantee or security in respect of such loans.	Transparency Rules: see in particular new *sections 89A and 89C* of FSMA, inserted by section 1266 of the Act.
17.	Requires issuers of shares admitted to trading on a regulated market to treat their shareholders, who are in the same position, equally. It provides for information to be distributed in particular ways and for shareholders to be able to exercise their rights in specified ways.	Transparency Rules.
18.	Makes similar provision as that contained in Article 17 but in respect of issuers whose debt securities are admitted to trading on a regulated market.	Transparency Rules.
19.	Requires issuers to file information that they are required to make public under the Directive, with the FSA and permits the FSA to publish that information itself. It also requires issuers to inform the FSA and the regulated market to which its securities are admitted of any proposed change to its instrument of incorporation.	Transparency Rules.
20.	Sets out the rules for determining which language the issuer must use to disclose regulated information in various circumstances.	Transparency Rules.
21.	Requires issuers to disclose regulated information in a manner ensuring fast access to such information on a non-discriminatory basis. Also requires each Member State to have an officially appointed mechanism for the central storage of regulated information.	Transparency Rules.

22.	Requires the competent authorities of the Member States (for the UK it is the FSA) to draw up guidelines to create an electronic network at national level to share information between the various competent authorities, operators of regulated markets and national company registers. Such guidelines must aim to further facilitate public access to be disclosed under this Directive, Directive 2003/6/EC (the Market Abuse Directive) and Directive 2003/71/EC (Prospectus Directive).	The FSA will draw up guidelines in accordance with the obligations under this Article.
23.	Enables the FSA to exempt issuers based in third countries from certain disclosure requirements if there are equivalent provisions in the third country. Requires the FSA to ensure that where a third country issuer is regulated in the UK for EU purposes, any information which may be important to the public in the Community is disclosed in accordance with Articles 20 and 21.	Transparency Rules.
24.	Requires each Member State to designate a central competent authority responsible for ensuring that the Directive is applied and to give that competent authority specified powers which are necessary for the performance of its functions.

Permits each Member State to designate a competent authority for examining that information is drawn up in accordance with the relevant reporting framework. | The central competent authority in the UK will be the FSA, by virtue of the amendments being inserted into Part 6 of FSMA.

The FSA already has various powers under FSMA. Other powers for the FSA to perform its functions are contained in new FSMA *sections 89H to 89N* inserted by sections 1267 and 1268 of the Act.

The Act provides power to designate a competent authority for reporting framework purposes by amending the Companies (Audit, Investigations and Community Enterprise) Act 2004. See Schedule 15 (Part 2) of the Act. |
| 25. | Imposes a requirement for professional secrecy on those who work for the competent authority and requires cooperation between the competent authorities of the various Member States. | FSMA already contains provisions relating to professional secrecy for those who work for the FSA and the Companies (Audit, Investigations and Community Enterprise) Act 2004 also contains provisions in relation to authorities appointed under that Act. |

26.	Provides for host Member States to take action in relation to infringements where an issuer or security holder continues to infringe the requirements of the Directive.	New *section 100A* of FSMA introduced by section 1271 of the Act.
27.	Sets out the committee procedure for the Commission to make implementing measures required by the Directive.	No implementing provision required.
28.	Requires, without prejudice to the right of Member States to impose criminal penalties, Member States to ensure, in conformity with their national law that at least the appropriate administrative measure may be taken or civil and/or administrative penalties imposed in respect of the persons responsible.	Schedule 15 (Part 1) of the Act amends section 91 of FSMA to enable the FSA to impose financial penalties for breach of the Transparency Rules.
29.	Requires a right of appeal to the courts to be in place.	No further implementation is required. FSMA already makes provision for appeals of FSA decisions to the Financial Services and Markets Tribunal and to the Court of Appeal.
30 – 35	These articles contain transitional and final provisions, including the date by which the Directive must be transposed – 20 January 2007.	No specific implementation is required for most of these provisions. New *sections 89B(4) and 89D(1)* introduced by section 1266 of the Act make provision for transitional arrangements.

ANNEX B: GLOSSARY

1985 Act	The Companies Act 1985
AGM	Annual General Meeting
BCLC	Butterworths Company Law Cases
C(AICE) Act 2004	Companies (Audit, Investigations and Community Enterprise) Act 2004
CFD	Contract for Difference
c.i.c.	Community Interest Company
CLR	Company Law Review
DTI	Department of Trade and Industry
EC	European Community
ECU	European Currency Unit
EEA	European Economic Area
EEC	European Economic Community

ESCB	European System of Central Banks
EU	European Union
FRC	Financial Reporting Council
FRRP	Financial Reporting Review Panel
FSA	Financial Services Authority
FSMA	Financial Services and Markets Act 2000
GB	Great Britain
IAS	International Accounting Standards
NI	Northern Ireland
PPERA	Political Parties, Elections and Referendums Act 2000
PSM	Professional Securities Market
QC	Queen's Counsel
RTE	Right to Enfranchise
RTM	Right to Manage
SE	Societas Europaea (European Public Limited-Liability Company)
SI	Statutory Instrument
UK	United Kingdom
UKHL	UK House of Lords

© Crown copyright 2007

Printed in the UK by The Stationery Office Limited
under the authority and superintendence of Carol Tullo, Controller of
Her Majesty's Stationery Office and Queen's Printer of Acts of Parliament.

1/2007   356518   19585